Birth of an Empire

Birth of an Empire

The State of Qin Revisited

EDITED BY
YURI PINES,
GIDEON SHELACH,
LOTHAR VON FALKENHAUSEN,
AND ROBIN D. S. YATES

Global, Area, and International Archive
University of California Press
BERKELEY   LOS ANGELES   LONDON

The Global, Area, and International Archive (GAIA) is an initiative
of the Institute of International Studies, University of California,
Berkeley, in partnership with the University of California Press,
the California Digital Library, and international research programs
across the University of California system.

University of California Press, one of the most distinguished
university presses in the United States, enriches lives around the
world by advancing scholarship in the humanities, social sciences,
and natural sciences. Its activities are supported by the UC Press
Foundation and by philanthropic contributions from individuals
and institutions. For more information, visit www.ucpress.edu.

University of California Press
Berkeley and Los Angeles, California

University of California Press, Ltd.
London, England

Library of Congress Cataloging-in-Publication Data

A catalog record for this book is available from the Library of
Congress.

ISBN : 978-0-520-28974-1

23 22 21 20 19 18 17 16 15 14
10 9 8 7 6 5 4 3 2 1

Contents

Illustrations

TABLES

Acknowledgments

In 2003 the editors of this volume began planning an international gathering of leading specialists on Qin history in which the cutting-edge achievements of archaeologists, paleographers, and historians could be integrated to provide a novel view of the Qin state and empire. Our efforts resulted in a ten-day international workshop that took place in the Institute for Advanced Study, the Hebrew University of Jerusalem, in December 2008. The workshop was supported by a joint grant (no. 1860/07) from the Israeli Science Foundation and the Institute for Advanced Study, by a grant from the American Council of Learned Societies and the Chiang Ching-kuo Foundation for International Scholarly Exchange in the program "New Perspectives on Chinese Culture and Society," and by the Louis Frieberg Center for East Asian Studies at the Hebrew University of Jerusalem. We are grateful to our donors, without whose generosity our gathering—and the resultant volume—never would have materialized.

Naturally, not all papers presented at the workshop could be included in this volume; but all of the participants contributed greatly to the volume's formation, and so we are grateful to them, specifically to Chen Songchang, Michael Nylan, Andrew H. Plaks, Charles Sanft, Griet Vankeerberghen, and Wang Hui. Our discussions also greatly benefited from the skill of Maxim Korolkov, who helped in the translations from Chinese to English and vice versa.

In preparing the volume for publication we benefited greatly from the work of our translators, Mei-yu Hsieh and William G. Crowell (both of whom volunteered to undertake the translation of Hsing I-tien's chapter), Susanna Lam, and Andrew H. Miller. Yitzchak Jaffe provided invaluable support in preparing maps and handling illustrations. We are also grateful to the reviewers of the Institute for International Studies, University of California, Berkeley, for their comments and encouragement. In working on this volume we were supported by the Israel Science Foundation (grant no. 1217/07) and by the Michael William Lipson Chair in Chinese Studies (Yuri Pines); by the Cotsen Institute of Archaeology at UCLA (Lothar von Falkenhausen); by the Louis Freiberg Chair in East Asian Studies (Gideon Shelach); and by the National Endowment for the Humanities, the Chiang Ching-kuo Foundation for International Scholarly Exchange, and the Social Sciences and Humanities Research Council of Canada (Robin D. S. Yates).

A Note on Conventions

Aristocratic ranks. It was common until recently to adopt European equivalents for Chinese aristocratic ranks: thus, *gong* 公 was rendered "duke," *hou* 侯 "marquis," and so on. This system, which is quite acceptable for imperial China, becomes counterproductive when applied to the pre-imperial eras, when the usage of major aristocratic ranks was much more fluid than later systematizing texts, such as the *Mengzi* ("Wan Zhang xia" 10.2: 235), suggest (see Li Feng 2008b). After a series of discussions, we opted to follow the lead of our colleagues, Stephen Durrant, Li Wai-yee, and David Schaberg, who adopted, in their forthcoming translation of the *Zuo zhuan*, "lord" for Chinese *gong*. Thus, we translate every ruler of a regional polity as "lord" except for those monarchs who adopted a "king" (*wang* 王) title. In a few cases when a specific rank matters (e.g., in the introduction to Part I and in chapter 1), we prefer to transliterate. As for the ranks of merit adopted in the state of Qin since the mid-fourth century BCE and used in the Qin and Han empires, we prefer numbers (e.g. "second rank of merit") over direct translation.

Administrative units. We opted for uniformity with the majority of other publications in the field; hence we invariably translate *jun* 郡 as "commandery," *xian* 縣 as "county," *xiang* 鄉 as "canton," and *li* 里 as "hamlet," although in a few cases alternative translations would be possible.

Names. Following Chinese conventions we normally refer to rulers by their posthumous names (*shi* 謚); an exception is the First Emperor of Qin prior to his adoption of the imperial title; during these years (246–221 BCE) we refer to him by his private name, King Zheng of Qin.

Transliteration. For renderings of Chinese terms we use *Hanyu pinyin*, except for those authors who prefer an alternative transliteration (e.g., Hsing I-tien and not Xing Yitian).

Translation. All translations are by the authors unless indicated otherwise. For the reader's convenience, we identify, whenever relevant, the scroll (*juan* 卷, indicated by Roman numbers), chapter (*pian* 篇), and section/paragraph (*zhang* 章) of the premodern Chinese texts; they are separated by a period and are followed by the page number of the modern edition, separated by a colon. Whenever we cite recently unearthed texts, we indicate the slip number according to the sequence proposed by the original publishers; the characters are rendered in their modern form according to the editors' or other scholars' suggestions.

Transcription of paleographic materials. In transcribing paleographic materials we use the modern form of Chinese characters. □ stands for undecipherable characters; ◇ stands for a broken slip.

Dates. Finally, all historical dates cited are Before the Common Era (BCE) unless otherwise indicated.

General Introduction

Qin History Revisited

Yuri Pines with
Lothar von Falkenhausen,
Gideon Shelach, and
Robin D. S. Yates

In the long history of what is now known as "Chinese" civilization, the state of Qin occupies a special place. Having conquered or otherwise subjugated most of the East Asian subcontinent by 221 BCE,[1] Qin put an end to centuries of turmoil, internecine warfare, and endless bloodshed between the so-called Warring States. Proudly proclaiming that warfare would never arise again, the king of Qin declared himself the First Emperor (Qin Shi Huangdi 秦始皇帝, r. 246–221–210), inaugurating thereby what he hoped to be a lengthy age of orderly rule, universal compliance, and prosperity for all. Although these goals were not fulfilled, and despite ongoing resistance to Qin's rule among some of the new subjects, the Emperor and his aides succeeded in a few years to lay the institutional and ideological foundations of all later "Chinese" empires, thus establishing the basis for the most durable succession of imperial polities worldwide. The Qin dynasty itself, however, was exceptionally short-lived: it started to crumble immediately after the death of the First Emperor, and in 207 it was toppled by a popular uprising of unprecedented scope and ferocity. Qin's remarkable success and its astounding collapse fascinated generations of statesmen, thinkers, and scholars and became the focus of controversies that continue to this day.

For two millennia, debates about Qin's history, its ideology, its cultural affiliation, and the appropriateness of its policies revolved overwhelmingly around conflicting interpretations of a single major source of Qin history—the *Historical Records* (*Shiji* 史記) by Sima Qian 司馬遷 (c. 145–90). In recent decades, however, this situation has changed dramatically. A series of remarkable archaeological discoveries of Qin material remains, of which the First Emperor's Terracotta Army is only the most famous, has radically expanded our knowledge of Qin's culture and of its historical trajectory. Of particular significance are discoveries of Qin paleographic materials. These materials are inscribed on almost every possible material—bronze and iron, stone and jade, bamboo, wood, and clay—and cover an extraordinarily broad range of topics: local and empire-wide administration, edicts, statutes, ordinances, other legal materials, popular and elite religion, political declarations, international relations, historiography, private letters, and much else. The sheer quantity of documents excavated and retrieved so far, which exceeds by far all Qin-related materials surviving in the received texts, explains their revolutionary role in reconstructing Qin history.[2] These new data, which come to us directly without the mediation of post-Qin ideological biases, and which bring to light aspects that the received texts do not address, allow us not only to expand our knowledge of Qin but, more important, to challenge some of the most strongly held beliefs about Qin history and culture.

The archaeological and paleographic revolution in Qin studies is duly reflected in the huge number of publications on Qin history in China and Japan, where several monographs and well over 100 articles are published annually.[3] In contrast, in the Western scholarly community the incorporation of new materials has been considerably slower. For decades, Derk Bodde's seminal *China's First Unifier: A Study of the Ch'in Dynasty as Seen in the Life of Li Ssu* (1938) remained the only scholarly monograph on Qin history in English, serving, together with Bodde's chapter on the Qin in the first volume of the *Cambridge History of China* (Bodde 1986) as the major source of information about Qin for the anglophone public. Even in recent years, and in spite of the worldwide renown of the Terracotta Army, the volume of Qin-related publication activity in the West remains minuscule. The three most notable exceptions are a translation of recently unearthed Qin legal materials (Hulsewé 1985) and two monographs on the earliest known Qin stone inscriptions—those carved on the famous fifth-century "Stone Drums of Qin" (Mattos 1988) and on the steles commemorating the First Emperor's inspection tours (Kern 2000). To these excellent works one should add several books devoted to the Terracotta Army, especially two recent exhibition catalogs in which experts on the Qin collaborated to present the latest findings related to the First Emperor's mausoleum (Portal 2007; Thote and Falkenhausen 2008; see also Khayutina 2013). In addition, a newly published introductory-level work presents a refreshingly novel and updated perspective on Qin (Lewis 2007). These publications are supplemented by a handful of articles and book chapters, many of which written by co-editors of this volume (e.g., McLeod and Yates 1981; Yates 1985/7, 1987, 1995; Falkenhausen 2004, 2006; Pines 2004, 2005/6; Shelach and Pines 2005). Yet the more we and others have been publishing on Qin-related issues, the clearer it has become that the Western audience needs to be informed of the latest developments in scholarship on the Qin by a volume that makes full use of the newly available materials and utilizes the most up-to-date approaches and methods from all fields, bridging the divides between history, archaeology, paleography, and anthropology.

It is, in particular, the desire to synthesize the scholarly achievements of Chinese and Western researchers that has inspired our endeavor. In December 2008, fifteen scholars from Canada, China (Mainland and Taiwan), Germany, Israel, and the United States gathered for a ten-day workshop at the Institute for Advanced Study of the Hebrew University of Jerusalem. The group included archaeologists and historians, specialists in paleography and religion, historiography and literature, and scholars working on administrative, intellectual, military, and legal history; they all presented cutting-edge analyses from their respective fields in an attempt to chart new areas of interdisciplinary consensus, to map ongoing controversies, and to explore still-challenging enigmas. Needless to say, we made progress, but Qin studies is now such a large field that we were obliged to focus our attention only on certain areas, while many issues and topics were left untouched, most notably questions relating to the Qin economy and the mausoleum of the First Emperor. The present volume contains some of the papers presented at the workshop and thus conveys, albeit by necessity incompletely, the joint insights of the participants.

The volume is divided into three parts of three chapters each. In the archaeological part I, we use material evidence to address the development of Qin from its earliest traceable origins to the collapse of the Empire. Part II, on the state and society of Qin, elucidates aspects of Qin religious, social, and administrative history, putting them in a broader perspective by comparing them with developments during the subsequent Han dynasty (漢, 206 BCE–220 CE). The chapters in part II primarily use paleographic evidence. Finally, the chapters in part III are based mainly on the transmitted textual data and focus on the image of the Qin Empire in later times and on its historical impact; this section ends with a chapter written by a historian of the Roman Empire, in an attempt to provide a comparative perspective on the Qin imperial enterprise. Each section is preceded by a short introduction that presents a broader picture of agreements and controversies around each of the topics involved.

In what follows we present a brief summary of the available sources and then provide an outline of Qin history as we understand it. These introductory sections are aimed primarily at students and a general audience who are not familiar with Qin history; those colleagues acquainted with the topic may wish to skip directly to the thematic sections.

SOURCES FOR QIN HISTORY

The Received Texts

The earliest references to Qin in transmitted textual sources appear in two canonical collections: the *Book of Poems* (*Shi jing* 詩經) and the *Venerated Documents* (*Shang shu* 尚書). The first contains a selection of Qin poems, the majority of which are indistinguishable in their style and content from those of other early Zhou 周 polities. Only one ode—the "Huangniao" 黃鳥 ("The Oriole," Mao 131)—is of great historical interest, as it supposedly laments the burial of three Qin ministers selected to escort Lord Mu 秦穆公 (r. 659–621) to his grave. Lord Mu, whose exceptional position in early Qin history will be discussed below, is also attributed with the authorship of the last of the *Venerated Documents:* the "Qin Pledge" ("Qin shi" 秦誓). The preservation of Qin-related materials in both collections (especially the latter) may be a result of editorial efforts of the imperial Qin court erudites (*boshi* 博士), who are likely to have contributed to the final shaping of the *Poems* and the *Documents* corpus (Kern 2000: 183–196); however, even if this assertion is correct, it is noteworthy that neither collection appears to single out Qin as particularly important.

While Qin is duly covered in the earliest canonical compilations, it appears quite marginal in the majority of other early preimperial texts. Thus, in the *Zuo zhuan* 左傳 (*Zuo Commentary*)—our most detailed source for the history of the Springs-and-Autumns (Chunqiu 春秋) period (770–453)—Qin is discussed less frequently than any other important polity of the age. Evidently, the *Zuo zhuan* author(s) did not use Qin materials, and the affairs of that state are mentioned, if at all, only in the context of its interactions with its neighbors, most notably the state of Jin 晉, or when Qin occasionally participated in a variety of interstate activities. By and large, neither the *Zuo zhuan* nor the *Guoyu* 國語 (*Discourses of the States*, another important compilation of historical anecdotes from roughly the same period) treat Qin as a significant polity. The same indifference toward Qin affairs characterizes most other early texts, such as the *Lunyu* 論語, *Mozi* 墨子, the slightly later *Mengzi* 孟子,

Map 0.1. The Warring States World around 350

and other such works. In this regard, Qin differs markedly from such states as Jin and its successors, Wei 魏, Han 韓, and Zhao 趙 in the north; Qi 齊 and Lu 魯 in the east; or Chu 楚 in the south (see Map 0.1), the affairs of which are discussed in much detail.

The apparent lack of interest in Qin affairs shown by most early pre-imperial texts may reflect a geographic bias. Most of the texts mentioned above were composed in the eastern part of the Zhou (Chinese) world, especially in the states of Qi and Lu, for which Qin, located on the western edge of the Zhou realm, remained a remote and largely unknown polity. As we shall see below, with the brief exception of Lord Mu's reign, Qin remained indeed a relatively marginal player in the affairs of the states in the Central Plains; the *Zuo zhuan* even predicts that after Lord Mu "Qin would never again march eastward," while Mozi (c. 460–390) omits Qin from the list of powerful regional states. It is noteworthy, however, that, in contrast to the common view of Qin as a cultural "other" during later periods, earlier sources from the Springs-and-Autumns and early Warring States periods do not contain any hint of Qin's cultural otherness.[4]

During the second half of the Warring States (Zhanguo 戰國) period

(453–221), the situation changes markedly. As Qin became the central player in contemporaneous interstate rivalries, its affairs are discussed, even if briefly, in most texts of that age. From that period we have also the first texts that were produced, at least partly, in the state of Qin itself. Of these, *The Book of Lord Shang* (*Shangjun shu* 商君書), attributed to the great Qin reformer, Shang Yang 商鞅 (d. 338) and his followers, is the most notable. Not only does it introduce the ideas of that major Qin statesman, but even some of those chapters that were definitely written long after Shang Yang's death clearly are of Qin provenance and are informative of socioeconomic and political conditions in the state.[5] More disappointing for social and institutional historians is another major Qin compilation: *Lüshi chunqiu* (*The Spring and Autumn Annals of Sire Lü* 呂氏春秋), produced on the eve of the imperial unification under the aegis of the Qin prime minister, Lü Buwei 呂不韋 (d. 235). This encyclopedic text was prepared primarily by guest scholars from other parts of the Warring States world (Knoblock and Riegel 2000: 1–55); hence it contains few references to Qin's past or to its contemporary conditions.[6] Additional information about Qin appears in texts ascribed to authors who had paid visits to the court of Qin, e.g., Xunzi 荀子 (c. 310–230) and Han Feizi 韓非子 (d. 233). Finally, the major compendium of historical anecdotes from the Warring States period, the *Zhanguo ce* (戰國策, *Stratagems of the Warring States*) contains no less than five chapters of anecdotes about and putative speeches by eminent statesmen who served the Qin.

One of the remarkable features of many of the late Warring States period texts is their predominantly negative view of Qin. Texts of that age often treat Qin as the ultimate cultural and political other, the "mortal adversary of the All-under-Heaven," the "barbarian" state, which "has common customs with the Rong 戎 and Di 狄 [alien tribesmen]; a state with the heart of a tiger or wolf; greedy, profit-seeking and untrustworthy, which knows nothing of ritual, propriety and virtuous behavior."[7] This negative view, which perhaps reflected both natural enmity to a state engaged in aggressive territorial expansion and more objective cultural judgment (see below), remained highly influential well into the early imperial era and beyond.

Despite increasing interest in Qin's conquests, most preimperial texts contain only scanty information about political, social, religious, and cultural life in Qin. It is with this background that Sima Qian's *Historical Records* become particularly important. Sima Qian dedicated two chapters of his "Basic Annals" to Qin, one to the preimperial state of Qin, and the other to the Qin dynasty. In addition, information about Qin is spread throughout other sections of this book, including the treatises and biographies of important political and military figures. Sima Qian not only incorporated many Qin-related materials from earlier texts, such as the *Zuo zhuan* and the *Zhanguo ce,* but, more significantly, used original Qin sources now unavailable elsewhere. His chapter on preimperial Qin, in particular, relies heavily on the *Qin Records* (*Qin ji* 秦紀), a historical text prepared by the Qin court scribes, which may have been saved by Xiao He 蕭何 (257–193), the future chancellor of the Han dynasty, from the Qin imperial archives before they were burned down in 206.[8] The *Qin Records* provided Sima Qian with relatively detailed information for the last century and a half of Qin history. For earlier stages of Qin history the value of the *Qin Records* is less apparent, as they may have undergone abridgment or other manipulations, possibly even at the Qin court itself, before being utilized by Sima Qian (Pines 2005/6); but they still contain precious information.

Scholars continuously debate to what extent the account of Qin in the *Historical Records* was shaped by the author's own agenda. We address this topic in part III of this volume (see especially chapter 7, by Hans van Ess); here it will suffice to note that in our opinion the simplistic reduction of Sima Qian's attitude toward preimperial and imperial Qin to uniformly "dolorous, grim and dismal" (Watson 1993: xix–xx) appears untenable. This view neither does justice to the complexity of Sima Qian's approach, nor does it take into account that the *Historical Records* incorporate diverse and multiple sources, resulting in a remarkably multifaceted view of Qin history. Thus, while our study is often critical of the biases and inaccuracies of the *Historical Records,* we cannot deny the perennial indebtedness of historians of Qin to Sima Qian, given that so many of the sources he utilized are no longer available.

The Archaeological Discoveries

Archaeological discoveries of Qin-related sites and artifacts started in the early decades of the twentieth century, but the rate of discovery has accelerated dramatically since the 1970s.[9] Decades of archaeological excavations and occasional finds resulted in a tremendous expansion of the sources for Qin history. Propelled by the accidental discovery in 1974 of terracotta soldiers and horses in Pit 1 to the east of the First Emperor's mausoleum in Lintong 臨潼 County (Shaanxi) (Zhao Huacheng and Gao Chongwen 2002; Ciarla 2005; Duan Qingbo 2011), Qin archaeology has become one of the most prestigious and vibrant subfields of archaeological research in the People's Republic of China (PRC). Dozens of Qin sites, such as capitals, towns, palaces, cemeteries and tombs, and remains of walls, roads (for the latter, see Sanft 2011), and canals, have been scientifically surveyed and excavated, yielding a huge sample of archaeological data; among these,mortuary data, especially from elite and subelite tombs, are the most prominent (see, for example, Teng Mingyu 2003). Qin-related excavations span the entire history of the state of Qin, from its earliest stages (Zhao, chapter 1, this volume; Chen Ping 2004) to the end of the Qin dynasty; and they cover a huge territory, from the core Qin settlement area in southeastern Gansu and western Shaanxi to the territories gradually incorporated into the state and empire, such as Sichuan, Hubei, Hunan, and even Guangdong and Liaoning.

Among the major projects of Qin archaeology, the excavation of the huge mortuary complex of the First Emperor is the most famous worldwide. This work is no longer confined to the immediate vicinity of the Emperor's tomb and to the pits of the terracotta soldiers and horses but encompasses an area of some 54 km^2 (Zhao Huacheng and Gao Chongwen 2002: 16–17). Other large-scale projects include surveys and excavations at the early Qin sites in Gansu (Zhao, chapter 1, this volume); at the site of Yong 雍, the capital of the Qin state between 677 and 383, and the nearby Nanzhihui 南指揮 necropolis, both in Fengxiang 鳳翔 County (Shaanxi); at another capital, Yueyang 櫟陽; and at Xianyang 咸陽, which served as the last capital between 350 and 206.[10]

The archaeological data pertaining to Qin are not confined to the core areas of Qin or to the huge royal and imperial sites. Remains associated with Qin commoners, both from the areas that are considered to be the homeland of Qin and from those incorporated later into the Qin realm, provide glimpses into the ethnic, cultural, and economic diversity of Qin society. Once these archaeological data are systematically analyzed, they provide us with refreshingly novel views of Qin's sociopolitical and cultural trajectory, allowing us to supplement Sima Qian's narrative, address issues not mentioned in the received texts, and at times suggest major modifications to the picture presented in the *Historical Records* and elsewhere (Teng, chapter 2, this volume).

Paleographic Sources

Aside from the wealth of material data, a variety of paleographic sources are of particular importance for studying Qin history. Some of these sources are not novel at all: the inscriptions on the Qin stone drums, for instance, have been known since the early Tang 唐 dynasty (618–907 CE), and several Qin inscriptions on bronze vessels and bells, on chime stones, and on stones were discovered during the Song 宋 dynasty (960–1279 CE) and are now preserved only in later woodcut illustrations based on ink-squeeze rubbings made at that time.[11] Yet it was only in the twentieth century that a series of astounding discoveries of Qin documents began to elucidate the pivotal importance of these sources for revising the historiography of Qin. For instance, newly discovered Qin bronze and chime-stone inscriptions have not only proved the reliability of the Song illustrations but also provided important clues about the self-image of Qin leaders and their ongoing cultural proximity to the Zhou sphere, *pace* the textual evidence (Kern 2000; Pines 2005/6; introduction to part I of this volume). Even more significant was the discovery of a cache of Qin administrative and legal documents and divinatory manuals, or "daybooks" (*rishu* 日書), from Tomb 11 at Shuihudi, Yunmeng 雲夢睡虎地 (Hubei). These documents, so far the only hoard of new Qin paleographic sources to have been studied to any extent in the West, provide invaluable, even if inevitably incomplete, information about the functioning of Qin administrative and legal apparatus, and aspects of Qin religious, economic, and social life.[12] In addition, letters from Qin conscripts discovered in Tomb 4 at the same site provide us with a rare glimpse into the concerns of simple soldiers who participated in the Qin conquests (Huang Shengzhang 1980; cf. Shaughnessy 1986: 181).

Since the discovery of Tomb 11 at Shuihudi, many more texts originating from preimperial and imperial Qin have resurfaced in different parts of China. Additional administrative texts were discovered in 1980 in Tomb 50 at Haojiaping, Qingchuan 青川郝家坪 (Sichuan), and in 1989 in Tomb 6 at Longgang, Yunmeng 雲夢龍崗 (Hubei); Tomb 1 at Fangmatan, Tianshui 天水放馬灘 (Gansu) (1986), yielded daybooks, maps, and a tale of the resurrection of a dead man, the first of its kind in China; a few more daybooks were discovered in Tomb 36 at Yueshan, Jiangling 江陵岳山 (Hubei) (1986), and additional divination texts were discovered in Tomb 15 at Wangjiatai, Jingzhou 荊州王家台 (Hubei), and Tomb 30 at Zhoujiatai, Jingzhou 荊州周家台 (Hubei) (both 1993). Many other Qin-related paleographic materials were discovered at other sites or found their way into private collections. Most notable among these are jade tablets (*yuban* 玉版) with the prayer of a king of Qin to the spirit of Mt. Hua 華山, the *Clay Document* (*washu* 瓦書) that narrates the grant of a "lineage settlement" to a Qin person in 334, inscriptions on weights and measures from the time of the Qin Empire, and a great number of clay seals inscribed with the titles of various office holders and with short "slogans" through which Qin officials expressed their ideals and expectations.[13] Although less comprehensive and exciting than the finds from Shuihudi Tomb 11, these discoveries, when systematically studied, can be extraordinarily informative on aspects of Qin history. In addition, many texts from Han tombs, most notably from Tomb 247 at Zhangjiashan, Jiangling 江陵張家山 (Hubei), contain materials relevant to Qin administrative and legal practices, and Qin history and intellectual life (see, e.g., Yates, chapter 6 in this volume).

The most recent decade has witnessed a new explosion in Qin-related discoveries. Of these, the single most important, which will probably dwarf even the Shuihudi texts, is the discovery in 2002 and in 2005 of portions of a local Qin archive in a well and in a defense moat at the town of Liye, Longshan 龍山里耶 (Hunan), which was apparently the site of an ancient Chu town conquered by Qin and renamed Qianling 遷陵 (*Liye* 2007; Wang Huanlin 2007; Zhongguo Shehuikexueyuan Kaogu Yanjiusuo 2009; Hsing, chapter 4, this volume). Of the reported 37,000 boards and slips, of which 18,000 are blank, only a tiny fraction had been published when we prepared this volume; yet even this small sample provides precious data about administrative, religious, and social life in the Qin Empire. In 2012, long after the draft of our volume had been completed, Chinese archaeologists and paleographers published the first of five planned volumes of Liye documents (*Liye* 2012; Chen Wei 2012), and we have done our best to update our study so that the reader may appreciate at least some of the extraordinary wealth of these new materials.

In addition to the Liye discoveries, two caches of Qin slips of unknown provenance were smuggled to Hong Kong and repatriated by the Yuelu Academy 岳麓書院 of Hunan University and by Peking University. The Yuelu Academy slips comprise legal and administrative texts, the earliest text on dream interpretation, the earliest work on mathematics, daybooks, and other materials (Chen Songchang 2009; *Yuelu shuyuan* 2011, 2012). The Peking University batch of approximately 800 smuggled Qin bamboo and wooden slips and boards has not yet been fully published; according to the preliminary publication they contain a manual for an official's training, a brief text concerning appropriate female behavior, poems, another tale of resurrection, mathematical and medical texts, and texts related to geography, to the production of garments, and more (Beijing Daxue 2012). Altogether the richness of these findings is such that no reliable study of Qin will henceforth be possible without systematically consulting them, despite their dubious provenance.

Given the exponential increase of new material and textual discoveries and given that only a fraction of the texts discovered so far have been published, it is still impossible to assess fully the impact that paleographic sources will have on our understanding of Qin history. Nonetheless, the currently available data are sufficient for a reassessment of Qin history, particularly during the six centuries that preceded imperial unification. Thus, in what follows we make a preliminary attempt to outline the history of Qin, synthesizing the textual, material, and paleographic data as much as possible. It would be foolhardy to claim that we are able at the current stage of our knowledge to produce a definitive interpretation of Qin history; our main goal here is to introduce our new understanding.

AN OUTLINE OF QIN HISTORY

Preimperial Qin history as narrated in Sima Qian's "Basic Annals of Qin" can be conveniently divided into three periods: the legendary origins of the Ying 嬴 clan, to which the ruling house of Qin belonged; Qin's history as a regional state (ca. 800–380); and Qin's rise to the position of a major power and the would-be unifier of the East Asian subcontinent in the aftermath of reforms under lords Xian 秦獻公 (r. 384–362) and Xiao 秦孝公 (r. 361–338). Below, we shall follow this division.

Early Origins

The Qin dynastic legend as presented in the *Historical Records* is somewhat confusing. On the one hand, we are told of the glory of the Qin ancestors: descendants of the legendary thearch (*di* 帝) Zhuanxu 顓頊, they gained merit in serving almost every important leader in China's mythical and semimythical past, such as the thearchs Shun 舜 and Yu 禹, and the kings of the Shang 商 (c. 1600–1046) and Western Zhou 西周 (c. 1046–771) dynasties. On the other hand, the Ying clan, or, more precisely, its segment to which the Qin ruling lineage belonged, appears as a relatively marginal player on the fringes of the Zhou world. Even more confusingly, the narrative provides two conflicting perspectives on the origins of the Qin ruling lineage: some statements strongly connect it to the Shang polity in the east, while others emphasize its proximity to the Western Rong 西戎, the major tribal group in the west (see Zhao, chapter 1, this volume). The confusion may be a result of the conflation of several early legends, or possibly of Qin leaders' search for transregional legitimacy.

Another possible clue for the early origins of the Qin ruling lineage is provided by the recently published historical text from the collection of Chu bamboo slips that were reportedly smuggled to Hong Kong and acquired by Tsinghua (Qinghua 清華) University. The text, named by its editors *Xinian* 繫年, is likely to have been composed in the state of Chu around 370 BCE, and it provides short summaries of major historical events in the Zhou world from the beginning of the Zhou dynasty to the early fourth century BCE. According to its narrative, the Qin ancestors were among the supporters of the Shang dynasty, who rebelled against the Zhou shortly after the elimination of the Shang. After the rebellion was suppressed, they were relocated to the West, to the location named Zhuyu 朱圉; thenceforth they "for generations acted as Zhou protectors" (*Qinghua daxue* 2011: 141, slip 15). Provided the *Xinian* slips are genuine, they shed new light—if not on early Qin history, then at least on a variant of the Qin dynastic legend as circulated in the early fourth century BCE. In the eyes of some researchers, the *Xinian* narrative appears reliable, particularly in light of a tentative identification of Zhuyu with an early Qin settlement at Maojiaping, Gangu County 甘谷毛家坪, Gansu Province, where Qin cultural remains coexist with remains from a distinct local culture (Li Xueqin 2011; for Maojiaping, see Teng, chapter 2, this volume). Ostensibly this story strengthens the position of those who support the "eastern" origins of the Qin ruling lineage; in addition, possible "Shang" influences on the recently discovered early Qin burials (Zhao, chapter 1, this volume) may further strengthen this assertion. Nonetheless, a word of caution is needed here.

In the twentieth century, as ethnicity became an important analytical tool to archaeologists in China and elsewhere (see, e.g., Heather 2010: 1–35), numerous attempts were made to find archaeological proof for either the eastern or the western origin of the Qin ruling lineage (i.e., of "Qin"). Supporters of each theory turned to material evidence to show that early Qin culture displays either "eastern" or "western" features. This is still a hotly debated topic among Chinese archaeologists, and it was addressed during our discussions. On the theoretical level, we would argue that this controversy, because it is focused on "archaeological cultures" and their correlation with prehistoric ethnic identities, is insoluble (Falkenhausen 2006). Archaeological cultures are at best a heuristic device, as their definition is based on the arbitrary classification of artifacts, usually pottery typology, and they encompass much variability. When such cultures are superimposed on ancient ethnic groups, which themselves are similarly arbitrarily defined and which are much more fluid than either the ancient writers or modern scholars would like to admit, the result appears to be a handy explanation while in reality it hinders our ability to analyze sociopolitical processes represented in the archaeological data (Shelach 2009: 75–80; see also the introduction to part I of this volume).

At a more practical level, we are faced with the incomparability of textual and archaeological data regarding this question. Because the early history of Qin deals only with the Qin ruling lineage, a small elite segment of the population, it is possible that, while this elite segment came from the east, as suggested in the *Xinian* text, the vast majority who produced and used the artifacts, structures, and graves on which our current definition of "early Qin culture" is based were local inhabitants of the upper Wei 渭 River basin and its tributaries (see Map 1.1). If indeed the Qin elite were "foreign" to this region, it may be indistinguishable in the archaeological record, or its members may have adopted the local cultural traits soon after they arrived in the region (cf. Zhao, chapter 1, this volume). But it is also possible that the story of its foreign origin was made up in order to answer Warring States–period political needs. In historical terms, insofar as we treat the Qin dynastic legend not as a reflection of ancient "truth" but as a legitimating device (or, more likely, several devices) employed by Qin leaders at different stages of their history, the very question of the "real" origins of the Ying clan and its various affiliated lineages appears irrelevant. Similar to societies in other parts of the world (cf. Connerton 1989; Hobsbawm and Ranger 1983; Mendels 2004), it was the invention and manipulation of those stories, rather than their historic "truth," which mattered most, not only during the rise of Qin to political and military dominance, but also after its demise

A Zhou Polity, circa 800–360 BCE

The *Historical Records* narrate the gradual empowerment of the Qin ancestors in the service of the Western Zhou, their ennoblement and later appointment as rulers of Qin. This process peaked under Lord Xiang of Qin 秦襄公 (r. 777–766), who is said to have provided crucial support to the Zhou dynasty during the crisis of 771, in the course of which the Zhou kings were obliged to relocate from the middle Wei River basin eastward, toward the area of modern Luoyang 洛陽 city (Li Feng 2006: 268–276). As a result, the *Historical Records* tell us, Lord Xiang was granted territories in the old Zhou heartland and elevated to the position of a regional lord (*zhuhou* 諸侯). Qin had become a state.

Sima Qian's narrative of the first four-odd centuries of Qin history remains laconic; significant portions of it derive from the *Zuo zhuan*, whereas there is little evidence for systematic coverage of that age in the

Qin Records. Yet despite the sketchiness of the account, we can discern the major topos of the narrative: Qin is treated as a political and cultural outsider by the rest of the Zhou world. The historian narrates gradual innovations that may testify to Qin's "acculturation," such as repeated shifts of the capitals from the "remote" west eastward toward the old Zhou heartland, the establishment of the office of scribes in 753, the abolition of human sacrifice in 384 (although the practice actually continued; see Huang Zhanyue 2004: 240–245), and so on. Yet these steps were not enough: hence the historian summarizes that on the eve of its ascendancy under Lords Xian and Xiao, "Qin was remote in Yongzhou; it did not participate in the assemblies and alliances with the lords of the Central States, who treated it like Yi 夷 and Di 翟 'barbarians'" (*Shiji* 5: 202). This view of Qin as backward and insignificant dominates the early part of the Qin-related narrative in the *Historical Records*.

That said, Sima Qian's narrative contains a few notable exceptions to the picture of Qin as a "barbarian" outsider. First, there is the story of Lord Mu—the single early Qin ruler whose reign is treated in considerable detail in the *Historical Records*. Lord Mu was by far the most successful of early Qin rulers: having intervened in succession struggles in the neighboring state of Jin, he had positioned himself as the major player in the politics of the Central Plains. This role was augmented by his support, in 635, of the restoration of the ousted King Xiang of Zhou 周襄王 (r. 651–619). Although in the later part of his reign, Lord Mu failed to advance farther eastward, he compensated this failure by an active expansion into the Rong territories to the west. Interestingly, in one of the anecdotes about Lord Mu, the *Historical Records* present him, contrary to the common picture of Qin rulers, as a representative of the "Central States" culture vis-à-vis the alien Rong (*Shiji* 5: 192–193). Thus, both culturally and in terms of his military successes and diplomatic importance, Lord Mu appears as a marked exception to the common picture of early Qin rulers as narrated by Sima Qian (Pines 2005/6: 31–32).[14]

Another important deviation from the pattern of limited knowledge of and limited respect for early Qin rulers is discernible in Sima Qian's accounts of religious activities of the lords of Qin. In several chapters, the narrative depicts the lords of Qin as exceptionally assertive in performing sacrificial rites to the supreme deity, *Di* 帝, ceremonies that were regarded as the exclusive prerogative of the Zhou kings. Sima Qian saw this as the "beginning of the usurpation": Qin, "being in a vassal position, carried out suburban sacrifices [appropriate to the Zhou king]: the superior men were overawed by this" (*Shiji* 15: 685; cf. Poo, chapter 5, this volume).

This notion may appear at first glimpse as a backward projection of the author's knowledge of Qin's eventual expansion eastward, but this is not the case. As we shall see, the archaeological and paleographic evidence suggest that Qin was even more assertive, and much less "barbarian" and "remote," than presented by Sima Qian.

The material and paleographic evidence provides a crucial corrective to Sima Qian's narrative. Most notably, it suggests cultural similarities and political proximity of Qin to the Zhou house, which contradicts the notion of its "remoteness" and "barbarism." This is most clearly seen in the observance by the Qin elites of the Zhou mortuary norms. The hallmark of these norms, established in the wake of the so-called Late Western Zhou "ritual reform" around 850 (Falkenhausen 2006: 29–73) are strict sumptuary gradations of bronze vessel assemblages, the so-called *lieding* 列鼎 system, which prescribed the precise number of bronze *ding*-cauldrons and other status-defining vessels to be used in the tomb and in the ancestral temple. From the analysis of the elite tombs of Qin, it is clear that they observed the *lieding* gradations, especially during the early stages of Qin history. While from the mid-seventh century on the usage of graded sets of bronze vessels in Qin tombs becomes less rigid, overall variations remain within the basic parameters of the Zhou system (Teng Mingyu 2003; Shelach and Pines 2006: 210–213). In certain aspects of Qin mortuary customs we even may observe considerable "Zhou conservatism": thus, Qin did not adopt typological and technological changes in bronze vessel production and usage that occurred elsewhere in the Zhou cultural sphere (Falkenhausen 2006: 326–369; cf. the introduction to part I of this volume). Similar conservatism is observable in the Qin script, as "Qin was the most faithful in carrying on the writing tradition of the Zhou dynasty" (Qiu Xigui 2000: 78). These conservative traits may have a technical rather than ideological explanation: having inherited the Zhou heartland and, perhaps, the Zhou artisans, Qin was prone to be influenced by material aspects of the Zhou cultural tradition. Yet in any case, the material evidence strongly undermines the notion of Qin's alleged "barbarism" as presented in the *Historical Records*.

While definitely belonging to the Zhou ritual-based cultural realm, Qin elites and subelites, whose tombs serve as a major source for our knowledge of early Qin society, were not slavishly following Zhou patterns. In some respects, many of them preserved what may have been indigenous mortuary practices, such as the predominant east–west orientation of graves, as opposed to the south–north orientation common during the Western Zhou and among the eastern states thereafter, and the so-called flexed burial as opposed to the extended supine posture of the deceased body common in other states. Whether or not these traits can serve as ethnic markers of the Qin population is debatable (cf. Falkenhausen 2006: 215–221; Teng, chapter 2, this volume), but in any case they do not undermine the notion of Qin's belonging to the Zhou cultural sphere. More interesting are apparent innovations made by members of the Qin elite, such as the widespread replacement of bronze vessels in the tombs with ceramic models ("numinous vessels," *mingqi* 明 器) from the middle of the Springs-and-Autumns period on. This separation between funerary vessels and bronzes used in the ancestral cult occurred in Qin earlier than in other parts of the Zhou cultural realm and may testify to an early reconceptualization of the ideas about the netherworld (Falkenhausen 2004, 2006: 293–321; cf. Poo, chapter 5, this volume). It is even possible that in this regard Qin acted as a sort of "cultural vanguard" of the Zhou world, rather than its backward periphery, although it is currently impossible to assess whether or not Qin's innovations directly contributed to adoption of *mingqi* elsewhere (cf. Thote 2009).

Another interesting aspect of early Qin history, unnoticed by Sima Qian, is the apparent political association of Qin rulers and the Zhou royal house. Qin-Zhou relations, which are attested primarily in several inscriptions (and are hinted at in such texts as *Xinian* and the *Zuo zhuan*), included ongoing marital ties between the Qin and the Zhou houses, and, even more significant, periodic visits by the Zhou kings to the state of Qin. Since royal "tours of inspection" had otherwise been discontinued after the end of the Western Zhou, royal visits to Qin appear ritually and politically significant. It is possible that Qin's position as a custodian of the Zhou heartland contributed to its special relations with the Zhou; and while the dearth of data prevents us from reconstructing the nature of these relations in full, their very existence testifies to Qin's position as a potentially important political actor in the Zhou realm (see more in Pines 2004: 4–23; cf. the introduction to part I of this volume).

Qin's ties with the Zhou may also explain what appears as a partial appropriation of the Zhou royal rhetoric by the Qin rulers. This appropriation is manifested primarily in a series of inscriptions on the bronze vessels and chime stones of the lords of Qin. These inscriptions identify the lords of Qin as bearers of Heaven's Mandate, who stay, just like the Zhou kings, in the vicinity of the [Supreme] Thearch; according to these inscriptions, the Qin leaders reside "within the footsteps of Yu 禹" (a possible reference to their claim to possess the entire All-under-Heaven), and they are "cautiously caring for the Man 蠻 and the Xia 夏" (namely, for aliens and Zhou-world peoples alike alike). Each of these claims is unparalleled in the official parlance of other regional states of the Springs-and-Autumns or early Warring States periods, and their combination testifies to the exceptional assertiveness of the Qin rulers.[15]

Material evidence provides further indications for the peculiarly assertive posture of the Qin rulers. Although the major Qin capital of that period, Yong, is smaller in size and less centralized in its layout than the capitals of some other contemporaneous polities (Shelach and Pines 2006: 207–208; Qu Yingjie 1991), the Qin rulers' graves far exceed in scale those in the eastern part of the Zhou world. What Falkenhausen defines in the introduction to part I of this volume as "gigantomania" of Qin rulers is evident already in the earliest known tomb of a Qin ruler, Tomb 2 at Dabuzishan, Li County 禮縣大堡子山 (Gansu). Although the tomb was exhaustively looted in the 1990s, its huge size is far in excess of the tombs of other regional lords and possibly even of the contemporaneous royal Zhou tombs (Falkenhausen 1999: 471–73; Dai 2000; introduction to part I of this volume; Zhao, chapter 1, this volume; Li Feng 2011).

Tomb 2 at Dabuzishan in turn is dwarfed by those from the Nanzhihui necropolis. The only large tomb so far excavated in this cemetery is Tomb 1, tentatively identified as the resting place of Lord Jing 秦景公 (r. 576–537). The tomb is huge: two sloping tomb passages that lead to the bottom of the tomb from the east and the west are respectively 156 m and 85 m long; the burial chamber itself is 60 m long (from east to west), 40 m wide, and 24 m deep. As the tomb was looted in antiquity, its ritual set of bronze vessels and other precious grave goods were not found. However, findings such as the inscribed fragments of chime-stones, 166 human victims each placed in their own coffins, as well as the huge wooden beams used to construct the burial chamber, and evidence for a wooden structure built above ground (Teng Mingyu 2003: 83), all suggest an extraordinarily rich burial. Even though we still lack a systematic perspective on rulers' tombs from the Zhou period, the evidence heretofore seems to strongly support Falkenhausen's (1999: 486) observation that Lord Jing's tomb "may well constitute an infraction, in spirit if not in letter, of the sumptuary privileges due to the rulers of a polity."

It may be tempting to interpret the evidence we have as indication of Qin becoming a ruler-centered polity already during the Springs-and-Autumns period when the position of most regional lords in the Zhou world was that of *primus inter pares* rather than of omnipotent monarchs (Pines 2002a: 136–163). Yet even though the idea of relative weakness of the hereditary nobility in Qin has been proposed in several studies (e.g., Thatcher 1985; Teng, chapter 2, this volume), one must be cautious in adopting it uncritically. Sketchy as it is, the evidence of the *Historical Records* suggests that during most of the fifth century, Qin suffered from the same process of deterioration of the sovereign's position vis-à-vis that of powerful aristocratic lineages as did the rest of the Zhou world (Yoshimoto 1995). Domestic struggles weakened the state militarily, and, by the beginning of the fourth century, it faced territorial losses and overall political deterioration. It is against this background that Lord Xian and his heir, Lord Xiao, initiated a series of reforms that propelled Qin into the position of a major superpower and the would-be unifier of the Zhou world.

A Warring Kingdom: 360–221 BCE

The last century and a half of Qin history is covered in our sources incomparably better than the earlier periods: the relatively detailed narrative of the *Historical Records* is supplemented by a few contemporaneous textual sources and, more significantly, by rich paleographic and material data. The outline of the history for this period can conveniently follow Sima Qian's "Basic Annals of Qin": it is a story of irresistible territorial expansion. Qin revitalized itself under two energetic leaders, lords Xian and Xiao, and especially thanks to a series of profound reforms launched by Lord Xiao's famous aide, Shang Yang (a.k.a. Lord Shang 商君 or Gongsun Yang 公孫鞅). Under Shang Yang's aegis, Qin became "a state organized for war and agriculture" (paraphrasing Lewis 2007), and the results quickly became apparent. Shang Yang personally led the Qin armies to strategically important victories over the neighboring powerful state of Wei 魏, causing the latter to relocate its capital farther to the east (Map 0.1), and restoring thereby Qin's position as a major power. Thus began a century during which Qin gobbled up in a "silkworm fashion" the territories of neighboring states, expanding into the heartland of the Zhou world (Lewis 1999a: 632–641).

After the initial successes of the Qin armies, the eastern states attempted to create a "Vertical Alliance" that was supposed to block Qin's advance; but perpetual disputes among the allies prevented them from effectively withstanding Qin. The latter benefitted enormously from the annexation in 316 of "Heaven's storehouse," the fertile land of Sichuan, which provided Qin with crucial economic advantages over its rivals (Sage 1992). Not only was Sichuan rich in natural resources, such as iron and salt, but, once the raging waters of the Min 岷 River had been controlled through the efforts of the governor of the region, Li Bing 李冰 (fl. 250) and his son, the Chengdu Plain produced an enormously abundant and reliable harvest of grain, which the Qin used to supply its armies. The colonization of Sichuan through the establishment of military settlements and through sending to the region many thousands of convicts to exploit its mineral and natural resources provided the Qin rulers with a viable model of effective incorporation of the newly conquered territories into their expanding realm (Sage 1992; Korolkov 2010: 58–98).

Sichuan's strategic location in the Upper Yangzi River basin further improved Qin's standing vis-à-vis its powerful southeastern neighbor, the state of Chu. In 278, the Qin armies, led by one of its most brilliant generals, Bai Qi 白起 (also transliterated as Bo Qi, d. 257), inflicted a major defeat on Chu, captured its capital, then located just north of modern Jingzhou, Hubei province, occupied the Chu heartland, and effectively neutralized Chu as a competitor of Qin. Two decades later, Bai Qi achieved another illustrious victory over the state of Zhao, the last of Qin's truly powerful rivals. Qin's final success was delayed by a series of military setbacks, domestic turmoil, and climatic problems; but once its armies set on the final war of unification, they proved to be almost unstoppable. Despite occasional tough resistance, most notably by Chu armies, and despite instances of postconquest guerilla-style warfare against the Qin government, the unification was achieved within just twelve years (233–221) (Map 0.2).[16]

Behind this narrative of territorial expansion we may discern several important developments that were of crucial importance for Qin's successes, and which had a lasting impact on the Qin Empire and beyond. Of these, the reorganization of the military is the most notable. Like other contemporaneous polities, Qin transformed a small army primarily based on aristocratic elite warriors mounted in light chariots into a large infantry-based army, filled by peasant conscripts. Military concerns, such as the establishment of universal conscription, ensuring the soldiers' loyalty, providing adequate supplies for the armies, and so on, had far-reaching impact on Qin's administrative, legal, social, and economic policies. To illustrate the degree of militarization of the society, it will suffice to mention that Qin divided its entire population into families of five, for the purposes of mutual surveillance and military recruitment (one man was taken from each family to fill a squad of five soldiers in the army), blurring the differences between social and military organizations. Like members of the general population, the members of the squads were obliged to denounce each other's crimes, particularly absconding

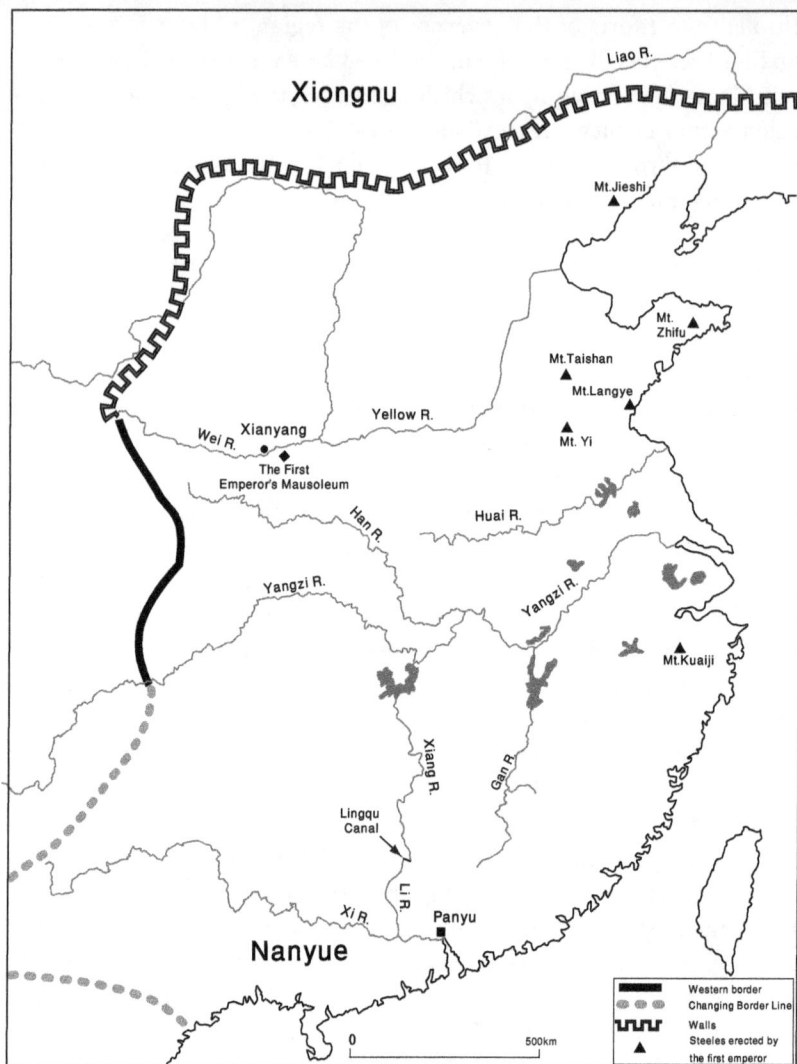

Map 0.2. The Qin Empire (adapted from Tan Qixiang 1991)

from the battlefield, greatly facilitating the state's control over the population (Lewis 1990: 53–96; Yates 1999, 2007, 2009c).[17] Another indicator
of the overall militarization of the society are Qin legal statutes, which
stipulate collection of fines in sets of armor or shields rather than in cash
or in grain (Yates 2009c). Military merit also became the major avenue

for entering the Qin sub-elite, as minor ranks were granted for cutting off enemies' heads (Zhu Shaohou 2008; cf. Teng, chapter 2, this volume).

Another major change was demographic. Archaeological data from the last two centuries of Qin history testify to a considerable increase in the number of Qin burials in the previously marginal areas in the Lower Wei River valley and into the loess highlands to the north. Qin burials are further found in the areas of its military expansion, most notably in Sichuan, the Han river basin, and further to the south and the east (Falkenhausen 2004: 110–115; Teng, chapter 2, this volume). While several explanations can be provided for the appearance of Qin graves in these areas, the most likely one is that they reflect demographic growth and increasing expansion of Qin population in the wake of concomitant military and economic changes.[18]

During the Warring States period, the population of Qin became increasingly mobile. While Qin settlers often followed the Qin armies, migrants from other polities were also lured into Qin lands, especially to the newly developed territories. The "Lai min" 徠民 chapter of *The Book of Lord Shang*, composed, according to the historical data contained therein, around 250, laments the scarcity of population in the Qin territories and proposes a series of measures aimed at attracting migrants. They duly arrived, as is suggested, among other evidence, from Qin burials of that period (Teng, chapter 2, this volume). Aside from voluntary migration, Qin populated the newly developed territories through the forced resettlement of convicts and of recently conquered populations. In turn, Qin also may have suffered from out-migration, which it tried to limit, but not always successfully. Qin legal documents record numerous cases of ordinary individuals who "left the country" (*chu bang* 出邦); and the crime of "absconding" (*wang* 亡) is also vividly present in Qin legal documents and the daybooks (Shi Weiqing 2004c; Zhang Gong 2006). It is impossible to assess the overall population dynamics of that age, but it is likely that the balance was in Qin's favor.

Migration aside, the population increase in Qin may reflect primarily the impact of contemporaneous technological and economic developments. Most notably, widespread introduction of iron tools, that since the fourth century BCE were produced in an industrial fashion (Wagner 1993), revolutionized agriculture, improving cultivation capabilities, increasing yields, and making it possible to turn virgin soils and swampy areas into rich farmland. Qin was exceptionally apt in responding to these opportunities. Its legal statutes testify to strict supervision over mining, production of iron tools, and their dissemination to the peasants (Hulsewé 1985: C14: 112; A8: 27; A47: 53). More broadly, the Qin government was concerned with all aspects of agricultural production, from the fitness of the draft animals to weather conditions, which were to be reported regularly by the county authorities to authorities in the capital (ibid, A7: 26; A1: 21). These efforts, which are stipulated in an ideal form in the *Book of Lord Shang*, surely contributed to the increasing productivity of Qin agriculture and to corresponding population increase.

One of the most immediate impacts of the "iron revolution" was the possibility to bring wastelands under cultivation through improving irrigation and undertaking other hydraulic projects. In this respect Qin appears to have been one of the most advanced places in the Zhou world, if not the most advanced. It is renowned for the masterful hydraulic construction of the Dujiangyan 都江堰 weir in Sichuan, which remains intact even today. Many other projects brought about similarly impressive results, at least in the short term. Sima Qian tells about Zheng Guo 鄭國, an agent of the state of Han 韓, who initiated a large-scale irrigation project in Qin lands with the aim of distracting it from military expansion. When his plot was discovered, Zheng was not executed but allowed to continue the project because of its obvious benefits to Qin: vast areas of previously unusable wasteland north and east of the capital were turned into fertile fields. The historian tells that after the project was finished "there were no longer any famines in the Guanzhong area [關中, the core Qin territory]" (*Shiji* 29: 1408; cf. Zhang Hua 2003).[19] The archaeologically attestable increasing density of Qin settlement in the lower Wei River valley may be directly connected to irrigation projects in that area.[20]

The government activism in developing the wastelands, in promoting agricultural production, and in mobilization of the population for economic (e.g., hydraulic) and military tasks may well be thought to make Qin an emblematic case study of "hydraulic" or "agro-managerial" despotism as analyzed by Karl Wittfogel (1957).[21] Indeed, certain indicators support such a characterization of Qin. Although, contrary to popular caricatures, Qin was neither "totalitarian" nor senselessly autocratic, it was nonetheless an extraordinarily well-organized and powerful state with an intrusive bureaucracy, whose tentacles penetrated the entire society, in a very "modern" fashion "down to the humblest inhabitant of the least of its villages" (Hobsbawm 1992: 80), and which attempted to reshape the social, economic, and even cultural life of the populace. Even a brief look at the Shuihudi regulations discloses an amazing degree of state activism. The officials were concerned with everything: from the fitness of the oxen, which were measured every season to the inch, with punishment inflicted on local officials and village heads if the oxen decreased in girth, to the number of rat holes in the granaries, to the amount of offspring of cows and ewes—the overseers were punished for insufficient birth rates among the animals (Hulsewé 1985, A7:26; D130: 162–3; C19:115). They closely supervised the life of rural hamlets, where even an appointment of a hamlet head and a postman required the approval of the county authorities (*Liye* 2012: 8-157; Giele 2005: 362–365; cf. Yates 1995).

Qin's economic policy certainly deserves its "agro-managerial" designation. The state apparatus was actively involved in agricultural production, and appears to have had an impressive impact on the life of peasant households. The economic power of Qin's bureaucracy derived primarily from its control of land resources. *Pace* Han accusations of the Qin as destroyer of the legendary "well-field" system and creator of the land market which "allowed the rich to amass myriads of fields" (*Hanshu* 24A:1162), Qin did not allow free transaction of land. From the currently available data it appears that the rights of Qin peasants with regard to their plots extended only to management and the reaping of harvests, but not necessarily to "alienation" (i.e., land could not be sold to non-kinsmen).[22] Part of land was managed directly by the state (the so-called "public fields" 公田 and probably also "fields of the conscripts" 卒田); the rest was possessed by the peasants but closely supervised by the authorities. The "office in charge of the fields" (*tian guan* 田官), which appears frequently in the Liye documents published so far, maintained registration of the plots, prepared cadastral maps (Yates 2012), and closely supervised annual harvest yields, adjusting tax quotas accordingly (Korolkov 2010). Overall, the impact of the state on agricultural production—either through "opening up" fields or through direct and indirect intervention into the lives of the peasants—appears as one of the singularly important features of the State and Dynasty of Qin.

Economic activism of the state was not confined to farming and to production of iron utensils. To assess its breadth suffice it to read a list of evaluations submitted to higher authorities by the Bureau of Finance of Qianling County (Liye): reports on lacquer and on workshops, on bamboo cultivated in groves and on ponds, on orchards and on markets, on convict laborers who died or absconded and on financial transactions, on mining and on ironworks, on arrows, weapons, chariots, craft materials and their equipment, and so on (*Liye* 2012: 8-454 [456]; 8-493 [491], etc.).[23] The state officials were engaged in manufacture, transportation and market transactions; few if any areas of economic life remained outside their interest. Yet Qin was not a simplistic "command economy," as is sometimes imagined; rather its officials were deeply involved in the vibrant market economy of their age, and their economic functioning appears quite sophisticated, on a par with that of the state apparatus under Emperor Wu of Han (漢武帝, r. 141–87) (Yates, 2012).

The Qin government's activism would not have been possible without an elaborate bureaucratic apparatus. While we lack precise data as for the evolution of Qin's bureaucracy, it is clear that by the end of the Warring States period it was impressively sophisticated and mature. Elaborate rules governed selection, promotion, and advancement of officials, their ranks and salaries, and, most notably their performance, and the precise amount of time, down to the day, they spent serving in each office (Yates 1995). Everything had to be reported to the superiors: from the amount of spoilt and worn iron tools loaned by the government to the peasants, to deaths of government horses and cattle, to transactions of grain, hay and straw (Hulsewé 1985, A8 and A9: 27, A19-A22: 34–39). In addition to an annual check, officials' performance was investigated at the end of their term; those responsible for inaccurate records were fined (Yates 1995). The state may have mistrusted its servants: hence, it demanded no less than four signatures to register grain coming into a granary and defined any misreporting of grain transfer as theft (Hulsewé 1985, A85: 79; A87: 81). Liye documents testify to meticulous recording of even minimal transactions, such as selling the leftovers from the state-sponsored sacrifices for a tiny amount of one coin (*qian* 錢) (*Liye* 2012: 8-1091 [1093]; Chen Wei 2012: 259-260 [who adds slip 8-1002 to 8-1091]; Jiang Feifei 2011). Violations of discipline were mercilessly punished: Liye materials testify to manifold fines imposed on local officials, and even indicate a sort of "inflation of fines" under the Imperial Qin (Yates 2012/13). The tightness of surveillance over the officials under the Qin is so impressive that it appears to some as dwarfing the efficiency of Chinese bureaucracy during the late imperial period (Jiang Feifei 2011), although it should be noted that we still lack sufficient data for a systematic comparison.

Perhaps the clearest indication of the power and assertiveness of the Qin government was its ability to orchestrate a profound social restructuring. This restructuring is attributed to Shang Yang, who reportedly proposed the abolition of the old hereditary aristocracy and its replacement with a new social order, based on twenty ranks of merit for which most males were eligible, regardless of pedigree or economic status. The eight lowest ranks were distributed in exchange for military achievements, particularly decapitation of enemy soldiers, or could be purchased by wealthy individuals; successful rank-holders could be incorporated into the military or civilian administration and thereafter be promoted up the social ladder. Each rank granted its holder economic, social, and legal privileges, such as the right to cultivate a certain amount of land and to be given slaves to assist in its cultivation, and the right to redeem certain punishments (see introduction in Loewe 1960; Yates 1999; cf. Loewe 2010).[24] Although Qin remained a highly stratified society, and ordinary commoners were normally not able to reach beyond the eighth rank in the hierarchy, the former power of the aristocratic lineages and of the close relatives of the Qin ruler had been fundamentally curtailed. More significantly, the state henceforth gained unprecedented control over determining an individual's social status, and, *mutatis mutandis*, over social life in general.

The new rank system, which eventually incorporated a majority of the male population, effectively transformed the society from one based on pedigree in which the individual's position was determined primarily by his/her lineage affiliation, into a much more open one, in which individual merits, especially military merits, for the most part determined social position (Yates 1987; Teng, chapter 2, this volume). The ranks were not fully inheritable; under normal circumstances a man could designate one heir to his rank, but the heir received one or two ranks lower than his father, and the decrease was sharper for the holders of higher ranks (except for the one or two highest ones). This system therefore generated a much higher degree of social mobility than had prevailed in the aristocratic age. Indeed, two of the Liye population registers suggest that the majority of households were headed by ranked individuals, approximately one quarter of whom were identified as "nobles" (*dafu* 大夫), i.e., holders of rank five and higher (*Liye* 2012: 8-19; 8-1236 + 8-1791; Chen Wei 2012: 32-33, 297; Yates 2012/2013). This high proportion of ranked individuals may reflect either particularly high possibilities of individual advancement in the wake of wars of unification, or lavish bestowal of ranks on the recently subjugated population in an attempt to legitimate the Qin regime (cf. Hsing, chapter 4, this volume); but it also suggests that Qin's ranks of merit did indeed encompass the majority, or at least a significant proportion, of the country's population.

The possibilities of upward (and downward) mobility are duly reflected in predictions of a child's future that appear in the Shuihudi *Daybooks*. These suggest the extraordinarily wide range of possibilities that faced a new born Qin baby: from becoming a high-ranking minister (*qing* 卿) or a noble (*dafu* 大夫), to becoming an official (*li* 吏) or a local bravo (*yi jie* 邑傑), or, in the opposite direction, becoming a mere bondservant, a fugitive, or, in the case of females, a female slave (Wu Xiaoqiang 2000: 291–311; Yates 2002: 310). Simultaneously, a strong downward mobility existed as well, as suggested by the regulations regarding unranked descendants of the ruling house (Hulsewé 1985, D164: 174). Most amazingly, even a bondservant could receive a rank of merit in exchange for his military achievements (Hulsewé 1985, A91: 83; Yates 2002: 313). Thus, although Qin retained several groups of hereditary occupations (most notably the scribes, see introduction to part II of this volume), overall the degree of social mobility in Qin appears to have exceeded that in other Warring States polities. This in turn may have made Qin an attractive destination for migrants and may have also generated considerable support of the Qin population for its government, despite the many draconian aspects of Qin's legal system (for which see below).

The Qin social reforms were fundamentally successful, at least insofar as they were aimed at dismantling the pedigree-based aristocratic order. The demise of the hereditary aristocracy is duly reflected archaeologically, as ritual bronze vessels and their ceramic imitations disappear from Qin mortuary assemblages in the aftermath of Shang Yang's reforms (Shelach and Pines 2006: 210–212).[25] The government's success in radically modifying the aristocratic order might have encouraged it to attempt social engineering in other fields. Thus, Shang Yang reportedly tried to divide large families by adding taxes on households with multiple male adults, so as to accelerate formation of new households, which could be encouraged by tax incentives to move into the wasteland areas. Qin further weakened family solidarity by requiring family members to denounce each other's crimes. While Qin rulers did not reject family solidarity altogether—unfilial behavior was potentially a capital crime (Yates, chapter 6, this volume)—they clearly wanted to subjugate the family firmly to the state. Thus, the authorities punished the parents for unauthorized killing or mutilating their children, as the latter were evidently conceptualized as a sort of state asset (Hulsewé 1985: D56: 139). Neither the family nor other social units could remain autonomous vis-à-vis the state authority.

Introduction of laws dealing with mutual responsibility of family members and of neighbors reflect yet another aspect of Qin's "despotism": the imposition of strict control over the population. Qin is notorious for the severity of its laws, which imposed harsh penalties even for the slightest offences. These laws were indeed draconian in many respects. For example, they stipulated a variety of mutilating punishments, from shaving the beard and side whiskers to tattooing, cutting off the nose, amputation of a foot, and castration; for many crimes, the entire property of the convict could be confiscated and his family members enslaved by the state. Yet punishments were not arbitrary: Qin statutes demanded careful investigation of legal cases, punished officials for failure to follow proper legal procedure, discouraged abuse of torture and distinguished between intended and accidental offenses (Hulsewé 1985: 1–18; Yates 2009a; 2009d). Moreover, in many cases Qin statutes allowed remittance of mutilations by forced labor for the state's needs; and it is conceivable that one of the aims of the harshness of the laws was to create an additional pool of involuntary laborers to augment the regular labor conscripts.

Qin maintained a huge army of convicts, whose labor was utilized in a great variety of public works: from working in the fields, tending to pasture animals, and building walls, to working in foundries and workshops, fighting in the army and acting as prison wardens (Yates 2002; Yates 2012), and it also owned a large number of public slaves. From the Liye documents it is clear that assigning jobs to convicts was among the major tasks of the county's Bureau of Granaries and Bureau of the Director of Works. The number of these laborers was huge: a single Register of the Convict Laborers (currently on display in the Liye Museum of Qin Slips) mentions no less than 4,376 male and female bondservants working under the Qianling County Bureau of Granaries in the year 213 (Yates 2012), and it is likely that the overall number of involuntary laborers in the county was even higher than this. It is impossible to calculate the contribution of convicts and slaves to Qin's economic and military prowess, but it was surely considerable.

Among manifold means of population control in Qin, mandatory registration appears as singularly important. This measure is stipulated already in the *Book of Lord Shang* but it was only with the Shuihudi and most notably the Liye discoveries that scholars could assess the degree of its actual implementation in Qin. A sample from Liye household registries is discussed by Hsing in chapter 4, this volume; and additional data published in 2012 can supplement his discussion. Thus, previously it was known that the authorities monitored population movements through a system of passports and checkpoints; now we have a sample of such passports, including one that was issued to a five-month old toddler (together with her parent): this may well be the earliest known registration of such

a young child worldwide![26] Another group of Liye documents demonstrate the ability of local authorities in Qin to trace debtors even when
those were relocated from one county to another (slips 9-1 to 9-12; Wang
Huanlin 2007: 57–93; Zhang Junmin 2003; Sanft, in progress). The
aforementioned division of the population into groups of five households,
the members of which were connected by the system of mutual responsibility, was also aimed at facilitating population control and preventing
free movement of individuals. As mentioned above, these measures were
not always sufficient to prevent migration and absconding by those who
were impoverished or who moved freely from one location to another
due to previous cultural or economic practices;[27] but the assertiveness of
the bureaucrats who aimed at controlling geographical mobility of their
subjects is undeniable.

Popular accounts and not a few scholarly publications tend to depict
the post-Shang Yang State and Empire of Qin as despotic and even "totalitarian" polities. These assessments are usually based on selective reading of a few passages from *The Book of Lord Shang* and the *Han Feizi* as
descriptive rather than prescriptive, as well as on a peculiar understanding of the infamous "book burning" in 213 as related to "thought control"
(see more in the introduction to part III of this volume). The real situation
was immeasurably more complex, however: Qin was not an ideologically
uniform entity and its intellectual atmosphere cannot be reduced to the
"Legalist" thought, which is misunderstood as an antipode of "Confucian"
ideology.[28] Thus, while strict Qin control over its officials may well reflect
a "Legalist" mindset, the manuals employed for the officials' self-cultiva-
tion are much more accommodative of "Confucian" and other ideologies;
and the seals of Qin officials commonly refer to such "Confucian" virtues
as benevolence (*ren* 仁), sincerity (*cheng* 誠), and loyalty (*zhong* 忠).[29]
Similarly, the *Lüshi chunqiu* 呂氏春秋 reflects a much more pluralistic
and less ruler-centered ideology than a caricature of "Legalist" Qin would
assume (Sellman 2002; cf. Pines 2009). Nor was Qin a senseless tyranny:
the need to "care for the people" and to "love the people below" is not just
strongly pronounced in its officials' manuals, but is even reflected in some
of its laws and regulations, which clearly protected the people's right not
to be over-exploited by the state apparatus.[30] Overall, Qin—much like
other contemporaneous or later polities on Chinese soil—was ideologically "mixed"; uniformity of values might have been a desideratum of
certain thinkers but it was never really achieved in practice.

Similar observations can be made with regard to another supposedly
"totalitarian" feature of Qin: its attempt at cultural unification of the

people below. There is no doubt that certain members of the ruling elite of Qin were supportive of this unification; not just Qin-related texts such as *The Book of Lord Shang* and the stele inscriptions of the First Emperor reflect the desire to "unify" or "correct" deviant popular customs, but even a speech of a commandery governor recorded in the "Speech Document" (*Yu shu* 語書) from Tomb 11, Shuihudi, advocates abolition of parochial practices which were considered detrimental "to the state and to the people" (*Shuihudi* 2001: 14–16). Qin moreover tried to impose centralized control over religious life, as is reflected both in its statutes (Hulsewé 1985: D141: 166), and in a few Liye documents: in particular, a very detailed list of the officials' duties to supervise an otherwise unidentified local "temple" (*miao* 廟) is suggestive of the state's regulatory functions in the realm of religion.[31] Yet while the drive to make local cults uniform and controlled from above is indeed observable in both the Qin and the subsequent Han dynasty (Yang Hua 2011), its impact should not be exaggerated: not only did religious pluralism remain palpable through these (and subsequent) dynasties, but also the official religion itself might have been too strongly influenced by popular beliefs (Poo, chapter 5, this volume) to allow meaningful "unification from above."

One final feature of the new state that was established in the wake of Shang Yang's reforms was its high degree of centralization and the consequent strengthening of the monarch's position. Like most contemporaneous polities, and probably even more resolutely, Qin was transformed from a loose aristocratic entity into what Mark Lewis (1999a: 597) aptly names a "ruler-centered" territorial state. Independent loci of power, which might from the very beginning have been weaker in Qin than elsewhere in the Zhou world, were largely eliminated; the administration became centralized at the capital, and the officialdom itself subjected to tight control (Yates 1995). The ruler's position was farther elevated above that of the elite, especially in the aftermath of the adoption of the royal title by Lord (later King) Huiwen of Qin 秦惠文王 (r. 337–311) in 325. This elevation is fully visible archaeologically. Thus, Tomb 1 at the Zhiyang 芷陽 Necropolis in Lintong 臨潼 (Shaanxi), identified as a tomb of one of late Qin monarchs, is the largest of the rulers' tombs of the Warring States era. It measures 278 m in length and up to 3107 m² in area; with four sloping passageways, as appropriate for kings rather than for regional lords, it displays the high ambitions of its occupant and distinguishes him critically from his subjects (Falkenhausen 2004: 120–121). The exalted status of Qin rulers is further reflected in the layout of the last Qin capital, Xianyang 咸陽 (350–207), which was dominated by towering palatial buildings (Lu Qingsong 2010). This tendency for rulers to engage in an ever-escalating "gigantomania" peaked in the aftermath of the imperial unification, as is evident from various famous projects associated with the First Emperor, such as his mausoleum complex and the never-completed Epanggong 阿房宮 palace (Sanft 2008; Shelach, chapter 3, this volume).

The scope and depth of sociopolitical transformation in the state of Qin during the fourth and third centuries allows us to speak of this period as a second birth of the Qin polity. This transformation was duly accompanied by manifold cultural changes, some of which are observable archaeologically. Thus, the disappearance of the hereditary aristocracy, the major bearer of the Zhou elite culture, is duly reflected in the afore-mentioned disappearance of old mortuary status-defining assemblages; while the influx of previously marginal strata into the Qin social elite is reflected, in turn, by the proliferation of new mortuary practices. For instance, the so-called catacomb burials—placing the deceased in a horizontal chamber adjacent to a vertical shaft, in distinction to a vertical grave [pit] burial common in Qin cemeteries theretofore—became strongly pronounced in Qin cemeteries of the late Warring States period (Shelach and Pines 2006: 214–215; see also Poo, chapter 5, this volume). These and other changes in Qin mortuary customs were not necessarily deliberately introduced from above, but rather were the results of multiple processes "from below," such as the ongoing re-conceptualization of death, the influx of migrants from the east, intensified cultural interaction with non-Zhou peoples, and, most likely, the new prominence of lower social strata that had been previously archaeologically invisible. Yet these changes, and the diversification of Qin burial customs in general (Teng, chapter 2, this volume), reflect a more culturally diverse society, one in which there was a place even for the customs and symbols associated with the cultures of non-Zhou peoples.

The cumulative effect of cultural changes of the Warring States period on the Qin place in the Zhou world was complex. On the one hand, it seems that these changes, most notably Qin's abandonment of the Zhou ritual system, might have contributed toward a more "nativist" outlook of the Qin people, increasing the gap between Qin and the core Zhou states of the east. This may explain why during the latter half of the Warring States period the notion of Qin's cultural otherness and alleged "barbarism" became strongly pronounced, and why it might have even influenced Qin's own self-image (Pines 2004/5: 23–35; Shelach and Pines 2006). On the other hand, the period under discussion witnessed also the converse process of increasing cultural integration of Qin into the Zhou world. Qin's ties with its eastern neighbors intensified through either conquest or immigration, in particular, through the influx of foreign advisors, some of whom climbed to the very top of the Qin government apparatus (Moriya 2001; Huang Liuzhu 2002: 41–50). These men served as a cultural bridge between Qin and the eastern and southern (Chu) states. Furthermore, the need to accommodate and incorporate the newly conquered eastern and southern populations required the preservation of the common cultural heritage of the Zhou realm. Hence, while Qin dis-tinguished itself from the Zhou world, it did not abandon its legacy alto-gether; and, by the end of the Warring States period, its rulers became engaged in what appears as a renewed Zhou "acculturation." This process is manifested in the activities of the Qin prime minister Lü Buwei, who assembled a group of eastern and southern thinkers at the court of Qin, in the hopes that their work would enhance the cultural prestige of Qin in the Zhou world and facilitate thereby the success of the impending unification.

The complexity of Qin's cultural dynamics explains why no general-ization can adequately summarize the cultural appearance of this state. Qin was both innovative and traditionalist; "barbarian-looking" and "Zhou-oriented"; "Legalist" and "Confucian." It was engaged in a bitter struggle with its neighbors, but welcomed as much elite migrants from the rival states as immiserated peasants; it implemented much of Shang Yang's "Legalist" program but continued to maintain "Confucian" virtues. This complex background may explain some of the contradictory assess-ments of Qin's cultural affiliation in the Warring States period and in Han literature, as well as in modern studies, and should caution us against the careless adoption of later categories and clichés while analyzing the Qin's political and cultural trajectory.

Many questions concerning the nature and organization of the Qin state on the eve of the imperial unification cannot be adequately answered at the current stage of our knowledge. For instance, more fine-tuning is necessary before we can understand properly the dynam-ics of resistance and accommodation to the Qin occupation among Qin's eastern and southern neighbors. How efficient was Qin in incorporating the local elites and officials of the conquered territories into its admin-istrative apparatus? How adaptive were its officials to local conditions when coming to impose Qin laws and regulations? When did they try to incorporate newly conquered territories fully into the Qin centralized administration, and when did they allow local customs and practices to continue *sub rosa?* Which social groups among the occupied populations resisted the Qin, and which were more prone to cooperate? What were, if any, the spatial and temporal fluctuations in Qin policies of conquest and annexation? While these questions still cannot be answered precisely due to the dearth of relevant sources, future studies may address them in a more systematic way.[32]

Epilogue: The Qin Empire and Beyond

The last stage of Qin's history, the fourteen years of the unified empire, is incomparably better studied than earlier periods. The *Historical Records* provide a detailed account of the rise and fall of the Qin Empire. Its major ingredients are: the successful conquest of the rival "hero-states" of the Warring States period by King Zheng 政 of Qin; his adoption in 221 of an imperial title (*huangdi* 皇帝, literally "August Thearch"); a series of reforms aimed at solidifying political and cultural unity; the military expansion northward and the building of the Great Wall; the parallel expansion southward into what is now Guangdong and Guangxi Provinces and the northern part of Vietnam; and the increasing tension between the First Emperor and the members of the intellectual community. Sima Qian narrates how the emperor's hubris led him to multiple excesses, which eventually brought about the dynasty's downfall soon after his death in 210. In two years of massive uprisings (209–207), the dynasty collapsed and, after five additional years of civil war, it was replaced by the new Han dynasty.

While the Qin imperial unification is sometimes erroneously presented as a "rupture" in Chinese history, current evidence suggests fundamental continuities on the institutional and cultural level between preimperial and imperial Qin (see introduction to Part I of this volume); hence the set of questions posed above with regard to Qin's territorial expansion during the late Warring States period is applicable, *mutatis mutandis*, to Imperial Qin as well. That said, the unprecedented territorial scope of Qin's empire makes the issue of the degree of its incorporation of the newly conquered lands all the more intriguing. Currently, both archaeological surveys and the paleographic data, particularly the Liye documents, suggest a very impressive degree of success in terms of radically reshaping administrative, social and cultural life of its new subjects.[33] However, before we draw sweeping conclusions based on these materials, a voice of caution is needed. First, only a small part of the Liye documents has been published so far; and, second, these documents overwhelmingly reflect the perspective of Qin officials, who naturally present the realm as much more ordered and well-ruled than it might have really been. Some scattered evidence to the persistent "banditry" under the Qin Empire may testify to much stronger resistance of the local population to the conquerors than we currently know about.[34] More data will be required before we can conclude to what degree Qin's "unification" was truly successful.

Aside from the debates over the effectiveness of the Imperial Qin rule over its new subjects, the major controversy over Imperial Qin history is of a different nature than that over the history of the preimperial state of Qin. Although scholars do disagree about certain details of Sima Qian's narrative and, more generally, about the reliability of this narrative (e.g., van Ess, chapter 7, this volume), the major debate revolves around ideological evaluations of Qin. Was it a legitimate dynasty, a laudable unifier, the founder of an immortal empire, or just a cruel and tyrannical entity, an aberration in Chinese history, a kind of a historical accident? Or was it, alternatively, a fundamentally conservative regime that restored a unity imagined to have been realized during earlier epochs (Pines 2008a)? These debates are treated in the introduction to part III, and they are echoed in several chapters in this volume (chapters 3, 7, 8 by Shelach, van Ess, and Pines, respectively), hence they will not be addressed here. Suffice it to mention that it is the dual position of the Qin dynasty, as both the founder of the imperial Chinese system and as a failed dynasty that barely outlived its founder, that make debates over Qin's imperial (and, to a lesser extent, preimperial) history exceptionally fierce. Yet as ideological cleavages of the past are losing their former sensitivity, it is becoming increasingly possible to address the impact of Qin's empire on Chinese history in an evenhanded fashion. This is what we hope to do in the present book.

A few words of caution are needed. In our enterprise, based as it is on contributors from distinct national schools and disciplinary affiliations, it is neither possible nor desirable to impose a uniform perspective, adopt a uniform style, or create a uniform narrative. While we did try to integrate the papers, to propose, whenever possible, a common terminology, and to focus on a common set of questions, differences of opinion, at times considerable, are evident throughout the volume. On certain issues, particularly those related to the reliability of textual data and to its relation with the material and paleographic evidence, we often agreed to disagree.

The very nature of our field, in which any major discovery, or the publication of previously discovered but not yet published manuscripts, can shed new light on many essential questions, cautions us against an attempt to create artificial consensus. This said, we believe that our cumulative efforts have resulted in a qualitatively new level of understanding of Qin's historical trajectory. In addition, we endeavor to outline some of the routes of inquiry for future research. We hope that this volume will encourage colleagues and students to focus anew on one of the most fascinating and promising fields in Chinese history.

PART I

Archaeological Reflections

Archaeological Perspectives

Introduction

Archaeological Perspectives
on the Qin "Unification" of China

Lothar von Falkenhausen
with Gideon Shelach

Qin's gigantomania dazzles. We are all aware of the tremendous scale of the First Emperor's construction projects—his palaces, his tomb, the roads and canals he had built, and the Great Wall—and, indeed, the strain they put on the empire's resources might have been one of the reasons for the rapidity of its downfall (see Shelach, chapter 3 in this volume). What is less commonly realized is that such predilection for the oversized distinguished the Qin ruling class throughout its history. That it was a persistent trend going back to the founding of the Qin polity is documented by recent archaeological finds, which heap example upon example in a continuous sequence stretching over the entire five-hundred-plus-year span of Qin's existence as a polity. Comparison of Qin rulers' residences and tombs to those of their peers in other parts of Zhou China shows, furthermore, that Qin consistently surpassed its peers by what seems to have been a considerable order of magnitude. This must have been a conscious strategy, perhaps intending to augment Qin's position at the same time as reflecting its insecurities as a relative latecomer to the competitive world of Zhou politics. In this sense, the First Emperor's gigantomania was no more than a continuation—albeit, no doubt, at an even further increased scale—of the well-established tradition of his forebears. Other aspects of Qin archaeology, as well, show the First Emperor as not only an innovator, but also, and perhaps more basically, a conservative ruler whose actions were guided to a considerable degree by historical precedent.

In general, archaeology—the study of a past civilization through its material remains—is prone to emphasize grand continuities over time and connections among different areas over singular individuals and one-time historical events. This is certainly true in the case of Qin, with respect to both its chronological position in Chinese history and its geographical context within continental East Asia. An archaeological approach to Qin's physical remains, by placing them into chronological sequences and by relating them typologically to similar phenomena elsewhere, can therefore provide a corrective to any tendencies to exaggerate Qin's newness and exceptionality. Overawed by sheer size, the modern observer might otherwise risk losing sight of the degree to which Qin was, all along, a fairly ordinary—indeed, somewhat conservative—example of a Zhou-type polity. In introducing this set of three chapters on archaeological topics, we would therefore like to emphasize Qin's conformity to royal Zhou standards. Rather than breaking the mold and advancing groundbreaking innovations in state administration and rulership, Qin and its rulers operated very much within the Zhou system; their shining model was the Zhou kingdom during its Western Zhou period (ca. 1046–771) florescence—or, rather, an idealized vision thereof. Even the founding of the unified Qin Empire, fundamental as it proved to be to later historical developments in China, appears, in light of its archaeological reflections, as determined at least in part by restorative tendencies.

True, the model of governance that Qin developed in the Warring States period differed tremendously from that of the Western Zhou in such aspects as the much higher degree of central control over the peripheries, the stronger control of the state over its economic and human resources, the nature of its sociopolitical hierarchy, the decreased importance of kinship in determining individuals' access to political power (see Teng, chapter 2, this volume), and its military organization (see the general introduction to this volume). We must certainly avoid the misleading image of an "eternal China." But by emphasizing continuities rather than ruptures, the following archaeological discussion hopes to contribute to a more balanced and nuanced picture of Qin and its developmental trajectory and its place in Chinese history. Briefly stated, the following are now obvious:

- Qin's development into a centralized empire was by no means primarily the First Emperor's personal achievement, nor is it chiefly to be credited to Shang Yang's 商鞅 (?390–338) reforms during the previous century, although the importance of these reforms should by no means be downplayed. Instead, it was a long and drawn-out process, guided by an explicit political agenda that had been clearly and very publicly promulgated as early as the beginning of the seventh century.

- This development was paralleled in other parts of continental East Asia. Other polities in Eastern Zhou–period (770–256) China pursued identical goals with very similar means. Some, notably Qi 齊 and Chu 楚, came close to realizing them. Qin's success was by no means preordained.

- Even before the rise of Qin, much of continental East Asia—the core area of "Chinese" civilization—was culturally and politically unified to a high degree. While it is moot to speculate about counterfactual historical alternatives, it nevertheless seems likely that the unified empire would not have turned out all that different had one of Qin's competitors prevailed. Zhou continuities would have likely asserted themselves under any unified regime, as they did under the Qin and Han.

- Most of the alleged Qin innovations in the realm of political administration were by no means new at the time of the unification. All the "unification" entailed was the imposition of Qin's institutions on the conquered areas to the east and south; one should realize that these institutions were, for the most part, but a slightly different variant of those which had previously been prevalent in these areas (an exception has to be made for formerly non-Zhou areas, e.g., in the southwest and farther to the south). In other words, the Qin "unification" merely universalized the Qin sociopolitical model, which was deeply rooted in the Zhou system.

Before we proceed, if not to demonstrate these points fully, then at least to illustrate them in a way that we hope will be compelling, a methodological point is in order. From an archaeological point of view, "Qin" is a problematic concept. Even though Chinese specialists (such as Zhao Huacheng and Teng Mingyu in chapters 1 and 2 of this volume, respectively) liberally use the term "Qin culture" and make highly suggestive attempts to define it through material data, the evidence shows that, strictly speaking, the material remains prevalent in areas governed by the Qin polity from the Late Western Zhou down to Warring States times are not distinctive enough to warrant defining a separate archaeological *culture;* they constitute at most a variant (or, more technically, a *regional phase*) of what, for want of a better term, we may call the archaeological culture of Zhou civilization. With some notable exceptions to be mentioned below, the development of material culture in Qin during Western Zhou through Eastern Zhou times by and large mirrors the transformations that occurred across the Zhou realm. In Qin as else-where, the Warring States period (453–221) was a time of major innova-tion in all realms of material culture, no doubt mirroring the exciting contemporaneous developments in the intellectual realm (for which see Poo, Yates, and Pines, chapters 5, 6, and 8 in this volume, respectively). Due to the sheer bulk of accumulated material, there is a certain tempta-tion to regard Qin archaeological evidence in isolation from these wider trends; to do so, however, risks serious distortion.

Moreover, it cannot be emphasized too often that changes in mate-rial culture do not necessarily go hand in hand with changes of political regimes. We should not expect, therefore, an archaeologically distinctive "Qin culture" to have emerged in tandem with the First Emperor's unifi-cation of China. Indeed, the Qin Empire, lasting only fifteen years, was shorter than any period archaeology can normally define through mate-rial parameters—no matter whether by means of typological seriation, stylistic analysis, or absolute dating, e.g., by the radiocarbon method. Qin-period sites and artifacts therefore do not stand apart from those of the Late Warring States and the Early Western Han. The fact that we can address some as belonging to unified Qin is invariably owed to more precisely dated written evidence.

"Qin culture" is thus difficult to define in properly archaeological terms. Although heuristically useful, a definition such as that implicit in the chapters 1 and 2 by Teng Mingyu and Zhao Huacheng in this volume—as the material remains used by the Qin ethnic group and its allies, or by the core population of the Qin territory—is, strictly speaking, inadmissible because it conflates material-culture and sociological (or even biological) categories; in principle, archaeological cultures should be defined based on material parameters alone, which means that we cannot include the human participants in a culture in its definition. When we identify certain cultural traits as Qin-related,[1] therefore, we must always remember that their "Qin-ness" does not provide an analytical tool for the better comprehension of these phenomena. It is merely a shorthand device, similar on an analytical level to the use of "Confucianism" and "Legalism" by our colleagues in the field of Qin intellectual history—terms that can be adopted for a preliminary labeling and classification of texts, but are useless (indeed sometimes worse than useless) for their in-depth investigation.

Proponents of a definition of "Qin culture" that rests essentially on a preconceived notion of the ethnic identity of the people who created it should consider the implications of the fact, which none of them contests (this much was confirmed during our workshop), that, save for their spatial distribution in what became the Qin core territory in eastern Gansu, the material remains at the earliest "Qin" settlements, such as Maojiaping in Gangu County 甘谷毛家坪 (Gansu Sheng Wenwu Gongzuodui et al. 1987), are virtually undistinguishable from those of their "Zhou" neighbors in Shaanxi. Other, more distinctive kinds of artifacts that stand apart from the standard Zhou inventory, such as the "*lì* vessels with spade-shaped feet" (*chanzuli* 鏟足鬲) once flagged by the late Yu Weichao 俞偉超 (1985: 180–210) as defining Qin-culture characteristics, are today ascribed, for good reason, to the non-Qin (i.e., non-Zhou) inhabitants of that area (Zhao Huacheng 1987, 1989). The earliest remains ascribed to Qin, in other words, constitute a westward extension of "Zhou culture." They mark the spread for the first time in history of a cohesive complex of systemically interrelated material-culture elements originating in central China into the upper Wei River basin. Even though the remains in question are fairly modest in nature—they are for the most part limited to household and funerary ceramics, as well as simple tombs—it seems safe to argue that they document an expansion of Zhou sociopolitical structures into this region. Whether this entailed a movement of "Zhou" people consisting of groups or individuals into the area or the conversion of some of its local residents to Zhou ways, or a combination of both, is impossible to tell with the evidence at hand. What is decisive is that the inhabitants of the alleged early Qin sites in eastern Gansu, in choosing material-culture items for their use, decided to behave like mainstream Zhou people (Falkenhausen 2008c). While we cannot, as a matter of strict methodological principle, be absolutely sure that these sites do indeed represent members of the Qin group, such a situation, if accurately characterized, would aptly prefigure what we observe later on in Qin throughout its history.

The eighth-century tombs of Qin rulers at Dabuzishan, Li County 禮縣大堡子山 (Gansu) in the Xihan 西漢 River valley discussed by Zhao Huacheng (chapter 1, this volume; q.v. for further references)—identifiable as such by inscriptions on the ritual bronzes found within—are another instantiation of the same phenomenon;[2] they are all the more significant because they document the Qin performance of Zhou cultural practices at the level of the highest elite. In their shape and—insofar as we can judge, given their hideously looted state—their contents, they conform completely with the sumptuary privileges what the orthodox Zhou ritual system accords to rulers of dependent polities (*zhuhou* 諸侯). The use of gold for coffin fittings normally made of bronze is slightly unusual, but it is unclear whether this constituted an infringement of some unknown sumptuary regulations or customs; since gold is found in the surrounding area, the patrons may have simply decided to use this local material in one area of funerary display that was not strictly governed by explicit sumptuary rules. The only truly significant aberration is the enormous size of the tombs, which in all likelihood exceeds that of the tombs of the Zhou kings, the nominal overlords of the Qin rulers. Similarly outsized tombs are seen at the later Qin rulers' cemeteries at Nanzhihui, Fengxiang 鳳翔南指揮 (Shaanxi), on the outskirts of the Springs-and-Autumns to Early Warring States–period Qin capital of Yong 雍 (Han Wei and Jiao Nanfeng 1988); and at Zhiyang, Lintong 陝西 臨潼芷陽 (Shaanxi) (Shaanxi Sheng Kaogu Yanjiusuo and Lintong Xian Wenguanhui 1987, 1990); and on the Shenheyuan plateau in Chang'an 長安神禾塬 on the southern outskirts of Xi'an (Guojia Wenwuju 2007: 87–90; Han Wei 2007). Some of the Late Warring States–period tombs at the last-mentioned two sites have four ramps leading into the tomb chamber, reflecting—once again strictly in terms of the Zhou system, which in this respect seems to have followed the precedent of the Shang dynasty—the privileges of royal rank, which the rulers of Qin had "usurped," rather belatedly, in comparison with their peers elsewhere in the Zhou realm, in 325. It is not irrelevant in this connection to note that the First Emperor's tomb, as well, had four ramps.

The earliest inscribed Qin bronzes, including those from Dabuzishan, are extremely close in style and method of manufacture to Late Western Zhou products from the time after the Late Western Zhou Ritual Reform (ca. 850; for the dating of the reform, see Falkenhausen 2006: 56–64)—even though all or some of them date to a time when bronze ornamentation styles had already changed elsewhere in the Zhou realm. This apparent retardation may be explainable in part by the notion that Qin came into possession of the metropolitan Zhou bronze workshops after it took over central Shaanxi in 770. But there is very possibly another element to this stylistic conservatism: the absence of any intention to change the forms transmitted from the royal Zhou for the sacred vessels and bells used at the ancestral temples of the Qin ruling family—or, to put it positively, a desire to adhere as closely as possible to Western Zhou royal precedent. This was no doubt a legitimizing device for a relatively new regime, but it was more: by manufacturing ritual paraphernalia that were indistinguishable from those of the Zhou kings during the time when they had last asserted their rule over much of the Yellow River basin and areas beyond, the rulers of Qin quite literally cast themselves in the role of the Zhou kings.

Such conscious emulation of the Zhou kings is particularly evident also in the long inscriptions on the early-seventh-century Qin Gong bells excavated in 1978 at Taigongmiao, Baoji (Shaanxi) 寶雞太公廟. This point has been extensively made elsewhere (see, e.g., Kern 2000); let us just quote here some phrases where the donor, a ruler of Qin (most likely Lord Wu 武公, r. 697–678) asserts equality with the Zhou kings by using the phraseology normally reserved to a royal speaker. The inscribed text is a long, boastful proclamation made by the ruler of Qin. It begins by stating that the donor's First Ancestor received the Mandate of Heaven (*Tianming* 天命), usually held to have been vested in the Zhou royal lineage alone. He then refers to three of his ancestors, who, by analogy to the kings' ancestors in Zhou royal inscriptions, are said to be "unfailing in their high positions" (i.e., in Heaven) (不墜於上) and "gloriously to cooperate with august Heaven" (邵合皇天) "so that we [sc. Qin] may exert our authority over the lands of the Man [tribes]" (以虩事蠻方)—again, a phrase usually associated with the rhetoric of Zhou royal power. In the following passage, the Qin ruler speaks of himself as "I, the youngest descendant" (余小子): a common royal Zhou form of self-reference; there follow several additional phrases normally associated with a royal speaker: "I harmonize the hereditary court officials and I assemble all my entourage" (龢胤士, 咸畜左右); "I ever-increasingly receive bright virtue; with it I peacefully strengthen and harmonize my state" (翼受明德, 以康奠協朕國); and "I have routed the Hundred Man [Tribes], who have already submitted all at once" (盜百蠻, 俱即其服). The reference to "Heaven's Mandate" is repeated at the end of the inscription, where it is combined with the wish, usually extended to Zhou kings, that the ruler of Qin "enjoy thoroughgoing longevity on his throne" (其畯齡在位); regional rulers are not normally thus characterized as being "enthroned."

The text inscribed on the bells from Taigongmiao documents, moreover, that the rulers of Qin in the early seventh century intermarried with the Zhou royal house. Under the rule of clan (*xing* 姓) exogamy prevalent in the Zhou realm, they were eligible to do so because the Ying 嬴 clan to which the Qin ruling house belonged was different from the Ji 姬 clan of the Zhou royal family. The preserved historical sources contain some information on Qin rulers' consorts from other lineages affiliated with the Ji clan, such as Jin 晉 in present-day Shanxi, but this inscription is the only record attesting the presence of a royal princess in Qin.[3] The part of the text introduced by the slightly unusual sentence *Qin Gong ji Wang Ji yue* 秦公及王姬曰 is a proclamation jointly issued by the ruler of Qin and the Royal Princess,[4] presumably addressed to the ancestors of the Qin ruling lineage. It is unclear whether she is his consort or his mother, but her appearance on ritual bronzes dedicated to the Qin ancestors makes it evident that she was part of the family, and from the place in the inscription where she appears it is clear that she was alive at the time of the proclamation. In the practice of the time, such marriage alliances were usually hereditary and were renewed from generation to generation; there is therefore some likelihood that the Qin-Zhou marriage attested in the Taigongmiao inscriptions was by no means a singular occurrence.[5] Such a kin relationship with the Zhou kings—propagandistically enounced on a Zhou-style object of orthodox shape and used for performing Zhou-type rituals—could have served to bolster the Qin rulers in their intention, evident from the inscribed text, to emulate and perhaps eventually to supplant the Zhou dynasty.

Qin at the turn of the seventh century thus saw itself—and projected an image of itself—as an eminently Zhou-type regime. This was a current topos in Springs-and-Autumns–period China, although claimants had a variety of strategies to choose from. The rulers of seventh- through fourth-century Chu, for instance, went even further: without explicitly claiming the Mandate of Heaven, they represented themselves as an alternative royal house analogous to the Zhou, requiring exclusive allegiance from their vassal polities, including some ruled by relatives of the Zhou royal house, and punishing those who attempted to pay reverence to the Zhou kings (Falkenhausen 1991; Cook 1999). Consistent with this stance, they opted to use the royal title for themselves, as did the rulers of several other, minor polities, and they apparently eschewed intermarriage with the Zhou royal house. Qin, by contrast, stretched its ostensible loyalty toward the Zhou to the point of identification with the Zhou—an identification that could, and eventually did, lead to the latter's replacement by a new Qin dynasty.

Qin and Chu both lodged their claims self-consciously within the terms of the Zhou system, adopting its culture of ritual display with very few modifications. Their intention in doing so, no doubt, was to communicate their claims in a code that any politically aware individual could understand. The conceivable alternative of establishing a new, completely different sumptuary system with its own distinctive rituals either did not occur to them or, more probably, was consciously rejected. It is not difficult to imagine the reason for this: the prestige, if not the actual power, of the Zhou royal house during much of Eastern Zhou must still have been considerable, probably more so than later historical accounts would suggest. Weak as it had become, the Zhou dynasty evidently retained the ritual power to define the parameters of kingship, and the memory of its early glory—to a large extent an *a posteriori* constructed memory, conflating the military prowess in the time of the dynasty's founding with the institution-building feats during Late Western Zhou—continued to provide the paramount model for political thinkers and ambitious rulers. The pre-Qin texts reflect this amply (see, e.g., Pines 2004; Falkenhausen 2008a), and archaeological and art-historical analysis can show how such conservative ideas of long standing were expressed in material form (for fundamental considerations on this point, see Powers 2006). Only during the final decades of the Warring States period—after Shang Yang's reform—does Qin material culture begin to evince significant departures from Zhou precedent, instead becoming more similar in some of its aspects to that of its less conservative neighbors to the east.

Since Qin was founded as a polity only in the early eighth century, all archaeological remains pertaining to the Qin elite postdate the Late Western Zhou Ritual Reform, which, a little more than half a century before, had created a new set of institutions for the management of social and religious relationships within the Zhou realm (Rawson 1990, pt. A: 108–111; Falkenhausen 2006: 29–73). These standards are archaeologically reflected, above all, in the sets of ritual paraphernalia found in elite tombs. Qin tombs, starting from the rulers' tombs at Dabuzishan, show a consistent, even rigid, adherence to standards imposed during the Late Western Zhou Ritual Reform even past the time of their partial abandonment in areas to the east after circa 600. It seems that Qin did not participate in the events one of us has described as the Middle Springs-and-Autumns Ritual Restructuring (Falkenhausen 2006: 326–369; 2009)—a transformation of the system through which the right to possess ritual bronzes, and, *partant*, the right to perform one's own ancestral sacrifices, was extended to previously disenfranchised lower-elite groups; these groups came to use simplified sets of stylistically modern and regionally distinctive vessels, while the orthodox bronze assemblages that had been in use since the Late Western Zhou Ritual Reform became restricted to the highest elite. In Qin, by contrast, the orthodox assemblages—increasingly in the form of low-value *mingqi* 明器 imitations—continue to reign supreme down to the mid-fourth century, when they became obsolete, most likely as a consequence of Shang Yang's reforms of the social system (Chen Ping 1984; Okamura 1985; Huang Xiaofen 1991; Falkenhausen

2004, 2008b). This Qin *Sonderweg* may signal that Qin was unaffected by the social developments in the eastern parts of the Zhou realm that necessitated the empowerment of new groups there. One possible reason, emphasized by Teng Mingyu (chapter 2, this volume) may have been the increasingly militarized character of the Qin elite and its inclusion of individuals and groups from outside the Zhou realm, which may have led to a weakening of more traditional kinship structures; but at the same time it seems possible to interpret the findings as an indication that significant aspects of a conservative, Zhou-style regime as ideally conceived by the promulgators of the Late Western Zhou Ritual Reform were maintained in Qin for 250 years after the system had already largely collapsed elsewhere.

Given the later Confucian excoriation of Qin, it is a delicious irony to observe, in light of the archaeological data, that Qin was the only part of China where the kinds of rituals that the Confucian ritualists considered orthodox were still being consistently reflected in elite funerary remains during the lifetimes of Confucius (551–479) and his early disciples. It appears that Qin played a role in the transmission of the Zhou ritual standards of the Late Western Zhou Ritual Reform to later Confucian China (Kern 2000), and it may have been in part due to this Qin impact that they later came to be regarded as orthodox (Falkenhausen 2008a).[6]

By contrast to the relative conservatism in the realm of the ancestral cult and its paraphernalia, Qin was apparently not exempt from other religious innovations that occurred during the Eastern Zhou period; to the contrary, in Qin these changes may be observed earlier, and their impact seems to have been more thoroughgoing, than elsewhere (cf. Poo, chapter 5, this volume). The already-mentioned transformation of funerary ritual vessels into *mingqi*, which became extremely prevalent after the middle of the Springs-and-Autumns period, is one manifestation of what seems to have been a new set of religious conceptions concerning death and the afterlife that downplayed the power of ancestors and placed an emphasis on the distinction between the living and the dead. Another consequence of these beliefs was the transformation of tombs into models of the world of the living, involving, *inter alia*, the use of figurines. These new ideas, which came to reign supreme in Qin in the aftermath of Shang Yang's reform, seem to have spread eastward from Qin to other parts of the Zhou realm, and we cannot exclude the possibility that they were in some way triggered by funerary customs from areas farther west; the specifics of this transmission urgently need further research.

Aside from these religious innovations reflected in tombs, Warring

States—and Imperial Qin—period trends in material culture more or less mirror those of the other Eastern Zhou states. They seem to vitiate the image of later historians of Qin as a semi-Barbarian backwater, nor do they necessarily confirm the long-standing prejudice that Qin was a drab, militaristic society without amenities or cultural life of any sort. Instead, it is becoming increasingly obvious that the material culture of Qin at the cusp of the unification was fully on par with that of the other Warring States kingdoms. Like them, Qin had a highly developed iron industry that supplied its peasantry with cheap and durable tools and its army with weapons (Wagner 2008: 115–170).[7] But at the same time, the Qin bronze workshops continued to operate, producing magnificently decorated vessels and bells as luxurious household furnishings (for examples, see *Zhongguo qingtongqi quanji* 1998: 38, 43–48, 50, 57–60; Li Xixing 1994: nos. 37, 86, 91, 146, 173, 201, 234; Thote and Falkenhausen 2008: nos. 37, 43–53). Bronze use was no longer limited to ritual and warfare, nor was the material restricted to a narrow elite; small but luxuriously executed bronze items such as belt hooks and, less frequently, mirrors are now also seen in association with low-ranking individuals (for examples, see Thote and Falkenhausen 2008: no. 67, 116). After the abandonment about 350 of the ritual-vessel forms promulgated in the Late Western Zhou Reform, the Qin bronze workshops' repertory of shapes became remarkably varied. It included vessels previously pioneered in the eastern neighboring kingdoms, such as new types of *dǐng* 鼎 and *hú* 壺, but also objects from the newly conquered areas to the south, such as *móu* 鍪 cauldrons and *chúnyú* 錞于 bells, as well as some original creations, such as "garlic-top bottles" (*suàntóupíng* 蒜頭瓶) (see Thote and Falkenhausen 2008: nos. 51, 87, 49). Qin workshops also produced some of the finest weaponry of the time—with blades so sharp that still today one could use them to shave; made of bronze, these were undoubtedly luxury objects and status items (Chen Ping 1987; Wang Xueli 1994: 233–419; Thote and Falkenhausen 2008: nos. 81–85; Zhang Weixing 2002; Zhang Weixing and Ma Yu 2003).

Qin artists, moreover, developed a new iconography of prestige, with swirling clouds as its main motif (Okamura 1991). This imagery had evolved from the dissolution of earlier animal-derived decor; it gave expression to new cosmological ideas, current all over the Chinese cultural sphere, according to which the entire cosmos is made of a uniform cosmic substance called *qi* 氣, a word that has been variously translated as "vapor," "ether," "pneuma," or "air." Even after the end of Qin, its elegant *qi* scrolls continued as the major artistic motif in the art of the Han Empire.

Also seen in Qin art are depictions of motifs associated with the cult of the four cosmic thearchs that was practiced at Yong, as well as in the Gansu homeland of the Qin ruling house. This innovative iconography in all probability does not constitute a cultural element specific to the Qin area or ethnic group, but it is more appropriate to interpret it as Qin's adaptation of intellectual and religious systematization efforts that were ongoing all over the Zhou cultural sphere during Middle to Late Warring States times and, indeed, beyond. This seems confirmed by recent manuscript finds, especially those from Fangmatan, Tianshui 天水放馬灘 (Gansu) (He Shuangquan 1989; *Tianshui Fangmatan* 2009).

The "Qin unification" was, in actuality, the conquest of all other Warring States kingdoms by Qin. Archaeology shows that the First Emperor's alleged innovations were not really new, but merely involved the imposition on the conquered areas of the Qin system as established in Qin earlier during the Warring States period. Cultural features traceable through the material record, such as the unified *banliang* 半兩 coinage (Thierry 2008), the Qin script (Venture 2008), musical pitches (Falkenhausen 1992), weights and measures (Sanft, forthcoming), and so on, were in fact Qin standards that had been instituted in Qin sometime in the Warring States and were gradually imposed on the conquered populations; in some cases they were updated to reflect new imperial realities.[8] Further, research has shown that many of these uniform norms were derived from an earlier system of standards, less systematized but similar in thrust, that was part of the royal Zhou institutions during the Late Western Zhou period (Matsumaru 1992), and which was followed with but minor variations in all the major polities of the Eastern Zhou realm. The practical impact of the so-called unification may not have been as revolutionary as has been previously thought. As archaeological finds are showing with increasing clarity, a considerable amount of unity and centralization had already prevailed during Western Zhou times, centuries before the Qin unification. Once again, therefore, it is likely that a conscious reference was made to the Zhou past, and one may state without undue exaggeration that there was—*pace* the First Emperor's own claim to innovation (Pines, chapter 8, this volume)—a clear "restorationist" aspect in the Qin unification. Similar considerations apply to less materially tangible aspects of the "unification," such as the bureaucratic order and the legal system, both of which, in spite of their important innovative features, harked back, in some of their aspects, to Western Zhou antecedents (for which see, e.g., Li Feng 2008a).

It is probably true, however, that the Qin conquests played a decisive role in extinguishing local cultural traditions that were completely distinct from the Western Zhou–derived Chinese traditions, such as the ancient cultures of Sichuan and of the Lower Yangzi River basin, which Qin conquered from the late fourth century on. These disappeared soon after the Qin conquest; their history was largely suppressed, and their (very scant) epigraphic traces—rendering languages as-yet unidentified—remain undeciphered today.

Qin is thus one of several not very distinct variations of what was common throughout the East Asian subcontinent. Perhaps unification was not ineluctable—perhaps Eastern Zhou China could have exhausted itself in an unresolved internecine struggle, another kingdom might have prevailed, or a hypothetical outside power might have taken over (Yates 2006). Nevertheless, the Qin unification, such as it was, merely consolidated Zhou-wide trends; it was very much a unification from within, extensively guided by royal Zhou precedents that the Qin adapted to new and much vaster cosmological conceptualizations. This brings us back to our initial observations on scale. In keeping with its centuries-old traditions and ambitions, Late Warring States–period Qin managed to outdo its competitors not so much on a qualitative level but on a quantitative and an organizational one. Herein, arguably, lies the innovative genius of Qin—the factor that gave it the decisive edge over its competitors. It was by putting this gigantomania to use in its sociopolitical reorganization and military exploits that Qin accomplished successfully what all major polities of Eastern Zhou China were attempting to do. The sheer volume of its operations, its heightened degree of application of all the techniques of governance available at the time, finally overwhelmed all opposition. Having accomplished its goals, Qin gigantomania had run its course; arguably Qin had overextended itself by reaching beyond the limits of the Zhou culture sphere that it had been its original aim to rule. This, from an archaeological perspective, may be the pattern of the Qin past. History tells the rest.

The three chapters in this section differ in their scope as well as in their theoretical and methodological underpinnings, but their authors share a common conviction—also expressed in the present introduction—that systematic collection and analysis of archaeological data can transform our understanding of Qin history and culture. In such a spirit, they have elevated material data that for a long time were viewed as a mere illustration of the written word to the position of an independent source of knowledge that can engender new insights on old questions and open up new research questions never addressed before.

Zhao Huacheng presents new primary data on the early phases of the Qin polity, when its center was located in southeastern Gansu. The evolution of Qin culture and early stages of Qin as a political entity in this region are among the least-known aspects of Qin history, and archaeological explorations, such as those described by Zhao, are crucial for shedding new light on them. As the chapter presents new data that have been discovered only since 2004, we are only at the primary stage of assessing their historical and cultural significance. Zhao's review of the new discoveries and his preliminary attempts to interpret them exemplify the new directions and immense potential of Qin archaeology.

Teng Mingyu's chapter utilizes archaeological data to address the social, political and cultural transformations Qin underwent between the time when it was established on the western fringes of the Zhou world and its conquest of All-under-Heaven. Rather than seeing material evidence as subordinate to textual or paleographic sources, Teng uses it as an independent source of information on important social developments that are largely undocumented otherwise. Thus she is able to trace Qin's transformation from a kin-based society to one in which sociopolitical organization was based on place of residence, and from a pedigree-based social system to one in which status was based primarily on personal achievements. This chapter is important not just because of its new insights on the social trajectories it spells out, but also because it demonstrates how archaeological data can be used to expand the scope of our historical understanding. It also touches upon important methodological issues related to the potential and limits of archaeological interpretations.

Gideon Shelach takes an anthropological approach to the collapse of the Qin Empire. While the quick demise of Qin after the death of the First Emperor has long attracted the attention of scholars and continues to be a hot topic in modern research, it has never been analyzed from a perspective that foregrounds archaeological data. Based on such data, Shelach attempts to quantify the amount of labor invested in the famous monuments constructed by Qin, such as the Great Wall and the burial complex of the First Emperor, and he goes on to examine the possible effects of such a huge investment in public works on the sociopolitical order of the Qin Empire. Considering the results of his analysis in a comparative perspective, Shelach points out ways in which such an analysis of the demise of Qin can contribute to a better understanding of, on the one hand, the political system that subsequently evolved in China, and on the other hand, of similar processes in states and empires in other parts of the world.

Full-scale incorporation of archaeological data into historical syntheses as a resource equal in importance to textual and paleographic evidence is just beginning. We hope that this volume, and particularly the chapters collected in the present section, will contribute toward the fuller integration of archaeology into the mainstream of the historical study of early China.

1 New Explorations of Early Qin Culture

Zhao Huacheng 趙化成

OVERVIEW OF ARCHAEOLOGICAL INVESTIGATIONS

According to the "Basic Annals of Qin" (Qin benji 秦本紀) in Sima Qian's 司馬遷 *Historical Records* (史記), the Qin people belonged to the Ying 嬴 clan, which in remote antiquity was a branch of the Eastern Yi 東夷 ethnic group. During the Shang 商 dynasty, the Ying clan had very close relations with the Shang. Yet later the Qin people became prominent in the Gansu and Shaanxi area, and it remains unclear when they migrated from east to west.[1] We only know that by the Western Zhou period (1046–771), the people of Qin were already active in eastern Gansu.

According to the "Basic Annals of Qin," during the reign of King Xiao 孝王 of Zhou (r. ca. 891–886), Qin Feizi 秦非子 was enfeoffed with a dependency in Qin 秦 (around Qingshui 清水, Gansu) on account of his service rearing horses for the king. The Eastern Zhou period began in the year 771 when the Western Zhou was forced by the Quanrong 犬戎 people (sometimes translated as "Dog Barbarians") to relocate its capital to Luoyang, Henan. Because of the service he had rendered in protecting King Ping of Zhou 周平王 (r. 770–720) during this eastward migration, Lord Xiang of Qin 秦襄公 (r. 777–766) is said to have been enfeoffed as one of the regional lords (zhuhou 諸侯) and awarded the "lands west of the Qi 岐 mountains." With the formal establishment of Qin as a state, the people of Qin thereafter began gradually migrating from southeastern Gansu to the western territory of Guanzhong 關中 in the vicinity of present-day Baoji 寶雞, Shaanxi.

During the early decades of this move to western Guanzhong, the Qin continued to regard their original home in southeastern Gansu as a rear base, and not until 677, in the Middle Springs-and-Autumns

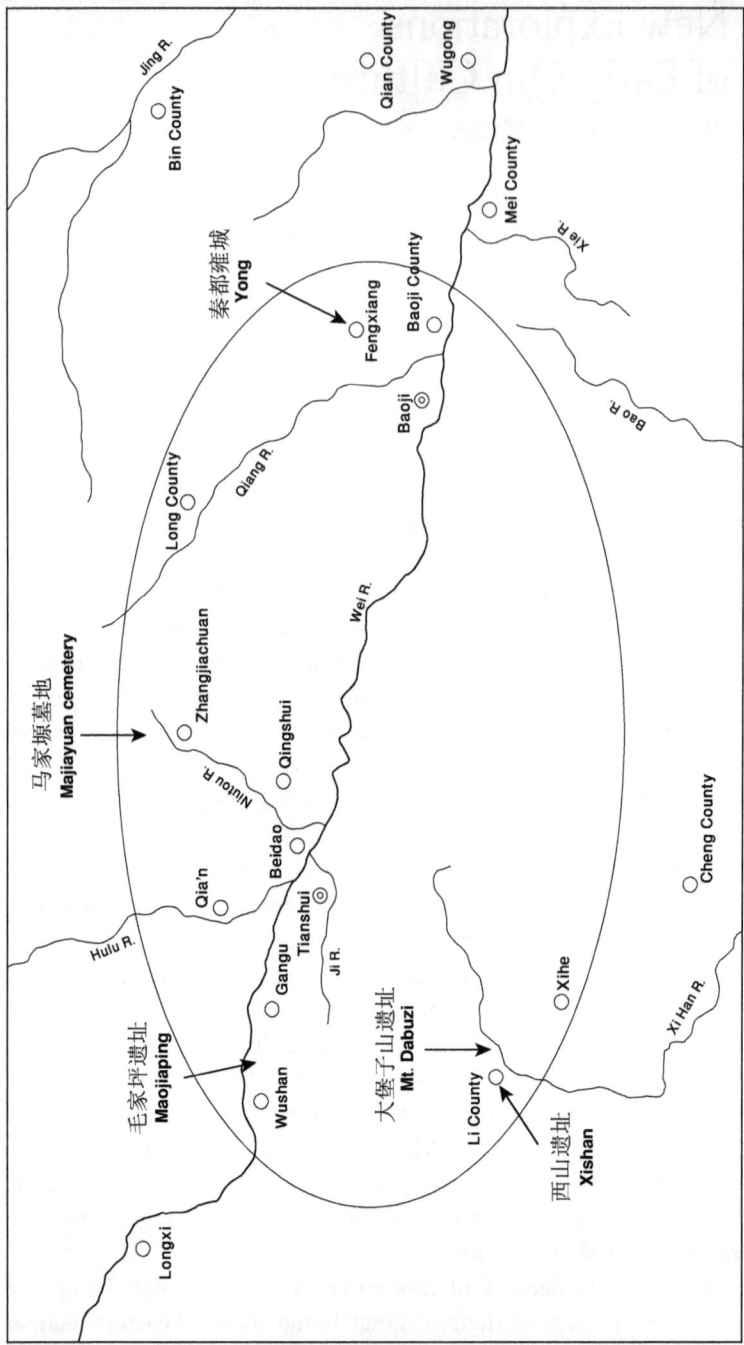

Map 1.1. Map of Early Qin Activities and Remains

period, when Lord De (德公, r. 677–675) established his residence in Yong 雍 (modern Fengxiang 鳳翔, Baoji, Shaanxi), did the Qin finally complete their migration. On account of this slow migration as suggested by historical accounts, the region along the upper reaches of the Wei 渭 and Xihan 西漢 rivers in eastern Gansu was the primary sphere of activity for the people of Qin for several hundred years from the end of the Shang dynasty through all of the Western Zhou and Early Springs-and-Autumns eras. The early Qin culture discussed here primarily refers to the archaeological culture of the Qin during this time and within this area (see Map 1.1).

The "Basic Annals of Qin" is the primary textual source recording the early history of the Qin, but because the account is very brief, one can learn very little from it about early Qin history and culture. In the early 1980s, Peking University's Department of Archaeology in cooperation with the Gansu Provincial Archaeological Team excavated Qin cultural remains dating to the Western Zhou period at Maojiaping 毛家坪, Gangu County 甘谷縣, in the Tianshui 天水 area along the upper Wei River (Gansu Sheng Wenwu Gongzuodui et al. 1987; Zhao Huacheng 1987, 1989). Some scholars even date these remains to as far back as the late Shang period (Teng Mingyu 2003). The discovery of these early Qin remains allowed us for the first time to see the features of early Qin culture from an archaeological perspective, and it inspired new ways of thinking in need of further investigation.

Between 1992 and 1993, two large tombs belonging to Qin lords were looted at Dabuzishan 大堡子山, Li County 禮縣, in the Xihan River valley. The looters had unearthed a sizable cache of important relics, including large ritual bronzes—such as *dǐng* 鼎 tripods, *guǐ* 簋 tureens, and *hú* 壺 liquid containers, all of which had inscriptions by Qin rulers of the *gong* (公) and *zi* (子) rank;[2] large bronze chime bells—including *yǒngzhōng* 甬鐘 and *bó* 鎛 bells; and sheet-gold ornaments for the coffins. Unfortunately, most of these precious cultural relics have been scattered (Lixian Bowuguan et al. 2004). From March to November 1994, the Gansu Institute of Cultural Relics and Archaeology cleared the two large tombs (M2 and M3) that had been robbed, as well as an adjacent chariot pit (numbered M1). Once cleared, it became apparent that the scale of the two tombs is enormous: the largest (M3) is 110 meters long (including the ramps), and the other (M2) is only slightly smaller at 88 meters in length (Figure 1.1). Both tombs have ramps descending into the graves from east and west. Tombs of this shape are ritualistically suitable for a resting place of a regional ruler (Dai Chunyang 2000). The discoveries of

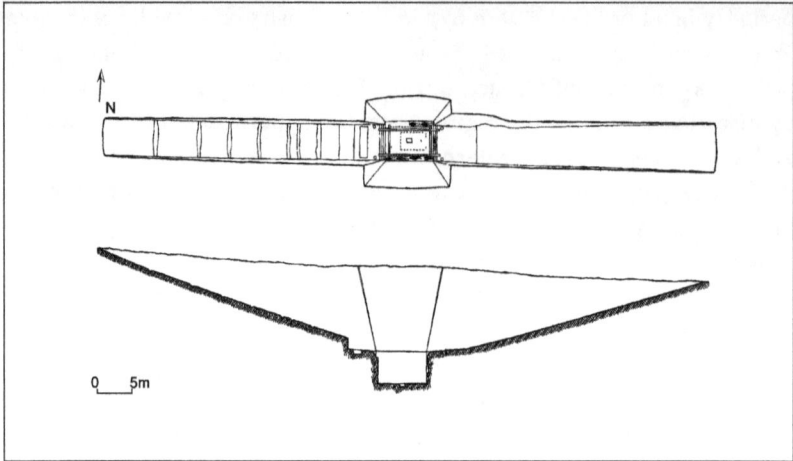

Figure 1.1. Drawing of the Looted M2 Tomb, Dabuzishan

the early Qin cultural remains at Maojiaping and these two large tombs at Dabuzishan largely verify Sima Qian's claim in the "Basic Annals of Qin" that eastern Gansu was the staging place of early Qin history.

At the beginning of 2004, under the auspices of the National Bureau of Cultural Heritage and the Gansu Bureau of Cultural Relics, a team of five work units—the Gansu Institute of Cultural Relics and Archaeology, Peking University's School of Archaeology and Museology, the National Museum of China, the Shaanxi Archaeological Institute (now the Shaanxi Archaeological Academy), and the School of Archaeology and Museology at Northwest University in Xi'an—was formed to initiate archaeological surveys, excavations, and research programs in order to further explore facets of early Qin culture and to locate early Qin cities as well as the tombs of other Qin nobles and their kin. During the first half of 2004, the group focused on surveying the upper reaches of the Xihan River in Li County and discovered dozens of new early Qin sites (Gansu Sheng Wenwu Kaogu Yanjiusuo et al. 2008). In 2004 and 2005, the team excavated an early Qin settlement at Xishan 西山 to the west of Li County and unearthed a Han dynasty site for imperial sacrifice to Heaven at Luantingshan 鸞亭山 (Zaoqi Qin 2005). The team focused on surveying and excavating the sites at Dabuzishan in 2006 and 2007 (Zaoqi Qin 2007). From 2007 to 2008 the basin of the Niutou River 牛頭河, a tributary of the upper Wei River, was explored in the administrative areas of Qingshui County and Zhangjiachuan Hui Autonomous County 張家川回族自治縣. Finally, from 2006 to 2008 the team excavated tombs ascribed to Western Rong 西戎 nobles and dated to the Warring States period at Majiayuan 馬家塬 in Zhangjiachuan (Gansu Sheng Wenwu Kaogu Yanjiusuo et al., 2008) (see Map 1.1). Let us review these new discoveries and their significance.

MAJOR ARCHAEOLOGICAL FINDS OF EARLY QIN CULTURE ALONG THE UPPER XIHAN RIVER

As a result of the 2004 archaeological survey conducted along the upper Xihan River and its tributaries in Li County, more than seventy pre-Han sites of various types were newly discovered, and among these, thirty-eight of the principal sites are considered to be those of the early Qin.[3] Moreover, investigators noticed the grouping of large sites into three relatively independent areas that nonetheless have some links. The sites forming the Liubatu 六八圖 cluster—the Feijiazhuang 費家莊 group, the Dabuzishan-Yuandingshan 圓頂山 (present-day Zhaoping 趙坪) group, and the Xishan-Shigouping 石溝坪 group—can be said to be the three central regions of early Qin culture. In addition to these finds, the survey also detected more than twenty sites of the early Bronze Age Siwa 寺洼 culture, which had close connections to the early Qin. Since the initial investigation, subsequent surveys at Xishan, Dabuzishan, and Shanping 山坪 have uncovered three early Qin settlements that have provided important clues about the potential location of the early Qin capitals.

Many other sites of early Qin culture were revealed during the course of the archaeological survey of the Niutou River conducted in 2007 and 2008. Among the many finds, the discovery of the Liya 李崖 site near the seat of Qingshui County is especially important. There are rich cultural deposits at this site occupying an area of more than one hundred hectares, and we believe there will be even more discoveries as the archaeological survey of the Wei River valley continues to be carried out in the future (see more in the appendix to this chapter).

The Sites of the Xishan-Luantingshan Group

The Xishan site is located in a zone along the hillsides west of the Li County town on the north bank of the Xihan River (Figure 1.2). The survey yielded a walled-city site, which has cultural deposits and burial areas scattered both within and outside the city walls. Mount Luanting (Luantingshan) stands across the Liujiagou 劉家溝 valley to the north of the Xishan site. The remains of a site dedicated to the worship of Heaven by the Han imperial household are located on its peak, but along its slopes

Figure 1.2. Xishan General View

is a wealth of early Qin cultural remains. In addition to these finds, early Qin cultural remains are also relatively plentiful at Shigouping along the south bank of the Xihan River to the southwest of the Xishan site. The sites of Luantingshan, Shigouping, and Xishan together form a cluster of early Qin settlements with Xishan as the center, and a large-scale excavation encompassing an area of nearly 3,000 square meters was carried out in 2005 and 2006 at the Xishan site.

The city site of Xishan is situated on an eastward sloping ridge in a long thin strip that varies in shape according to the terrain; it runs approximately 1,000 meters from east to west, ranges from 80 to 120 meters in width from north to south, and covers an area of nearly ten hectares. The eastern and western portions of the city's north wall as well as the east wall are well preserved and run continuously with the exception of the center section of the north wall. The depth of the rammed earth filling the foundation trench extends more than three meters below ground, and the overall width of the wall is typically between five and six meters. Only intermittent traces of the west wall and western section of the south wall survive, and the eastern portion of the south wall has yet to be located. Judging by the current terrain, it is possible that this section of wall has completely disintegrated. The wall was constructed by pounding earth in wooden frames, resulting in a tightly compacted and firm structure. Each layer of tamped earth is typically seven to eight centimeters thick, and the thickest stratum is approximately ten centimeters.

The tamping tools left shallow circular impressions with a diameter of 4.5 to 5 centimeters in the rammed earth. It is still not clear when the wall was first constructed, but judging by the Late Western Zhou ash pits that have cut into the rammed earth in places and by the foundations of the small structures built on top of the rammed earth in the Early Springs-and-Autumns period, the wall could not have been built later than the Late Western Zhou, and it was most likely built in the Middle Western Zhou period or slightly thereafter (Zaoqi Qin 2008a).

The 2005–2006 excavation primarily concentrated on clearing the northeast area within the city site. In addition to prehistoric remains, the work uncovered significant artifacts from the Western Zhou period, including six tombs and several ash pits. The remains dating to the Eastern Zhou period consist of more than 170 ash pits, 28 tombs, 10 animal pits, and the foundations of five structures.

Among the Western Zhou tombs, tomb M2003 is the largest in scale. Having an east-west orientation, it is 11.10 meters deep, 5.05 meters long, and 2.60 meters wide, and it contained both an inner and an outer coffin, with the former having lacquer decorations. An adult male lying in an extended position with his head oriented toward the west occupied the tomb along with burial objects placed inside the coffin, in the compartment between the head of the coffin and the outer coffin, and on the lid of the outer coffin. The bronze offerings included three *dǐng*, two *gǔi*, one short sword, one *gē* 戈 dagger-axe, and sixteen bronze fish. The recovered jade artifacts consisted of *bì* 璧 disks, *gūi* 圭 tablets, *zhāng* 璋 tablets, *gē* dagger-axes, *jué* 玦 rings, and *guǎn* 管 tubes. The ceramic offerings included *lì* 鬲 pouch-legged tripods, *yú* 盂 basins, *yǎn* 甗 vessels, and *guàn* 罐 jars. Shells and other items were found as well. Judging by the style of the grave goods, we can date the tomb to the Late Western Zhou, which, at present, makes this the earliest Qin tomb to contain bronze ritual vessels.

Seven horse pits, one cattle pit, and three pits for dogs and other animals were unearthed at the site. The pits approximately date to the Early Springs-and-Autumns period. Since no tombs have been discovered in the vicinity of the animal pits, they may have been related to some significant sacrificial activities. In addition to these pits, rammed-earth foundations and Late Western Zhou ceramic drainage pipes were discovered within the Xishan city site, but because of severe damage, the nature of these finds is not clear.

In 2005, the site of the Han dynasty imperial sacrifice to Heaven at Luantingshan in Li County was also excavated, resulting in the uncovering of more than fifty sacrificial items of jade, such as *guī* tablets, *bì* disks, and jade figurines, as well as roof tile end caps inscribed with "boundless joy" (*changle weiyang* 長樂未央). On the slopes of this mountain is an early Qin culture site, which, during the course of the investigation, yielded some rammed-earth structures, ash pits, and looted tombs. Because Han imperial sacrifices often adopted the sacrificial locations used by the preceding Qin dynasty, the Han site on Luantingshan offers a valuable clue for locating Xizhi 西畤, the place where Lord Xiang of Qin performed the sacrifice to the White Thearch (Bai Di 白帝) in the early years of the Springs-and-Autumns era (*Shiji* 14: 532; 28: 1358; Poo, chapter 5 in this volume). Needless to say, the early Qin culture site on the slopes of Luantingshan is a place of tremendous significance deserving further attention.

The Dabuzishan Site

The Dabuzishan site is located on the north bank of the Xihan River, 13 kilometers to the east of the Li County seat. The 2004 archaeological survey revealed extensive remains of an early Qin city, but the Dabuzishan site itself is just the center of an area with many other remains. The most noteworthy among them are Shanping 山坪, an early Qin settlement on the south bank of the Xihan River; the Springs-and-Autumns Qin elite burial ground at Yuandingshan (Gansu Sheng Wenwu Kaogu Yanjiusuo et al. 2002; 2005); and the Yantuya 鹽土崖 site on the west bank of the Yongping River 永坪河, a tributary of the Xihan River.

A comprehensive campaign of coring for underground soil and artifacts samples, covering an area of 150 hectares, was carried out at the Dabuzishan site in 2006. Rammed-earth foundations of twenty-six structures, more than four hundred tombs of all sizes, as well as a wealth of cultural deposits in general were located by this research (Figure 1.3). Based on this information, extensive excavations of more than 3,000 square meters were conducted in 2006. These excavations exposed the ruins of one large-scale structure (F 21), seven small and medium-sized tombs, and the remains of one sacrificial ground, which included one pit for musical instruments and four pits for human sacrifices.

The City Site. The Dabuzishan city site is situated on a mountain running from the northeast to the southwest. The site is very irregular in shape because the city encompasses the mountain and was built to conform to its topography. The city wall was constructed by ramming earth between formwork. As a result of extensive landslides, large sections of the wall

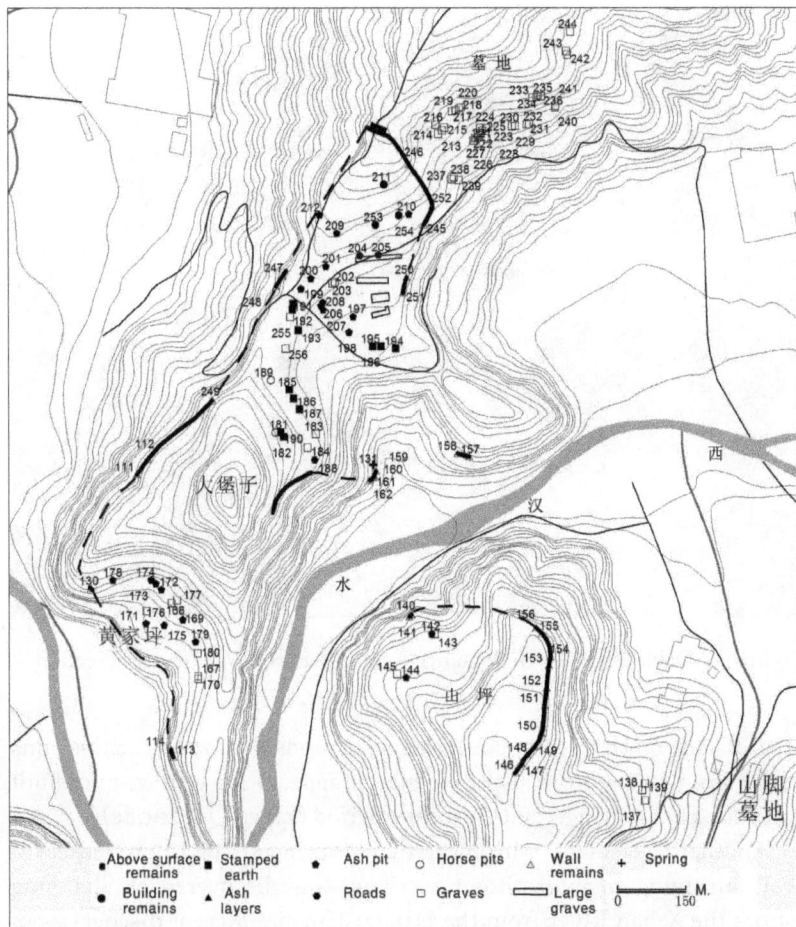

Figure 1.3. Drawing of the Remains in the Dabuzishan Qin Town

have been lost, but a portion of the north wall has been well preserved (Figure 1.4). The original length of the north wall was approximately 250 meters and the west wall 1,300 meters. Only a few sections of the south and east walls have been found, as both were situated along the periphery of the mountain in more rugged and steep terrain. Nevertheless, it is estimated that the east wall was originally 870 meters in length and the south wall 2,600 meters. The overall area of the site is roughly 55 hectares. The construction of the wall could not have begun earlier than the Late Western Zhou since the rammed earth of the wall contained ceramics with Late Western Zhou traits, such as the rough relief of cord

Figure 1.4. Dabuzishan Town Remains: Rammed-Earth Wall, Eastern Section

impressions on the legs of pouch-legged tripods (*li*) and distinctive rims on basins. Judging from such evidence, it appears the wall was not built until the Early Springs-and-Autumns period (Zaoqi Qin 2008a).

Another settlement, with more than 300 meters of a rammed-earth wall surviving in intermittent sections, was discovered at Shanping across the Xihan River from the Dabuzishan site. Recent discoveries of early Qin cultural relics suggest that this is also a site of early Qin culture.

The Structural Remains of Site Number 21. The structural remains of site number 21 are at a relatively high elevation within the southern part of the Dabuzi city site. The excavation uncovered a structure with four rammed-earth walls. The above-ground remains of the west wall are 30 to 60 centimeters in height and around 1.5 meters in width, with a foundation wall 3 meters wide. A foundation trough filled with rammed earth, roughly 3 meters wide, is all that remains of the north wall, the northern half of the east wall, and the eastern half of the south wall. The foundation measures 107 meters from north to south and 16.4 meters from east to west. Eighteen large pillar bases, separated approximately five meters apart, were discovered running parallel to and centered between the east

Figure 1.5. Remains of Large-Scale Structure F21, Dabuzishan

and west walls (Figure 1.5). From the stratigraphic evidence and an analy-sis of the composition of the rammed earth, Building 21 was probably constructed in the Middle or Late Springs-and-Autumns period, and it was abandoned during the Warring States era. Despite the relatively poor preservation of the remaining edifice, its basic structural form is never-theless clear—it was a pitched-roof building using a ridgepole-and-rafter construction. No tiles have been found within the site area, nor is there any evidence of internal partitions or of special treatment of the floor, so researchers have inferred that the building was a large storehouse of some type (Zaoqi Qin 2008b).

The Sacrificial Site. The sacrificial site is about 20 meters from the south-west corner of the large tomb (M2) belonging to a Qin lord, which was looted in the 1990s. The primary components of this site are one musical-instrument pit and four pits for human sacrifices. The former is oriented along an east-west axis and measures 8.8 meters long by 2.1 meters wide by 1.60 meters deep (Figure 1.6). Arrayed at the south side of the pit next to the rotted remains of a wooden chime rack were three bronze *bó* 鎛 bells, three bronze tigers (next to the *bó*), and eight *yǒngzhōng* 甬鐘 bells. Each of the *bó* and *yǒngzhōng* bells has a bronze suspension hook affixed to it (Figures 1.7, 1.8). At the north end of the pit, ten intact chime stones

Figure 1.6. Picture of the Musical Instrument Pit,
Dabuzishan

divided into two groups lay under the decayed remains of a chime rack
(Figure 1.9). The assemblage of bronze *bó* consists of one large and two
small bells; the largest is 65 centimeters in height and has coiled dragon
ornamentation in relief on the body of the bell as well as on its flat top
(*wǔ* 舞). The design of the four flanges projecting from the spines of the
bell is exceptional with its reticulation of intertwining dragons. The
bells' striking surface has been cast with an inscription of twenty-six
characters, including "The Prince (*zi*) of Qin made this precious harmonious bell" 秦子做寶龢鐘. Because these *bó* closely resemble a set of
three *bó* bells believed to have been made for Lord Wu of Qin 秦武公 (r.
697–678), which was unearthed in 1978 at Taigongmiao 太公廟 in Baoji,

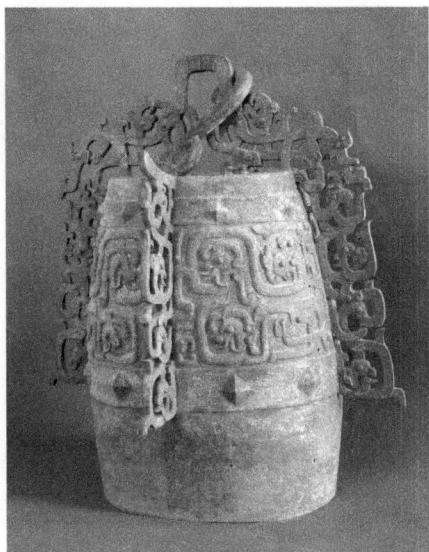

Figure 1.7. The *bo* Bell of the *Zi* of Qin from the Musical Instrument Pit, Dabuzishan

Figure 1.8. One of the *yongzhong* Bells from the Musical Instrument Pit, Dabuzishan

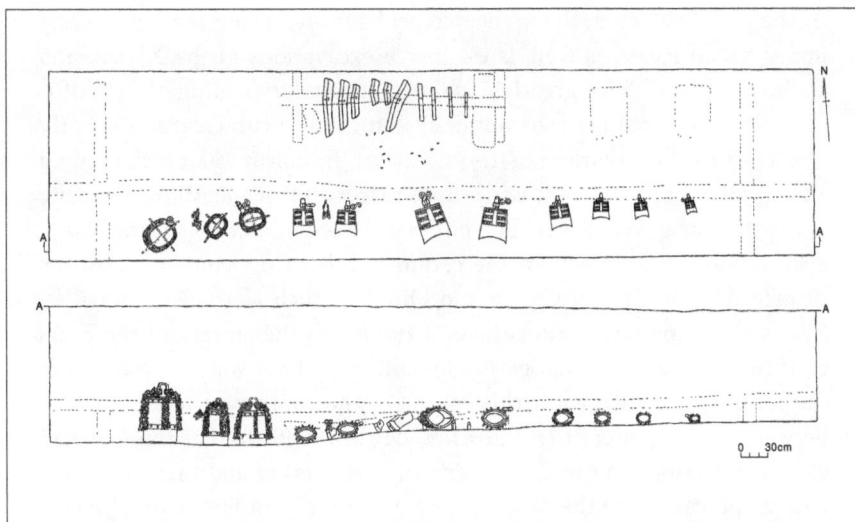

Figure 1.9. Drawing of the Musical Instrument Pit, Dabuzishan

Shaanxi, they probably date to the Early Springs-and-Autumns period. The four pits for human sacrifices were excavated at the same time as the pit for musical instruments. One or two skeletons were buried in each pit, and the placement of the bodies in a flexed position suggests these were human sacrifices. Since the pit for musical instruments shares characteristics with the pits for human sacrifice, this suggests that it too was of a sacrificial nature (Zaoqi Qin 2008c).

The Small and Medium-Sized Tombs. Of the seven small and medium-sized tombs excavated, three remained untouched by looters. The largest of the tombs (I M25) is located in the burial ground to the northeast beyond the city wall. The tomb is 4.8 meters long, 2.7 meters wide, and 10.1 meters deep. It contained 9 bronze vessels (three *dǐng*, one *yǎn*, one *yú*, and one short sword), more than 130 stone *guī* tablets 石主, and 6 pieces of pottery, all of which are dated to the Early Springs–and-Autumns era (Zaoqi Qin 2008d).

ANALYSIS: A NEW UNDERSTANDING OF THE EARLY QIN CULTURE

The Connections between Early Qin Culture and Zhou Culture

In the past few years, the archaeological surveys along the Niutou and upper Xihan rivers as well as extensive excavations of the Xishan and Dabuzishan sites have greatly expanded our understanding of the diffusion, settlement patterns, economic system, and cultural features of early Qin culture. The characteristics of early Qin culture along the Xihan River valley are consistent with those discovered at the Maojiaping site along the upper Wei River. The pottery style found at these sites, however, obviously differs from the ceramic style of the contemporaneous Bronze Age cultures of Gansu and Qinghai, such as the Xindian 辛店, Kayue 卡約, and Siwa cultures, yet it resembles the pottery of the Zhou culture. This suggests that early Qin culture did not simply evolve from the indigenous cultures in this area. On the contrary, the similarities between early Qin culture and Zhou culture indicate that the Qin had close connections to the Zhou from an early period and that the dominant Zhou culture of the time exerted tremendous influence on Qin culture. The Qin people nevertheless did maintain some of their traditions, such as having tombs oriented along an east-west axis, burying corpses in a flexed position, and including waist pits and human sacrifices in the larger tombs. However, the corpses excavated from the tombs of Qin elite at Xishan and Yuandingshan are in an extended position, which was also a popular manner of burial for Qin nobles in the Guanzhong region during the Eastern Zhou period.

The Origins of the Qin People and Culture

According to the written record, there should be no doubt that the men of Qin in remote antiquity belonged to the Ying clan and were a group of the Eastern Yi peoples who had close relations with the Xia 夏 and Shang. However, trying to identify their origins archaeologically is extremely difficult. Taking the history of Qin westward migration into account, it is possible that some of the remains of Shang culture in the western portion of Guanzhong are the product of the early Qin (Liu Junshe 1994).

The Dating of the Westward Migration across Longshan

The recent surveys and excavations have determined that the remains of early Qin culture along the upper Wei River generally date to a slightly earlier period than those found in the Xihan River valley. Although Early Western Zhou remains have been discovered in the latter location, they are negligible. In other words, during the migration across the Longshan range, the Qin people first settled along the upper reaches of the Wei River in an area around Tianshui. Not until the beginning of the Middle Western Zhou period did a large contingent of Qin people move from the upper reaches of the Wei River to the Xihan River valley and establish the capital there. This migration is likely related to the fact that the upper Xihan River has rich deposits of salt and gold (Gansu Sheng Wenwu Kaogu Yanjiusuo et al., 2008).

The Relationship between the Rong and Qin Peoples

There is a regular pattern to the distribution of the remains of the Siwa culture, which was contemporaneous with the early Qin culture in the Xihan River valley. There are a few vestiges of Siwa culture along the upper reaches of the Xihan River, where early Qin culture sites predominate, but Siwa remains are mainly distributed along the middle and downstream reaches of the river, where we almost never see traces of early Qin culture. More and more scholars have accepted my idea, first proposed in an article published in 1989, that Siwa culture is perhaps the remains of the Quanrong, a group of the Western Rong peoples (Zhao Huacheng 1989). Historical documents describe Qin's rise to power through its incessant struggles against the Western Rong during this early period (Shiji 5: 177ff.). Yet, in light of the coterminous remains of both Siwa culture and early Qin culture along the upper Xihan River, it seems that the Qin and Rong peoples not only had periods of struggle, but also enjoyed times of peaceful coexistence.

The Location of Xiquanqiu

The discovery of the three walled cities in the Xihan River valley has provided useful material for locating the early Qin capitals—Xiquanqiu 西犬丘 ("West Dog Mound") and Xixinyi 西新邑 ("New Town in the West")—mentioned in historical documents (*Shiji* 5: 178; 6: 285). The establishment of the city at Xishan before the Late Western Zhou period corresponds to the time frame of Xiquanqiu as documented in the textual sources. More importantly, the city's rammed-earth structures, its Western Zhou–style ceramic drainage pipes, its medium-sized tombs containing ritual bronzes of the Late Western Zhou, the sacrificial horse pit of the Early Springs-and-Autumns period, along with other significant finds, all indicate an important city and perhaps the location of the early Qin capital of Xiquanqiu (Zaoqi Qin 2008a). As mentioned, the excavation of the Han dynasty site for sacrificing to Heaven on the summit of Luanting Mountain in Li County and the presence of an early Qin culture site along the slopes of Luanting Mountain suggest the possible location of Xizhi, the place where Duke Xiang of Qin sacrificed to the White Thearch in the opening years of the Springs–and-Autumns period. If we could verify Xizhi's location, it would be a boon to explaining the precise nature of the city at the Xishan site. Unfortunately, the city's remains are relatively poorly preserved due to looting and due to the city's location on a mountain susceptible to natural erosion and to destruction by humans. A few key relics have been seriously damaged, which has further hampered the determination of the site's precise nature.

The Location of Xixinyi

The city wall at the Dabuzishan site was constructed later than the Xishan city wall. The wall itself dates roughly to the Early Springs-and-Autumns period, and all the major finds within the scope of the city—including the excavated foundation of the large warehouse (site F21), the two looted tombs belonging to Qin lords, the sacrificial site with the pit for musical instruments belonging to a Qin prince, and the recently excavated tomb with bronze vessels—also date to this period or slightly later. The recent discoveries seem to undermine the argument of those who previously held the Dabuzishan site to be the earlier capital Xiquanqiu. On the basis of the material revealed during the 2004 survey of the upper reaches of the Xihan River, some scholars have deemed the Yuandingshan site across the river from Dabuzishan in present-day Zhaoping to be Xixinyi, the residence of Lord Xian 秦憲公 (r. 715–704), but the discoveries from the more recent surveys and excavations of 2006 and 2007 increase the likelihood that the Dabuzishan site is Xixinyi.

Identifying the Occupants of the Looted Tombs

Prior to the discovery of the pit for musical instruments belonging to a "prince" (*zi*) of Qin, scholars intensely debated questions relating to the tomb occupants and the bronze vessels belonging to a lord and a prince of Qin that had been unearthed at the Dabuzishan site before being stolen in the 1990s. The discovery of the large pit for musical instruments, however, has provided valuable information for identifying the occupants of, and bronze vessels from the looted tombs. As I have written elsewhere, the "prince of Qin" in question is actually Lord Jing 靜公, the son of Lord Wen 秦文公 (r. 765–716) from the Early Springs-and-Autumns period, who was awarded the title of lord posthumously (*Shiji* 5: 180). The two large tombs, M2 and M3, thus belong to Lord Jing and Lord Wen, respectively (Zhao Huacheng, Wang Hui, and Wei Zheng 2008).[4]

Further Research Plans

The first five-year plan of archaeological survey of early Qin cultural remains, promulgated in 2004 by the National Bureau of Cultural Heritage, has been completed. The second ten-year period of survey has now started. The survey will be conducted by the joint team with members from the five above-mentioned units. The team will continue investigation of the Xihan River basin, and expand it to neighboring areas of the upper reaches of the Wei River and its tributaries: the Hulu 葫蘆 River, Jing 涇 River, and Qian 汧 River (Map 1.1). The main goal is to explore the cultural landscape of the early Qin state further and to look for remains of early Qin capitals and settlements, in addition to the rulers' mausolea and other burial sites. Because of the close connection between the Qin and Rong cultures, we include in our investigation cultural remains of the Western Rong from the Western and Eastern Zhou periods.

While the Terracotta Army of the Qin became a source of worldwide attention, our knowledge of the origins and early development of the Qin culture remains meager due to the dearth of textual data. Archaeological surveys and excavations will allow us to recover aspects of the early history of the people and the state of Qin and of their cultural landscape, expanding the prospects for historical study.

2012 APPENDIX: 2010–2011 EXCAVATIONS OF EARLY QIN REMAINS

The Liya 李崖 cemetery is located in the northern part of Qingshui 清水 County (Gansu) near the confluence of the Fan 樊 and Niutou Rivers. This cemetery was excavated in 2010–2011. The archaeologists excavated about one dozen pit burials, all of which were oriented from east to west; all the corpses were in the extended supine position and faced west; each tomb contained a waist pit with a dog sacrifice inside. These characteristics are largely shared by more than sixty tombs in an area in which a preliminary survey has been conducted. These burial customs are identical to those of the bronze-yielding tombs from the Late Western Zhou period excavated at Xishan, Li County, depicted above, and to those of the dozens of known bronze-yielding tombs of Qin aristocrats from the Springs–and–Autumns period. Therefore it is highly likely that this cemetery belongs to the Qin people of the Ying clan, and that the tomb occupants were Qin aristocrats.

Scholars are still debating the exact date of these burials; preliminary estimates place them either in the Middle Western Zhou period, or even earlier, in the early Western Zhou period; for a more precise dating we must wait until carbon-14 dates are obtained. What is most remarkable about these finds is that among the burial goods there are many pottery vessels that have clear Shang characteristics, such as *lì* 鬲 vessels with pouch-shaped feet and square lips, and pottery *guǐ* tureens with triangular patterns; these, in addition to the burial custom of using waist pits with dog sacrifices in them are indicative of the possible common origins of the early Qin and the Shang cultures. It should be noticed, however, that such a feature as the westward tomb orientation is distinct from the normal practice in Shang burials. Textual evidence confirms the proximity of the Qin ancestors to the Shang royal house;[5] hence it can be affirmed that the Qin people and Qin culture originated from the East. After relocating to the west, the Qin people became subordinate to the Zhou, and therefore were greatly influenced by the Zhou culture; hence, naturally, their culture reflects the pronounced impact of the Zhou.

Translated by Andrew H. Miller

2   From Vassal State to Empire

An Archaeological Examination
of Qin Culture

Teng Mingyu

During the Western Zhou period, Qin was a small principality located in eastern Gansu. After the beginning of the Eastern Zhou period in 771, Qin slowly advanced toward the east and continued to expand, eventually uniting China and forming its first imperial state in 221. As a result of the establishment of the Qin dynasty, social and political structures in ancient China shifted from the vassal-states system[1] of the Western Zhou age to the centralized system of administration that oversaw commandery- (*jun* 郡) and county- (*xian* 縣) level administrative units (He Huaihong 1996: 29). The shift from a kinship-based political system to a system based on place of residence paralleled and contributed to the transition from the system of vassal states to that of an imperial state (Guan Donggui 1998). As scholars have pointed out, the significance of the First Emperor's historical achievement in uniting China cannot be exaggerated (Xu Pingfang 1999). Given the importance of that event, research aimed at shedding light on Qin's transition from a weak and dependent vassal state to a strong one that eventually united China and completed the shift to imperial rule not only should be a task for historians, but also deserves enthusiastic archaeological pursuit.

The transition from kinship-based to residence-based social organization in ancient China is duly reflected in the archaeological record. According to Yu Weichao (2002: 180), "Historically, the means by which communities of people manifesting themselves in archaeological cultures were integrated, changed from kinship bonds to residence bonds. The formation trajectory of archaeological cultures, as well as the constituting elements and contents of these cultures, also for this reason underwent a corresponding change." Thus, when analyzing the basic social structure of an archaeological culture based on the structure of its internal diachronic development, emphasis should be placed on whether it is fundamentally kinship- or residence-based. Moreover, through an analysis of the internal ranking structure of Qin culture, it is possible to determine whether the different social strata in Qin society were opened or closed to one another, and also to shed light on the membership composition of its ruling apparatus and on whether its members achieved their elite status due to heredity or due to ability and individual achievements. This chapter attempts to investigate and explain ancient China's transition on the basis of current archaeological evidence from Qin-related burials. The evidence reflects two interrelated shifts: from kin-centered to place of residence-oriented society, and from heredity to personal achievement as determinants of elite status.

ARCHAEOLOGICAL STAGES OF THE EVOLUTION OF QIN CULTURE

Archaeological interpretation of the data traces the earliest evidence for Qin culture to the late Shang period (eleventh century BCE), and evidence of its demise to the early Western Han (second century BCE). Within this span of nine hundred years, archaeological research has revealed ancient remains created, utilized, and left behind by the Ying clan, which existed prior to the foundation of the Qin principality and then became its ruling core and eventually the ruling core of the Qin Empire. These remains constitute the main components of the indigenous Qin culture. The ancient remains of other groups who, for various reasons, came under the sway of the Qin principality and Empire—groups that either were closely related to the Qin core group or essentially accepted its cultural influence—should also be considered part of Qin culture inasmuch as they date to the same period, were used in the same area, and exhibit identical or similar features to those of the Qin core group (Teng Mingyu 2003: 4).

The Qin remains that date from the Late Shang dynasty to the early Han period can be divided chronologically into ten periods: (1) Late Shang to Early Western Zhou (c. 1100–950); (2) Middle Western Zhou (c. 950–870); (3) Late Western Zhou (c. 870–770); (4) Early Springs-and-Autumns period (c. 770–678); (5) Middle Springs-and-Autumns period (c. 677–621); (6) Late Springs-and-Autumns period and transition to Early Warring States period (c. 620–475); (7) Early Warring States period (c. 475–403); (8) Middle Warring States period (c. 403–325); (9) Late Warring States period (c. 325–221); and (10) imperial Qin and Early Western Han periods (c. 221–118). Four major stages of Qin's cultural development can be delineated based on the epoch-making changes that occurred within that developmental sequence.

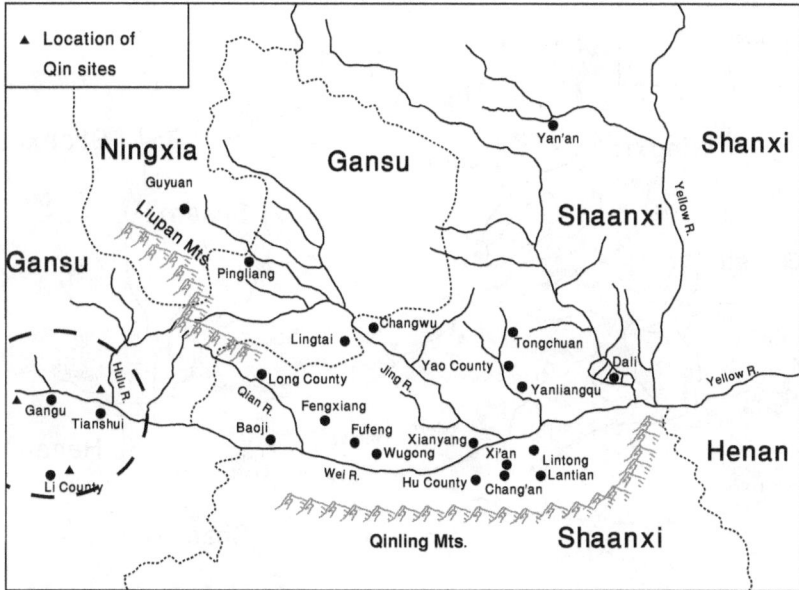

Map 2.1. Distribution of Qin Culture, Stage 1

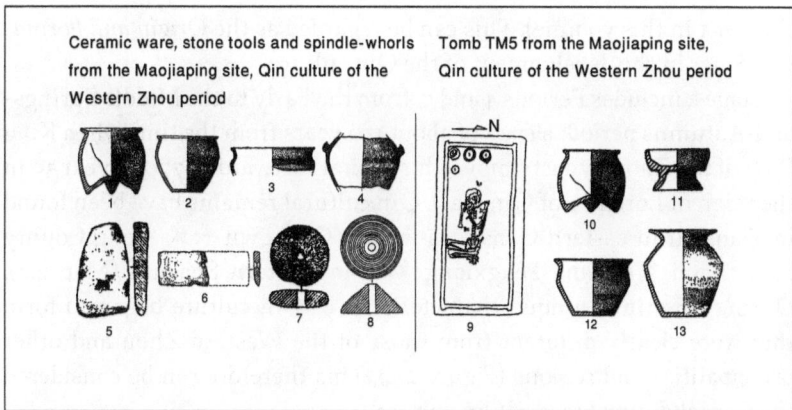

Figure 2.1: Funerary Goods of Qin Culture, Stage 1. (1) *lì;* (2) *pén;* (3) *yú;* (4) *guàn* with ears; (5) stone axe; (6) stone sword; (7, 8) spindle-whorls; (9) Tomb TM5; (10) *lì* ; (11) *dòu;* (12) *yú;* (13) *guàn* (11–13 are from TM5)

Stage 1 ranges from Periods 1 to 3, spanning the Late Shang and entire Western Zhou periods. Qin remains from this time can be found primarily in the Tianshui 天水 area in eastern Gansu (Map 2.1). Although these archaeological remains confirm the existence of Qin culture, its cultural characteristics are very similar to those of the Zhou (Figure 2.1; cf. Zhao,

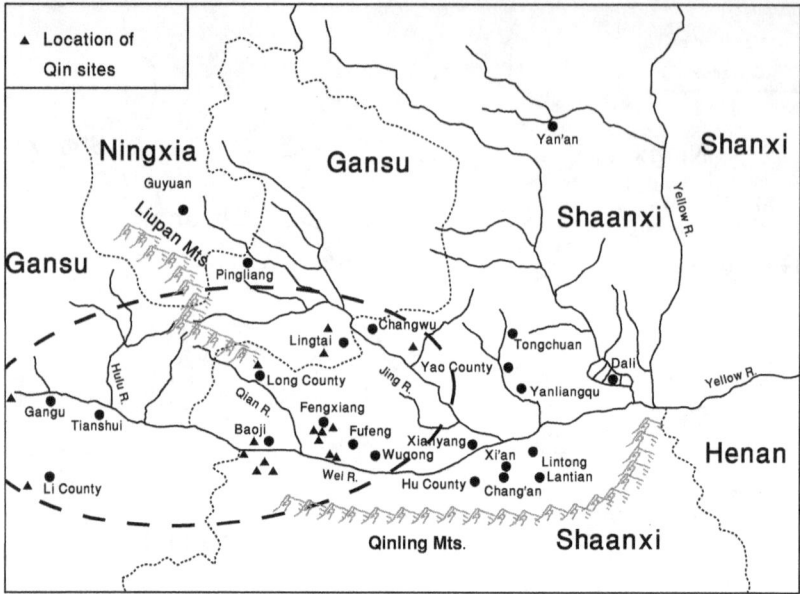

Map 2.2. Distribution of Qin Culture, Stage 2

chapter 1 in this volume). This can be regarded as the *Origin and Forma-tion Stage* in the development of the Qin culture.

Stage 2 includes Periods 4 and 5, from the Early to the Middle Springs-and-Autumns period, a span of about 150 years from the time when King Ping of the Zhou dynasty moved his capital eastward in 770 to year 39 in the reign of Lord Mu of Qin (621). Qin cultural remains have been found in Tianshui in eastern Gansu, as well as Changwu 長武, Long County 隴縣, Baoji 寶雞, and Fengxiang 鳳翔 in western Shaanxi (Map 2.2). During this time, unique characteristics of Qin culture began to form that were clearly different from those of the Western Zhou and other principalities and regions (Figure 2.2). This therefore can be considered the *Consolidation Stage* of Qin culture.

Stage 3 encompasses Periods 6 to 8, corresponding roughly to the Late Springs-and-Autumns through Middle Warring States periods, a 300-year span from the enthronement of Lord Kang of Qin in 620 to the time when the rulers of Qin took the royal title in 325 (year 13 in the reign of King Huiwen 惠文王). Except for Dali 大荔 County on the western bank of the Yellow River in eastern Shaanxi, Qin cultural remains can now be found throughout the entire Wei River basin in Shaanxi and eastern Gansu (Map 2.3). During this time, Qin culture continued to develop

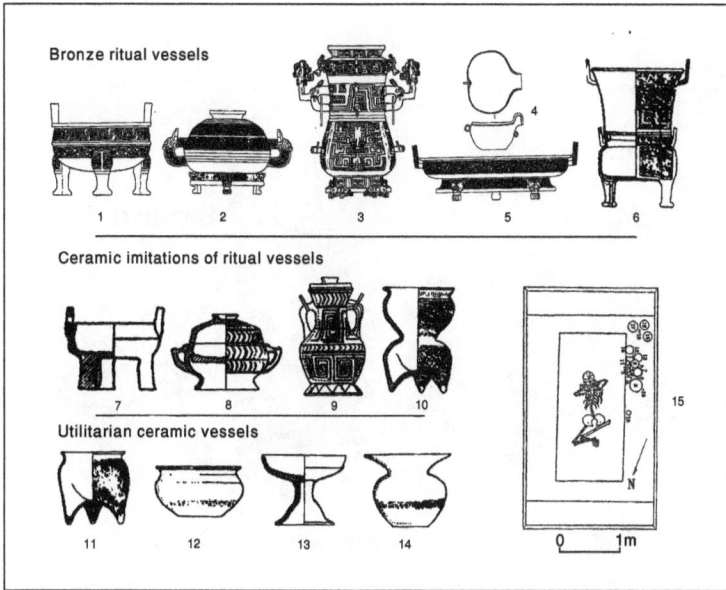

Figure 2.2. Funerary Goods of Qin Culture, Stage 2. *Bronze ritual vessels:* (1) *dǐng* with no lid; (2) *gǔi*; (3) square *hú*; (4) *yí*; (5) *pán*; (6) *yǎn*. *Ceramic imitations of ritual vessels* (7) *dǐng* with no lid; (8) *gǔi* with false abdomen; (9) square *hú* (10) *yǎn*. *Utilitarian ceramic vessels:* (11) *lì*; (12) *yú*; (13) *dòu*; (14) *guàn* with large bell-shaped mouth; (15) Tomb M2, Qinjiagou. Sources: (1–5) Yuandingshan 98LDM2; (6) Long County Bianjiazhuang M1; (7, 8) Dianzi M218; (9) Dianzi M268; (10) Dianzi M215; (11–13) Dianzi M287; (14) Dianzi M215

steadily; thus this stage can be considered the *Florescence Stage* of development (Figures 2.3a, b).

Periods 9 and 10 constitute Stage 4, encompassing the Late Warring States, imperial Qin, and Early Western Han periods, and corresponding roughly to the 200 years from the time when Qin conquered the states of Ba 巴 and Shu 蜀 in 316 (nine years after King Huiwen's change of title) to the promulgation of the *wǔzhū* 五銖 coinage system in the Western Han (year 5 in the Yuanshou 元狩 reign of Emperor Wu, 118). Qin remains can be found throughout eastern Gansu and central Shaanxi (Map 2.4). Because Qin expanded actively outward during this time, leading to the founding of the Qin Empire, it, on the one hand, introduced its own culture into the territories it expanded into, and, on the other, adopted the cultural traits of its subjects, thus bringing about obvious changes in the overall characteristics of Qin culture. This signifies the arrival of the

(text continues on page 80)

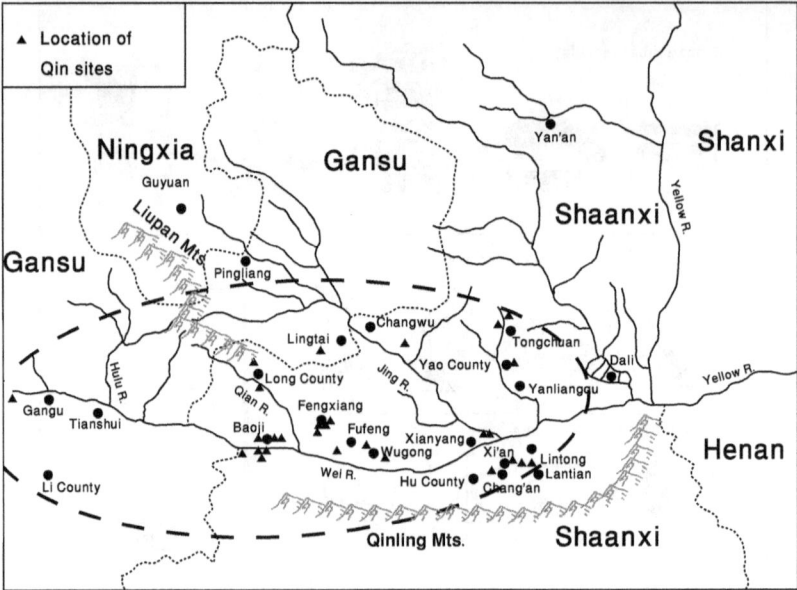

Map 2.3. Distribution of Qin Culture, Stage 3

Figure 2.3a *(opposite, top)*. Funerary Goods of Qin Culture, Stage 3 Bronze Vessels. (1, 5) *dǐng* with no lid; (2, 6) *gǔi*; (3) square *hú*; (4, 8) *yǎn*; (9) *dǐng* with lid; (10) *fóu*; (11) *zhou*

Figure 2.3b *(opposite, bottom)*. Funerary Goods of Qin Culture, Stage 3: Ceramic Imitations of Ritual Vessels and Utilitarian Pottery. (1) *dǐng* with no lid (Long County, Dianzi M185); (2) *gǔi* with false abdomen (Fengxiang Gaozhuang M18); (3) square *hú* (Fengxiang Baqitun CM4); (4) square *hú* (Fengxiang Gaozhuang M48); (5) *yǎn* (Baoji Rujiazhuang M5); (6) 6 *dǐng* with lid (Fengxiang Baqitun BM31); (7) *dòu* with lid (Fengxiang 79 Gaozhuang M1); (8) orbicular *hú* (Fengxiang Baqitun BM31); (9) *lì* (Long County, Dianzi M157); (10) *fǔ* (Long County, Dianzi M58); (11) *guàn* with large mouth (Long County, Dianzi M167); (12) *yú* (Long County, Dianzi M58): (13) *fǔ* with two ears (Long County, Dianzi M157)

1

2

3

4

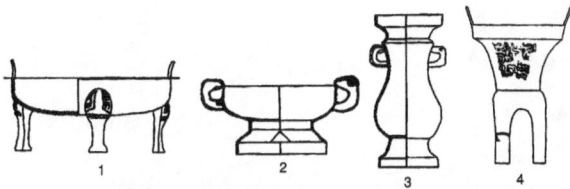

Chang'an Keshengzhunag M202

5

6

7

8

Fengxiang Xigoudao M26

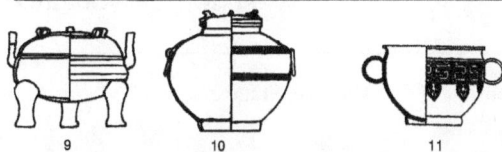

9

10

11

Fengxiang Xigoudao M26   Fengxiang Gaozhuang M10

Ceramic imitations of ritual vessels

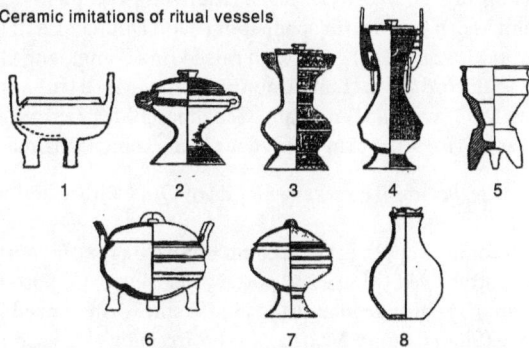

1   2   3   4   5

6   7   8

Utilitarian ceramic vessels

9   10   11   12   13

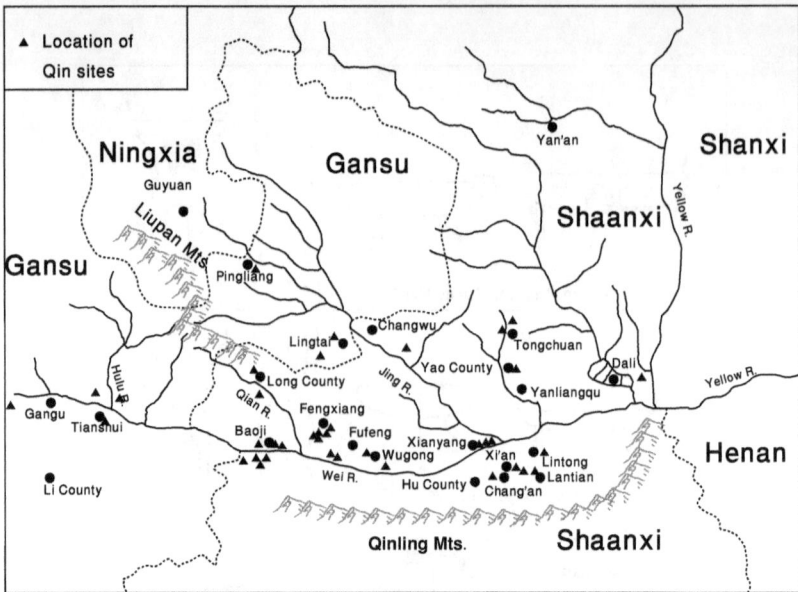

Map 2.4. Distribution of Qin Culture, Stage 4

Figure 2.4a *(opposite, top)*. Funerary Goods of Qin Culture, Stage 4. (1) *dǐng* with lid (Xianyang Huangjiagou M43); (2) orbicular *hú* (Fengxiang 79 Gaozhuang M1); (3) square *hú* (Xianyang Huangjiagou M43); (4) garlic-head *hú* (Fengxiang Gaozhuang M46); (5) *móu* (Fengxiang 79 Gaozhuang M1); (6) *yǎn* made of two separate parts (Fengxiang Gaozhuang M46); (7) 7 *dǐng* with lid; (8) *hé*; (9) orbicular *hú* (Xianyang Ta'erpo M28057); (10) *lì* (Xianyang Ta'erpo M34223); (11) 11 *fǔ* (Lantian Xiehu M14); (12) *lì* with spade foot (Baoji Doujiatai A3); (13) *pén* (Xianyang Ta'erpo M34223); (14) *guàn* with raised line (Fengxiang Gaozhuang M47); (15) *guàn* with cord mark (Long County, Dianzi M81); (16) *wèng* (Yaozhi'anchengdong M8); (17) *fóu* (Fengxiang Gaozhuang M6); (18) garlic-head *hú* (Dali Zhaoyi M202); (19) silkworm-shaped jar (Fengxiang Gaozhuang M39)

Figure 2.4b *(opposite, bottom)*. Funerary Goods of Qin Culture Found in Other Regions, Stage 4
A: (1) Vertical pit tomb (M443); (2) Catacomb tomb (M4172); (3) pottery *fǔ* (M4240); (4) pottery *pén* (M441); (5) pottery *hé* (M453); (6) pottery garlic-head *hú* (M4263); (7) bronze *móu* (M4238); (8) silkworm-shaped jar (M310)
B: (1) bronze *dǐng* (Shan County M3002); (2) bronze *móu* (Shan County M2001); (3) bronze garlic-head *hú* (Shan County M3410); (4) pottery *lì* (Sifaju M16); (5) pottery *pén* (Shan County M4015); (6) pottery *fǔ* (Shangcunling Qin tomb); (7) pottery *wèng* (Shan County M3411); (8) silkworm-shaped jar (Shan County M3101); (9) pottery *fóu* (Shan County M3002)
C: (1) bronze *dǐng* (M1); (2) bronze *móu* (M26); (3) pottery *fǔ* (M50); (4) pottery *hé* (M40); (5) pottery *pén* (M17); (6) pottery silkworm-shaped jar (M50); (7) pottery *fóu* (M64)
D: (1) bronze *dǐng* (M11); (2) bronze garlic-head *hú* (M9); (3) bronze *móu* (M11); (4) pottery *fǔ* (M36); (5) pottery *pén* (M11); (6) pottery silkworm-shaped jar (M9); (7) pottery *fóu* (M11)

Bronze ritual vessels   Utilitarian bronze vessels

1   2   3   4   5   6

Ceramic imitations of ritual vessels

7   8   9

Utilitarian ceramic vessels

10   11   12   13   14   15

16   17   18   19

A- Houma Qiaocun cemetery, Shanxi

B- Sanmenxia area, Henan

C- Qinchuan Haojiaping cemetery, Sichuan

D- Shuihudi Yunmeng cemetery, Hubei

Transformation Stage in the development of Qin culture (Figures 2.4a, b). It is thus classified because at the time when the Qin dynasty collapsed, Qin cultural elements were incorporated into the various cultures that existed in different areas of China during the first sixty to seventy years of the Western Han dynasty, constituting a major ingredient in the emergent Han culture.

FROM KINSHIP-BASED TO RESIDENCE-BASED SOCIAL ORDER

First, let us investigate changes in the membership composition of basic social groups that constituted Qin society. Based on a careful analysis of archaeological finds, particularly from the burial sites near major Qin settlements from each stage of development of Qin culture, we can observe the following changes.

During Stage 1, Qin cultural remains were limited to Eastern Gansu. Since data are scant, it is difficult to analyze basic social structure thoroughly. What is known is that evidence of other cultures coexisting with the Qin culture was not found at the Western Zhou–period settlement at Maojiaping in Gangu County. The burials from this period display great homogeneity in their layout, burial style, and burial goods (Figure 2.1). This shows that the group who inhabited the Maojiaping site during the Western Zhou period was quite homogenous in composition (see also Zhao, chapter 1 in this volume).

Evidence reflecting the basic social group during Stage 2, corresponding roughly to the Early and Middle Springs-and-Autumns period, is still scarce. However, Qin cultural remains from this time begin to display extraneous cultural elements, particularly those that can be traced to the Zhou and to areas to the north (Figure 2.2). This is evidence that the territory governed by Qin already comprised both leftover Zhou populations who remained in this region and new occupiers who arrived at the time when Qin culture infiltrated these areas (Teng Mingyu 1999).

During Stage 3, distinct cultural remains belonging to both Qin (identified as Group A) and indigenous northwestern cultures (Group B), datable from the Late Springs-and-Autumns to the Warring States periods, are found together in the same stratigraphic layers as well as the same pits at the Maojiaping site (Gansu Sheng Wenwu Gongzuodui 1987; Zhao Huacheng 1989). This scenario is an indication that members of a non-Qin group, represented by Group B remains, coexisted with Qin people at the Maojiaping site. Besides cultural layers, houses, and pits,

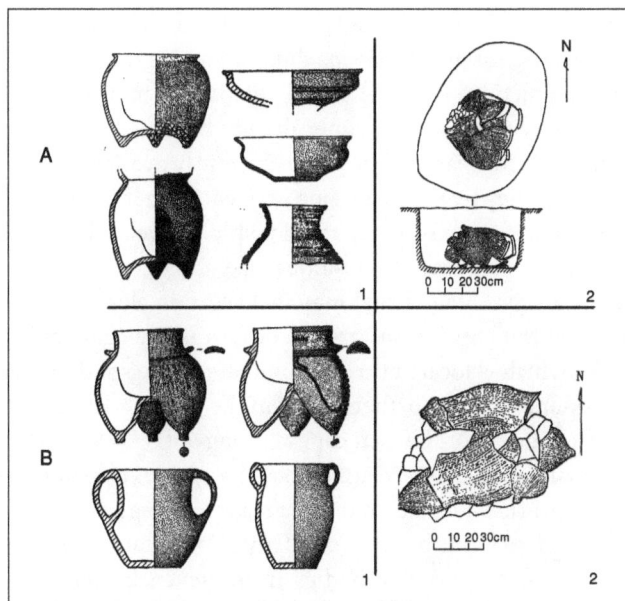

Figure 2.5. Ceramics and Urn Burials from Maojiaping A and B groups. (A1) The Qin culture ceramics from Maojiaping; (A2) Urn burials of Qin culture from Maojiaping; (B1) Ceramics of the Maojiaping B group; (B2) Urn burials of Maojiaping B group

vertical-pit graves, and infant burials covered by broken *lì* 鬲 vessels were found in the settlement. All the vertical-pit burials can be attributed to Qin people. The infant burials in *lì* vessels that belong to the category of Qin vertical-pit burials were constructed first by digging an irregular-shaped flat pit; the skeletal remains of infants were then placed inside a *lì* or *yǎn* 甗 vessel and buried in the pit. By contrast, infant burials in *lì* vessels belonging to the Group B remains were found in unsealed deposits during excavations; rather than placing the remains inside vessels, the Maojiaping residents associated with Group B remains used pieces of broken *lì* or *yǎn* vessels to cover the skeletal remains of infants and covered them in a makeshift fashion with earth and dirt without digging a specially dedicated pit—a custom that is completely different from Qin-style infant burial in *lì* vessels (Figure 2.5). From this it can be inferred that a separate burial ground must have existed for the group of inhabitants who produced Maojiaping Group B finds.[2] This suggests that people who were bearers of Qin culture and the producers of the

Maojiaping Group B finds already coexisted in the same settlements, but due to certain unknown reasons did not engage in cultural exchange or fusion and practiced separate burial customs specific to their groups. Whether these two groups of people already belonged to the same basic social grouping is unclear, but, based on currently available data, it can be ascertained that they lived side by side with each other in the same settlement. Therefore, if there was any relationship between them, it could be based only on co-residence at the same place.

Another site from Stage 3 that may yield certain clues about changing composition of the basic social groups of Qin is the cemetery of Deng-jiaya 鄧家崖, which is located three kilometers to the south of the county seat of Fengxiang, on the northern bank of the Yong 雍 River and close to the southern suburbs of the Qin capital, Yong City 雍城. In 1988, seven burials were discovered as a result of local farmers extracting earth from the location for brick making, and salvage archaeological excavation was subsequently carried out by the Yong City Work Station of the Shaanxi Institute of Archaeology. The bodies in all seven burials were in the supine position and can be dated generally from the Late Springs-and-Autumns to Middle Warring States periods. Two of those entombed were buried with coarsely made bronze ritual vessels, including *dǐng* 鼎, *dòu*豆, *pán*盘, *yí* 匜, and *yǎn*. The remaining five tombs contain ceramic imitations of *dǐng*, *guǐ* 簋, *hú* 壶, *pán*, *yí*, and so on. There were also utilitarian ceramic vessels such as *lì* and flared *guàn* 罐 (Shaanxi Sheng Kaogu Yanjiusuo Yongcheng Gongzuozhan 1991). The above-mentioned burial goods are completely identical to those excavated from other Qin graves (Figures 2.3a, 2.3b, and 2.6). Due to limited published data, we do not know the order and layout of these seven graves, their positions in relation to the entire cemetery, or whether any flexed burials were found in the cemetery. Indeed, this information may prove difficult to obtain because of the accidental nature of the discovery and the subsequent salvage excavation of these graves. Nevertheless, it is noteworthy that all the bodies were buried in the supine position. Since the bodies found in all other Qin burials dated to this time period are strongly flexed, there must be a reason behind the practice of this different burial style in the Dengjiaya cemetery. Yet while practicing a burial tradition that was different from the rest of the Qin culture area, the people utilizing the Dengjiaya cemetery used burial goods manifesting the classical Qin style. This is an indication that they shared with the Qin people a certain degree of similarity, perhaps even close affinity, but were nonetheless different in other aspects of life.

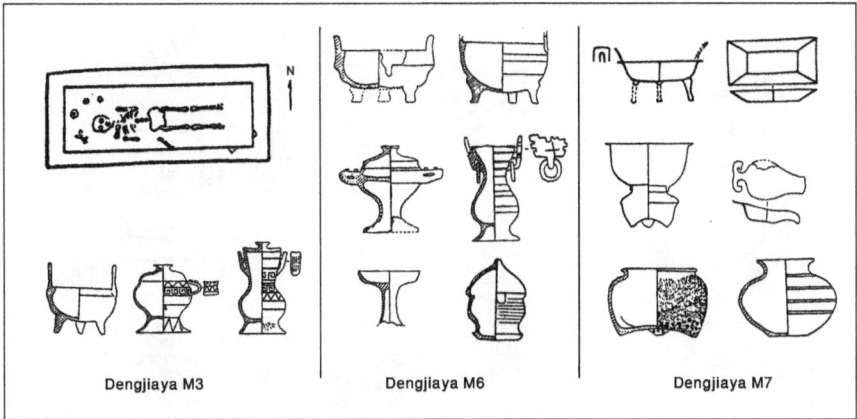

Figure 2.6. Funerary Goods from the Dengjiaya Cemetery

As Dengjiaya is located on the northern bank of the Yong River and was approximately only three kilometers from the Qin capital of Yong, the people who were buried at Dengjiaya most likely lived either in Yong City or nearby. Based on the observation that these people were buried in their separate cemetery, on the location of this cemetery in the southern outskirts of Yong, and on the presence of bronze ritual vessels and ceramic imitations of these vessels in the graves, one may infer that the social status of these people was most likely the same as those who were buried in flexed position at other cemeteries nearby. These people with different burial style must have come from different cultural origins. They probably inhabited the same settlements, yet maintained their own cemetery and burial customs while embracing certain aspects of Qin culture. This shows that the Qin community in this period already comprised people practicing supine burial alongside the flexed-burial practicing majority.

Stage 4 is represented by the Ta'erpo 塔兒坡 cemetery in Xianyang, located about ten kilometers to the west of the Qin capital Xianyang. The cemetery itself was in use from the Late Warring States to the Qin imperial period (Xianyang Shi Wenwu Kaogu Yanjiusuo 1998: 226–227). Both vertical shaft tombs and chamber ("catacomb") tombs were found at the Ta'erpo cemetery, and the burials were aligned facing the four cardinal directions, with the skeletal remains buried in both supine and flexed positions. Aside from the presence of bronze ritual vessels in one grave, the remaining 197 graves contained various types of burial goods, including ceramic imitations of bronze ritual vessels, everyday utilitar-

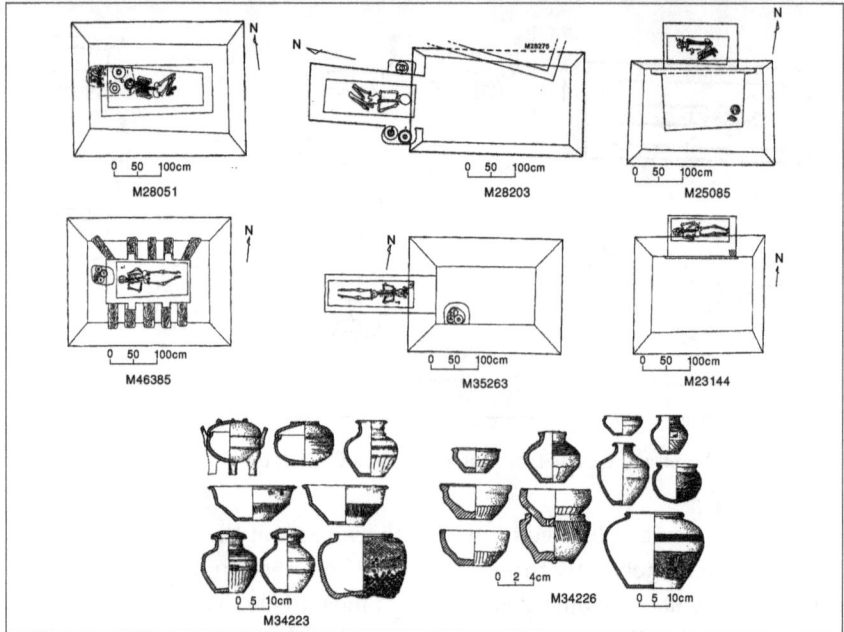

Figure 2.7. The Different Shapes of the Tomb and Funerary Goods from the Ta'erpo Cemetery

ian ceramic wares, as well as small ceramic models known as *mingqi* (Figure 2.7). Since most of these ceramics bear inscriptions indicating the workshop where they were made, it is possible to deduce that these wares were manufactured for commercial purposes. Although the burials can be differentiated into various rank categories based on the types and varieties of burial goods found, and thus shedding light on the social status of the tomb occupants, the commercial nature of these burial goods and the great variety in body treatment and tomb style all point to diverse cultural origins of those buried within (Teng Mingyu 2004). Therefore the cemetery at Ta'erpo is different from Dengjiaya where the deceased all belonged to the same social group, or were buried together because they shared a common cultural tradition. In contrast, at Ta'erpo it is difficult to argue that people were buried in the same cemetery by dint of belonging to the same social stratum; nor does the situation seem to be that which prevailed from the Han dynasty onward, when people of similar economic means bought and sold tomb plots close to one another. The variety in the typology, burial style, and the combination of burial goods seen here demonstrate how people of different cultural traditions could be buried in the same cemetery, linked together because they had been living in the same location over a period of time, thus creating a place-based relationship. A similar scenario is seen in other cemeteries from the same time period, such as Dianzi 店子 in Long County (Teng Mingyu 2002), Gaozhuang 高莊 in Fengxiang (Teng Mingyu 1993), and Renjiazui 任家咀 in Xianyang (Teng Mingyu 2009). The fact that people of different cultural origins could be buried at the same cemetery is not only an indication of a certain degree of cultural openness and tolerance in Qin culture, but also proof that people of non-Qin origin coexisted with Qin people in the same communities, where they had already been fused into the basic organizations constituting Qin culture and society.

In summary, beginning with the Late Springs-and-Autumns period, Qin people and those from other cultural traditions were living within the same communities. We cannot confirm whether they still lived in separate groups at the settlements, but it is clear that at first they still buried their dead separately. Some of the non-Qin groups preserved their own cultural traditions, others adopted those of the Qin. Only toward the end of the Warring States period is there ample evidence that people from different cultural traditions were living harmoniously in the same settlements and were also buried in the same cemeteries. This indicates that at this time, the most basic Qin social organization had already absorbed groups of people originating from different cultural traditions who had come to inhabit the same territory. The fact that they were no longer occupying a settlement based on kinship ties shows that the Qin social structure was now maintained on the basis of place of residence.

CHANGES IN THE MEMBERSHIP COMPOSITION OF THE QIN RULING ELITE

The people who constituted the social fabric of Qin society can be divided into two groups, namely the rulers and the ruled. The ruling stratum included the lord (*gong* 公)[3] and other members of the elite. The lord occupied the highest social position as head of the Qin ruling lineage. From the Qin founder Lord Xiang down to the founding of the Qin Empire, in Qin, like in other Zhou polities, rulership was consistently maintained through hereditary succession (Lin Jianming 1981: 447–48). Our discussion here does not deal, however, either with members of the ruling lineage or with the upper segments of the Qin ruling elite in general, because we lack sufficient data about this group: not just the textual data for the early periods of Qin history is scanty (see the general introduction to this volume), but so also are archaeological discoveries of the tombs of the leading nobility. Yet luckily we have ample archaeological evidence from the tombs of lower elite members, and our discussion focuses largely on these tombs. Through an analysis of small- to medium-scale Qin burials, it is possible to identify those tomb occupants who used ritual bronzes as the principal members of the Qin ruling stratum aside from the ruler and the leading nobility (Teng Mingyu 2003: 21–28). This group became the ruling elite through which Qin established its leadership and control in the newly occupied areas, as it expanded eastward and southward from eastern Gansu along the upper reaches of the Qian 千 and Wei 渭 rivers.

Since information that can help explain the social structure cannot be found during the initial stage of the development of Qin culture, it is difficult to discuss and illustrate such issues as the groups constituting the upper echelons of Qin society and the internal ranking of that elite during the Western Zhou period. Yet when Qin cultural development reached Stage 2, it is possible to observe through an analysis of burial goods such as bronze ritual vessels that there were at least three groups who made up the elite of Qin culture during that time. A number of tombs, including 98LDM1, 98LDM2, and 2000LDM4 at Yuandingshan 圓頂山 in Li County (Gansu Sheng Wenwu Kaogu Yanjiusuo et al. 2002, 2005), M1 and M5 at Bianjiazhuang 邊家莊 in Long County (Yin Shengping and Zhang Tian'en 1986; Shaanxi Sheng Kaogu Yanjiusuo Baoji Gongzuozhan et al. 1998), M1 and M2 at Qinjiagou 秦家溝 in Yangping 陽平 (Shaanxi Sheng Wenwu Guanli Weiyuanhui 1965), M1 at Fulinbu 福臨堡 in Baoji (Zhongguo Kexueyuan Kaogu Yanjiusuo Baoji Fajuedui 1963), the Qin tomb at Jiangchengbu 姜城堡 in Baoji (Wang Guangyong 1979), and M1 at Nanyang 南陽 Village in Baoji (Baoji Shi Kaogu Gongzuodui et al. 2001), display evidence of the tomb occupants using bronze ritual vessels according to prescribed Zhou ritual rules, as they were buried with *dǐng, guǐ, hú, pán,* and *yí* (in some instances *pán* and *yí* are missing) (see Appendix, Table 2.1). Sometimes *hé* 盉 vessels were used instead of *yí;* some tombs additionally yielded *yǎn* vessels. These are complete ritual assemblages comprising meat-cooking vessels, grain-offering vessels, wine vessels, and water containers. The number of vessels followed an established pattern, with odd-numbered sets of *dǐng,* even-numbered sets of *guǐ* and *hú,* and single *pán, yí* (or *hé*), and *yǎn.*

The regularity in the number and types of bronze ritual vessels found in these tombs is evidence of the importance placed on the hereditary patriarchal lineage system that had become the core of ancient Chinese culture since the Western Zhou. The vessel assemblages testify to the implementation of sumptuary rules according to which the number of *dǐng* vessels indicated their owner's status and identity within the aristocratic hierarchy. Apparently, the power and privilege to use these bronze ritual vessels and to be buried with them derived from the fact that the tomb occupants, while alive, belonged to the elite core of Qin society. Moreover, the reason why these members of Qin society were able to attain their social status was probably due to their kinship ties within the hereditary patriarchal lineage system, signifying that the membership in the Qin ruling elite was obtained through kinship ties.

Another group of tomb occupants, however, such as those of MI at Xigaoquan 西高泉 in Baoji (Baoji Shi Bowuguan et al. 1980), MI at Jingjiazhuang 景家莊 in Lingtai 靈臺 (Liu Dezhen and Zhu Jiantang 1981), BM27 at Baqitun 八旗屯 in Fengxiang (Wu Zhenfeng and Shang Zhiru 1980), the Bianjiazhuang Springs-and-Autumns tomb found in Long County (Zhang Tian'en 1990), and 98LDM3 at Yuandingshan in Li County (Gansu Sheng Wenwu Kaogu Yanjiusuo et al. 2002), were buried with bronze ritual vessels apparently chosen more or less at random and not assembled according to specific rules (see Appendix, Table 2.1). The burial goods found in these tombs include northern-style straight-bladed short swords as well as other bronze weapons,[4] all pointing to extraneous cultural influences. Although these tomb occupants were buried with some bronze ritual vessels, it does not seem that they followed the sumptuary rules governing the usage of *dǐng* vessels. Therefore it can be argued that these people attained the privilege of possessing and utilizing these bronze vessels for a different reason from the group mentioned previously. The presence of northern-style straight-bladed short swords and other bronze weapons in these tombs perhaps suggests that the tomb occupants were granted the privilege to use their bronze ritual vessels due to their engagement in military activities in areas to the north. They were most likely members of a warrior nobility who were able to enter the elite stratum of Qin society through their military interaction with extraneous cultures, especially those to the north, during the course of Qin's expansion.

In addition, there was a third group of tombs such as CM2 and AM9 at Baqitun in Fengxiang (Wu Zhenfeng and Shang Zhiru 1980), M2 and M3 at Nanyang Village in Baoji (Baoji Shi Kaogu Gongzuodui et al. 2001), and M27 at Shangmeng 上孟 Village in Changwu (Yun Anzhi 1984), in which the occupants were buried with groups of bronze ritual vessels or their ceramic equivalents in fairly regular arrangements that show relatively numerous elements introduced from the Zhou culture (see Appendix, Table 2.1). However, bronze weapons are absent in these burials. The tomb occupants were buried in the supine position. Since these people followed the sumptuary stipulations regarding the usage of *dǐng* vessels, they presumably obtained the privilege of using bronze vessels due to their social status; they were most likely the local ruling elite of the areas into which Qin culture had expanded. Since many elements related to Zhou culture were found in these tombs, it seems likely that the tomb occupants were descendants of the Zhou people who had inhabited Central Shaanxi during Western Zhou times (Teng Mingyu 1999). Based on this evidence, it can be inferred that during the Early to Middle Springs-and-Autumns period, the Qin ruling stratum comprised three groups of people, namely those related through kinship ties to the indigenous Qin nobility, individuals who had attained high social status through military achievements, and the local ruling elites of areas the Qin had conquered. This situation was very different from that of the social composition of the elite during the Western Zhou period, when authority was handed down solely through one dominant patriarchal lineage through kinship ties.

When Qin cultural development reached Stage 3, roughly at the transition to the Early Warring States period, the ruling elite of Qin still consisted of a number of different groups. Some tomb occupants, such as those of tombs M10 and M49 at Gaozhuang, Fengxiang (Yongcheng Kaogu Gongzuodui 1980), M26 at Xigoudao 西溝道, Fengxiang (Shaanxi Sheng Yongcheng Kaogudui 1986a), CM9 at Baqitun, Fengxiang (Wu Zhenfeng and Shang Zhiru 1980), and M202 at Keshengzhuang 客省莊, Chang'an 長安 (Zhongguo Kexueyuan Kaogu Yanjiusuo 1962: 131–140), were buried with Qin-style bronze ritual vessels (see Appendix, Table 2.2). These vessels were increasingly made for exclusive use as burial goods, but the burial sets were still comprised of meat-cooking vessels, grain-offering vessels, and wine containers; water containers were also found occasionally. The numerical constellations of these different types of bronze ritual vessels, however, no longer displayed the same regularity as before. For example, there are instances when ceramic imitations of bronze ritual vessels are absent, and others where all vessels other than *dǐng* are ceramic imitations.[5]

Among the various extraneous cultural elements seen in these burials, bronze ritual vessels and weapons from north-central China (the territory of Jin and its three successor kingdoms, Han, Wei, and Zhao, and of the Zhou royal domain) are dominant.[6] We may infer that these tomb occupants belonged to the group within Qin society that had already pre-

viously been empowered to utilize bronze vessels, but they had to vary-
ing degrees adopted, and identified with, extraneous cultural elements
in the course of their ongoing interactions with non-Qin others, mainly
from north-central China. Since bronze weapons were found in most of
these tombs, such interactions may be assumed also to have included
military activities.

Another group of individuals, such as those found in M48 and M18
at Gaozhuang, Fengxiang (Yongcheng Kaogu Gongzuodui 1980), M1 at
Zhaojialai 趙家來, Wugong 武功 (Zhongguo Shehuikexueyuan Kaogu
Yanjiusuo Wugong Fajuedui, CASS 1996), M4 and M7 at Dengjiaya,
Fengxiang (Shaanxi Sheng Kaogu Yanjiusuo Yongcheng Gongzuozhan
1991), BM31 at Baqitun, Fengxiang (Wu Zhenfeng and Shang Zhiru 1980),
81M14 at Baqitun, Fengxiang (Shaanxi Sheng Yongcheng Kaogudui
1986b), and M56 at Renjiazui, Xianyang (Xianyang Shi Wenwu Kaogu
Yanjiusuo 2005: 55–56), were buried with bronze ritual vessels that
appeared to be chosen in a more random manner, with many of these
objects being extraneous imports. In particular, the Early Warring
States–period burials such as M48 and M18 at Gaozhuang in Fengxiang
and M1 at Zhaojialai in Wugong, and others, each contained one complete set of ceramic imitations of bronze ritual vessels, including *dǐng*,
guǐ, and *hú*, sometimes with the addition of *pán*, *yí*, and *yǎn*. The main
evidence of the incorporation of extraneous cultural elements is seen in
the bronze-imitating ceramics and in the weapons. Examples include the
Jin- and Zhou-style covered *dǐng* found in BM31 at Baqitun in Fengxiang,
a Wu-Yue 吴越-style *gē* dagger-axe with nose-shaped protrusion and
spear with curved tip found together with a Ba-Shu 巴蜀-style bronze
short sword in M18 at Gaozhuang in Fengxiang. It should be noted that
besides these bronze weapons, Qin-style *gē* dagger-axes were also found.

From these burial goods it can be inferred that the tomb occupants
already had the privilege to be buried with ceramic imitations of bronze
ritual vessels, but, as a result of the important roles they played in the
interactions with other cultures, particularly by means of military-
related activities, they were able to attain the privilege of owning actual
bronze ritual vessels as well. It is also possible that the deceased acquired
these vessels from other cultures and included them as part of their
repertoire of burial goods. Such a scenario shows that the practice of
individuals gaining access to bronze ritual vessels as a result of military
achievements that was practiced during the Early and Middle Springs-
and-Autumns periods was still rather common in this time, but also that,
rather than populations to the north of Qin, the main counterparts with

whom these Qin elites engaged in military activities were now their eastern neighbors in the Zhou-allied principalities of north-central China. The decline of importance of Qin-style bronze ritual vessels during Middle Warring States period and the prominence of vessels of north-central Chinese styles shows not only that the Qin users of these vessels had come to identify with bronze ritual vessels of north-central Chinese origin, but also that a change had occurred in how the group of people who had previously used Qin-style ritual vessels perceived the ability of such Qin-style bronze ritual vessels to serve as a marker of social status and power. In addition, since these extraneous-originated bronze ritual vessels could not possibly have been acquired through inheritance within the kin group, it is likely the power of those elite groups who previously had obtained the privilege of using Qin-style bronze ritual vessels through their hereditary position in the kinship system had already begun to decline.

From the Late Warring States period until after the Qin unification of China, those groups who were allowed to use ritual bronzes were buried with assemblages altogether lacking in regularity. Traditional Qin-style vessels completely disappeared from tombs, with the majority of the objects displaying styles that can be attributed to north-central China. Examples include the bronze *dǐng* produced in the Zhongshan 中山 area found in 79M1 at Gaozhuang, Fengxiang (Figure 2.8: 1 and 2) (Yongcheng Kaogu Gongzuodui 1980), the compressed-profile *dǐng* found in tombs M203 at Chaoyi 朝邑, Dali 大荔 (Figure 2.8: 3) (Shaanxi Sheng Wenguanhui et al. 1978) and M6 at Shangyuanjia 上袁家, Qin'an 秦安 (Figure 2.8: 4) (Gansu Sheng Wenwu Kaogu Yanjiusuo 1997), the *lìdǐng* 鬲鼎 (or *liándāngdǐng* 連襠鼎) unearthed from M6 at Miaozhuang 廟莊, Pingliang 平涼 (Figure 2.8: 5) (Wei Huaiheng 1982), the round *hú* with a flat covers from M203 at Chaoyi, Dali, and M6 at Miaozhuang, Pingliang (Figure 2.8: 6 and 7), as well as the *yǎn* consisting of a *zèng* 甑 superimposed upon a lower body resembling a *fǔ* 釜 found in M18 at Shangjiaocun 上焦村, Lintong (Figure 2.8: 8) (Qinyong Kaogudui 1980). It is possible that these objects were imported from north-central China, or perhaps they were manufactured in Qin in imitation of imported originals (see Appendix, Table 2.3). Their ubiquity is clear evidence that the belief in Qin-style bronze ritual vessels as indicators of a tomb occupant's social status had disappeared by this time period.

Besides extraneous-influenced bronze ritual vessels, bronze vessels of daily utilitarian function attributed to cultural influences from the Ba

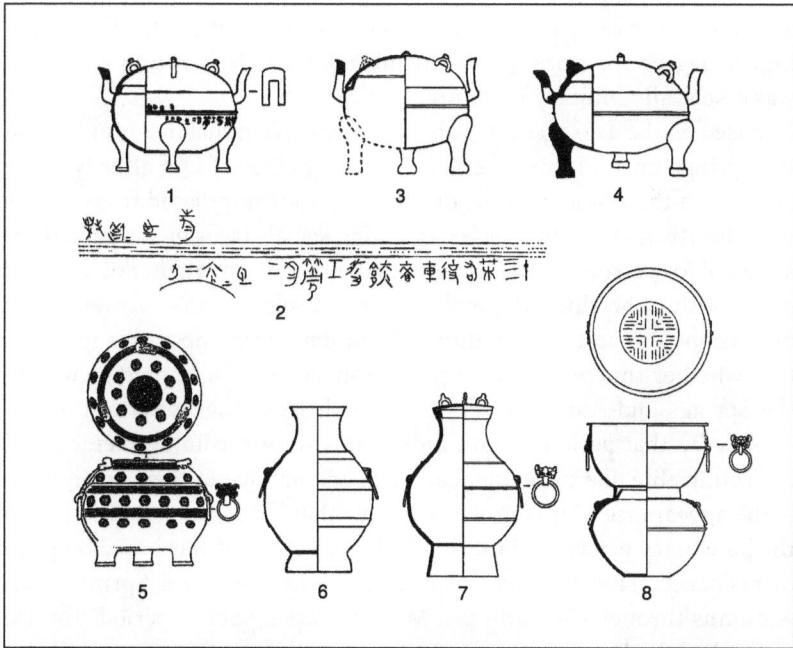

Figure 2.8. Non-Qin Ritual Bronzes Unearthed from Qin Tomba. (1) Bronze *dǐng* from the Zhongshan area (Fengxiang, Gaozhuang 79M1); (2) Rubbing of the inscription from the Zhongshan bronze *dǐng*; (3) Compressed-profile *dǐng* from tomb M203 Chaoyi, Dali; (4) Compressed-profile *dǐng* from tomb M6, Shangyuanjia, Qin'an; (5) 5 *Lìdǐng* 鬲鼎 (or *liándāngdǐng* 連襠鼎) from tomb M6 Pingliang, Miaozhuang; (6) Round *hú* with a flat covers from tomb M203 Chaoyi, Dali; (7) Round *hú* with a flat covers from M6 Pingliang, Miaozhuang; (8) *Yǎn* consisting of a *zèng* 甑 superimposed upon a lower body resembling a *fǔ* 釜, tomb M18, Lintong, Shangjiaocun

and Shu region in modern Sichuan were also found in large numbers, particularly the *móu* 鍪 and *fǔ* 釜 vessels that were used in cooking. However, bronze weapons, which are known to have been used by the Ba and Shu nobility to signify their social status, are rarely encountered in Qin archaeological contexts in this time. The advantages of bronze *móu* and *fǔ* vessels over their ceramic equivalents are their sturdiness and ease of transportation, which catered to the basic needs of an army on the move. Hence the individuals who were able to acquire these exotic bronze ritual and daily utilitarian vessels must have been involved, either directly or indirectly, in the military activities related to Qin's expansion into Sichuan and its conquest of the six rival kingdoms to the east, and thus in the campaigns leading up to the Qin unification. To an even higher degree than previously, membership in Qin's ruling apparatus was essentially military in nature.

Based on the data presented above, it can be seen that, beginning from the Springs-and-Autumns period, the ruling elites of Qin already broke away from the Zhou tradition of exclusively kinship-based transference of authority. Instead, the conferral of high social status on individuals as a reward for personal achievement resulted in the emergence of a special group within the elite, who took a powerful role in Qin's vast territorial expansion. Due to the limitations of our data, it is impossible to ascertain whether this group of people had indeed begun to emerge during the Springs-and-Autumns period. Nevertheless, what is certain is that already by that period certain individuals were becoming members of the ruling elite due to personal abilities and not due to their pedigree. It is the appearance of this group of people that led to the transition from the hereditary patriarchal lineage system to one that was based on place of residence. This continuous process lasted from Late Springs-and-Autumns through the Early and Middle Warring States period. Toward the end of the Warring States until after the Qin unification of China, the ruling elite of the Qin Empire already displayed a great degree of openness, as members of this group consisted of individuals who were able to attain their status through personal accomplishments rather than the pedigree, thus completing the transition from kinship-based to place-based mode of rule.

CONCLUSION

To conclude, during the approximately 900 years of Qin's cultural development, the mechanism that sustained the basic social structure shifted from a society based on kinship ties to a society based on one's place of residence. During the Late Warring States period, burials that indicate the tomb occupants' diverse cultural origins can be found at the Ta'erpo cemetery in Xianyang, signifying that Qin society had entered a new phase: the ruling elite whose members were related to one another through kinship ties had given way to an elite composed of individuals who had attained power through personal achievement, particularly through their accomplishments in military affairs. Such people now formed the major component of the Qin ruling class. Just like the policy of delegating officials from the Qin capital to oversee the administration of commanderies and counties solidified the basic social and political structures of Qin, so can the increasing openness and inclusiveness of the Late Warring States period Qin culture, as expressed in gradual transformation of basic social units from kinship to place of residence-based ones, be seen as the foundation of the unified Qin Empire, which transcended initial cultural confinement (Xu Zhuoyun 1998).

Since the founding of the Qin principality was not a consequence of investiture by the Zhou king during the Early Western Zhou period, Qin was not compelled to adhere strictly to the kinship-based governing policies that were characteristic of the Western Zhou state system. This resulted in the early decline of kinship-based mode of rule. When Qin was finally invested by the Zhou king at the beginning of the Eastern Zhou period, this merely was an empty formality; actually, warfare with its Rong and Di neighbors had a decisive effect on the early formation of the Qin principality. This situation was conducive to the formation of a new ruling stratum wherein status was attained at least in part through personal achievement in military affairs; the members of this new elite were subsequently assigned by the Qin ruler to govern the newly conquered territory. During the process of its territorial expansion, Qin continued to interact with neighboring groups and the local inhabitants of areas that came under its rule, resulting in an early change in Qin's basic social structure that included a shift from kinship-based to place-based status reckoning and an unprecedented openness and acceptance of extraneous cultural elements.

The decline of a political system that was based exclusively on kinship ties and hereditary rules, the rise of individuals to elite status as a result of personal accomplishments, as well as the embrace of extraneous cultural elements, all constituted the basic requirements for the founding of an empire that exercised centralized control over its various commanderies and counties. Since Qin culture already possessed the above-mentioned characteristics during the Late Warring States period, it was able to expand into the Central Plains, to conquer its six powerful eastern and southern rivals, and eventually to unify China, paving the way for the transition from a system of vassal states to an imperial state.

Translated by Susanna Lam

APPENDIX: TABLES

A key to the abbreviations used in these tables follows table 2.3.

TABLE 2.1. Funerary Goods from Qin Tombs with Bronze Ritual Vessels,
Stage 2

Tomb	Tomb Orientation	Coffin and Outer Coffin	Body Position	Gender and Age
Li County Yuandingshan 98LDM1	275	One coffin and one outer coffin	unknown	unknown
Li County Yuandingshan 98LDM2	275	One coffin and one outer coffin	unknown	unknown
Li County Yuandingshan 2000LDM4	275	unknown	unknown	unknown
Long County Bianjiazhuang M1	unknown	unknown	unknown	unknown

	Bronze Ritual Vessels													Ceramic Imitations of Ritual Vessels							
	A 鼎	B 簋	C 壺	D 盥	E 盉	F 匜	G 舟	H 簠	I 盆	J 盂	K 甂	L 罐		A 鼎	B 簋	C 壺	D 盥	E 盉	F 匜	K 甂	M 豆
	5*+ / 1*	2	2*+ / 1*	1	1	1	1	-	-	-	-	-		-	-	-	-	-	-	-	-

ADDITIONAL BRONZE RITUAL VESSELS 2 square boxes 方盒

OTHER ARTIFACTS jade *guī* tablets, jade fish, bronze jingle, jade coffin ornaments, etc.

REMARKS The grave was looted. Secondary ledge on the south and the north sides; 3 human skeletons (sacrifice) in niches south and north of the coffin; a dog placed in a waist pit at the middle of the tomb.

*5 *dǐng* are without lid; one is with lid; 2 *hú* are square; one is orbicular.

| | 4*+ / 1* | 6 | 2*+ / 1* | 1 | 1 | 1 | - | 1 | - | - | - | - | | - | - | - | - | - | - | - | - |

OTHER ARTIFACTS 4 straight iron swords with bronze handle; 4 bronze *gē* dagger-axe; 2 scrapers; 8 jingles; jade *guī* tablets; jade and stone artifacts

REMARKS The grave was looted. Secondary ledge on four sides. 7 human skeletons (sacrifice) in niches south of the coffin, a dog placed in a waist pit at the middle of the tomb.

*4 *dǐng* are without lid; one is with lid; 2 *hú* are square; one is orbicular.

| | 5 | 4 | 2*+ / 1* | - | - | - | 1 | - | 1 | - | - | - | | - | - | - | - | - | - | - | - |

OTHER ARTIFACTS jade *guī* tablets, jade fish, jade and stone artifacts, etc.

REMARKS The grave was looted and destroyed.

*2 *hú* are square; one is orbicular.

| | 6 | 4 | 2 | 1 | 1 | - | - | - | 1 | - | - | - | | - | - | - | - | - | - | - | - |

OTHER ARTIFACTS 2 bronze spears; 4 bronze *gē* dagger-axes, 71 bronze arrowheads; chariot and horse utensils

REMARKS The grave was destroyed. Perhaps it had a chariot pit.

(continued)

TABLE 2.1. *(continued)*

Tomb	Tomb Orientation	Coffin and Outer Coffin	Body Position	Gender and Age
Long County Bianjiazhuang M5	335	One coffin and one outer coffin	Extended	unknown
Yangping Qinjiagou M1	southeast	One coffin and one outer coffin	Extended	unknown
Yangping Qinjiagou M2	southeast	One coffin and one outer coffin	Flexed	unknown
Baoji Fulinbu M1	west	One coffin and one outer coffin	unknown	unknown
Baoji Jiangchengbu (tomb of the Springs-and-Autumns period)	unknown	unknown	unknown	unknown
Baoji Nanyangcun M1	15	unknown	unknown	unknown

Bronze Ritual Vessels												Ceramic Imitations of Ritual Vessels							
A 鼎	B 簋	C 壺	D 盉	E 盉	F 匜	G 舟	H 簠	I 盆	J 盂	K 甗	L 罐	A 鼎	B 簋	C 壺	D 盉	E 盉	F 匜	K 甗	M 豆
5	4	2	1	1	-	-	-	-	-	1	-	-	-	-	-	-	-	-	-

OTHER ARTIFACTS chariot and horse ornaments; bronze jingle, jade ornaments on the outer coffin

REMARKS A two layer burial chambers, a chariot placed in the upper layer.

A	B	C	D	E	F	G	H	I	J	K	L	A	B	C	D	E	F	K	M
3	4	2	1	-	1	-	-	-	-	-	-	-	-	-	-	-	-	-	-

OTHER ARTIFACTS bronze jingle, jade fish, jade *guī* tablets, chariot and horse utensils, jade ornaments on outer coffin, etc.

REMARKS Secondary ledge, internal wooden structure, a sacrificed dog.

A	B	C	D	E	F	G	H	I	J	K	L	A	B	C	D	E	F	K	M
3	4	2	1	-	1	-	-	-	-	-	-	-	-	-	-	-	-	-	-

OTHER ARTIFACTS Ceramic *guī* tablets, stone and shell ornaments, etc.

REMARKS Secondary ledge, internal wooden structure, a sacrificed dog

A	B	C	D	E	F	G	H	I	J	K	L	A	B	C	D	E	F	K	M
3	2	2	1	-	1	-	1	-	-	1	-	-	-	-	-	-	-	-	-

ADDITIONAL BRONZE RITUAL VESSELS 1 ladle 勺

OTHER ARTIFACTS Stone *guī* tablets, jade fish, jade ornaments, bronze jingle, chariot and horse utensils, etc.

A	B	C	D	E	F	G	H	I	J	K	L	A	B	C	D	E	F	K	M
3	2	2	1	1	-	-	-	-	-	-	-	-	-	-	-	-	-	-	-

OTHER ARTIFACTS A *gē* dagger-axe, a spear, chariot and horse utensils, ornaments on outer coffin

REMARKS Found during house construction therefore the tomb orientation and the position of the body are unknown .

A	B	C	D	E	F	G	H	I	J	K	L	A	B	C	D	E	F	K	M
3	2	2*	1	-	1	-	-	-	-	-	-	-	-	-	-	-	-	-	-

REMARKS Tomb destroyed.

*2 square *hú*

(continued)

TABLE 2.1. *(continued)*

Tomb	Tomb Orientation	Coffin and Outer Coffin	Body Position	Gender and Age
Long County Bianjiazhuang (Springs-and-Autumns period)	unknown	unknown	unknown	unknown
Baoji Xigaoquan M1	unknown	unknown	Flexed	unknown
Lingtai Jingjiazhuang M1	220	One coffin and one outer coffin	Flexed	unknown
Fengxiang Baqitun BM27	292	One coffin and two outer coffins	Extended	unknown
Lixian Yuandingshan 98LDM3	275	One coffin and one outer coffin	unknown	unknown
Fengxiang Baqitun CM2	288	one coffin and two outer coffins	Extended	unknown

Bronze Ritual Vessels												Ceramic Imitations of Ritual Vessels							
A 鼎	B 簋	C 壶	D 盉	E 盂	F 匜	G 舟	H 簠	I 盆	J 盂	K 瓿	L 罐	A 鼎	B 簋	C 壶	D 盉	E 盂	F 匜	K 瓿	M 豆
5	4	-	-	-	-	-	-	-	-	-	-	-	-	-	-	-	-	-	-

OTHER ARTIFACTS Straight iron sword with a bronze handle, chariot and horse utensils

REMARKS See Zhang Tian'en 1990: 227

A 鼎	B 簋	C 壶	D 盉	E 盂	F 匜	G 舟	H 簠	I 盆	J 盂	K 瓿	L 罐	A 鼎	B 簋	C 壶	D 盉	E 盂	F 匜	K 瓿	M 豆
-	-	1	-	-	-	-	-	-	-	-	-	-	-	-	-	-	-	-	-

ADDITIONAL BRONZE RITUAL VESSELS 1 *dòu* vessel; 1 *yǒngzhōng* bell

OTHER ARTIFACTS Straight iron sword with a bronze handle, bronze fish, bronze scraper bronze axe, chariot and horse utensils

REMARKS Tomb destroyed

A 鼎	B 簋	C 壶	D 盉	E 盂	F 匜	G 舟	H 簠	I 盆	J 盂	K 瓿	L 罐	A 鼎	B 簋	C 壶	D 盉	E 盂	F 匜	K 瓿	M 豆
3	-	-	-	-	-	-	-	-	1	-	-	-	-	-	-	-	-	-	-

OTHER ARTIFACTS Straight iron sword with a bronze handle, a *gē* dagger-axe, a bronze jingle, stone *guī* tablets, stone *gē* (dagger-axe), stone ornaments

REMARKS bones of cat, dog and chicken, and skulls of cattle and sheep were placed inside a waist pit in the middle of the tomb. Nearby there was the horse pit

A 鼎	B 簋	C 壶	D 盉	E 盂	F 匜	G 舟	H 簠	I 盆	J 盂	K 瓿	L 罐	A 鼎	B 簋	C 壶	D 盉	E 盂	F 匜	K 瓿	M 豆
3	-	-	-	-	-	-	-	1	-	1	-	-	-	-	-	-	-	-	-

OTHER ARTIFACTS Ceramic chime stones, stone *guī* tablets, jade *bì* disc, straight iron sword with a bronze handle, a bronze *gē* dagger-axe, spear, arrowheads, bow, shield, jingle, sea shells, chariot and horse utensils

REMARKS Associated chariot pit

A 鼎	B 簋	C 壶	D 盉	E 盂	F 匜	G 舟	H 簠	I 盆	J 盂	K 瓿	L 罐	A 鼎	B 簋	C 壶	D 盉	E 盂	F 匜	K 瓿	M 豆
1	-	-	-	-	-	-	-	1	-	-	3	-	-	-	-	-	-	-	-

OTHER ARTIFACTS straight dagger, bronze *gē* dagger-axe, roebuck tooth

A 鼎	B 簋	C 壶	D 盉	E 盂	F 匜	G 舟	H 簠	I 盆	J 盂	K 瓿	L 罐	A 鼎	B 簋	C 壶	D 盉	E 盂	F 匜	K 瓿	M 豆
3	1	-	1	-	1	-	-	-	1	-	-	-	-	-	-	-	-	-	-

OTHER ARTIFACTS 4 *lì* 鬲 vessels with bag legs, stone *guī* tablets, jade *jué* earring, jade *huáng* pendant, bronze jingle, etc.

REMARKS Bronze jingles in four corners of the outer coffin. 2 skeletons of human sacrifice

(continued)

TABLE 2.1. *(continued)*

Tomb	Tomb Orientation	Coffin and Outer Coffin	Body Position	Gender and Age
Fengxiang Baqitun AM9	298	One coffin and one outer coffin	Extended	unknown
Baoji Nanyangcun M2	305	One coffin and one outer coffin	Extended	unknown
Baoji Nanyangcun M3	295	One coffin and one outer coffin	Extended	unknown
Changwu Shangmengcun M27	282	One coffin and one outer coffin	Extended	Male, unknown age

Bronze Ritual Vessels												Ceramic Imitations of Ritual Vessels							
A 鼎	B 簋	C 壺	D 盨	E 盉	F 匜	G 舟	H 簠	I 盆	J 盂	K 甗	L 罐	A 鼎	B 簋	C 壺	D 盨	E 盉	F 匜	K 甗	M 豆
1	-	-	-	-	-	-	-	1	-	1	-	2	-	-	1	-	2	-	-

OTHER ARTIFACTS 2 *lì* 鬲 vessels with bag legs, stone *guī* tablets, stone *zhāng* tablet, jade *jue* earring, bone hairpins, bronze jingle, shells

REMARKS The grave was looted. 1 skeleton of human sacrifice

2	-	-	-	-	-	-	-	-	-	-	-	3	4	2	1	1	-	1	2

OTHER ARTIFACTS 1 bronze *gē* dagger-axe; stone *guī* tablets; jingles, shells, etc.

REMARKS Waist pit

5	-	-	-	-	-	-	-	-	-	-	-	5	4	2	1	1	-	1	2

OTHER ARTIFACTS 1 bronze *gē* dagger-axe, stone *guī* tablets, jingle

REMARKS Waist pit

1	-	-	-	-	-	-	-	-	1	-	-	2	-	-	-	-	-	-	-

OTHER ARTIFACTS bronze jingle, stone *guī* tablets, shell ornaments, clam shells, bone beads

REMARKS Waist pit and sacrificed dog skeleton

TABLE 2.2. Funerary Goods from Qin Tombs with Bronze Ritual Vessels, Stage 3

Tomb	Tomb Orientation	Coffin and Outer Coffin	Burial system	Gender and Age
Fengxiang Gaozhuang M10	274	One coffin and one outer coffin	Flexed burial	unknown
Fengxiang Gaozhuang M49	280	One coffin and one outer coffin	Flexed burial	unknown
Fengxiang, Xigoudao M26	292	One coffin and one outer coffin	Flexed burial	Male unknown age
Fengxiang Baqitun CM9	285	One outer coffin	unknown	unknown
Chang'an Keshengzhuang K202	280	One coffin and one outer coffin	Flexed burial	unknown

Bronze Ritual vessels												Ceramic Imitation of Ritual Vessels							
A 鼎	B 簋	C 壺	D 盤	E 盉	F 匜	G 舟	H 簠	I 盆	J 盂	K 瓿	L 罐	A 鼎	B 簋	C 壺	D 盤	E 盉	F 匜	K 瓿	M 豆
3	-	2	-	-	-	1	-	1	-	1	1	-	2	2	-	1	-	-	-

OTHER ARTIFACTS Bronze dagger, bronze scraper, bronze belt hook, jade *jīngōu* hook, jade *jué* earring, jade *huáng* pendant, jade string ornaments; gold *jīngōu* hook, ceramic cartwheel, etc.

REMARKS Two coffins, joint burial tomb; 2 skeletons of human sacrifice

A 鼎	B 簋	C 壺	D 盤	E 盉	F 匜	G 舟	H 簠	I 盆	J 盂	K 瓿	L 罐	A 鼎	B 簋	C 壺	D 盤	E 盉	F 匜	K 瓿	M 豆
2	-	2	1	-	1	-	-	1	-	1	-	-	2	2	1	1	-	-	2

OTHER ARTIFACTS Bronze belt hook, bronze *jīngōu* hook, scraper, jingles, stone ornaments, etc.

A 鼎	B 簋	C 壺	D 盤	E 盉	F 匜	G 舟	H 簠	I 盆	J 盂	K 瓿	L 罐	A 鼎	B 簋	C 壺	D 盤	E 盉	F 匜	K 瓿	M 豆
3	-	2	3	-	1	-	-	1	-	1	-	-	-	-	-	-	-	-	-

ADDITIONAL BRONZE RITUAL VESSELS 2 *dòu* vessels, 1 *fǒu* jar

OTHER ARTIFACTS Bronze *gē* dagger-axe, bronze sword, arrowheads, bronze scraper, bronze *pào* bosses, iron belt decoration, iron ring, stone *guī* tablets, jade *bì* disc, ornaments,

REMARKS One bronze *dǐng* is the Central Plains type ritual vessel, the bronze *fǒu* jar is a Chu type

A 鼎	B 簋	C 壺	D 盤	E 盉	F 匜	G 舟	H 簠	I 盆	J 盂	K 瓿	L 罐	A 鼎	B 簋	C 壺	D 盤	E 盉	F 匜	K 瓿	M 豆
3	-	2	1	-	-	-	-	-	-	1	-	-	-	2	-	-	-	-	-

ADDITIONAL BRONZE RITUAL VESSELS 2 *dòu* vessels, 1 *dǐng* shaped as *lì* 鬲

OTHER ARTIFACTS Bronze sword, scraper, bronze *pào* bosses, iron ring, stone *guī* tablets, jade *bì* disc

REMARKS The sword is inscribed with "吉為乍元用"; *dǐng* shaped as *lì* is an artifact for daily use.

A 鼎	B 簋	C 壺	D 盤	E 盉	F 匜	G 舟	H 簠	I 盆	J 盂	K 瓿	L 罐	A 鼎	B 簋	C 壺	D 盤	E 盉	F 匜	K 瓿	M 豆
2	2	2	1	-	1	-	-	-	-	1	-	-	-	-	-	-	-	-	-

ADDITIONAL BRONZE RITUAL VESSELS 2 mirrors

OTHER ARTIFACTS Bronze sword, belt decoration, stone *guī* tablets

(continued)

TABLE 2.2. *(continued)*

Tomb	Tomb Orientation	Coffin and Outer Coffin	Burial system	Gender and Age
Fengxiang Gaozhuang M48	282	One coffin and one outer coffin	Flexed burial	unknown
Fengxiang Gaozhuang M18	272	One coffin and one outer coffin	Flexed burial	unknown
Wugong Zhaojialai M1	100	One coffin and two outer coffins	Flexed burial	unknown
Fengxiang Dengjiaya M7	west	One coffin	extended burial	unknown
Fengxiang Dengjiaya M4	west	One coffin	extended burial	unknown
Fengxiang Baqitun BM31	295	One outer coffin	Flexed burial	unknown

Bronze Ritual vessels												Ceramic Imitation of Ritual Vessels							
A 鼎	B 簋	C 壺	D 盘	E 盉	F 匜	G 舟	H 簠	I 盆	J 盂	K 甗	L 罐	A 鼎	B 簋	C 壺	D 盘	E 盉	F 匜	K 甗	M 豆
1	-	-	1	-	1	-	-	-	-	1	-	1	2	2	1	-	1	1	2

ADDITIONAL BRONZE RITUAL VESSELS 1 *dǐng* shaped as *lì* 鬲

OTHER ARTIFACTS bronze belt hook, bronze *jīngōu* hook, scraper, jingle; stone ornaments

A	B	C	D	E	F	G	H	I	J	K	L	A	B	C	D	E	F	K	M
-	-	-	-	-	-	1	-	-	-	-	-	2	2	2	1	-	1	1	1

ADDITIONAL BRONZE RITUAL VESSELS 1 three-legged *fǔ* vessel, 1 *dǐng* shaped as *lì* 鬲

OTHER ARTIFACTS Bronze willow-leaf-shaped dagger, lance with curved handle, bronze belt hook, bronze *jīngōu* hook, scraper, jingle, stone *guī* tablets, stone ornaments, etc.

REMARKS 3 skeletons of human sacrifice.

A	B	C	D	E	F	G	H	I	J	K	L	A	B	C	D	E	F	K	M
3	-	-	-	-	-	-	-	1*	-	-	-	1	2	2	-	-	-	1	1

OTHER ARTIFACTS Bronze belt hook, stone *guī* tablets

*pén basin with a circle bottom

A	B	C	D	E	F	G	H	I	J	K	L	A	B	C	D	E	F	K	M
1	-	-	1	-	1	-	-	-	-	1	-	-	-	-	-	-	-	-	-

OTHER ARTIFACTS Scraper

A	B	C	D	E	F	G	H	I	J	K	L	A	B	C	D	E	F	K	M
1	-	-	1	-	-	-	-	-	-	-	-	-	-	-	-	-	-	-	-

ADDITIONAL BRONZE RITUAL VESSELS 1 *dòu*

OTHER ARTIFACTS bronze belt hook

A	B	C	D	E	F	G	H	I	J	K	L	A	B	C	D	E	F	K	M
-	-	-	1	-	1	-	-	-	-	1	-	2*	-	3	-	-	-	-	1

OTHER ARTIFACTS stone *guī* tablets, stone belt hook, bronze jingles;

*2 ceramic *dǐng* with lids

(continued)

TABLE 2.2. *(continued)*

Tomb	Tomb Orientation	Coffin and Outer Coffin	Burial system	Gender and Age
Fengxiang Gaozhuang M48	282	One coffin and one outer coffin	Flexed burial	unknown
Xianyang Renjiazui M56	285	One coffin and one outer coffin	unknown	unknown
Xianyang Renjiazui M230	285	One coffin and one outer coffin	Flexed burial	Male, about forty years
Xianyang Renjiazui M232	290	One coffin and one outer coffin	Flexed burial	unknown

Bronze Ritual vessels												Ceramic Imitation of Ritual Vessels							
A 鼎	B 簋	C 壺	D 盤	E 盉	F 匜	G 舟	H 簠	I 盆	J 盂	K 瓿	L 罐	A 鼎	B 簋	C 壺	D 盤	E 盉	F 匜	K 瓿	M 豆
I	-	-	I	-	I	-	-	-	-	I	-	I	2	2	I	-	I	I	2

ADDITIONAL BRONZE RITUAL VESSELS I *dǐng* shaped as *lì* 鬲

OTHER ARTIFACTS bronze belt hook, bronze *jīngōu* hook, scraper, jingle; stone ornaments

A	B	C	D	E	F	G	H	I	J	K	L	A	B	C	D	E	F	K	M
3	-	-	-	-	-	-	-	-	-	I	-	-	-	-	-	-	-	-	-

OTHER ARTIFACTS Ceramic *guī* tablets; stone *guī* tablets, ring-handle knife, bronze belt parts, jade and stone artifacts

REMARKS One bronze *dǐng* is a Central Plains type ritual vessel

A	B	C	D	E	F	G	H	I	J	K	L	A	B	C	D	E	F	K	M
I	-	-	2	-	-	-	-	-	-	-	-	-	-	-	-	-	-	-	-

ADDITIONAL BRONZE RITUAL VESSELS I *zèng* steamer

OTHER ARTIFACTS bronze belt decorations

A	B	C	D	E	F	G	H	I	J	K	L	A	B	C	D	E	F	K	M
-	-	-	I	-	-	-	-	-	-	3	-	-	-	-	-	-	-	-	-

OTHER ARTIFACTS Bronze scraper, iron belt hook

TABLE 2.3. Funerary Goods from Qin Tombs with Bronze Ritual Vessels, Stage 4

Tomb	Tomb Orientation	Coffin and Outer Coffin	Burial system	Gender and Age
Fengxiang Gaozhuang 79M1	west	One coffin	Flexed burial	unknown
Dali Zhaoyi M203	west	One coffin	Flexed burial	unknown
Qin'an Shangyuanjia M6	355	unknown	Extended burial	Old Female
Pingliang Miaozhuang M6	west	unknown	Extended burial	unknown

	Bronze Ritual vessels												Ceramic Imitation of Ritual Vessels							
	A 鼎	*B* 簋	*C* 壺	*D* 盉	*E* 盃	*F* 匜	*G* 舟	*H* 簠	*I* 盆	*J* 盂	*K* 瓿	*L* 罐	*A* 鼎	*B* 簋	*C* 壺	*D* 盉	*E* 盃	*F* 匜	*K* 瓿	*M* 豆
	1	-	1*	-	-	-	-	-	-	-	-	-	-	-	-	-	-	-	-	-

ADDITIONAL BRONZE RITUAL VESSELS 1 *móu* 鍪, 2 ladles, set of 6 cups

OTHER ARTIFACTS Bronze belt hook, bronze *jīngōu* hook, bronze mirror

REMARKS Catacomb burial, Zhongshan-type bronze *dǐng*, *guàn* 罐 jar inscribed with "亭"; a small niche on one side of the tomb,

*"garlic-top" *hú*

	1	-	1	-	-	-	-	-	-	-	-	-	-	-	-	-	-	-	-	-

ADDITIONAL BRONZE RITUAL VESSELS 1 *fǔ* 釜

OTHER ARTIFACTS Bronze belt hook, iron *dǐng*, iron dagger

REMARKS *dǐng* is similar to the Ping'an Jun-*dǐng* 平安君鼎 from the Biyang 沁陽 Qin tomb

	2	-	-	-	-	-	-	-	-	-	-	-	3	-	-	-	-	-	-	-

OTHER ARTIFACTS 4 lacquer goblets with bronze buckle; 4 belt hooks; 1 bronze mirror ; 1 iron spade; iron spoon

REMARKS *dǐng* are of the north-central type; buried with the chariots and harnesses and many bones of cattle, sheep and dogs

	-	-	2	1	-	1	-	-	-	-	-	-	-	-	-	-	-	-	-	-

ADDITIONAL BRONZE RITUAL VESSELS 1 *dǐng* shaped as *lì* 鬲

OTHER ARTIFACTS Bronze dagger arrowhead; iron spear, bronze and iron chariot parts; skulls of cattle and sheep

REMARKS Looted. A lacquer chariot with four horses found in a chariot pit in front of the tomb.

TABLE 2.3. *(continued)*

Tomb	Tomb Orientation	Coffin and Outer Coffin	Burial system	Gender and Age
Pingliang Miaozhuang M7	west	unknown	Extended burial	unknown
Shangjiaocun M18	west	One coffin and one outer coffin	unknown	unknown

Bronze Ritual vessels													Ceramic Imitation of Ritual Vessels							
A 鼎	B 簋	C 壺	D 盉	E 盃	F 匜	G 舟	H 簠	I 盆	J 盂	K 瓿	L 罐		A 鼎	B 簋	C 壺	D 盉	E 盃	F 匜	K 瓿	M 豆
I	-	I	I	-	-	-	-	-	-	-	-		-	-	-	-	-	-	-	-

OTHER ARTIFACTS Bronze *ding*-shaped lamp, bronze mirror, belt hook, bronze seal, iron scraper, golden ring, different kind of jade and stone artifacts, many chariot parts, sheep bones

REMARKS A lacquer chariot with four horses found in a chariot pit in front of the tomb.

A 鼎	B 簋	C 壺	D 盉	E 盃	F 匜	G 舟	H 簠	I 盆	J 盂	K 瓿	L 罐		A 鼎	B 簋	C 壺	D 盉	E 盃	F 匜	K 瓿	M 豆
-	-	-	-	-	-	-	-	-	I*	-	-		-	-	-	-	-	-	-	-

ADDITIONAL BRONZE RITUAL VESSELS 1 *móu* 鍪, 1 ladle

OTHER ARTIFACTS Bronze sword, arrowhead; iron adz

REMARKS no skeleton was found

*yǎn steamer consists of two separable parts.

Key to Abbreviations and Glossary

MAJOR BRONZE VESSELS OR THEIR CERAMIC IMITATIONS (ENUMERATED IN THE TABLE)

A	鼎 *dǐng*	meat-stewing tripod
B	簋 *guǐ*	grain-offering tureen
C	壺 *hú*	a tall liquid container
D	盤 *pán*	shallow basin used for hand-washing during rituals
E	盉 *hé*	water-pouring vessel with tubular spout
F	匜 *yí*	sauceboat-shaped water-pouring vessel
G	舟 *zhōu*	boat shaped serving plate
H	簠 *fǔ*	round vessel with flat bowl on high openwork foot
I	盂 *yú*	coverless vessel with curved profile and laterally attached handles
J	盆 *pén*	high-walled basin
K	甗 *yǎn*	grain steamer
L	罐 *guàn*	jar, storage vessel
M	豆 *dòu*	high-stemmed covered vessel or coverless pottery vessels with ring feet

OTHER VESSELS AND UTENSILS

bì 璧	jade discs
fǒu 缶	jar; squat-proportioned liquid–container vessel
fǔ 釜	ceramic vessel with globular bottom, made to fit a stove top
gē 戈	dagger-axe
guī 圭	pentagonal tablet of jade or stone
huáng 璜	jade semicircle pendant
jīngōu 襟钩	garment pin or hook
jué 玦	earring
lì 鬲	tripodal cooking vessel with pouch-shaped feet
móu 鍪	globular vessel with ring handle, originating from Sichuan
pào 泡	bronze boss
sháo 勺	ladle
yǒngzhōng 甬鐘	obliquely suspended chime bell with round shank and arch rim
zèng 甑	grain steamer
zhāng 璋	jade tablet

3   Collapse or Transformation?

Anthropological and Archaeological
Perspectives on the Fall of Qin

Gideon Shelach

> Collapse studies are important not only because they deal with
> significant but often poorly understood sociocultural phenomena,
> but also because they provide excellent points of entry into
> the social configuration of the societies that were doing the
> collapsing.
>
> YOFFEE 2005: 131–132

The collapse of powerful states and ancient civilizations is a fascinating topic. It is among the few themes in history that easily lend themselves to the human imagination, arousing strong and conflicting feelings. Small wonder, then, that historic collapses are the subject of some of the more successful popular scientific bestsellers, as well as of fiction and film.[1] It may be precisely because of this popularity that academic studies into the demise of complex societies, and especially their rapid "collapse," are few and quite often anecdotal. The demise of the Qin Empire is a prime example of such a tendency: The dramatic nature of the empire's collapse and the emotions attached to it make its objective academic assessment all the more difficult. Thus, while the fall of Qin is a very common topos in popular narrations of Chinese history, few if any academic studies have gone beyond the received texts and systematically analyzed its various dimensions.

The rapid demise of the Qin Empire was as dramatic and as memorable an event as the first unification of "All under Heaven" by Qin just slightly more than a decade earlier. Amazement at the fate of China's mighty first empire can be clearly heard in the voice of Jia Yi (賈誼 200–168), whose essay on the subject is the locus classicus for all subsequent studies: "Qin united and incorporated the lands of the feudal lords East of the Mount into more than thirty commanderies, mended ferries and forts, and refined their armor and weapons to guard them. Nevertheless, when Chen She 陳涉, with a group of a few hundred unorganized militia raised their arms and cried out loud, with hoe handles and simple clubs instead of bows and pole hammers, looking to the next village for their food, they swept across the world."[2]

How could a small group of ill-equipped peasants bring a mighty empire to its knees? There are good reasons as to why this enigma has fascinated scholars and aroused popular imagination in China throughout the imperial era and still continues to do so today. The story of the fall of Qin and the subsequent civil war is indeed most dramatic, full of unexpected twists, extraordinary heroes, and tragic losers. Yet it also poses a serious intellectual challenge. While the inevitability of decline of any polity was taken for granted in Chinese historiography—as reflected in the idea of the transferability of Heaven's Mandate—the fall of Qin was exceptional. In China, as in other classic civilizations, the trajectory of states was normally expected to be very long, whereby states or dynasties rose to power, reached maturity, and then slowly declined until they were replaced by a new and vigorous dynasty (Yoffee 2005: 132). Qin, which disintegrated when it was at the apex of its vitality, defied this pattern. Perhaps because of this paradox, most traditional and modern explanations tend to focus on ideological, political, and personal faults of Qin's leaders rather than attempting to generalize and examine Qin's collapse in a systematic way. In other words, the fall of Qin is treated as sui generis, an accident that should be studied to prevent the recurrence of similar accidents in the future, but which does not lend itself to broader generalizations.

This chapter argues that although some, or even most, of the explanations put forward by Jia Yi and reiterated by generations of historians ever since are valid, a search for more general models can further our understanding of the process of Qin's collapse. This approach has the potential to make the Qin case more amenable to cross-cultural comparison. At the same time, as the epigraph from Yoffee at the beginning of this chapter suggests, it may also help us better understand the Qin system before its collapse. Below, I examine a number of models based on anthropological and archaeological theories. I shall then test the fit between these abstractions and the developments that led to the fall of the Qin, and, more important, whether and how they can help us generate new insights about Qin and its downfall.

TRADITIONAL EXPLANATIONS FOR THE FALL OF THE QIN

Before we address anthropologically derived models, a short survey of traditional explanations is in order. As mentioned, most of the elements used to explain the rapid demise of the Qin are found in Jia Yi's famous essay *Guo Qin lun* 過秦論 (*Faulting the Qin*), which was written not long after the events themselves. This exceptionally influential essay, arguably the earliest and the most systematic attempt to address the fall of Qin, remains essential for any discussion about the reasons for Qin's collapse well into our days. I have divided the explanations put forward by Jia Yi and elaborated by modern scholars into four major groups: personal factors, moral and ideological reasons, excessive exploitation and oppression, and cultural tensions and old opposition.

Personal Factors. Focusing on the personality faults of the First and Second Emperors and other main figures, such as Li Si 李斯 and the dynasty's "evil genius," Zhao Gao 趙高, is surely the most common traditional explanation for the rapid fall of the Qin. Jia Yi, for instance, blames not just the two emperors' inadequacy, but even faults the hapless Ziying 子嬰, who ruled as a "King of Qin" for a mere forty-six days before the final collapse. Jia Yi asserts that had Ziying been but a mediocre ruler, then even at this late stage he could have saved the Qin kingdom (Nienhauser 1994 I: 164). Apparently, however, he was less than mediocre, and worse still was the Second Emperor. Therefore, Qin could not be saved. This attitude is frequently echoed in modern scholarship. Patricia Ebrey, for instance, notices that "[t]he legalist institutions designed to concentrate power in the hands of the ruler made the stability of the government dependent on the strength and character of a single person" (Ebrey et al. 2006: 49; cf. Bodde 1986: 86; Ray Huang 1997: 37; Xu Weimin 2005: 132). In other words, if the Second Emperor had been more capable, the empire could have remained stable and the achievements of the First Emperor would have been maintained. Yet while we cannot ignore the importance of the human factor and personal faults in shaping history, reducing the fall of Qin to such factors alone sounds more like a story than an historical explanation.

Moral and Ideological Reasons. Throughout his essay, Jia Yi emphasizes Qin's immoral ideology as the reason for its downfall. In one of his most quoted sentences, Jia Yi asserts that this mighty and strategically positioned state was ruined by a one-man rebellion because "benevolence (*ren* 仁) and righteousness (*yi* 義) were not extended" to the people (Nienhauser 1994 I: 168). This summary was not just popular with moralizing traditional scholars, but is still discernible nowadays, both in the West (Bodde 1986: 85) and, more intensely, in China. Thus, Cao Ying (2004) argued that despite its very efficient mechanisms for controlling the population and recruiting the best people for its bureaucracy, the Qin

Empire collapsed because of its moral deficiencies. Its Legalist ideology, which focused on the evil side of humanity, compelled the bureaucrats to adopt harsh methods that lacked moral considerations, a policy that cost Qin its popular support and led to the uprising. Others argue that while the Legalist ideology itself was appropriate, its corruption by the First Emperor led to the downfall of the Qin (Ding Nan 2008), while yet others, in contrast, emphatically reject the possibility that moral considerations played an important role in the demise of Qin (e.g., Song Liheng 2007; Xu Weimin 2005). The very fact that this heated debate continues suggests that examining the fall of Qin through moralistic lenses is still perfectly acceptable. The problem with such views is not that they are necessarily wrong, but that they do not specify the mechanisms by which immoral ideology or conduct might affect the stability of a state. It is, therefore, difficult to address such models academically.

Excessive Exploitation and Oppression. Harsh policies have been identified by many traditional and current scholars as one of the main factors, if not the most important one, behind Qin's collapse. Such policies included cruel and disproportionate punishments, the excessive use of force, large-scale recruitment of manpower to work on megalomaniacal imperial projects, and a very high taxation rate, which deprived many peasants of all their property and prevented them from providing for their families. Interestingly, Jia Yi does not appear to emphasize such aspects with respect to the First Emperor. Although the harshness of Qin laws is mentioned, this is done in the context of personality flaws of the First Emperor and his inability to change (Nienhauser 1994 I: 168), rather than in the context of excessive exploitation of the people.[3] More direct accusations of exploitation and excessive use of manpower are launched by Jia Yi against the Second Emperor: "He renewed the building of the Epang Palace (阿房宮), increased punitive laws, and stiffened punishments, made judicial rulings harsh and stern, awards and punishments improper, taxation limitless, the world full of labor projects . . . the common people were destitute and poor" (Nienhauser 1994 I: 169). Later scholars rarely distinguished between the policies of the First and Second Emperors, talking instead in general terms about the effects of Qin's large-scale projects and harsh punitive laws. Mark Lewis, for example, describes the Qin state as "engaged in an orgy of expansion and building that had little logic" (Lewis 2007: 71). This, he argues, exhausted the strength of the state and alienated its population. Similarly, Zhao Dingxin (2004: 62–63) argues that after conquering "All under Heaven," the Qin simply tried to do too much at once, and concludes that "no regime of such a brutal nature could survive for long" (cf. Xu Weimin 2005). Other scholars mention the heavy burden imposed on the peasants by public works projects and high taxes, but they place more emphasis on the cruel punishments employed by the Qin—or "severe negative sanctions" to use a more scientific term—as the main reason behind the popular unrest that led to the collapse of the empire (e.g., Kiser and Cai 2003: 530). While this explanatory framework is clearly related to the previous one (Qin's moral flaws), it has an advantage for a scholar, because such issues as excessive coercion and overburdening of the population with public works are verifiable through historical documents and archaeological data (see below). Even so, we should still try to explain how such policies affected the stability of the state.

Cultural Tensions and Old Opposition. Jia Yi does not emphasize the role that the "old guard" of the defeated Warring States–period kingdoms could have played in the upheaval that led to the fall of the Qin, except for mentioning that after Chen She had started the revolt, the "powerful and the elite to the east of the Mount all rose up to destroy the Qin clan" (Nienhauser 1994 I: 167).[4] However, evidence for the active role played by the nobility and elites of the defeated states, especially Chu, and the resistance to the imposition of Qin culture over the conquered territories can be found elsewhere in the *Historical Records*. Some modern scholars argue accordingly that resentment against the Qin occupation might have been the main factor behind its downfall (Song Liheng 2007; Wu Yi 1999). In one of the more sophisticated attempts to elaborate on this, Jack Dull (1983) analyzed the biographies of the leaders and participants in the revolt against the Qin. He concluded that they came from three groups: people already on the margins of society—hiding in the "mountains and marshes"—who wanted to improve their personal lot; local officials who joined because the Qin had failed to inspire them with confidence and loyalty; and members of the preimperial elite and nobility. Members of these groups, which overlapped considerably, were all motivated by personal interests; but in the final analysis, Dull argues that their success was due to strong local sentiments and resentment against Qin culture. "Both those who came from the old elite and those who did not, availed themselves of a common desire to maintain old identities as 'men of Qi' or 'men of Chu' in order to develop their followings. It was this powerful movement in favor of politically restoring 'the good old days' that produced the collapse of the first empire" (Dull 1983: 316–317). There are clear advantages to this analysis, as it demonstrates how identities are maintained and manipulated to gain sociopolitical power. However, I doubt whether such an analysis in itself is able to provide an explanation for the systematic collapse of the Qin.

To be fair, many discussions of the fall of Qin do not focus on a single cause; instead, they integrate two or more of the abovementioned aspects. While some merely present the explanations one after the other (e.g., Bodde 1986: 85–90), others attempt to integrate different aspects and pay attention to the changing circumstances after the imperial unification (e.g., Lewis 2007), or try to develop a more sophisticated understanding of processes within the political and bureaucratic system of the Qin (e.g., Wang Shaodong 2007). However, even the more sophisticated and synthetic treatments often sound more like stories than explanations. That is, while they narrate the events and suggest the causes and effects of different actions, they still echo Jia Yi's assertion that had only the First Emperor (or the Second, or Ziying) acted differently, then the Qin could have survived for many generations. To my mind, this still amounts to seeing the fall of the Qin as an historical accident rather than looking for a more processual or systematic explanation.

UNDERSTANDING "COLLAPSE": A SYSTEMS THEORY APPROACH

As mentioned above, the collapse of ancient states and empires can easily inspire strong feelings. Images of ancient cities ravaged by war or deserted by their starving populations immediately come to mind. But how can we define a "collapse"? The common usage of the term refers to an abrupt breakdown of sociopolitical and economic institutions and a return to a much more simple form of social organization. In contrast to a slow decline, this is a rapid process, although this "rapidity" should be understood in archaeological and historic terms: it may be quite a long time, as in the case of the Maya, the collapse of whom spanned at least "several generations" (Webster 2002: 186). A more critical issue is what we mean by sociopolitical and economic breakdown. As pointed out by Yoffee (2005: 134), in most cases, even when the entire society appears to disintegrate, only some institutions do actually fail or revert to a much simpler form, while others remain more or less intact. In other words, different components of society are affected differently by the "collapse": some devolve, some remain unchanged, while some may even evolve. It is therefore important to ask which parts of the society actually do collapse, and how their collapse is expressed in the interactions between the various social, political, and economic institutions. I discuss this idea in more detail below; suffice it here to emphasize that once collapse is addressed in this way, we are implicitly depicting human society as a system constructed of subsystems that interact with one another, and which are regulated by higher-order units.

I believe that the time is ripe to begin thinking of sociopolitical and economic collapse in systemic terms. It should be admitted, however, that systems theory (or general systems theory), as a formal framework directly derived from such fields of knowledge as cybernetics, engineering, industrial organization theory, and epidemiology, has not been embraced by mainstream anthropological thinking. After briefly flirting with its ideas during the 1970s (e.g., Rodin et al. 1978) anthropologists subsequently marginalized it to such an extent that today not a single entry in the many volumes of the *International Encyclopedia of the Social and Behavioral Sciences* is devoted to the application of systems theory in any field of anthropological research. Systems theory has had greater success in anthropologically oriented archaeology, however. During its heyday, especially in seminal papers by Flannery (1968, 1972) and others, they enjoyed a certain influence and catalyzed early experiments at building computerized simulations of the development and change of human societies (Renfrew and Bahn 1996: 455–461). While such theories have since been widely criticized for being "mechanistic" and leaving no place for human agency, as well as for assuming rigid relations among different social actors and institutions, systems theory has remained ingrained in the work of many archaeologists, albeit more often implicitly than explicitly. This tendency may be explained by the fact that, despite our best efforts, human agency is much less visible in archaeology than it is in cultural anthropology or ethnology; hence the emphasis on larger social institutions and long term processes.

The concept of *feedback*, borrowed from cybernetics, is key to many systemic models in archaeology. Feedbacks are reactions to the inputs and outputs of subsystems, and they regulate their activity within larger systems (Renfrew and Bahn 1996: 457). Negative feedback prevents too much activity in the system or parts of it and keeps the system in a stable state (homeostasis). However, under certain conditions—for example, when one subsystem is under severe stress—positive feedback can cause the system to evolve through the creation of a new regulatory unit that alleviates some of the pressure from the lower-level unit, or by creating more lower-level units (Flannery 1972: 411).[5] Conversely, according to this model, because all subsystems are internally connected, if the system fails to react adequately to increased pressure on one or more of its subsystems, then it is liable to collapse entirely. This is especially true in a large and well-integrated system where subsystems "are coupled more closely to each other and/or to the central hierarchical control until, like an old-fashioned string of Christmas tree lights set in linear sequence, change in one does in fact affect all the others too directly and rapidly" (ibid: 420).

Flannery has been criticized, among other faults, for his overemphasis on societies as mechanisms for processing information, as well as for his assumption that the collapse of one part of the system will automatically affect all other parts. However, the idea that extreme stress on one part of the system can cause changes that transcend the subsystem and extend to the entire system (or many of its subsystems) is valid. One such source of stress is an increased demand for resources and manpower posed by higher levels of the system on its lower subsystems. Although this is by no means the only possible source of stress, or even the one most commonly used in models of collapse, I focus on it here because it fits well with one of the reasons suggested for the collapse of the Qin.

A famous explanation for the alleged collapse of the classic Maya civilization is based on the systems-theory approach as adapted to archaeology by Flannery.[6] This model is based on the observation, made in the 1940s but still held to be true by contemporary researchers, that the Long Count dates on Lowland Maya monuments started during the third century CE and steadily increased in number until they dramatically peaked between 730 and 790 CE. This was followed by an abrupt fall in monument construction until monuments completely ceased to be made in the beginning of the tenth century (Webster 2002: 209). In other words, there was a dramatic increase in the rate of monumental construction, and presumably in the labor invested in such activity, just prior to the collapse of the system.

Hosler, Sabloff and Runge developed a quantifiable systemic model that addresses the feedback relations among different variables and endeavors to explain how such interrelations might have led to the collapse of the classic Maya. They look at several variables and subsystems, including long-distance trade, the production and exchange of prestige goods, population dynamics (growth and decline), health conditions, agricultural production, and the productivity of agricultural lands, monumental construction, and the exploitation of the commoners by the elite (Hosler et al. 1977: 559–561). However, the key feedback loop, in the view of these authors, was the relationship between resource pressure, elite prestige, and monumental (or prestige) building activity. Initially, monumental construction was a kind of regulatory mechanism (negative feedback). Presented in religious terms—monuments were supposed to placate the gods—it helped the Mayan elite control the population and ensure social cohesion. During the eighth century CE, the cessation of long-range trade, combined with population growth and a decline in agricultural productivity, put increasingly severe restraints on available resources. The system reacted to this stress with more monumental construction, which in turn led to greater pressure on resources, increased exploitation of the common people, and a decline in their nutrition and health, which in turn led to more construction (ibid: 567–568). This feedback loop of increased stress affected other subsystems and might have caused the system to collapse due to popular unrest, inter-elite conflicts, a decline in size of the effective population, or large-scale migration out of the Maya lowlands (ibid: 577–578).[7]

During the workshop that preceded the development of this volume, many participants resisted the comparison between the Maya and the Qin. I agree that the two cases differ greatly: while the Maya were constituted in city-states, the Qin state covered a much larger territory and was ruled by a single emperor. The Qin political system was also much more centralized and hierarchical than the Maya. However, the point of this comparison is not to suggest that the two systems are similar, but rather to use the model developed for the explanation of the collapse of the Maya as a heuristic device with which to test the collapse of the Qin. We need not subscribe to all the details of this "vicious circle" model in order to see that it may be relevant to our understanding of the fall of the Qin. In order to test it, however, we need first to examine how heavy the burden of public works that the Qin regime imposed on its population, including monumental construction, really was.

The Direct and Indirect Costs of Qin's Imperial Monuments and Public Works

Most of the written information on Qin's public works and the amount of labor invested in them is found in chapter 6 of the *Historical Records* (*Shiji*), the "Basic Annals of the First Emperor of Qin" 秦始皇本紀. Thus, for the year 212, it records that "more than 700,000 mutilated or banished criminals (*tuxingzhe* 徒刑者)[8] were assigned to build either the Epang Palace or [the Emperor's mausoleum at] Mount Li" (Nienhauser 1994 I: 148). Later the same chapter mentions again the number of 700,000 workers, this time in association with the construction of the Emperor's mausoleum (ibid: 155).

The Great Wall on the northern and western frontiers of the empire is another famous monument of Qin. Here the number of 300,000 workers is usually given, although it is less clear than in the case of the mausoleum and the Epang Palace that this refers to the number of wall-builders. The *Historical Records* says that in 215, general Meng Tian 蒙恬 was sent with 300,000 men to attack the tribes on the northern frontiers. Immediately following that, albeit in an entry from the following year (214), Meng Tian's victories are described, followed by a statement that the Qin built a wall north of the Yellow River. In the next year (213), more people were reportedly sent to work on the wall. In his biography, Meng Tian is explicitly portrayed as being in charge of constructing the wall, and the length of the wall is said to be 10,000 *li* 里 (*Shiji* 88; Watson 1993: 207–213). From all these references it is not at all clear whether the 300,000 men in Meng Tian's army were also the workers who constructed the wall.

Other large-scale constructions of the Qin included the construction of the "Straight Road" (Zhidao直道) and the imperial highways (*chidao* 馳道). The first was a very wide road leading north from the capital for some 800 km and "cutting through mountains and filling in valleys" (Watson 1993: 209). This ambitious project was also carried out by Meng Tian. The construction of this road may never have been completed, but in the conclusion to *Shiji* 88, Sima Qian describes a journey along it, so it would appear that substantial parts of it were indeed finished; some of its traces can still be seen today (Sanft 2011).[9] According to estimates based on place names mentioned in the *Historical Records*, the total length of all the imperial highways constructed by the Qin was some 6,800 km (Bodde 1986: 61; cf. Sanft forthcoming).

Another transportation project associated with the First Emperor is the so-called Lingqu 靈渠, or "Magic Canal." While it is not specifically mentioned in the *Historical Records*, a roughly contemporaneous source attributes this water project to the time of the Qin's penetration south of the Yangzi River basin (*Huainanzi*, "Renjian xun" 人間訓 18: 617). According to modern studies, the Lingqu connected the southward flowing Li River 灕江 and the northward flowing Xiang River 湘江 in current Guangxi province, thus creating a transportation route that connected the Yangzi River with the Xi River 西江 in the Far South (Needham 1971: 299–306). While the canal itself was not very long, it was distant from the capital, built in a region that was probably still sparsely inhabited, and cutting through the mountain ranges that separated the two rivers must have required a substantial amount of work. The canal was a major feat of organization; in engineering terms as well, connecting two rivers flowing in opposite directions was an ingenious achievement (ibid: 306).

A considerable investment of manpower and resources must also have gone into the construction of palaces and other imperial structures. A familiar example is that of the 120,000 noble families of the six conquered states who were transferred to Xianyang, where they were housed and taken care of by the state, and for whom palaces were constructed that imitated those of the conquered regional lords (Nienhauser 1994 I: 138). The construction of many other palaces and royal temples, perhaps up to 700, is mentioned throughout the *Historical Records* and elsewhere (Xu Weimin 2005: 132).

In spite of the numbers provided by Sima Qian, it is difficult to estimate the direct expenses of these public works, let alone their indirect costs. Some calculate that between 1.5 and 2.5 million people were mobilized, and that in order to support these and other government expenditures the tax rate had to be as high as 60 percent of the farmers' production (e.g., Kiser and Cai 2003; Xu Weimin 2005). Others question the numbers provided by Sima Qian and suggest that the burden imposed by such projects has been vastly exaggerated by modern scholars (Dull 1983: 189–190; Waldron 1990: 18–26).

The construction of the Great Wall of the Qin dynasty can serve as a good test case. Modern scholarship has not only challenged estimations of the number of people who worked on the project, which in any case is not clear from the original text, but also the length of the wall and of the portions of it that were actually constructed during the Qin Empire. The figure of 10,000 *li* given by Sima Qian as the length of the wall is clearly a symbolic number. As many have pointed out, the word *wan* 萬, which today means "ten thousand," did not originally have such a precise signification and even in later literature is often used as an expression meaning "myriad" or "a lot" rather than referring to an exact figure (Bodde 1986: 62). Moreover, many scholars believe that Qin made extensive use of walls constructed before the imperial unification on the northern borders of the states of Qin, Zhao, and Yan, and that the actual work carried out by Meng Tian and his workforce was therefore relatively small. This view has been summarized and expanded upon by Waldron (1990: 16–29), who argued that not only were the portions constructed during the Qin dynasty relatively short, but also that in many places where the Qin fortified its borders it constructed individual forts and not a continuous long wall.[10]

Such minimalist views are not supported by the text. The fact that the *Historical Records* refer only to the building of walls and not to the use of existing structures may be attributed to the laconic nature of the text's description of the wall. However, the *Historical Records* do make it clear that the wall was built only after Meng Tian had defeated the northern tribes, so it is logical to assume that it was built in territories taken from Qin's enemies and not on the borders of the pre-unification states. Careful analysis of the descriptions in chapters 6 and 88 of the *Historical Records* show that they describe three different sections of the wall that cover its entire length from the upper Yellow River area in the west to Liaodong in the east (Xu Pingfang 2002: 260). Recent archaeological works identify sections of this Qin wall and confirm that they are located north of the walls constructed by the states of the Warring States period (ibid: 261) (see Map 3.1). We may therefore conclude that the entire length of the Qin wall was constructed during the five years between 214 and the beginning of the revolt against the Qin in 209.

Based on the maps of the archaeological remains provided by Xu Pingfang (2002: 263–264), I have drawn the approximate course of the wall on a map of Qin China (Map 3.1). Its length comes to a little more than 2,800 km, much less than the 10,000 *li* (or 4,100 km) of the *Historical Records*, but still a very large number. As the text and the archaeological record make clear, the construction techniques and the investment of labor were not the same in all places. The architects of the wall made use of the natural features of the terrain: in places that are naturally more difficult to cross, the artificial barrier constructed was probably modest; while in flat areas, where armies were more likely to launch an invasion, more extensive fortifications were built, which may have included several lines of walls, as well as moats and other types of fortification. In places where stones could be easily collected, they were the main raw materials, but in other places only the outer and inner faces of the wall were made of stone and the inner core was made of earth and rubble, and in yet other places the entire wall was made of stamped earth (Li Yiyou 2001).

Making an accurate calculation of the amount of labor needed to construct the Qin wall is quite difficult because of this variability. Moreover, because we usually have little or no direct information about the techniques used and the way the work was organized, any effort to calculate the ancient labor investment will be inherently uncertain. However, archaeologists working in different parts of the world have used basic engineering knowledge and ethnographic observations to develop ways of estimating the labor investment required to build different kinds of monuments (cf. Abrams et al. 1999; Erasmus 1965). Using such methods,

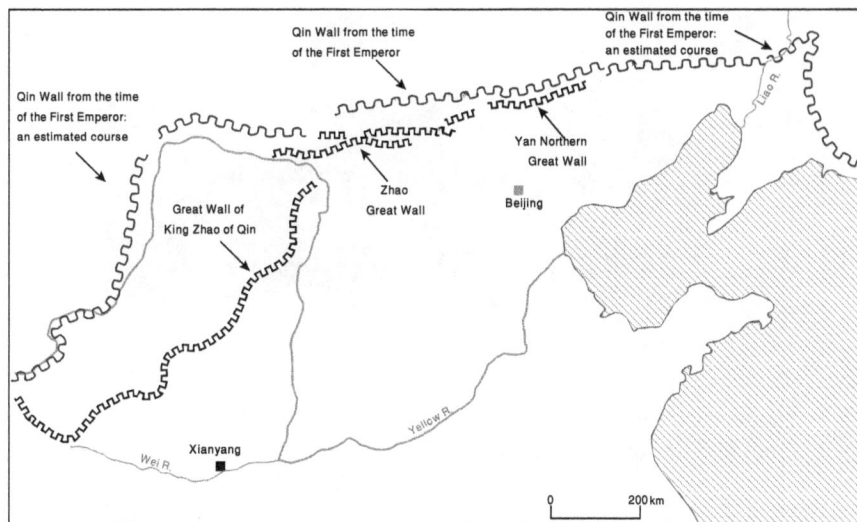

Map 3.1. The Qin Great Wall

and making assumptions on the "average" size of the wall, we can apply such numbers to the entire length of the wall. Even if we accept that such calculations involve large margins of error, they can nevertheless provide us with a general impression of the cost of construction.

In one of the more comprehensive surveys of the remains of the Qin wall, Li Yiyou (2001: 9) identifies the section at Wulate Front Banner 烏 拉特前旗 in Inner Mongolia as one of the best-preserved parts, which may be representative for other locations. At this section the wall is five to six meters high; it is some six meters wide at the bottom and three meters at the top. Similar measurements are reported at other well preserved localities as well (idem: 10, 13, 21). If this is typical, then 21.42 m³ of materials would have been needed to construct one meter of wall (see Figure 3.1).[11] To calculate the direct cost of constructing the wall, we need to know how much work went into (1) the acquisition of raw materials, (2) the transportation of raw materials to the construction site, (3) the preparation of raw materials, and (4) the construction of the wall itself. Such estimates are mediated by the type of raw materials—stones, for example, are more difficult to quarry and more heavy to carry than earth—the type of preparation needed, and the method of construction. In order to produce minimal and maximal limits for our estimations, I developed different scenarios: For the raw materials used I tested the possibilities that the entire wall was made of stone, that it was made entirely

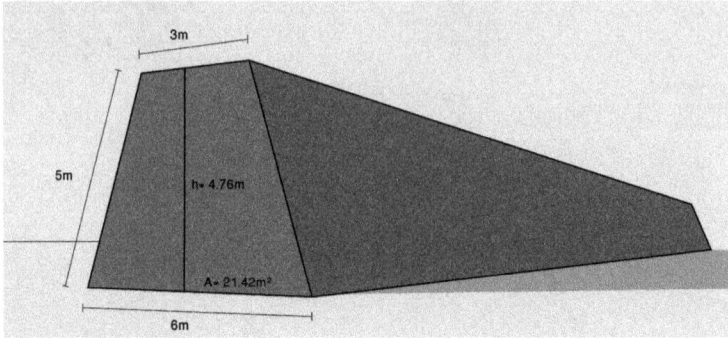

Figure 3.1. Schematic Drawing of a Well-Preserved Wall Section, Wulate Front Banner, Inner Mongolia

of earth, and that it was made of equal parts of stone (for the external and internal walls) and of earth and rubble (for the fill). For the transportation, I assumed that earth would be locally available, and so the distance it would need to be transported would be no greater than 100 m. Because stones would not necessarily be available in the immediate vicinity of the route of the wall, however, I estimated that they would have to be brought from a distance of 500 m to 1,000 m. No preparation would be needed for the earth fill, but even rough cobble stones would have to be hewed before they could be used for construction. The amount of labor needed for each of the work phases is described in Table 3.1.

Based on these numbers, the investment in one meter of wall made of stone would be as follows: for acquisition, 21.42/6.6 = 3.25 person-days; for transportation to 500 m, 21.42/0.46 = 46.54 person-days (93.08 for 1,000 m); for preparation, 21.42/0.86 = 24.9 person-days; and for construction, 21.42/0.8 = 26.76 person-days. Altogether, 101.45 person-days would have been needed to construct one meter of a wall (or 147.99 if the source of stones was at a distance of 1,000 m).

Building the same wall from earth would have required: for acquisition, 21.42/2.6 = 8.23 person-days; for transportation to 50 m distance, 21.42/3.17 = 6.75 person-days (or 12.16 for 100 m); and for construction, 21.42/1 = 21.42 person-days. Altogether, 36.39 person-days would have been needed to construct one meter of wall (or 41.8 if the source of earth was at a distance of 100 m). According to the Han mathematical manual *Jiuzhang suanshu* 九章算術 (Nine Chapters on the Mathematical Art), a single conscript worker was expected to excavate, transport, and con-

TABLE 3.1 Labor Estimates for Building the Qin Wall

	Acquisition	Transportation	Preparation	Construction
Stone	6.6 m³/person-day	0.46 m³/person-day (500 m) 0.23 m³/person-day (1000 m)	0.86 m³/person-day (for roughly hewn cobbles)	0.8 m³/person-day
Earth	2.6 m³/person-day	3.17 m³/person-day (50 m) 1.76 m³/person-day (100 m)	none	1 m³/person-day (for stamped earth)

SOURCES: Based on Abrams 1994; Erasmus 1965.

struct 7.55 m³ of pounded earth wall in a month, which means 0.25 m³ per worker per day (Shen Kangshen et al. 1999: 258–259). If this number is correct, then constructing one meter of the earthen parts of the Qin wall would have taken 85.1 person-days (21.42 : 0.25 = 85.1). This is double the amount of time estimated for the construction of a wall made from earth, but is still within our range for wall construction (including stones).[12]

Yuan Zhongyi (1983) arrived at much higher workload estimates for the construction of the stamped-earth walls that surrounded the burial mound of the First Emperor. Drawing on Han and pre-Han documents, as well as on ethnographic observations of the construction of walls by Chinese peasants, he estimated that the construction of a stamped-earth wall 10 m high and 8 m wide would have taken Qin workers 1,080 man/working days (Yuan Zhongyi 1983: 46). However, much of this high estimate is derived from his estimate of the cost of transporting the earth, given that he thought it would have been brought from a distance of 2.5 km (ibid: 45). Using Yuan's numbers but assuming that the earth was only brought from a distance of 100 m, a wall like the one we use as a model would have needed 76.5 person days to construct: very similar to the numbers provided by the *Jiuzhang suanshu* (Shen Kangshen et al. 1999: 254–260).

The construction of the walls of the Western Han capital of Chang'an is another comparable example for work investment. According to the *History of the Former Han Dynasty*, the major work on this project was carried out in several phases during the reign period of Emperor Hui (惠帝, r. 194–188) (*Hanshu* 2: 89–91). According to this source, during one of the episodes of work on the wall, an entire section was constructed by 145,000 workers who were conscripted from a 600 *li* radius around the capital and worked for 30 days. Researchers estimate that the western section of the wall was constructed during this work episode (Barbieri-Low 2007: 391). Archaeological surveys of the remains of this wall have produced estimates that its western side measured 4,900 m. The wall was made entirely of stamped-earth; it was about 12 m high, and from 12 m to 16 m wide at its base (Wang Zhongshu 1982: 2). According to these measurements (taking the wall at the base to be 15 m and 10 m at the top), the entire length of the western wall contained 735,000 cubic meters of soil. Altogether, 4.35 million working days would have been invested in this wall, some 888 days per meter of wall. However, because the volume of earth in this wall is seven times larger than in our example of the Great Wall, if the same calculation is projected to our example, then 126.8 days would have been required in order to construct 1 m of wall. This, again, is higher than our estimate for the construction of an earthen wall, but within the range of our estimate for the construction of a stone wall.

If we average the two estimates presented above for the construction of walls that were made half of stone and half of earth, then the low estimate is 68.92 person-days per 1 m of wall and the high estimate is 94.9. Based on those averages, 192,976,000 to 265,720,000 person-days would have been needed to construct the entire Great Wall of Qin. Assuming that each person worked 350 days per year, and that the project was completed in 5 years (214–209), it follows that between 110,272 to 151,840 people would have been needed to construct the entire wall. Taking into consideration the higher estimates for the construction of earth walls found in the *Jiuzhang suanshu,* as well as the abovementioned estimates for the construction of the enclosure walls of the First Emperor (Yuan Zhongyi 1983) and of the Chang'an walls, I tend to think that my higher range is more accurate, and that it may even be an underestimation.

This calculation does not take into account the construction of camps, beacon towers, and other installations that are known to have accompanied the line of the wall of the Warring States, Qin and Han (Di Cosmo 2002: 144; Li Yiyou 2001). More importantly, as Bodde (1986: 63) has pointed out, building such a wall in remote locations and in difficult terrain, such as mountains and deserts, would have required far more resources than those directly invested in the construction of the wall itself. In contrast to roads, which create their own lines of supply as they progress, the further a wall is built, the more investment is needed in creating transportation routes to it and in transporting supplies to the construction sites. This was especially true in the sparsely populated areas in which the wall was built, where there were no local food resources to draw upon. According to Bodde, this implies that "for every man whom Meng Tian could put to work at the scene of actual construction, dozens must have been needed to build approaching roads and to transport supplies" (ibid). All in all then, it seems that the number of 300,000 men working on the wall for five years is not an exaggeration, and the direct and indirect expenses of constructing the wall may have been even higher.

In the 1980s, Derk Bodde considered the size of the Epang throne hall, said to have measured 675 × 112 m, too big to be realistic (Bodde 1986: 64). However, recent excavations at the site of the palace have revealed a much larger complex that included, among other buildings, a single pounded earth foundation platform sized 1,270 × 426 m, with some of it still preserved to the height of 12 m (Zhongguo Shehuikexueyuan Kaogu Yanjiusuo 2004: 4). While the palace, the construction of which started only three years before the Qin Empire started to fall apart, was probably never completed (Sanft 2008), its planned size attests to the scale of the work carried out there. An even more impressive example is the so-called mausoleum of the First Emperor. In the past, the only evidence for this monument was Sima Qian's brief description and the extant above-ground earth mound. Following the initial discovery of the Terracotta Army pits in 1974, intensive research was carried out in the huge area around the central earth mound, and our understanding of the organization and content of this burial complex increased dramatically. The area of the mound itself and the two concentric walls that surrounded it is some 2 km² in size. However, other constellations, including the famous "Terracotta Army" pits, are spread around this core in an area that is now estimated at some 54 km² (Zhao Huacheng and Gao Chongwen 2002: 16–17).[13] Such estimates make this probably the largest burial complex of a single ruler ever to have been constructed anywhere in the world. Even without taking into account the badly preserved above-ground structures, the construction of the below-ground pits, most of which are not merely trenches excavated in the ground but real underground houses with paved floors, stamped earth walls and wooden roofs, and the wealth of artifacts placed in them, attest to investment on a grand scale.

A recent study of the DNA of bones of 121 individuals found in a Qin dynasty kiln site can add an important piece of information to our discussion. Because the site is located only 500 m from the Terracotta Army pits, archaeologists working there assume that it served the production of artifacts for those pits. Given that the people whose bones were recovered were not formally buried, and because analysis of the bones suggests that they suffered from pathologies associated with hard manual labor, it is assumed that those individuals were part of the workforce brought in to construct the First Emperor's mortuary complex (Xu Zhi et al. 2008: 1). From the initial group of 121 individuals, Xu Zhi and his colleagues have been able to extract sequences of mitochondrial DNA from 19 individuals and to compare them with one another and other reference groups of current Han and non-Han populations from different parts of China. Because the size of the sample is small and the reference groups may not always be appropriate, it is difficult to accept the identification of some of those individuals with current groups in southern China (ibid: 5). However, the observation made by researchers that the mitochondrial DNA sequences of the nineteen Qin workers were more diverse than any of the current thirty-two populations (ibid: 5) suggests that they were brought to the construction site from different regions of the newly conquered empire. Indeed, in order to recruit such a large workforce as the *Historical Records* describe, workers would have had to come from far away regions, as sufficient human resources would not have been locally available.[14]

While the 700,000 criminals mentioned by Sima Qian might have performed unskilled manual labor, the more professional work would have required highly trained craftsmen. For example, in the production of the ceramic statues of the so-called Terracotta Army, preparing the clay and pressing it into the moulds are tasks that could have been performed by criminals or regular conscripts. However, other tasks, such as designing and preparing the moulds, retouching the fine details on the statues' faces, building the giant kilns for firing the statues, and supervising the work, must have been executed by professional artisans. Indeed, recent research on the ceramic statues, and especially on the inscriptions stamped and incised on them, suggests that two distinct groups of specialists were responsible for their manufacturing: (1) palace artisans employed by the Qin bureau in charge of producing water pipes, roof tiles and hollow bricks; and (2) private artisans, who normally worked in private workshops and who were probably conscripted for the task from areas up to 200 km from the site (Barbieri-Low 2007: 7–9). Other more technologically advanced artifacts, such as the two bronze chariots found in a pit close to the burial mound, required workmanship of the highest quality for their construction, which must have necessitated assembling a large group of highly trained artisans and skilled laborers. Comprising 7,000 parts and weighing 2.4 tons, these chariots surely would have required substantial labor for their construction. All this evidence suggests that, in addition to the forced labor of convicted criminals and unskilled conscript laborers, many more skilled workers, artisans, and supervisors must have been employed (cf. Li Xiuzhen et al., 2011). While these people may have received payment for their work (in cash or in kind) or have performed their tasks as part of their corvée labor obligations, the resources needed for such a project, including the acquisition and transportation of materials, in addition to paying and feeding the workers, must have placed a heavy burden on the state and, in consequence, on the entire population.

If we add to the above-mentioned projects the imperial highways and transportation routes, temples and palaces, as well as the people who carried out other services for the court, produced court paraphernalia, and so on, an estimate of two million people does not sound terribly off target, and may in fact be overly conservative even if we do not include soldiers in the Qin armies as well (see more below). Based on this estimate, I think that we can clearly reject Dull's assertion that "the human labor used in the huge construction projects was not conscript labor but convict labor . . . It is thus difficult to accept the notion that Qin conscription policies created inordinately heavy burdens which were decisive causes in the downfall of the Qin dynasty" (Dull 1983: 290). While further fine tuning of Qin's workload would be attained when we distinguish between the amount of mobilized convicts (obliged to work for 365 days a year) and conscripts (who could only be employed for a certain amount of days each year), from a systemic perspective, if two million people were mobilized for these projects, the difference becomes less significant.[15] In any case, a large proportion of the able-bodied adult male (and some of the female) population was taken out of regular economic activity and put to work in these projects. Current estimates of the size of the Qin population vary greatly between about 20 to 40 million people (Falkenhausen 2006: 405; Ge Jianxiong 2002: 300–312; Lu Yu and Teng Zezhi 1999: 73–75).[16] Assuming that only about one-third of the entire population were adolescents or adult males able to work on the projects,[17] we can estimate that 15–30 percent of the productive population was conscripted or directly involved in public works.[18] This is a very high proportion of the workforce to have been taken out of the production of food and basic resources, and in itself must have placed the people who were left behind to produce food and basic resources under great pressure. The indirect burden of the projects must also have been quite severe. Regardless of whether the people working on them were convicts or conscripts, or even if they were artisans that received payment for the work they did, the need to equip, feed, clothe, and house them, even at a minimal level, must have been very expensive. We do not even have to estimate that taxes reached rates of up to 60 percent (Kiser and Cai 2003: 530) in order to see that the burden on the peasants may well have been extremely heavy.

One crucial component of the "vicious circle" model of the fall of the Maya is the acceleration of public works just prior to the collapse. Although to the best of my knowledge such a pattern has not been suggested for the Qin, an examination of the "Basic Annals of the First Emperor" in the *Historical Records*, where the events are described in chronological order, can be interpreted in this way. As pointed out above, the construction of the Great Wall started in 214, seven years after the unification and only five years before the empire started to unravel.[19] The construction of the "straight road," the largest and most costly of Qin's imperial highways, started in 212, the same year that the allocation of 700,000 people to work on the grave complex of the First Emperor and the Epang Palace was first mentioned. As the *Historical Records* make clear, work on the grave started even before the unification of the empire (Nienhauser 1994 I: 155); yet probably the entry in 212 refers to a dramatic increase in the scale of work, as well as the commencement of work on the Epang palace. Moreover, from 215 on, the First Emperor also resumed large-scale military campaigns. As mentioned above, Meng Tian was sent to fight on the northern frontiers of the empire in 215. During the following year, 214, the First Emperor initiated a bold campaign in which larger territories in the far south were conquered and the commanderies of Guilin 桂林, Xiang 象, and Nanhai 南海 were established in today's Guangdong and Guangxi provinces (ibid: 145–146). Such campaigns also employed large armies and would have required considerable investment in terms of equipment and supplies. Moreover, if this timetable is accepted, then the construction of the Lingqu canal in this area must have started no earlier than 214.[20] It seems, therefore, that all of the major construction projects of the Qin started or were dramatically expanded just prior to the fall of the empire.

Can such an acceleration of public work and military campaigns be attributed to a feedback loop, such that instead of stabilizing the system it actually made the situation worse? It is difficult to say. The *Historical Records* do not describe any major crisis before the death of the First Emperor, apart, perhaps, from the psychological crisis that the Emperor himself might have experienced, and so it is difficult to speak about the initial stress that might have triggered such a response. Researchers often quote Jia Yi's dictum that "acquisition and conservation require different techniques" (Nienhauser 1994 I: 158), and his accusation that the First Emperor did not succeed in making the transition from conquering the empire to sustaining it. Lewis explicitly connects this idea to the grand-scale public works when he argues that the "direct administration of peasant households who were mobilized for military service continued as the organizing principle of the state, with a large servile labor pool formed from those who violated any of the numerous laws. No longer necessary for inter-state warfare, this giant machine for extracting service had become a tool in search of a use" (Lewis 2007: 71). However, if the gap I have identified between the unification of the empire and the beginning of large-scale public works is real, then we have to modify Lewis's explanation. Perhaps even a minor stress was able to revert the system—which was indeed based on pre-unification foundations—to the way it traditionally coped with stress, namely, the large-scale mobilization of manpower.

Another issue to be addressed is how so heavy a burden of public works projects affected other subsystems of Qin, and how this may be related to the collapse of the entire system. In the case of the Maya, the model suggests that large-scale public works brought about real economic crises, especially in the context of a gradual increase in population density at Maya centers and the decline of agricultural productivity. We can imagine that a food shortage that was exacerbated by the fact that fewer people were able to work in the fields might have caused popular unrest or forced portions of the population to abandon the lowland centers in search of better land. While we have no direct historical evidence that there was a similar pressure on basic resources during the last years of the Qin, it is conceivable that it was at the background of mass participation in anti-Qin rebellions—if not on the leadership level, then at least among the rank-and-file. We should look more carefully how the pressure, created by one subsystem within the Qin Empire, could have affected other subsystems; and in order to do so and to present a more complete explanation of the apparent collapse of the Qin system, we need to consider more advanced notions about the workings of large-scale social systems.

MODELS OF LARGE-SCALE SOCIAL SYSTEMS AND A SYNTHETIC VIEW OF THE FALL OF THE QIN

In his comments to a paper on system theories in anthropology, Stanley West touches on the difference between tightly integrated systems and what he terms fuzzy or soft systems (Rodin et al. 1978: 758–759). He argues, for example, that "although scientists too often assume that more precision is better than less precision, there is considerable evidence that certain fuzzy systems outperform sharp or precise ones." More specifically, regarding sociopolitical systems, he asserts that "the virtue of fuzzy rules and fuzzy instructions is that each can be given multiple interpretations, thereby admitting variety and permitting enough freedom to enable control to be flexibly attuned to compelling empirical conditions" (ibid: 759). The other side of the coin is that systems that are too precise or tight may ultimately severely malfunction and collapse. I would like to argue that this is the perspective we should adopt in understanding the collapse of the Qin Empire: The attempt to create a hyper-precise system, coupled with increased pressure on the extraction of human and natural resources, led the low-level bureaucratic units to severely malfunction and finally brought about the collapse of the entire political system.

In his book *Seeing like a State,* James C. Scott argues that our scheme of sociopolitical evolution, whereby entities develop from simple to complex forms, is mistaken, at least from a certain perspective; in fact, he maintains that modern states actually wanted to *simplify* their sociopolitical systems. Scott depicts the premodern state as immensely complex and as characterized by much variability and a very large number of autonomous or semi-autonomous subsystems. Because of this, their system was *fuzzy*, to adopt West's terminology. "The premodern state was, in many crucial respects, partially blind; it knew precious little about its subjects, their wealth, their landholders and yields, their location, their very identity. It lacked anything like a detailed 'map' of its terrain and its people, a measure, metric, that would allow it to 'translate' what it knew into a common standard necessary for a synoptic view. As a result, its interventions were often crude and self-defeating" (Scott 1998: 2). In contrast, the modern state tries to simplify the system in order to create a "rational" or "legible" system. "Processes [. . . such] as the creation of permanent last names, the standardization of weights and measures, the establishment of cadastral surveys and population registers, the invention of freehold tenure, the standardization of language and legal discourse, the design of cities, and the organization of transportation [are] attempts at legibility and simplification. In each case, officials took exceptionally complex, illegible and local social practices . . . and created a standard grid whereby it could be centrally recorded and monitored" (ibid).

I think that any Sinologist will immediately be struck by the resemblance—even in the specific examples given—between Scott's description of modern states and the Qin system. Indeed, if observed from this perspective, the Qin state and Empire represent an enormous project of social simplification, probably the largest of its kind in the premodern world. Just as in the modern states described by Scott, the aim of the Qin Empire was to allow the state to make society legible so that it could be efficiently recorded, monitored, controlled, and utilized by the state. The standardization and unification of measurements, the monetary system, writing, and so on, was one aspect of this project. Reducing human variability by organizing people into groups and assigning ranks even to people from the society's lower strata (Yates 1987; Hsing, chapter 4, this volume) was another. Creating a unified bureaucratic system that acted according to the same laws and regulations and recorded the same information for all places was the mechanism that enabled the empire to reap the benefits of the now "simplified" society.

The paleographic records of Qin laws and administration, not known prior to their discovery in the last thirty years, flesh out the modern-looking nature of the Qin bureaucratic system and its numerous efforts to intervene in the minutest details of the local societies that it controlled. Documents such as those discovered at Shuihudi, Liye, and elsewhere show the amount of information that was recorded and reported by low-level officials, as well as how tight the system was, how closely local levels were monitored by higher ones, and how rapidly orders and information traveled in both directions (see, e.g., Fujita 2010). The empire's intervention into peasants' everyday lives extended to such details as checking the weight of oxen or the number of rat holes in the local granaries, and the Qin administrative apparatus was so efficient as to be able to trace debtors even in the remotest corners of the empire.[21] The very system of Qin land taxation, investigated by Korolkov (2010), with its desire to assess annual grain yields in every location and adjust the taxes accordingly, presupposed extraordinarily tight and effective monitoring of the peasant economy.

Why is such a system problematic? While in the short run it is much more efficient than more heterogeneous systems, in the longer run it may encounter fatal problems (e.g., Scott 1998: 19–21). The main issue here is stability. Scott offers examples from natural systems, arguing that systems that are variable and complex are "demonstrably more stable, more self-sufficient, and less vulnerable to epidemics and environmental stress . . . A roughly similar case can be made, I think, for human institutions—a case that contrasts the fragility of rigid, single-purpose, centralized institutions to the adaptability of more flexible, multipurpose, decentralized social forms" (ibid: 352–353). He concludes by asserting that "[e]ven in huge organizations, diversity pays dividends in stability and resilience" (ibid: 354). A similar conclusion, although from a less well-developed and somewhat different perspective, can also found in Flannery's discussion of systems theory. As pointed out above, according to Flannery, once a system is well integrated—that is, when interdependency prevails among subsystems of the same level and among subsystems of higher and lower orders—then a failure of one subsystem or a group of lower-level subsystems can cause a chain effect that destabilizes the entire system.

The underlying logic of both approaches is that when a sociopolitical system is variable and complex (or not well integrated), it is much less efficient in controlling the population. Because it has *fuzzy* information about lower-level units, such as individual villages, let alone individual families and people, the state does not know what surpluses exist. Moreover, even if the state knows how much surpluses it can extract, its mechanisms for collecting and transporting them are inefficient. However, while such systems are inefficient, they are very stable. Because low-level units are self-sufficient and more or less manage themselves, they are less likely to be affected by crises, even when higher levels of the system are quite severely affected. In other words, *fuzzy* systems have internal buffers that, while inefficient, mitigate the effects of turmoil.

Clearly, the Qin system created an unprecedented interdependency among subsystems and reduced the ability of the lower-level units to self-regulate. Excessive pressure on the population, caused by the large-scale construction of monuments, but also by the activities of the extensive bureaucracy, could well have caused a small-scale upheaval, such as the Chen She uprising. In a less well-integrated system, such a rebellion would have probably been handled at the local level and perhaps not even have been reported to the center, as was the case throughout most of the imperial era. Yet because Qin society was so integrated, sub-parts of it were so interdependent, and the functioning of lower-level bureaucrats was so tightly controlled by the center, the upheaval could cause the entire system to malfunction severely, with ultimately grave results.

CONCLUSION: COLLAPSE OR TRANSFORMATION?

The perspective adopted here on the fall of the Qin Empire transcends the ideological debates that have colored discussion of it since the early years of the Han (see the introduction to part III of this volume). By adopting such a perspective, I also hope to set aside issues related to the personalities of the main historical figures, such as the First and Second Emperors of the Qin. It is not that the personalities of leaders and their advisors and enemies cannot affect historical events—they certainly can—but focusing much of the discussion on personal traits, as has been the case in many discussions on the Qin and its rapid demise, masks the systematic aspects of the process.

While much of this chapter has been devoted to an analysis of the scale of the Qin's public works, my argument is that the huge scale of such works and the burden they put on the population did not cause the rapid disintegration of the Qin's political system by itself. Rather, this disintegration was brought about by the combined impact of the scale of public works, their acceleration during the last years of the First Emperor, and the peculiar political and bureaucratic system of the Qin. No other premodern system in China was so tightly integrated, so efficient in extracting resources and manpower, and so capable of controlling the population. However, those same properties that made the Qin system so powerful also made it prone to unprecedented internal pressures.

As suggested by this chapter's epigraph, from looking at the collapse or the demise of the Qin we can learn much about the fundamentals of its system. It is from those insights that I approach the debate that arose during the discussions that led to this volume and is reflected in some of its chapters (see, e.g., chapter 8, by Pines) about whether or not the Han represented a continuation of the Qin or a rupture from it. While many of the institutions and cultural attributes of imperial and preimperial Qin were definitely carried on into the Han, some fundamental principles of the system changed in very significant ways. For example, the symbolic framework established by the burial complex of the First Emperor borrowed many of its components from Eastern Zhou traditions (of Qin and other states), but synthesized them in a way that was novel not only in scale but also in the overall impression it projected. As can be seen in the burial complex of Emperor Jing 景帝 (r. 157–141) of the Han, the Yangling 陽陵, this Qin tradition regarding what an emperor's tomb should contain and how it should be organized and oriented was carried on to the early Han (Yan Xinzhi et al., 2009). The scale of Yangling is quite impressive, and the work invested in it must have been substantial, although I doubt it came anywhere near the amount of work that went into the various aspects of the First Emperor's burial complex.[22] However, a clear difference between the Qin and the Han emerges when we look at the way large-scale public works were organized. The construction of the city walls of Chang'an, discussed above, is a good example. It seems that the Han were much more conscious of the burden that such work would impose on the population. To alleviate this burden, the 145,000 workers conscripted for the project were employed for only 30 days during the first month of the lunar year (February), a period when peasants are free from the most urgent and time-consuming agricultural works (Barbieri-Low 2007: 392). Such observations are in line with a system that takes into account not only the demands of the imperial court but also the needs of the lower-level segments of the population.

The most notable systematic transformation seems to be that in the Han attempts were no longer made to control comprehensively all levels of society, and that much more autonomy was bestowed on lower levels of the political and bureaucratic system. The details of this process of administrative relaxation require further fine-tuning; in some respects it might have spanned much of the Former Han period amidst strong continuities with the Qin (Hsing, chapter 4, this volume); in others—for example, abandonment of the Qin attempts to annually update the tax quotas for every locality—the change might have been particularly swift (Korolkov 2010). In any case, viewed from this perspective, the fall of the Qin appears not as a total collapse but rather as a process that culminated in the early years of the Han, when the system returned to a less homogeneous and more complex form. Perhaps because of lessons learned from the rapid fall of the Qin, or due to objective constraints, such as the difficulty to recover from post-Qin civil wars, the new system was less centralized and less tightly integrated, and it included many more safety buffers. This does not mean that the Han system was intrinsically "better" or "worthier" than that of the Qin, but the system of the Han, and that of most other Chinese imperial dynasties that followed it, was clearly more stable and shock-resistant than that of the Qin. Arguably, the early Han emperors were willing (consciously or unconsciously) to sacrifice some of the efficiency of the Qin system for greater stability.

PART II

State and Society of Qin

Introduction

The Empire of the Scribes

Robin D. S. Yates

In the general introduction we have outlined our understanding of certain fundamental aspects of the sociopolitical trajectory of the Qin state that culminated in its success in unifying the East Asian subcontinent and founding the first empire. To recapitulate: from the early fourth century BCE, Qin became engaged in parallel processes of socioeconomic transformation and radical political reforms, which brought into existence an unprecedentedly powerful, centralized, and hierarchically organized bureaucratic state that replaced the loose polity of the preceding aristocratic age. That state expanded exponentially in territorial size, and, as it expanded, it attempted to subject, control, and exploit the physical and material resources of all individuals and groups living within its boundaries. While the formation of the new state is commonly associated with the name and reform program of the so-called Legalist Shang Yang, or Lord Shang, the minister of Lord Xiao (d. 338), it is clear that this was a lengthy process, which spanned more than a century and continued well into the aftermath of the imperial unification of 221. Very large numbers of officials at all levels of the hierarchy, as well as ordinary commoners and immigrants to Qin, participated in helping to establish the structure of the new state and empire. The Qin model as a consequence strongly influenced the subsequent Han dynasty (and, *mutatis mutandis*, later imperial regimes) despite ongoing modifications and partial abandonment of some of its policies, laws, and bureaucratic procedures.

The above narrative itself is not controversial; but its details are continuously disputed and being refined as new evidence comes to light, especially through archaeological discoveries (see part I).[1] Still, many questions remain unanswered: What was the degree of continuity versus rupture between the prereform and postreform state of Qin? To what extent was the Qin model exceptional in the world of the Warring States and to what extent typical? What was the process of the state penetration into local societies and how did local societies respond to, negotiate with, manipulate, and modify the Qin system as it was formulated at the capital and regional administrative centers? How successful were Qin magistrates in their attempts to regulate social, economic and even the cultural life of their subjects? How meritocratic and mobile was Qin society and what was the role of pedigree in determining one's status? Which sources of social prestige existed outside the Qin system of ranks of merit? Were there social elites in the state of Qin who were not dependent on the central state, and, if so, what was their role in the life of local society? How did gender relations develop and transform and what role did women play in the creation of the empire? Which aspects of the Qin model continued into the Han dynasty, which were modified, and which were abandoned, and why? A comprehensive answer to these questions is currently impossible; yet a few partial answers are presented in the chapters in this section.

Scholars who analyze state-society relations in the Qin have benefited enormously from the paleographic revolution of recent decades. While earlier generations of researchers had to rely primarily on the Han and later—often biased—interpretations of the Qin realities (e.g., the *Historical Records* of Sima Qian; see van Ess, chapter 7 in this volume), or to utilize prescriptive rather than descriptive Qin texts (e.g., *The Book of Lord Shang*), today we possess thousands of Qin documents, including many administrative and legal materials (Chen Wei 2009; 2012). Yet these documents pose not a few problems of interpretation, which partly explains ongoing controversies.

First, most of the recently unearthed or recovered paleographic texts from the Warring States and imperial Qin periods come from the region of modern Hubei and Hunan provinces, which were ruled prior to 278 by the state of Chu and later incorporated into Qin.[2] This creates a significant Qin (and to a lesser degree Chu) bias; in the absence of comparable data from eastern parts of the Zhou world we are unable to fully assess the peculiarity of Qin developments. Second, as almost all of the Qin-related documents come from the conquered Chu territories, we need to assess the extent to which they reflect the regulations and practices that were common and of long standing in the Qin core region surrounding the capital at Xianyang, Shaanxi, against the extent to which they reflect rather the specifics of regulations imposed by the Qin authorities on recently annexed areas. Third, inasmuch as almost all of the Qin paleographic materials reflect the perspective of Qin administrators, it should be assessed how much social life they were able to influence or control and how much remained outside their purview. Fourth, only a portion of the Qin archive found in Well 1, Liye, in modern Hunan Province, the ancient town of Qianling which had been captured by the Qin from the Chu and made into a Qin county in 222 (see this volume's general introduction), has been published so far. Once the complete archive has been published, we will be in a much better position to assess the workings of a county-level town during the Qin Empire. Until that occurs, we are obliged to rely on other excavated paleographic sources, most of which derive from the tombs of Qin scribes. The mortuary provenance of most of these documents poses certain questions regarding their overall reliability (see below). Finally, in order to assess the reliability of the unearthed documents we should learn more about their producers, the Qin scribes. It is on this particular question that we shall focus below, hoping to elucidate thereby certain rarely noticed social, administrative and cultural phenomena from the state and the empire of Qin.

As indicated above, many of the newly recovered paleographic materials were originally placed in the tombs of low-level bureaucrats, in the Qin and early Han probably most of whom were hereditary scribes (*shi* 史);[3] yet others were discarded archives of local or military administration.[4] Some of these new texts were scientifically excavated and have been properly recorded in site reports;[5] others were looted and retrieved from the Hong Kong antiques market.[6] All of them provide insights into the daily workings of the Qin state and imperial administration as well as the beliefs and practices of the lower orders of Qin society that are not referred to at all in transmitted historical sources, mentioned only in passing, or critiqued in other literary sources.[7]

These new materials reveal a far greater complexity of bureaucratic organization and richness of cultural and religious life in the Qin and Han than we could possibly have imagined without them or that can be reconstructed based solely on transmitted sources. Yet, to this point, almost all scholars who have worked on these new materials that have been retrieved from tombs, or which probably originated in tombs (for example, the Yuelu hoard of Qin slips), have devoted themselves solely to the contents of the texts and have not considered the more general implications of the fact that these latter materials were found in the tombs of scribes. Who were these scribes and where were they located in Qin state and society? How representative is the information contained in the texts deposited in their tombs, and how reliable is the information in those documents that they wrote which were later discarded?[8] What does the nature of the texts deposited in their tombs tell us about their value system and world view? How might they differ from other members of Qin and early Han society?

At this point, we are far from answering these questions, but the content of the texts is revealing to a certain extent. First, let us consider the types of texts deposited in their tombs. They include calendars of significant moments in their lives and activities (*zhiri* 質日 or *shiri* 視日) (Li Ling 2008); legal documents, including statutes (*lü* 律), ordinances (*ling* 令), form books of transcripts showing how legal cases should be written up (*Fengzhen shi* 封診式), questions and answers on points of law (*falü dawen* 法律答問), cases submitted for decision by higher authorities (*Zouyan shu* 奏讞書), and administrative handbooks or training manuals[9] and other miscellaneous legal and administrative materials (Yates, chapter 6 in this volume), such as registers (Hsing, chapter 4 this volume); mathematical texts; almanac texts or *Daybooks* (*Rishu* 日書) (Poo, chapter 5 in this volume); medical texts; military texts; and stories.[10] Of these, the largest number consists of legal texts.

Who were the scribes? They were the low-status bureaucrats who were expected to manage the daily administration of the Qin state and empire, including keeping detailed records of all state financial matters, such as tax records, income and disbursement of salaries, and food rations of officials and those working for the state, such as convicts and slaves; and they were obliged to investigate all illegal activity and record all legal actions taken by authorities in the area under their jurisdiction. They were, in short, completely indispensable for running the administrative machinery of the Qin state and empire. Hence the presence not only of legal documents in their tombs but also of mathematical works: they had to be trained in techniques of calculation in order to perform their daily tasks.[11] The calendars, on the other hand, give dates in specific years according to the king or emperor's reign, together with months and days according to the stem and branch (*tiangan dizhi* 天干地支) system. Under certain years or days, there are brief annotations on the official activities of the scribe, including his sometimes extensive travels on official business to different locations.[12] Again, this type of text seems to be intimately connected to the official life of the tomb owner.

According to the Shuihudi Tomb No. 11 and Zhangjiashan Tomb No. 247 legal documents, scribes belonged to a hereditary occupation, and only their sons were permitted to enroll in the school for scribes.[13] There existed detailed statutes on their training, the examination of their skills and competence to perform their tasks, and appointment to office at different levels of the bureaucratic hierarchy. From these rules, it appears that these hereditary scribes were not permitted to be appointed into high ranking policy or executive positions, from assistant prefect (or magistrate) in a county to prefect (magistrate), on up to similar positions at the regional (commandery) or central administration levels; rather they were the personnel responsible for record-keeping and writing the official correspondence of the office to which they were seconded (Yates 2011; Yan Buke 2001: 33–82). That this essential, highly skilled and technical occupation was hereditary shows that the Qin continued to lay emphasis on family background and hereditary status: it was not a purely meritocratic state or social system. It is actually possible that the hereditary occupation of the scribes was a necessary complementary feature in a mobile society in which persons of limited literary skills could climb, due to their military merits, to high positions in the state hierarchy.[14] Scribes, in short, were the specialists who managed the daily administration at all levels of the state hierarchy, as well as the individuals responsible for managing the legal system for which the Qin later gained special notoriety.

Let us consider now the state structure maintained by the scribes. At the bottom of society were individual families which the Qin administration organized into five-family units (*wu* 伍). The Qin state appointed the heads of these units, or at least approved their appointment, for it recorded their names on the household registers (Hsing, chapter 4 in this volume).[15] All births and deaths had to be reported to Qin authorities so that the Qin could exploit the tax and labor power of the population (Yates 1987; Shelach, chapter 3 in this volume), and all members were responsible for each other's behavior. Crimes of family members had to be denounced to the authorities; if they were not, then the family members were held guilty of the crime. The Qin developed minute distinctions in the levels of responsibility that family members held for each other, depending on whether they lived together (*tongju* 同居), their age, and the status they held in the family (Kim Yop 1994).[16] Crimes committed in groups of five or more were punished more severely than those by individuals. Thus the Qin state administration penetrated into the heart of the family and, over time, attempted to assert control over the head of the household's right to punish family members. Heads of households and senior generations in a family could still punish their junior members, but they had to ask permission of the Qin state authorities; and the Qin state also eventually took over the punishment as well, as can been seen from several cases in the Shuihudi *Forms for Sealing and Investigating* (*Fengzhen shi*) (McLeod and Yates 1981). Was the Qin actually able to enforce these rules? From the cases that have been discovered, it certainly seems that it tried and did, but it is also clear that people resisted, as evidenced in the numbers of individuals who committed the crime of "abscondence" (*wang* 亡), running away and refusing to perform the duties that the Qin state tried to impose upon them (Shi Weiqing 2004c; Zhang Gong 2006). Whether such resistance was confined to the areas conquered by the Qin, or whether this situation also held true in the core area of Qin remains unknown. Nevertheless, we do know from several cases in the Shuihudi *Forms for Sealing and Investigating* that it was the responsibility of the magistrate's scribe (*lingshi* 令史) in the first instance to investigate crimes, determine responsibility, and report the details to their superiors.

The five-family units were organized into hamlets (also known as villages or wards) (*li* 里), which were subordinate to cantons (also known as districts) (*xiang* 鄉), counties (*xian* 縣) or marches (*dao* 道) if minorities composed a significant portion of the population, and commanderies (*jun* 郡) at the regional level. At each level of the hierarchy, the state explicitly delineated the area of jurisdiction of officials and their obligations. Boundaries were carefully drawn and it was a crime both to physically cross those boundaries without permission, or, more symbolically, to perform the duties of another without specific written permission.

At the top of the administrative hierarchy, the central government was based in the capital, Xianyang, modern Shaanxi Province, and the capital area was separately administered by the "Clerk of the Capital" (*neishi* 內史). In addition, some offices at the local level were directly administered by the state, and often these were of particular economic and military or other significance, such as salt and iron offices. These were known as "metropolitan offices" (*duguan* 都官), and had the same status and a similar complement of officials, with similar ranks, as the county, whose seat itself was also known as a "metropolitan canton" (*duxiang* 都鄉)—at least in Qianling.[17] Thus scribes, being posted in offices from the bottom to the top of the administrative hierarchy and having such extensive responsibilities, had intimate knowledge of the entire structure of the Qin state as well as of the society that they helped to administer.

The final component of the Qin was the court and the palace and the royal, later imperial family. Again, not much is known about their structure and practices from either transmitted or excavated texts. We do know that Shang Yang proposed that relatives of the Qin royal house should not have rank unless they won it by means of military success.[18] This would suggest a system of meritocratic ranking and abandonment of the hereditary principle. We do have some evidence for unranked members of the royal house; yet we also have the Zhangjiashan legal statutory stipulation that, unlike most holders of the ranks of merit, whose descendants were eligible only to a reduced rank, those in two upper categories (*che hou* 徹侯 and *guannei hou* 關內侯) could bequeath their full rank on their heir.[19] If the Zhangjiashan regulations are applicable for the Qin, they suggest an attempt to create a tiny, but powerful, super-elite which would have been at least partly hereditary. Currently, the details of the system, as well as the relations between the old elite and the new one, for example, foreigners who climbed to the very top of the Qin government apparatus (Moriya 2001), remain exceedingly obscure.

An interesting clue to the latter question may be provided by a wooden placard that was found in Well No. 1, Liye. Numbered 8-455 by the excavators (but subsequently given number 8-461 in the *Liye* 2012 publication), this placard lists the old and new names for royal Qin ancestors, deities and for other terms, which appear to have been renamed after the unification of the empire in 221, probably as the result of the promulgation of an edict, at the same time as King Zheng declared himself the First Emperor (Zhang Chunlong and Long Jingsha 2009; Hu Pingsheng 2009; You Yifei 2011). As this placard has yet to be fully analyzed, its value for understanding the structure of the Qin court and palace, and their religious practices, has yet to be determined. Nevertheless, while some of the changes in nomenclature were hardly earth-shattering, for example, royal hounds (*wang quan* 王犬) were now to be known as "imperial hounds" (*huangdi quan* 皇帝犬), and "do not venture to say 'pig' [*zhu* 豬], say 'swine' [*zhi* 彘]," others have more serious implications. One example is that both the "royal house" (*wangshi* 王室) and the "lord's house" (*gongshi* 公室) were now to be referred to as *xianguan* 縣官, in other words "the state." This seems to have been a major institutional innovation, for now all matters concerning the imperial family were to be considered state matters, thus changing the previous apparent tripartite division between the private sphere of the individual family or person, the state, and the royal house.[20]

Going back to the scribes, it is noteworthy that the "Statutes for Scribes" also specified the rules for the training of religious specialists called prayer-makers or invocators (*zhu* 祝), who were required to be less highly literate than scribes in the sense of knowing how to write and recognize graphs; they were required to be able to recognize 3,000 graphs from each of the "scribe's texts" (史書) and the "diviner's texts" (卜書) and be capable of chanting 30,000 words.[21] It is my suspicion that they were expected to memorize the prayers that they would use in the rites of the cults to which they had been assigned. It appears that there was a close relationship between the two types of occupation, an association that went back far in time to the Springs-and-Autumns, if not Western Zhou, period or beyond (Xu Zhaochang 2006; Zhao Ping'an 2009).[22] Further, sacrifices were regulated by legal statute (the "Statutes on Sacrifices" ["Ci lü" 祠律]), and thus scribes also had to know the regulations that applied to different types of sacrifices, from local, to commandery, to central and royal, later imperial sacrifices. Thus it is not surprising that so many of the texts placed in scribes' tombs have been found to be almanac or day-books, for it seems as though scribes were obliged to be familiar with all the different types of esoteric belief systems and practices of the peoples with whom they had to manage and interact as well as with current state religious policy.[23]

Finally, it seems as though scribes were also legally responsible for determining the reasons for an individual's death or injury. In this way, one of their obligations was to act as coroners, as their descendants, the clerks, did in later imperial times (McKnight 1981). It is possible, there-fore, that the reason why medical texts and medical prescriptions were deposited in scribes' tombs was because they were obliged to be aware of methods of treating sick persons in the areas under their jurisdiction and be capable of assessing the reasons for an individual's injury or death, in ways similar to doctors and shamans (cf. Lin Fu-shih 2009). Of course, some scribes might simply have had a personal interest in medicine and thus medical texts were deposited in their tombs by those they had left behind.

By no means do all tombs of scribes contain all the types of materials listed above. Nevertheless, the list is sufficient to appreciate that most of the texts retrieved from their tombs are related to the scribes' profession, while others may have been enjoyed by them in their leisure hours, for example the military texts and the historical romances. Indeed, a number of the tombs also include artifacts, such as brushes, knives, and counting rods, which they might have used during their lifetime, or perhaps were deposited to indicate their status and occupation, or that they might have been expected to use in the afterlife. Furthermore, the contents of those tombs that have been scientifically excavated, which include pottery, lac-querware, and even bronze swords, as well as their size, indicate that these scribes were possessed of a certain wealth, but by no means were they as wealthy as the highest elite that they served, whose tomb complexes served to distinguish them from their social inferiors.[24] However, their social status was clearly well above that of the peasants and urban townsfolk whose lives they managed. We must read their texts, therefore, bearing this information in mind.

In short, therefore, it is to the scribes that we owe most of the new paleographic evidence for the functioning of the state and empire and for understanding state-society relations in the late Warring States and imperial Qin times. It is imperative to understand their role in the administration and to analyze the texts that they composed or had deposited in their tombs, if we are to eventually answer the historical questions posed above.

In the following three chapters, the authors analyze three of the types of documents for which scribes were responsible or which were found in their tombs, and in those of local functionaries of the lower ranks later in the Han, in the case of the second half of chapter 4, by Hsing I-t'ien. In the first part of his chapter, Hsing provides a detailed explanation of what appears to be original household registration documents of Nanyang 南 陽 that were excavated from the northern moat of the ancient Qin county town of Qianling, modern Liye. Hsing carefully reviews the various problems in interpretation of these newly discovered materials, the oldest household registration documents yet discovered. The Qin had ordered all households to register themselves with the state approximately four decades earlier. Although so far no such statutes on households from the Qin have been found, it is hard to imagine that the Qin did not have Statutes on Households ("Hu lü" 戶律) and other similar statutes that regulated registration and the compilation and composition of the household registers.[25] Qin could only have been able to control, manage, and exploit its own population, in addition to the huge number of conquered peoples that it inherited after it had defeated its rivals and founded the empire, if it had been able to develop a sophisticated system of household registration founded on law. Indeed, from unpublished documents exhibited in the newly established Liye Museum of Qin Slips (里耶秦簡 博物館), it appears that a Qin county administration was organized into various bureaus, one of which was the Bureau of Households (hu cao 戶 曹), managed by a Magistrate's Scribe or Foreman Clerk (ling shi 令史); others were the Bureau of the Commandant (Wei cao 尉曹), presumably in charge of military affairs and security; the Bureau of the Director of Works (*Sikong cao* 司空曹); the Bureau of Granaries (*cang cao* 倉曹), which was in charge of county finances; and the Bureau of Officials (*li cao* 吏曹), which would have been in charge of day-to-day administration, keeping track of the movement of officials and their performance records, and so on.[26]

Further, the document translated and analyzed in part by Hsing, J1(16)9 (also known as 16–9),[27] suggests that there were also Qin ordinances (*ling* 令) in addition to statutes, that regulated unusual circumstances regarding household registration, in this case of migration of seventeen households from one location to another. Although before the discovery of the Liye documents some scholars doubted that the Qin had ordinances, considering them to be an innovation of the Han, this and other Liye documents, as well as the more recently retrieved Yuelu hoard, leave no doubt that ordinances were Qin legal instruments. In the case of J1(16)9, there appears to have been an ordinance that regulated the transfer of household registers.

Hsing proceeds to analyze other types of documents and registers that have been excavated from the tombs of local officials later in the Han dynasty. Of significance is his finding that the average size of a family generally matches the empirewide census of 2 CE recorded in the "Treatise of Geography" in the *History of the Former Han Dynasty* (*Hanshu* 漢書) by Ban Gu (班固, 32–92 CE). Thus we can presume on the reliability of the general figure for the Han population at that time.

Equally significant is Hsing's analysis of the funerary, i.e., ritual, nature of the documents deposited in the tombs of these local functionaries. The documents were not original official documents but copies, probably produced after the death of the deceased by family members or colleagues, which were intended to show the achievements of the deceased perhaps to the officials of the underworld. Their figures may not have been completely accurate and copyists' errors appear to have crept in. However, Hsing's analysis shows that we can be sure of the format of these types of document, as well as the general statistics. He also allows us to answer one of the questions we raised above regarding the reliability of the documents that have been discovered by archaeologists. The documents from Liye are genuine originals that were discarded for whatever reason in Well 1. The same is true for the documents abandoned in the forts and limes of the northwestern regions in the Han, the so-called Juyan documents, and the registers thrown away by the Commandery of Changsha 長沙 of the Wu 吳 Kingdom of the Three Kingdoms period (220–280 CE) discovered in the downtown Changsha site of Zoumalou

走馬樓. We can rely on these without a doubt. On the other hand, all documents deposited in tombs must be treated as funeral objects first and foremost. While they can be relied on to provide general information about the legal and social system of the Qin and Han, they cannot be taken as complete and absolutely accurate copies of the statutes and ordinances that were promulgated and applied by the Qin state and the later Qin and Han empires. Their analysis requires sophistication and care, with due recognition that they may contain inaccuracies or outright falsehoods, as Hsing so masterfully demonstrates in his chapter.

In chapter 5, Mu-chou Poo considers two aspects of Qin religion, the state cults sponsored by the Qin ruling house and its related aristocratic elite members, and the beliefs and practices of the commoner population as a whole. First, he observes that Qin religious practices and culture, and their underlying cosmological foundations, cannot be disassociated from the Northern Plains Zhou culture of which they were a part and that the two aspects cannot really be differentiated in their essential nature and in their fundamental view of the relations between the human and suprahuman realms. Thus the Qin royal house imitated practices of the Zhou court, adding to these whatever convenient or "extraordinary" religious practices that could give it legitimacy in the eyes of its own members or associates and dwellers of rival states.

After his analysis of the development of Qin burial customs, Poo turns to consider the mentality and religious beliefs that lay behind the *Daybooks*. He notes that certain assumptions underlay the relationship between humans and the greater cosmos and that what ordinary Qin and Han people were most concerned about was to obtain a happy life. He identifies three basic assumptions, first "the progress of time structures human destiny;" second, "the varieties of the nature of days are confined to what is allowed by the sexagesimal calendrical system"; and, third, "all . . . activities are often connected with the will of the spirits and gods." After giving some examples of the numerous, often contradictory systems, based on alternative astronomical and numerological methods of reckoning, found in the *Daybooks*, Poo suggests that most of systems presume that if an individual adheres to the requirements to perform activities on certain days and to avoid the taboos or inauspicious days, then the world was entirely predictable. However, he complicates this view by bringing attention to the "Demonography," also included in the *Daybooks* in Tomb 11, Shuihudi, where various ghosts and spirits are presented as attacking, injuring or killing humans randomly, without warning, and completely arbitrarily. He resolves the apparent contradiction between these two views of the natural world, the one that it is entirely predictable and the other that the non-human world is filled with a host of unpredictable dangers, by suggesting that the "Demonography" provides the user with various powerful means of exorcizing these unpredictable spirits. Thus it was a matter of power relations between humans and non-human world. While hesitating to call this religious view "fatalism," Poo concludes that the *Daybooks* reveal a mentality that saw the human and non-human world as consisting of a fixed structure of numerical systems that could be analyzed and predicted. It was a rather amoral and materialistic view of the world with little evidence of any transcendental power that could be appealed to or used to explain the meaning of life.

This is certainly a very interesting analysis of the religious world view of the Qin and early Han people. However, I would like to note by way of conclusion, without offering my own analysis of the phenomena presented in this type of text, that a number of the systems found in the daybooks were of direct relevance to the lives of scribes and low-level officials in whose tombs so many of these daybooks have been discovered. Among these can be counted the "Entering Office" (i.e., "Taking up a Post," ["Ru guan" 入官]) system found in both the Kongjiapo 孔家坡 and Shuihudi Tomb No. 11 "Book A" slips;[28] "Officials" ("Li" 吏), "Escaping and Absconding" ("Tao wang" 逃亡), which allowed the user to determine whether he would be able to catch an individual who had taken flight; "Robbers" ("Dao" 盜), which allowed the user to determine what sort of individual had committed a robbery on a particular day and where he or she had stashed the loot; when was most auspicious to register households ("Fu hu" 傅戶); which directions were most auspicious at what times to travel, travelling long distances on official business seemingly, from the evidence of the calendars deposited in the tombs, being the continuous duty of many scribes, and so on. All of these systems certainly would have been of assistance in carrying out a scribe's official duties, but whether they actually decided their actions on the basis of the daybooks, as Poo observes for the general user or reader of these texts, is yet to be determined.

Chapter 6 is by Yates and is titled "The Changing Status of Slaves in the Qin-Han Transition." In a previous study (Yates 2002), Yates adopted the sociocultural approach of Orlando Patterson to make a number of points about the status of slaves in Qin and Han times (Patterson 1982). He noted, for example, that the Qin had several different terms for slaves and that slaves could not be legally married: a slave wife was always called a *qie* 妾 ("concubine") in Qin legal parlance. Recent archaeological finds of Han statutes from such sites as Zhangjiashan Tomb 247 have required a re-evaluation of his previous analysis. The early Han made some significant alterations in the nomenclature and legal status of slaves, simplifying the complex and harsher Qin system. His chapter compares the Qin and Han systems of slavery by analyzing the articles in the Zhangjiashan statutes relating to the status of slaves and argues that the Han made a conscious effort to assimilate slaves into the family system. Not only were slaves distinguished from movable and immovable property, such as houses and animals, but they were also included as persons on the household registers. If an ordinary commoner lacked a viable heir, the longest-serving slave could be manumitted and made his/her heir. In punishments relating to a lack of filial piety, slaves were also treated similarly to male and female children. Thus the changing legal attitude towards slaves also transformed intra-family relations.

In assessing aspects of Qin religious, administrative, and social realities, the three contributions in this section try also to contextualize these realities within a broader sweep of early Chinese history. In general, they tend to reject Qin's exceptionality: Poo explicitly considers it a part of a broader Zhou pattern, while Hsing and Yates indicate important continuities between the Qin and the Han. Yet there were changes as well: of a more immediate nature in the case of slaves' status; and a less explicit and more gradual change in the administrative activism in the course of early Han history. We hope that future studies will further fine-tune spatial and temporal contextualization of the Qin model, and allow us to understand better the Qin's place in China's history.

4 Qin-Han Census and Tax and Corvée Administration

Notes on Newly Discovered Materials

Hsing I-tien

In recent years local census, tax, and conscript service records on bamboo slips and wooden boards have been unearthed variously from the site of the Qin dynasty seat of Qianling County 遷陵縣 in Liye 里耶, Longshan 龍山, Hunan; from Western Han Tomb 10 at Fenghuangshan 鳳凰山, Jiangling 江陵, Hubei; from Western Han Tomb 1 at Songbocun 松柏村, Ji'nan 紀南, Jingzhou 荊州; from Western Han Tomb 19 at Tianchang 天長, Anhui; and from the Western Han Tomb 6 at Yinwan 尹灣, Lianyungang 連雲港, Jiangsu, among others. These discoveries have made possible a general understanding of the operation of census and tax/corvée administration at the hamlet, canton, county, and commandery levels. The present discussion begins with the most basic level—the hamlet *li* 里.[1]

QIN HAMLET HOUSEHOLD REGISTRATION DOCUMENTS FROM THE LIYE EXCAVATIONS

The most recent publications of new materials pertaining to Qin-Han household registrations have included (1) household registrations on wooden boards unearthed in the remains of the ancient city moat of Liye at Longshan, Hunan; (2) census and capitation tax records on wooden boards excavated from a mid-Western Han tomb at Tianchang in Anhui; and (3) collection registers, et cetera, on wooden boards from the tomb of one Shi Rao 師饒, a late Western Han clerk or scribe (*shi* 史) of the Bureau of Merit (*gongcao* 功曹) of Donghai Commandery 東海郡, excavated at Yinwan, in Lianyungang, Jiangsu. Although the levels of detail and the character of the three sets are not entirely the same, they do offer an unprecedented opportunity to uncover the reality of Qin-Han local state and commandery population administration and household registration.[2]

Of these, the Liye household registration documents are of the greatest significance, because for the first time they give us a clear view of a comparatively early stage of the Qin-Han household registration system.[3]

The Liye household registries were excavated from Pit K 11, at the bottom of the middle section of the northern moat of the ancient county town of Qianling, modern Liye. Household registries on ten slips have been completely restored; fourteen slips remain fragments.[4] The restored slips are 46 cm long, which is exactly twice the length of the normal Qin-Han wooden slip, and are 0.9 to 3.0 cm wide. Plates of fourteen of the slips having relatively more content have been published. The following discussion is based on the published transcriptions.

The originals of these household registries are quite possibly a portion of the official household registration documents of the Qin local government. First, the documents are written on wood, unlike the usual documents recorded on bamboo slips. According to the "Statutes of the Minister of Works" of the Qin laws found in Tomb 11, Shuihudi, documents used by county and commandant (i.e., commandery) offices had to be made from willow or soft wood made rectangular or on boards (Hulsewé 1985: A77: 76; *Shuihudi* 2001: 83). This must refer only to official records or documents; for copies or documents for other uses, bamboo might also be used. Second, their length was to be two Qin/Han feet (2 *chi* = 46 cm).[5] Many Qin-Han official documents used two *chi* as the standard. For example, the "Statute on Fields" of the *Statutes and Ordinances of the Second Year* 二年律令田律 from Zhangjiashan 張家山 Tomb 247 directs: "Each office is to write down separately on two-foot boards the amount of straw used in one year by its horses, oxen, and other animals, and the amount of the surplus hay and straw, and report it up to the Minister of Finance (*Neishi* 內史).[6] The deadline is always the full moon of the eighth month." (*Zhangjiashan* 2001: 168, slip 256; Barbieri-Low and Yates, forthcoming). If the formal documents which report the amount of hay consumed annually by horses and cattle required the use of two *chi* slips, reporting population figures ought to have been the same. If we can determine that these were formal household registers, then we shall have an important standard for the material, length, and format adopted for documents that will enable us to distinguish the formal documents and copies of this sort for the Qin. Curiously, the width of these household registration documents is not very consistent, running from 0.9 to 3.0 cm. Why is this? Ancient texts mention only the length of documents and not their width. Is this because the length was of greater institutional significance and width requirements were less strict? These questions merit further study.

There are several elements of these documents that differ from received or other excavated texts. In the following examples selected from among the Qin state household registries, one can see the family structure of seven households from Nanyang 南陽 hamlet, Qianling County, Dongting 洞庭 Commandery (*Liye* 2007: 203–208):

1. (K27)   Column 1: 南陽戶人荊不更蠻強
                       Nanyang, household head, fourth merit rank in Jing, Man Qiang

                  Column 2: 妻曰嗛
                       Wife called Qian

                  Column 3: 子小上造□
                       Child X, minor second merit rank.[7]

                  Column 4: 子小女子駝
                       Child, minor female, Tuo

                  Column 5: 臣曰聚
                       Servant called Ju
                     伍長
                     Squad [i.e., five-family unit] leader
                     [Intact slip]

2. (K1/25/50) Column 1: 南陽戶人荊不更黃得
                       Nanyang, household head, fourth merit rank in Jing, Huang De

                  Column 2: 妻曰嗛
                       Wife, called Qian

                  Column 3: 子小上造台
                       Child, minor second merit rank, Tai
                     子小上造
                     Child, minor second merit rank
                     子小上造定(?)
                     Child, minor second merit rank Ding (?)

                  Column 4: 子小女庠
                       Child, minor female, Hu
                     子小女移
                     Child, minor female, Yi
                     子小女平(?)
                     Child, minor female Ping(?)

                  Column 5: 伍長
                     Squad leader   [Intact slip]

3. (K43) Column 1: 南陽戶人荊不更大囗
Nanyang, household head, fourth merit rank in Jing, Da+X
弟不更慶(?)
Younger brother, fourth merit rank, Qing (?)

      Column 2: 妻曰[ ]
Wife, called [ ]
慶妻規
Qing's wife, Gui

      Column 3: 子小上造視
Child, minor second merit rank, Shi
子小上造囗
Child, minor second merit rank, X
[Intact slip]

4. (K42/46) Column 1: 南陽戶人荊不更囗囗
Nanyang, household head, fourth merit rank in Jing, XX

      Column 2: 妻(?)曰義
Wife (?), called Yi

      Column 3: . . .

      Column 4: 母睢
Mother, Sui

      Column 5: 伍長
Squad leader [Intact slip]

5. (K30/45) Column 1: 南陽戶人不更彭奄
Nanyang, household head, fourth merit rank, Peng Yan
弟不更說
Younger brother, fourth merit rank, Yue

      Column 2: 母曰錯
Mother, called Cuo
妾曰囗
Concubine (female slave?), called X

      Column 3: 子小上造狀
Child, minor second merit rank, Zhuang
[Fragment]

6. (K4) Column 1: 南陽戶人荊不更[ ]喜
Nanyang, household head, fourth merit rank in Jing, [ ] Xi
子不更衍
Child, fourth merit rank, Yan

Column 2: 妻大女子媅
Wife, adult female, Dan
隸大女子華
Servant (?),[8] adult female, Hua

Column 3: 子小上造章
Child, minor second merit rank, Zhang
子小上造
Child, minor second merit rank

Column 4: 子小女子趙
Child, minor female, Zhao
子小女子見
Child, minor female, Jian   [Fragment]

7. (K2/23) Column 1: 南陽戶人荊不更宋午
Nanyang, household head, fourth merit rank in Jing, Song Wu
弟不更熊
Younger brother, fourth merit rank, Xiong
弟不更衛
Younger brother, fourth merit rank, Wei

Column 2: 熊妻曰□□[9]
Xiong's wife, called XX
衛妻曰□
Wei's wife, called X

Column 3: 子小上造傅
Child, minor second merit rank, Chuan
子小上造逐
Child, minor second merit rank, Zhu
□子小上造□
X's child, minor second merit rank, X
熊(?)子小上造□
Xiong's (?) child, minor second merit rank, X

Column 4: 衛(?)子小女子□
Wei's (?) child, minor female, X

Column 5: 臣曰[ ]
Male slave called [ ]   [Intact slip]

These household registries, which were found in the pit, had probably been retired and discarded. The Han bureaucracy maintained a system for the regular retirement and disposal of official documents.[10] Many of the Han slips found on the frontier had been tossed into trash heaps. Some of the Liye slips had been used to practice writing (*Liye* 2007: 208, slip K19); similar examples are seen among slips from Juyan 居延 and Dunhuang 敦煌 (Hsing 1993, 2011). This is evidence that after a document had been retired, the slips on which it had been recorded might be put to another use before being finally discarded.

The content of these discarded registries is very simple, but we should not assume that Qin household records were limited to this. In the Zhangjiashan *Statutes and Ordinances of the Second Year,* which largely follow the Qin statutes, we find mentioned various types of registry, including "Dwelling and Garden Household Registry," "Age Details Registry,"[11] "Register of Field Boundaries," "Field Tax Registry," and "Field Ownership Registry."[12] This suggests that "household registry" 戶籍 was in fact a broad concept and a general term that covered a range of records with different content and designations. Further support for such a conclusion comes from an injunction in the chapter on "Eliminating the Powerful" (去強) of the *Book of Lord Shang:* "Enumerate the entire population. Register [commoners] at birth and erase the deceased. . . . A strong state should know thirteen figures: the number of granaries within its borders, the number of able-bodied men and women, the number of old and weak people, the number of officials and officers, the number of those earning a livelihood through rhetoric, the number of useful people, the number of horses and oxen, and the quantity of fodder and straw" (*Shang jun shu* 4: 32; Duyvendak 1928: 203, 205). If the state required such data as the numbers of granaries, of able-bodied persons, births and deaths, social status and professions and the like, then it needed to record far more than the limited information found in the Liye documents.[13] Surely, one type of household registration would not have sufficed. Moreover, in order to obtain the numbers of different kinds of livestock and the amounts of hay and fodder, it would have been necessary to know what property people owned. This would have required registration as well and would have fallen under household registration.[14]

Which types of household registration did the Qin have? Under which category should the records presently seen fall? What were they called? None of these questions can be answered with any certainty. The only point that we can be sure of from the Liye records is that at birth the populace had to register the year, which was entered in the "Age Registry" 年細籍:

廿六年五月辛巳朔庚子,啟陵鄉□(應?)敢言之:都鄉守嘉言渚里□□劾等十
七戶徙都鄉,皆不移年籍∠.令曰移言∠,今問之劾等徙□書告都鄉,曰啟陵鄉
未有萊(牒),毋以智(知)劾等初產至今年數,□□□□□謁令,都鄉具問劾等
年數,敢言之.

On the day *gengzi* of the fifth month, first day *xinsi*, in the twenty-sixth year [of King Zheng, 221], Ying(?) of Qiling canton respectfully submits this report: Jia, the Probationary [Bailiff] of Du [metropolitan] canton, states that He and others, of Zhu hamlet XX, seventeen households, have moved to Du canton; none of their *age registries* has been forwarded ∠. The ordinance says, "Forward statements ∠. Now we have asked He and others about their movement [. . .] written report to Du canton. I state: Qiling canton does not yet have documents. *There is no way to know the age and birth years*[15] *of He and the others*. [. . .] reports ordinance (?),[16] Du canton is to thoroughly inquire of He and others the year numbers. I [X of Qiling canton] respectfully submit this report. (Recto) (italics added)

遷陵守丞敦狐告都鄉主以律令從事／.建手囗

甲辰水十一刻,刻下者十刻,不更成里午以來／犟手

Qianling Temporary Magistrate Dunhu instructs the chief of Du canton to handle the matter according to the statutes and ordinances. / Jian signs X.

The day *jiachen*, at the tenth-unit time of the eleven-unit clepsydra,[17] received from Wu of Cheng hamlet who holds the fourth merit rank *bugeng*. / Si signs. (Verso) (*Liye* 2007: 194, slip 16-9)

This document, which dates from just after the empire was unified (221), has a few lacunae, but the gist is that seventeen households from Du 渚 hamlet had migrated to Du 都 canton (i.e., possibly the canton that held the county seat), but their age registries had not been forwarded with them, resulting in an inquiry. The italicized statement is further confirmation of the account in the *Historical Records* that in the sixteenth year of King Zheng of Qin, "for the first time men were ordered to register according to their age" (*Shiji* 6: 232). Given the existence of a specific category "age registry," other demographically related registration categories probably existed as well. In any case, in light of this material, there are certain features of the Liye documents that are worth noting.

First are format characteristics. Intact slips are divided top to bottom into five horizontal columns by lines of black ink. The exception is slip K33; its second and third columns are delineated using a hard instrument. The first column records the household head 戶人 of a specified place, including surname and given name as well the names and ranks of brothers in the same household. The second column records spouses, including brothers' spouses and, in one case, the household head's mother and concubine (female slave?). Column three records sons, including those of the brothers, and the fourth column records daughters, as well as the household head's mother and his brothers' daughters. The final column notes with larger graphs whether the household head was a squad (five-family unit) leader (*wuzhang* 伍長) or records servants registered in the same household. The content of the five columns is arranged according to household members' taxation status starting with adult males, followed by adult females, minor males and minor females (Liu Xinning 2008).

In the Qin and early Han, male adults were termed *da nanzi* 大男子, female adults *da nüzi* 大女子, minor (non-adult) males *xiao nanzi* 小男子, and minor females *xiao nüzi* 小女子. From the early Han on, these terms were abbreviated into *da nan* 大男, *da nü* 大女, *xiao nan* 小男, and *xiao nü* 小女 (Hsing 2009; cf. Yates 1987, Liu Xinning 2008, and Wang Zijin 2008). From the Shuihudi and Zhangjiashan documents we can see that the terms *da nüzi* (female adult), *xiao nanzi* (minor male), and *xiao nüzi* (minor female) were formal terms for referring to an individual's administrative or tax/corvée status; hence we may assert that the word *zi* 子 in Liye documents is not part of a person's name. Further investigation is required to determine at what point the terms were abbreviated into *da nan, da nü, xiao nan,* and *xiao nü* (Hsing 2009).

The household registries begin with *Nanyang huren* 南陽戶人. The term *huren* means household head, and is frequently seen in other excavated Qin and early Han documents. A household head was an adult with children whose status perforce was usually "adult male" or "adult female."[18] When either the household head or the sons held a merit rank, the rank was used in lieu of "adult male" or "minor male," a clear indication that ranks were normally bestowed only on males. Another point to note is that the household registries recorded only hamlet names (e.g., Nanyang), merit ranks (e.g., Jing *bugeng, bugeng, shangzao,* etc.), household heads, surnames and given names, taxation and service status (e.g., *wu* squad leader, adult female, or minor female), and kinship (e.g., wife, son, brother, mother, or male or female slave). Completely absent are age, height, complexion and appearance, and property. During the Qin there should have been separate registries for recording fields, dwellings, or other property.[19]

It is especially worth noting that the term "squad leader" appears in the household registries, confirming that from Lord Xian of Qin (r. 384–362) on, commoners were indeed organized into five family units or squads (*Shiji* 6: 289). Nonetheless, the Liye documents can only confirm that the residents within the city wall were so organized. Further evidence will be required to determine whether communities outside the city wall were grouped into squads as well, and whether other groupings, such as units of ten (*shi* 什) might also have existed. Each squad had a leader. Acting as squad leader was probably an obligation of the populace and thus should be viewed as one form of levy status.[20]

Another question raised by the Liye slips is the meaning of the terms "Jing *bugeng*" 荆不更 and "Jing *dafu*" 荆大夫. *Bugeng* and *dafu*, of course, were merit ranks bestowed on people for a variety of reasons and carried with them privileges, such as tax or conscript service reductions (Loewe 1960; Loewe 2010). The *Liye Excavation Report* says that "Jing" refers to the state of Chu 楚. Furthermore, it states: "*Bugeng* was the fourth level of the Qin ranks. The compound term 'Jing *bugeng*' may indicate that following Qin's conquest of Chu, when the people of Chu were registered, their original ranks were recorded, rather than indicating the Qin rank *bugeng* in the Chu region. Later in the text, the terms *xiaoshangzao* 小上造and 'Jing *dafu*' on slip 17 may also be Chu ranks" (*Liye* 2007: 208). I believe, however, that following the Qin conquest of the Chu state, only Qin ranks would have been recorded in the household registries. In order to win over the support of the Chu populace, Qin guaranteed the privileges held by those who submitted. Rather than eliminating the ranks they already held, it registered them anew using Qin equivalents. If one says, as does the excavation report, that "the Chu populace was registered based on their original ranks," this creates the misunderstanding that *bugeng*, *dafu* and *shangzao* were also Chu ranks. In fact, these terms denote Qin merit ranks. To indicate that the registrant was originally from Chu, the word "Jing" was added as a prefix to his rank.[21]

Also striking is a case in which all the minor sons in a single household held the rank of *xiaoshangzao* (minor second merit rank). This situation differs strikingly from the regulation in the "Statutes on the Appointment of Heirs" 置後律 from the Zhangjiashan *Statutes and Ordinances of the Second Year*, according to which only one son could inherit a merit rank, albeit with a demotion of two ranks. Moreover, the *Statutes and Ordinances of the Second Year* mandate that "sons of those who hold the ranks from *bugeng* to *shangzao* (i.e., ranks 2–4) shall be made *gongzu* 公卒."[22] But what we see in the Liye documents is quite different. The household heads mostly held the fourth rank of *bugeng*, and the sons—minor second rank, *xiaoshangzao*. We can conclude, then, that the system of ranks must have gone through several changes between the Qin and the early Han of the *Statutes and Ordinances of the Second Year*. *Xiaoshangzao* may have been one of the minor merit ranks (*xiaojue* 小爵) mentioned in the *Statutes and Ordinances of the Second Year*, that is ranks granted to minors or those who were unregistered.[23] This may have been one way for Qin to gain the acquiescence of residents in the conquered Chu region: all males were granted ranks, regardless of whether they had earned merit as military men or whether they were registered for corvée and military services. Yet we cannot exclude another possibility: namely, that the Chu rank system was different from that of the Qin and that under Chu *all* minor sons held rank, which they were allowed to keep after submitting to Qin.[24]

According to the *Historical Records*, in the ninth month of the sixteenth year (231 BCE) of King Zheng of Qin "for the first time males were ordered to register their ages" (*Shiji* 6: 232). If this order applied to the entire empire and was thoroughly enforced, does it mean the Liye registries, which do not include the ages, were compiled prior to the order? If this were the case, these documents—written in clerical script *li shu*—would prove once again that this script was already in common use before the empire's unification in 221 BCE. If not, then orders of the Qin government must not necessarily have reached all the way down to the local level.

Another striking feature of the Liye documents is that brothers might marry and have wives and children and yet not be separately registered (see slips K43, K2/23, and K5). But, as is well known, the reforms that Shang Yang carried out in Qin in 356 ordered: "If a commoner family has two or more sons but fails to establish a separate household, its taxes are to be doubled" (*Shiji* 68: 2230). Are these household registries an indication that many families preferred having their taxes doubled to dividing their households? Or, should we perhaps rethink our understanding of Shang Yang's order? Might there have been merely a failure of the order to extend to distant small frontier towns such as Qianling? The matter will require further study.

Moreover, the information about *chen* 臣 was also recorded in the household registries (e.g., slips K27 and K2/23). If the term *chen* is understood to refer to slaves or bound servants (i.e., servants who cannot freely leave their master), as is generally the case, this would be proof that the household registers recorded servants as well (cf. Yates, chapter 6, this volume). This would resolve the long-running debate over whether servants were registered as household members.[25] One slip (K30/45) registers a *qie* 妾. Depending on the context, this term can refer to either a concubine or a servant. In this case, the term appears in the second column under the mother. Accordingly, here *qie* should mean a concubine as in *qiqie* 妻妾 and not a female servant as in *chenqie* 臣妾 (for a different view, see Yates, chapter 6, this volume). In some intact slips, the entire household—including servants—could range from five to eleven members. This recalls a question in the Shuihudi *Questions and Answers concerning the Qin Statutes* 法律答問, which mentions households of five members and ten members. Apparently the questions in the Shuihudi documents fairly accurately reflect the actual situation.

A final point is geographical. All the household heads were from Nanyang. But where was Nanyang? According to the *Liye Excavation Report*, "Nanyang may be the name of a hamlet or of a commandery. Given its association with the Jing region, it is more likely that Nanyang represents the name of a commandery. But why do the household registries of people from Nanyang commandery appear here? This question warrants further investigation" (*Liye* 2007: 208). If we consult the context in other Han documents in which the term "household head" appears, we can be confident that in this case Nanyang was the name of a hamlet.

First, in Qin-Han administrative documents the usual practice was to write the commandery, county, hamlet and, occasionally, canton before the name and rank of the person. There are no examples of the name of the household head written immediately after the commandery. Second, Nanyang was a commonly used place name at the canton and hamlet levels in the Qin-Han times. In Sun Weizu's *Collection of Ancient Seals* there are as many as six seals that read: "Seal of Nanyang canton" (南陽鄉 印; Sun Weizu 1994: 302–303, nos. 1798–1803). One can also find in the Juyan documents an example of Nanyang hamlet.[26] Third, evidence of inscribing the name of the hamlet immediately before a household head can be seen, e.g., in the granary account of a Zheng hamlet household head dating to the early Western Han from Fenghuangshan Tomb 10 (see below). This format recurs in other Han slips which undoubtedly follow an early document format.[27]

EARLY WESTERN HAN CANTON AND HAMLET CENSUS AND TAX/CORVÉE DOCUMENTS FROM FENGHUANGSHAN TOMB 10

In 1973, nine Han tombs were excavated at Fenghuangshan, near Ji'nan-cheng, Jiangling, in Hubei province. Of these, Tombs 8, 9, and 10 yielded more than 400 bamboo slips. Tomb 10 held 170 slips in a bamboo case in a side chamber of the coffin. This tomb also yielded six wooden boards; their content included the inventory of grave goods, the watermen's covenant 服約,[28] and accounts for capitation tax cash *suan qian* 算錢, fodder and so forth.[29] From the content of the grave documents, we know that the occupant was a canton functionary with the rank of *wu dafu* 五大

夫, the ninth grade (Qiu Xigui 1974). Qiu Xigui 裘錫圭 believes that the occupant may have been one Zhang Yan 張偃, who was bailiff or petty official with rank (*youzhi* 有秩) of the Xi 西 canton of Jiangling, the capital of the Linjiang 臨江 princedom at the beginning of the reign of Emperor Jing 景帝 of the Western Han (r. 157–141). One bit of evidence for this is that the tomb surprisingly contained records for poll tax payments during different months for Shiyang, Dangli and Zheng hamlets in the Xi canton (boards 4 and 5, *Jiangling Fenghuang* 2012: 97–102), accounts of field straw and household hay levied on Ping and Gaoshang hamlets (board 6, numbered as 5 in *Jiangling Fenghuang* 2012: 103), records of tax grain for Shiyang hamlet (slip 7, or 6 in *Jiangling Fenghuang* 2012: 104–105), records of corvée performed by each household in Shiyang hamlet, records of grain lent to each household in Zheng hamlet, and so on. This fits closely with the description given in the "Treatise on the Bureaucracy" of the *History of the Later Han* (*Hou Hanshu* 118: 3624) of the types of records that should fall within the purview of the bailiffs and petty officials with rank. Concerning the capitation tax, the front and back of board 4 includes the following records:

市陽二月百一十二算二 卅五錢三千九百廿正偃付西鄉偃佐纏吏奉卩 受正忠(?)二百卅八

Shiyang, 2nd month, 112 capitations, each capitation 35, 3920 [cash in total]; the [canton] head Yan pays the salaries to Yan's assistant in Xi canton, Chan. 卩* Giving the chief Zhong (?) 248 [cash].

[* The 卩 symbol, here and below, was a check mark used to indicate verification of the operation recorded.]

市陽二月百一十二算二 十錢千一百廿正偃付西鄉佐賜 口錢 卩

Shiyang, 2nd month, 112 capitations, each capitation 10, 1120 [cash in total]; the head Yan pays to Yan's assistant in Xi canton, Ci, poll tax 卩

市陽三月百九算二 九錢九百八十一 卩

Shiyang, 3rd month, 109 capitations, each capitation 9 cash, 981 [cash in total] 卩 . . .

市陽四月百九算二 八錢八百七十二. . .

Shiyang, 4th month, 109 capitations, each capitation 8 cash, 872 [cash in total] . . .

市陽五月百九算二 九錢九百八十一. . .

Shiyang, 5th month, 109 capitations, each capitation 9 cash, 981 [cash in total] . . .

市陽五月百九算二廿六錢二千八百卅四 . . .

Shiyang, 5th month, 109 capitations, each capitation 26 cash, 2,834 [cash in total] . . .

市陽五月百九算二八錢八百七十二 . . .

Shiyang, 5th month, 109 capitations, each capitation 8 cash, 872 [cash in total]

鄭里二月七十二算二卅五錢二千五百廿 . . .

Zheng Hamlet, 2nd month, 72 capitations, each capitation 35 cash, 2,520 [cash in total] . . .

鄭里二月七十二算二八錢五百七十六 . . .

Zheng Hamlet, 2nd month, 72 capitations, each capitation 8 cash, 576 [cash in total] . . .

鄭里二月七十二算二十錢七百廿 . . .

Zheng Hamlet, 2nd month, 72 capitations, each capitation 10 cash, 720 [cash in total] . . .

On the front side of the wooden plate 5, the expenses of poll tax money read as follows.

當利正月定算百一十五

Dangli, the first month, the fixed tax units are 115.

正月算卅二給轉費 尸

The first month, tax units of 42 are for paying freight charges. 尸

正月算十四吏奉 尸

The first month, tax units of 14 are for salaries for functionaries. 尸

正月算十三吏奉 尸

The first month, tax units of 13 are for salaries for functionaries. 尸

正月算囗傳送 尸

The first month, tax units of [. . .] for submitting to a higher authority. 尸

We shall address in the next section the significance of those tax and corvée accounts from Xi Canton, Jiangling, that are related to individual household taxes and corvée, but there are some other records as well.

One type that has not been previously seen among excavated materials is the "Zheng Hamlet Granary Account Books" (鄭里稟(廩)簿). That is the original title found on the bamboo slips, which record, for twenty-five Zheng hamlet households, the total amounts of seed grain loaned to each household, the name of the head of household, the number of those able to cultivate, the number of household members, the number of *mu* 畝 of fields, and the amounts of loaned grain, followed by a sign 卩 that indicates it was distributed (*Jiangling Fenghuang* 2012: 106–112; see table 4.1). Scholars early on determined, based on the ratio of amount of grain to field size, that it was surely seed grain that was being loaned in the amount of one *dou* 斗 (= 1996.875 cc) of grain per *mu* (= 480 m²). This possibly corroborates received textual records of Han central and local government officials continually lending the populace grain for food and for seed.[30]

More important, however, is what this record reveals about household numbers and demographic structure of an early Western Han hamlet. Although we cannot be certain that the twenty-five households of Zheng hamlet constitute the total for the hamlet, the number should not be too far off. From the figures quoted above for the poll tax cash receipts for the three hamlets, poll tax of 72 cash was paid in Zheng, 112 or 109 cash in Shiyang, and 115 cash in Dangli. If we apply the household/tax ratio for Zheng to the other two hamlets, then Shiyang ought to have had thirty-eight or thirty-nine households and Dangli, about forty households. This scale is close to that of the forty households per hamlet for the five new hamlets for the poor established in Chang'an 長安 by Wang Mang 王莽 (*Hanshu* 12: 353; Dubs 1938/55 III: 74). The assumption in making this calculation is that the demographic composition of each household in these hamlets was roughly the same. Data for each household are tabulated below.

In this case, the term *neng tian* "able to cultivate" must refer to those physically able to work the fields. As such, it should include the *shinan* 使男 and *shinü* 使女, *danan*, and *danü* often seen in the Juyan and Dunhuang slips; it probably indicates able-bodied males and females, from age seven up but not yet "elderly" 老. A household might include able-bodied males and females, as well as the elderly and children too small to farm. Each household in Zheng hamlet on average comprised four to five persons, of whom three or so were "able to cultivate." This demographic composition is in line with the numbers of household members found in the Qin household registers from Liye, the late Western Han collected accounts

TABLE 4.1 Statistical Chart Based on the "Zheng Hamlet Granary Account Books"

Head of household 戶人	Number of "able to cultivate" 能田人數	Household size 口數	Mu of fields 田畝數	Amount of grain lent in dan 貸糧數(石)
Sheng 聖	1	1	8	0.8
X [才 + 得]	1	3	10	1
Jiniu 擊牛	2	4	12	1.2
Ye 野	4	8	15	1.5
Yanye 厭冶	2	2	18	1.8
X □	2	3	20	2
Li 立	2	6	23	2.3
Yueren 越人	3	6	30	3
Buzhang 不章	4	7	30	3.7
Sheng 勝	3	5	54	5.4
Lu 虜	2	4	20	2
X [禾 + 貴]	2	6	20	2
Xiaonu 小奴	2	3	30	3
Tuo 佗 (?)	3	4	20	2
Dingmin 定民 (?)	4	4	30	3
Qingjian 青肩	3	6	27	2.7
X + nu □奴	4	7	23	2.3
X + nu □奴	3	□ (3–6) ※*	40	4
XX □□	4	6	33	3.3
Gongshi Tian 公士田	3	6	21	2.1
Pian 駢	4	5	30	missing
Zhushi 朱市	3	4	30	missing
X + nu □奴	3	3	14(?)	missing
XX □□	2	3	20	missing
Gongshi Shiren 公士市人	3	4	32	missing
TOTAL 總計	69	112–115	[617]	61.7 (Original total)
Average fields per household			24.68	
Average household size	2.76	4.48–4.60		

*※ = the number is missing in the original; 3-6 persons is based on an estimate.

from Yinwan, the household registries from the Wu 吳 state of the Three Kingdoms period (220–280 CE) found at Zoumalou 走馬樓, the Han household numbers in records discovered at Juyan and Dunhuang, and with the standard "family of five" *wukou zhi jia* 五口之家 referred to in received texts (cf. Lewis 2006: 89–93). This once again affirms the high degree of reliability of the empire-wide population figures recorded for the end of the Western Han in the "Treatise on Geography" of the *History of the Former Han*.[31] They also confirm that the family comprising a father and mother and three minor children was the principal form of the family household from the Qin to the Three Kingdoms period. During these several hundred years, the "great lineage" *dazu* 大族 or "magnate lineage" *haozu* 豪族 must have been formed by rather large groups of such nuclear families of the same clan 姓 living together, to share political and economic advantage.

HAN HOUSEHOLD AND CAPITATION TAX RECORDS FROM TOMB 19, TIANCHANG

In 2004 a vertical earthen pit tomb dating from the early part of the mid-Western Han was discovered at Jizhuang 紀莊 Village, Anle Town 安樂鎮, Tianchang City, Anhui. The funerary goods found in the tomb were rather rich; they included eight pieces of pottery, eight bronze items, seven iron pieces, forty-seven pieces of lacquerware, and forty-nine wooden pieces. Indications of the status of the tomb occupant include an iron sword and an iron knife found on either side of the skeleton. In a burial chest containing funerary objects placed at the head of the casket were piled wooden boards, a lacquer inkstone container, and lacquerware and wooden boards containing the name Xie Meng 謝孟. The most important finds among the wooden boards were Western Han capitation and household records for Dongyang County 東陽縣, Linhuai Commandery 臨淮郡. These unquestionably attest to Xie Meng's position as being a first-rank county local official similar to Shi Rao, clerk of the Bureau of Merit of Donghai Commandery (see below). The reason for concluding that Xie Meng was a first rank county official is that the household and capitation records that were found buried with him clearly cover only the cantons of a single county.

The household and capitation accounts are written on opposite sides of the same wooden board. Since it is not long, the full text is given here (Tianchang 2006):

戶口簿

•戶凡九千一百六十九少前　鄉[32]

口四萬九百七十少前

南[33] 鄉戶千七百八十三口七千七百九十五

都鄉戶二千三百九十八口萬八百一十九

楊池鄉戶千四百五十一口六千三百廿八

挶[34]鄉戶八百八十口四千五

垣雍北鄉戶千三百七十五口六千三百五十四

垣雍南[35]鄉戶千二百八十二口五千六百六十九

HOUSEHOLD RECORD

•Households total 9169. Less than previously.　Qing

Population 40,970. Less than previously.

Nan Canton: 1783 households, 7795 persons

Du (Metropolitan) Canton: 2398 households, 10,819 persons.

Yangchi Canton: 1451 households, 6328 persons.

Ju Canton: 880 households, 4005 persons.

Yuanyong North Canton: 1375 households, 6354 persons.

Yuanyong South Canton: 1282 households, 5669 persons

算簿

集八月事算二萬九復算二千卌五

都鄉八月事算五千卌五

南鄉八月事算三千六百八十九

垣雍北鄉[36]八月事算三千二百八十五

垣雍南[37]鄉八月事算二千九百卅一

挶鄉八月事算千八百九十

楊池鄉八月事算三千一百六十九

•　右八月

•　集九月事算萬九千九百八十八復算二千六十五[38]

CAPITATION RECORD

Assembled 8th Month: Service capitation 20,009; exempt capitation 2045

Du Canton 8th month service capitation 5045

Nan Canton 8th month service capitation 3689

Yuanyong North 8th month service capitation 3285

Yuanyong South 8th month service capitation 2931

Ju Canton 8th month service capitation 1890

Yangchi 8th month service capitation

- Above Eighth Month
- Assembled 9th Month: Service capitation 19,988; exempt capitation 2615

According to the "Treatise on Geography" of the *History of the Former Han*, Emperor Wu in 117 established Linhuai Commandery, comprising twenty-nine counties, of which Dongyang was one. At the end of the Western Han, the commandery had a population of 268,283 households and 1,237,764 persons (*Hanshu* 28A: 1589). The averages would have been 9,251 households per county, and 4.61 persons per household. According to table 4.2, Dongyang County had six cantons ranging from 800 plus households to upwards of 2,000 households, with an average of 1,500-plus households per canton. The entire county comprised 9,169 households for an average of 4.46 persons per household. These figures are very close to the county and household averages in the "Treatise on Geography." As with the later Western Han materials from Donghai Commandery excavated at Yinwan (see below), these records are evidence of the relative accuracy of the population data in the "Treatise on Geography." Comparing the averages for the *shi suan* service capitation to household averages, we know they refer to household members who were required to perform the corvée service from which the elderly and very young were exempt. That is, they are the *shinan* and *shinü*, or *dingnan* 丁 男 and *dingnü* 丁女, referred to in the records.

Since the population and capitation records are written on the two faces of the same board, their content is probably related. If we take the two together, we have for each canton the totals for the census and for the service capitation. This presents us with excellent material to advance our discussion of the debate over the significance of "service" and "capitation" that has been engendered by the capitation cash slips unearthed from Tomb 10 at Fenghuangshan and the Three Kingdoms–period Wu slips from Zoumalou.

First, the recording of individual amounts of service *shi* and capitation *suan* for each person in a household in the Wu slips is a continuation of the Han system. But while there is an intrinsic nexus to the service and the levy in the earlier records, the substantive content differs somewhat. In the case of the Wu documents, each person's service and capitation are

TABLE 4.2 Household and Tax Data for Each Canton, Dongyang
County, Linhuai Commandery

Canton	Households 戶數	Persons 口數	Persons/ Household 一戶平均口數	8th month service 八月事算	9th month service 九月事算	Avg. service capitation/ household 一戶平均事算數
Nan 南	1,783	7,795	4.37	3,689		2.06
Du 都	2,398	819	4.51	5,045		2.10
Yangchi 楊池	1,451	6,328	4.36	3,169		2.18
Ju 掬	880	4,005	4.55	1,890		2.14
Yuanyong N 垣雍北	1,375	354	4.62	3,285		2.38
Yuanyong S 垣雍南	1,282	5,669	4.42	2,931		2.28
TOTAL 總計	9,169 少前 less than before	40,970 少前 less than before	4.46	20,009 復算 2,045 exempted	19,988 復算 2,065 exempted	2.18

separately recorded. Service refers to corvée, and capitation refers to the poll tax.[39] In contrast, in the Dongyang capitation records, the service and poll tax are combined and recorded together as a single number. In such a case, there must have been some convertibility between the service and the tax that would have permitted them to be combined into a single amount and recorded.

Second, if we compare the poll tax cash amounts on the slips from Fenghuangshan Tomb 10, the capitation accounts from Dongyang County, and the capitation mentioned in the received texts, it is possible to determine that *suan* can either refer to the poll tax and other types of taxes,[40] or it can be a unit of calculation for government levies. It does not indicate a fixed amount of cash.[41] For example, in the *History of the Former Han*, "Annals of Emperor Hui," we find, "Unmarried women aged 15 to 30, five capitations *suan*" (*Hanshu* 2: 91; Dubs 1938/55 I: 183–84). In this case, "five capitations" means that an unmarried woman is levied five times the amount of other individuals, who pay one capitation. As for the how much cash constituted one *suan*, the amount could vary in different periods. The comment by Ying Shao 應劭 (c. 140–206 CE) on the cited passage quotes the Han Statutes (Han lü 漢律): "A person pays one *suan*; a *suan* is 120 cash. Merchants and slaves pay two times" (*Hanshu* 2: 91; Dubs 1938/55 I: 184n1). The Tang commentator Li Xian 李賢 (654–684 CE) cites the *Glosses on Han Protocols* (Han yizhu 漢儀注) as saying one *suan* is 120 cash (*Hou Hanshu* 1B: 74). Both texts clearly state that the amount of the *suan* was fixed at 120 cash, which means that they refer to the period, probably after Emperor Wu's reign, when this amount had been fixed.[42] It differs from the *suan* seen on the Fenghuangshan board which referred to amounts of cash that varied monthly from eight to nine, ten, twenty-six, thirty-five, thirty-six, and so on.[43]

Third, concerning the significance of *shi*, others have already pointed out this term refers to conscript service. Among the Han slips found at Juyan were numerous travel permits—passport 傳 or transit tallies 過所 (Loewe 1967: 205n1)—on which the canton bailiff or petty official with rank had to certify that the bearer "is not subject to imprisonment or to service levy" *zheng shi* 徵事, before he was permitted through the control barriers at passes and fords. The "service levy" meant the corvée levy. Before a permit could be issued, a person had to prove that he did not owe corvée or taxes and that he had not been sentenced for a crime for which he was awaiting punishment. If the bearer were identified as "non-service" 不事, that meant he enjoyed the privilege of exemption from corvée. This is already very clear from received texts and requires no further comment. The problem is the linking of *shi* to *suan* and the combining of their totals; *shi* and *suan* could only have been convertible if the accounting units of the two were the same. That is, if one *suan* were 120 cash, then one *shi* must have had a cash value. Only then would it have been possible for *suan* and *shi* to have been combined into a single amount in the *suan* records.

From Ru Chun's (如淳, 3rd c. CE) commentaries on the *History of the Former Han* we know that during the Han dynasty a system existed through which a conscript could hire for a fixed amount of money a substitute to perform frontier service in his stead; the same source tells of a "transferred rotation" 過更 money paid to the government instead of annual frontier garrison service (*Hanshu* 8: 230; Dubs 1938/55 II: 170, nn8.7–9, 176–177). Epigraphic evidence, such as the Zhangjiashan "Record of Submitted Doubtful Cases" 奏讞書 indicate that such practice might have begun already at the early years of the Han dynasty or even under the Qin (*Zhangjiashan* 2001: 221–222). Thus, capitation accounts, *shi*, could be converted to *suan* with cash. In the capitation account of the

Dongyang County, amounts in the 1000's or 100's recorded for the *shi* or *suan* of each canton undoubtedly used cash as the unit for the total.

Limitations of space prevent me from discussing in detail the possible dating of the Dongyang County capitation accounts, but it should be noticed here that I disagree with the dating proposed in the archaeological report according to which the documents come from the time of Emperor Wu. The rate of annual service capitation as reflected in these documents is in the range of 27–30 cash, which is much lower than the levels of Emperor Wu's time; it may well reflect the general relaxation of taxation burden in the last decades of the Western Han, in the aftermath of the wars with the Xiongnu.[44] Nor will I explore here differences between the Tianchang records and those from the Zoumalou documents from the state of Wu, which suggest that by the time of the Three Kingdoms it was no longer possible to convert service to *suan*, and *suan* and *shi* had to be recorded separately. Suffice it to mention that the discovery of materials related to canton and hamlet census, tax, and conscript service allows us to understand fully the operation of these levies.

Moving from the hamlet and canton levels to the county and commandery, there has been new light shed by the materials from the early part of Emperor Wu's reign discovered from the tomb of a petty functionary from Nan 南 Commandery, Zhou Yan 周偃 (Jingzhou Bowuguan 2008), and the collection registries on wooden boards recovered from the tomb of Shi Rao, clerk in the Bureau of Merit of Donghai Commandery that come from the last years of the Western Han (*Yinwan* 1997). We shall move now to these materials.

COUNTY RECORDS FROM THE REIGN OF EMPEROR WU FROM TOMB I AT SONGBOCUN

In 2004 a cluster of ancient tombs were found in Songbocun Village 松柏村 near modern Ji'nan Town in Jingzhou City, Hubei Province (Jingzhou Bowuguan 2008). Four tombs were surveyed, and from Tomb M1 archaeologists unearthed sixty-three wooden boards and ten wooden slips. Boards ranged from 22.7 cm to 23.3 cm in length and 2.7 cm to 6.5 cm in width, and were 0.2 cm thick. Six boards were blank, thirty-one had writing on one side only, twenty-six, on both sides. Based on their position in the tomb, they most likely had been bound together according to document category. After a preliminary analysis, scholars organized the boards into the following categories: (1) inventory of grave goods 遣書; (2) miscellaneous registries from the Nan Commandery, the Xi canton of

Jiangling, and other places, including household registries, records from
Zheng 正 hamlet, registries of exempted elders 免老簿, records of the
newly registered 新傅簿, registries of exempted disabled population 罷癃
簿, registries of the submitted non-Chinese population 歸義簿, records of
service and tax exemptions 復事算簿, rosters of current soldiers 見卒簿,
and records of authorized positions of functionaries and soldiers 置吏卒
簿; (3) the *die* 牒 document, chronicling reigns from King Zhaoxiang 昭襄
of the Qin to the seventh year of Emperor Wu of the Han; (4) ordinances,
primarily statutes and ordinances promulgated under Emperor Wen; (5)
almanacs, primarily from Emperor Wu's reign; (6) a record of Zhou Yan's
merits and service; and (7) copies of documents pertaining to Zhou Yan's
appointments and promotions during the reigns of Emperors Jing and
Wu. Although the contents are rich, unfortunately the only published
transcription and photos in the 2008 report were of board 35 and a single
slip (for later publications, see, e.g., Peng Hao 2009a; Yuan Yansheng
2009; Yang Zhenhong 2010 [q.v. for further references]).

Based on the recovered texts, the excavation summary report speculates that the tomb occupant must have been a petty official with rank
or a bailiff in Xi canton, Jiangling, whose name was Zhou Yan. If the
tomb occupant was indeed a canton bailiff, his status was the same as the
occupant of Fenghuangshan Tomb 10. All the texts unearthed there concern the population and taxation of a canton. Why, then, did bailiff Zhou
Yan's tomb also contain Nan Commandery-level records for the exempted
elderly, exempted disabled, and newly registered population? As the bulk
of the material has yet to be published, for the present we shall have to
set this question aside and focus on the content of the wooden board 35.

The most obvious characteristic of the board 35 is that on one side of
the board, the surface is divided horizontally into four columns, written
from right to left; the top two columns are a record of exempted elders,
and the lower two columns, a record of newly registered population. On
the other side is a registry of exempted disabled in the same format. In
other words, three different categories of record for Nan Commandery
are inscribed on the two faces of a single board. The three records follow
the same sequence in listing the numbers for twelve counties, one march
道 (a county-level jurisdiction for alien tribesmen), and four marquisates.
Examination of the records raises some questions. First, why is there the
discrepancy between the established counties, march, and marquisates in
the Nan Commandery listed in this text and those found in the "Treatise
on Geography" in the *History of the Former Han?* Second, are the correla-
tions among the numbers of exempted elderly, exempted disabled, and

newly registered population and what they can tell us about phenomena related to the population age structure? The third question concerns the real nature of this wooden board. Was it an official document belonging to the tomb occupant during life? Or was it a funerary object made specifically for burial?

Let us begin with the third question, since clarifying the nature of the board will facilitate discussion of its contents. First, as noted already, this board is not itself an official registry. Rather, for whatever reason, three different kinds of registry were copied onto the two sides of this board. This was also the case with the household and taxation registries of the Tianchang document discussed earlier. It is also similar to the Yinwan "Collected Registries" 集簿 and the "Yongshi Year 4 Armory Collected Inventory of Chariots and Weaponry" 永始四年武庫兵車器 集簿 for the Donghai Commandery discussed below. The difference is that the Yinwan records are inscribed on separate boards; there are no cases of three registries copied onto a single board. But whether the registries are written on the same or different boards, finding boards of a similar nature coincidentally in tombs of different regions is enough to reflect a popular burial custom during the Qin–Western Han period. Official documents or maps, such as the Fangmatan 放馬灘 Tomb 1 maps on boards and paper, and the silk maps of the south of the Changsha princedom from Mawangdui Tomb 3, related to a local official's position were reproduced as funerary goods and placed in the tomb along with the grave-goods inventory (Hsing 2007a). These funerary objects were meant to demonstrate to those overseeing the underworld (the Lord of Mount Tai 泰山 or other imagined rulers of the nether world) that the tomb occupant used to be the master of someplace—a village, canton, county, or commandery—and in charge of its land and people. The hope was that in the underworld they would be able to continue in a position of authority or even rise higher (cf. Poo, chapter 5, this volume).

Increasingly I am persuaded that the fundamental nature of these objects is that they are funerary objects rather than being records or original official documents used by the tomb occupant in life. Still, although they may be funerary objects, their content is not as formulaic as the deeds for tomb lands (*diquan* 地券) unearthed from tombs of the Wei-Jin 魏晉 (220–420 CE) and later periods. In the texts seen thus far, except for similarity of document categories, there is no evidence of repeating content or following a particular template. They are more likely duplicates or excerpts of real official documents used during the tomb occupant's lifetime. The content includes local household and taxation registries, statutes and ordinances, almanacs, daybooks, the "chronicle of important events" 大事記 of the individual, or classical texts, and so forth. I assume that all excavated bamboo, wooden, and silk documents from Western Han or even Qin tombs are funerary objects in nature. Because funerary objects were intended to be symbolic and not intended for use, they cannot avoid revealing their impracticability. For instance, hundreds of slips were tied together as one book with no regard to ease of use (e.g., the daybooks from the Kongjiapo 孔家坡 site in Suizhou 隨州 City, see Suizhou Kongjiapo 2006). Moreover, there are errors and missing graphs in the documents that were not corrected, as would have been done had the documents been in use (Hsing 2007b).

If this interpretation of the essential nature of the recovered documents is correct, we can presume that most buried texts were made after the tomb occupant's death in the course of the burial preparations.[45] Unless the deceased had prepared the documents beforehand or had left a will (called a *xianling* 先令 in Han times), it would naturally have been impossible for the tomb occupant himself to have selected or copied the documents. Family members or those arranging the funeral must have chosen the texts according to prevailing custom. This would explain why so many documents of similar type have been unearthed from the tombs of Qin or Western Han local officials.

How were documents selected? We have no way of knowing, but I would suggest three possibilities: (1) Select and reproduce materials the tomb occupant handled while alive. (2) Select and reproduce documents used by the tomb occupant at the peak of his government career. Officials could neither control promotions nor avoid demotions; thus, their last position held before death might not represent the peak of their career. (3) Choose for reproduction records that best manifested the tomb occupant's professional achievements. For example, if his evaluation in a particular year was "outstanding" 最, the household and taxation registries for this year would be selected to be buried with the tomb occupant. Given all these various possibilities, one should not simply assume that such documents date from the death or the burial of the tomb occupant, although they ought not be too far apart.

In light of these possibilities, there are three points about the records of exempted elderly, exempted disabled, and newly registered population on board 35 worth noting: First, while the tomb occupant may have been a bailiff of Xi canton, as the excavation summary report suggests, this should not be thought to be necessarily the highest position he reached. Otherwise it is difficult to explain why copies of records for the whole of Nan Commandery were found in his tomb. The excavation summary report mentions that a record of the tomb occupant's promotions and achievements was also among the unearthed documents. Once this text is published, it should greatly help us understand the tomb occupant's status.[46]

Second, the boards may have been the records of which the tomb occupant and his family were the most proud and not necessarily his final records. The reason for this supposition is the board numbers for those who "can serve" (*keshi* 可事) and for "exempted disabled" (*pilong* 罷 癃). These numbers, presented in table 4.3 below, remind us of the Han fashion to employ severe officials who "regarded laws and ordinances as *Poems* and *Documents*" 以法律為詩書 (*Hanshu* 77: 3247). These so-called capable officials did not promote the reduction of tax burdens but considered severity to be a sign of competence. Wang Mang criticized the Han for claiming to reduce the land tax to only one-thirtieth while in reality "constantly there were conscript service and taxes; even the infirm all paid" (*Hanshu* 24: 1143, 99B: 4111). In the counties, marches, and marquisates in Nan Commandery, 2,708 persons were categorized as infirm *pilong*, meaning those who were exempted from taxation because of congenital disability (Yu Haoliang 1985: 138–139). The tomb occupant Zhou Yan carefully investigated and then identified only 480 among the more than 2,700 persons who were genuinely "unable to serve" (*bukeshi* 不可事). This means that as many as 2,228 persons were determined to be capable of performing service! In other words, he added more than 2,000 persons to the labor force for the state and greatly reduced the number exempt from corvée. This board further supports Wang Mang's criticism, although from the point of view of the Han court this was undoubtedly a competent and praiseworthy official. The tomb occupant and his family were quite possibly very proud of this.[47]

Third, looking at the figures in table 4.3, it is easy to spot errors in the totals for the exempt elderly and the newly registered among the five categories of figures. The graphs written in ink on the original board are clearly legible; all the numbers are distinguishable and there is no misinterpretation. Although such errors might have come from the original official documents, we cannot exclude the possibility they were copyist errors. Indeed, the likelihood that they are dittographic errors is rather greater. But since these were copied to be buried with the deceased, there was comparatively less concern about mistakes, and they were not necessarily corrected.

Regardless of the accuracy of the figures, the three types of record on

TABLE 4.3 Data from Board 35 from Western Han Tomb at Songbocun, Ji'nan, Jingzhou

	Counties, Circuit, and Marquisates	Population				
		Exempted Elderly	Newly Registered	Exempted Disabled	Able to Serve	Unable to Serve
1	巫 Wu	278	203	116	74	(42)
2	秭歸 Zigui	246	261	160	133	(27)
3	夷道 Yi March	66	37	48	40	(8)
4	夷陵 Yiling	42	45	22	17	(5)
5	醴陽 Liyang	61	25	26	15	(11)
6	孱陵 Chanling	97	26	76	62	(14)
7	州陵 Zhouling	74	15	61	48	(13)
8	沙羨 Shaxian	92	50	51	40	(11)
9	安陸 Anlu	67	19	28	24	(4)
10	宜成 Yicheng	232	546	643	570	(73)
11	臨沮 Linju	331	116	199	134	(65)
12	顯陵 Xianling	20	12	45	40	(5)
13	江陵 Jiangling	538	255	363	316	(47)
14	襄平侯 Xiangping Marquisate at 中廬 Zhonglu	162	78	218	169	(49)
15	邔侯國 Qi Marquisate	267	220	275	223	(52)
16	便侯國 Bian Marquisate	250	123	307	264	(43)
17	軑侯國 Dai Marquisate	138	56	70	59	(11)
	total as in original	2,966	2,085	2,708	2,228	480
	correct total	2,961	2,087	2,708	2,228	480

the board provide firsthand material that allows us to understand population figures for the exempt elderly, newly registered, and infirm from the single jurisdiction of Nan Commandery during the late-middle period of the Western Han. Their value goes without saying. The exempt elderly and the newly registered population were both subject to age limits. If the documents from this tomb—the household registries of the Nan Commandery and Xi Canton—continue to be published, we shall be able to advance our study of the age structure of the population. Important questions remain unanswered regarding the numbers and names of counties, marches, and marquisates in the Nan Commandery: why are there rather significant discrepancies between this document and the geography treatise of *History of the Former Han?*[48] Why is the first listed county Wu and not Jiangling? This may involve an unrecorded redrawing of commandery and princedom boundaries in the mid-to late Western Han. But these questions require separate treatment and for the present will not be addressed.

DEMOGRAPHICS OF THE ELDERLY AND YOUNG: "COLLECTED REGISTRIES" FROM YINWAN, LATE WESTERN HAN

In 1993, a group of Western Han tombs was discovered southwest of Yinwan Village, Lianyungang City, Jiangsu Province. From Tomb 6 were recovered several types of important documents relating to the duties of a functionary of the Bureau of Merit of Donghai Commandery, including a "Collected Registries" 集簿, a "Roster of County and Canton Officials of the Commandery" 郡屬縣鄉吏員定簿, a "Records of Transfers and Postings of Senior Functionaries" 長吏遷除簿, a "Records of Evaluations of Functionaries and Staff" 吏員考績簿, and the "Yongshi Year 4 [13 BCE] Armory Collected Inventory of Chariots and Weaponry." The text that concerns us here is the board entitled "Collected Registries." It not only reflects an important link in the Han institution of the submission of reports to the central government, but for the Western Han it also allows us concretely to see from the hamlet and canton levels upward through the county and commandery a well-ordered system of administrative control.

Based on the "Collected Registries," a commandery-level Bureau of Merit was doubtlessly in charge of collecting statistics on population and taxation for counties, cantons, and hamlets under the commandery's jurisdiction, combining the totals and submitting the figures to the central government. The commandery totals included (1) the number of counties, appanages 邑, marquisates, cantons, and relay stations 亭 under its jurisdiction; (2) county and canton population figures for those holding the ranks of Thrice Venerables 三老, the Filial and Fraternally Respectful 孝悌, and Diligent Farmer 力田; (3) the number of functionaries and staff in the commandery, counties, and marquisates; (4) census figures; (5) figures for the total area of orchards and fields; (6) number of *mu* planted in winter wheat 宿麥; (7) numbers of males and females; (8)

population figures for those aged six and below, aged seventy and above, eighty and above, and ninety and above; (9) the number of trees planted in the spring; (10) the number of households formed in the spring; (11) annual cash receipts and disbursements; and (12) annual grain receipts and disbursements. The information in the Collected Registries about household registration, farming, cash and grain is far more detailed than that recorded in the received texts. Rather than taking them one by one, here I shall offer some thoughts concerning the male/female population ratio and ages in a single commandery.

The "Collected Registries" contain population statistics from the Donghai Commandery; an excerpt is reproduced here:

> Households: 266,290; 2629 more than before; of households, 11,662 recovered refugees[49]
>
> Population is 1,397,343; of [?] 42,752 recovered refugees
>
> Age 80 and above, 33,871; age 6 and below, 262,588; total 296,459
>
> Age 90 and above, 11,670; age 70 and above who are granted staffs, 2,823; total is 14,493; 718 more than before

A general principle of population age structure is the higher the age, the smaller the number of persons. Given ancient conditions of hygiene, nutrition, medicine, and reproduction for common people, to live into one's 80s or 90s must not have been easy and those who did must have been few.[50] In the Donghai Commandery, however, 2.42 percent of the total population were aged 80 and above, and 0.83 percent aged 90 and above. When this ratio is compared with modern population age structures (e.g., Mainland China in 1953 and 1990; Taiwan in 1999), the figures seem unusually skewed (Gao Dalun 1998; Hsing 2002: 541–547). Take the case of Taiwan in 1999 for example: only 0.11 percent of the entire population was in their 90s, and 1.15 percent in their 80s. Accordingly, the percentage of people aged 90 and above in the Donghai Commandery during the Han would have been seven times and that for those aged 80 and above two times that of modern Taiwan. Obviously the records in the Collected Registries of the Donghai Commandery are problematic.

If one were to object that Han and modern societies are too different for comparison, we can refer to the population age structure of the early Qing, which was also an agrarian society. Research indicates the population age structure of traditional Chinese villages tends to be stable, so there should not be much difference between Western Han and Qing villages. One study has concluded that in early Qing about 2 percent of the population was aged 70 and above (Liu Cuirong 1998). Thus, the percentage of population aged 80 and above ought to be less than 1 percent. The percentage for elders aged 80 and above in Donghai was as high as 2.42 percent, more than two times that of the early Qing. This is clearly an exaggeration.

Why was this? A plausible explanation is that under certain circumstances Han local officials falsely reported the numbers of elderly and children. According to Han regulations, both the elderly and children were exempted from taxation. The greater the exempted population, the less tax local governments reported and passed on to the central government. During Emperor Wen's reign, one son could be exempted from corvée service if someone in the household were ninety. In the case of someone over eighty, two household members could be exempted from poll taxes. If having an eighty-year old gained the household two poll tax exemptions, a ninety-year old must have earned even more tax exemptions. From the reign of Emperor Yuan, it was further ordained that only commoners seven and above should pay poll taxes; six and below were exempt (see, e.g., Huang Jinyan 1988: 206–218). One way to submit less tax revenue to the central government would be to falsely increase the numbers of elderly and children in the reports. Of course, if found out, such local officials would hardly be evaluated "capable" 能, much less "outstanding" 最.

From an examination of the figures for the elderly let us turn to the figures for those aged six and below in the Collected Registries. The first question is why were children six and below counted and not those seven and below? There is no way to know; we can only guess there might have been a change in the age of poll tax liability sometime between the reign of Emperor Yuan and compilation of the Collected Registries under Emperor Cheng.[51] The Donghai Collected Registries record 262,588 persons under six, which accounts for 18.79 percent of the entire population (1,397,343 persons). In the 1999 census of Taiwan, the population under age 6 was 2,157,536 persons, forming 9.76 percent of the entire population. Infant mortality was much higher in the ancient world, yet the Donghai percentage is twice that of modern Taiwan. Surely this was an inflated report similar to figures for the elderly.[52] Falsely reporting population figures for the elderly and for children was precisely what Emperor Xuan (r. 73–49 BCE) sternly criticized when he said the submitted reports "seek to lie and deceive in order to avoid levies."[53]

A second and perhaps more important reason for falsifying figures is that local officials might have wanted a reputation for benevolent governance. In the Han evaluations of officials, one crucial criterion was the increase or decrease of population. When the numbers of the elderly and of children were high, it meant that local officials had duly encouraged population increase and cared for the elderly, goals proclaimed since Emperor Gaozu.[54] By achieving this goal, local officials could gain a reputation of caring for the aged and children and improve their evaluations. Real benefits and an empty name were both enough to cause distortion of the age statistics.

In sum, the Donghai Collected Registries are an extremely valuable source and contain much that is incontrovertible. For instance, the documents prove that during the Western Han the elderly were in fact granted dove-headed staffs and that this practice probably dates from Emperor Gaozu's time. On the other hand, the population age statistics fly in the face of demographic common sense and their reliability is questionable. Another question worth asking is whether false reporting of the elderly and children occurred at the canton and hamlet levels or only after the reports reached the county or commandery levels. Unfortunately, at this point it is difficult to answer this question with any certainty.

It may be interesting here to speculate about the differences between Zhou Yan's records from Songbocun and Shi Rao's from Yinwan. In the first case, the official was proud to be able to increase the amount of taxpayers by drastically reducing the exemptions; in the second, the official was acting either consciously or due to being duped by his underlings, in a contrary way: his manipulated records were depriving the government of some of its revenues. While the nature of our data precludes systematic comparison, it may be observed that the records seem to indicate a shift from an active and even "aggressive" state, aimed at maximizing its share of resources at the population's expense, to a more lenient one. This observation adds another dimension to the frequently discussed transformation of the Western Han state from the Qin model to a more relaxed one (cf. Bu Xianqun 2009). Further publications of the recently discovered materials that concern the functioning of the Qin and Han governments at the lower social levels would allow us to fine-tune this observation.[55]

CONCLUSION

What conclusions are to be drawn from our discussion of these documents? I think now we can almost be certain that the spatial arrangements of rural communities in the Qin-Han times varied and were not as uniform as portrayed in the received texts. The hamlet 里 described in the received texts, such as "houses and residences ranged next to one another, gates and alleys orderly and straight" 室居櫛比, 門巷修直 (*Sanfu huangtu* 2: 99) probably existed mainly in the capital cities of Chang'an and Luoyang, commandery or county seats, the newly established imperial mausolea towns such as Yangling 陽陵 or Maoling 茂陵 to which wealthy and powerful families and high-ranking officials were relocated, or areas newly settled by displaced persons or agricultural colonists *tun hu* 屯戶 and brought into cultivation either on the frontiers or in internal commanderies. In the Shuihudi documents, the phrase *li men* 里門 (ward gate) appears together with the phrase *yibangmen* 邑邦門 (city gate), indicating that here *li* 里 should be understood as wards in a city (Hulsewé 1985, D140: 166). The *li* frequently mentioned in the Juyan documents inadvertently reveal the *li* structure. But this type of *li* apparently refers to residential areas for those who were cultivating wastelands in the frontiers. The frontier *li* was thus more similar to the well-planned and organized emigrant communities discussed in Chao Cuo's 晁錯 (d. 154) proposal for frontier settlement (*Hanshu* 48: 2286–2289). But even after existing agricultural villages were drawn into the canton and hamlet administrative system, their original residential patterns, which had been shaped by geographical conditions and agricultural requirements, probably remained unchanged. In other words, those communities were not relocated, divided, or combined for administrative convenience or the requirements of uniformity. This leads us to consider the different natures of the urban and rural *li* (ward/hamlet). The urban *li* (wards) were planned and organized in a uniform manner, while the layout and spatial distribution of the rural *li* (hamlets) remained those of agricultural settlements that followed their natural surroundings.

Although these differences did exist, it should be emphasized that since the Springs-and-Autumns and Warring States periods, the rulers of the different states, seeking to gain better control over manpower and material resources, generally tended to extend the canton-hamlet system of the capitals 國 outward into the surrounding countryside 野 (see, e.g., Tian Changwu and Zang Zhifei 1996). By establishing a hierarchical administrative system of counties and commanderies, they ultimately blurred the boundaries between the capital and countryside. This long-term change evolved at different rates according to time and place. During the Qin-Han period, although the hamlets (villages) *li* and cantons were marked on maps of the frontier regions, still they were different from the *li* (wards) found in various levels of cities (imperial capital, commandery and county capitals).

In terms of canton-hamlet administration, the excavated documents firmly attest to the existence of the hierarchical system of submission of reports from the cantons upward to the counties and from the counties to the commanderies. It is no exaggeration to say that the Qin and Han empires would have not existed without such a system for recording population, landholdings, and property ownership in the cantons and hamlets. The content and titles of the unearthed documents reveal a far more nuanced picture than is recorded in the transmitted texts, and they fill many gaps in our knowledge. As such evidence continues to be uncovered, an ever clearer understanding of Qin-Han society is sure to emerge.

Translated by Hsieh Mei-yu and William G. Crowell

5 Religion and Religious Life of the Qin

Poo Mu-chou

While there are strong indications in the archaeological material that suggest the existence of a "Qin culture" (Wang Xueli 1994; Shelach and Pines 2006), there are still some doubts as to the distinctiveness of this "Qin culture" from that of other Central Plains states since the establishment of the Qin state early in the Eastern Zhou period. It seems more appropriate to consider the Qin state and culture (material as well as non-material) as developing within the larger cultural sphere that was dominated by the Shang and Zhou tradition, and amidst continuous interactions with peoples or ethnic groups further to the west and southwest. "Qin culture"—if we still want use this term—should best be seen as a subculture of the Shang-Zhou tradition, with local variations (Falkenhausen 2004, esp. pp. 155–156; Falkenhausen 2006: 204–243; and the introduction to part I of this volume). It is important to remember that political events usually cannot serve as proper indications of cultural development. The establishment of the Qin state therefore can tell us little about the actual character or any change that happened to the culture of the Qin people. Moreover, political boundaries can rarely be regarded as identical to cultural boundaries, especially in an early period when boundaries are but hazy zones of interactions. Instead, larger areas defined by geographical features, environmental conditions, and modes of production may be more tangible physical bases for the development of distinctive cultural phenomena, as the "Treatise on Geography" in the *History of the Former Han Dynasty* (*Hanshu* 28) tried to demonstrate.

A discussion of the "Qin religion" necessarily involves its position in relationship to the religious tradition of the Shang and Zhou. It is by trying to clarify this position that our understanding of "Qin religion" may gain some substance. Moreover, I would like to emphasize that we need to define clearly the use of the term "religion" in the Chinese context. I use the term to refer to those activities and conceptions that have to do with the human search and striving for certain extra-human forces to be involved in human destiny—whether prescribed by these forces or not. When I use the term "popular religion," I refer to those religious activities and conceptions that are not part of the state- or court-sponsored religious activities and rituals. This does not mean, however, that the nature of the popular religion is fundamentally different from the "official religion" (the religious activities engaged in by the court and/or the high officials and social elite) either in its cosmological outlook or in the human–extra human relations that it posits.

We thus begin our inquiry by contemplating the meaning and substance of "religion" in the context of early China. As one way to study past society and people, the investigation of religion gives us the opportunity to try to understand the fears, hopes, and desires of the people we study. Although often we make distinctions between the official and the popular, or the elite and the commoner in religious practice, no religious expressions can be devoid of certain sense of hope and desire for a better life, or fear of punishment, from certain extra-human power(s).

Previous studies have shown that for the Shang period, there existed among the elite class a cosmology that posited a number of cosmic powers (the Thearch/Di 帝, Sun, Moon, Thunder, etc.), nature deities (the River, the Mountain, etc.) and eminent dead (the royal ancestors) that constituted the divine sphere with which people on earth were obliged to interact.[1] People in different situations developed their own ways to make contact with the deities, including offering sacrifices, pronouncing prayers, and performing divinations of different sorts. That the commoners of the Shang period shared essentially the same cosmology as that of the elite can only be assumed based on the tombs of the commoners. If similar burial style indicates similar religious mentality—since burial style inevitably reflects certain understandings, though mostly in a conventional sense, of the fate of the dead and the relationship between the living and the dead, as well as the structure of the cosmos—then we may assume that the religion of the Shang society was rather uniformly structured.[2]

The political transition from Shang to Zhou did not mean a fundamental change of religious mentality, as has been discussed time and again. The often invoked "humanistic turn" of the Zhou religious character or the emergence of the concept of the "Mandate of Heaven" (tian ming 天命), for example, have to be examined against evidence that points to a continuation of the Shang religious framework: divination by oracle bones and yarrow stalks, invoking the Supreme Thearch (Shangdi 上帝)

in the ceremonial bronze inscriptions, and burial customs. As more textual evidence becomes available for the Zhou period, a picture of the religious life of the commoners begins to emerge, which, to a certain extent, reflects what happened during the earlier period (Poo 1998: 41–68).

The ritual revolution of late Western Zhou suggested by Rawson (1999: 433–440) was a change most observable in the styles of ritual bronze vessels (cf. Falkenhausen 2008a, esp. pp. 142–143). Yet it is uncertain what exactly was involved in this "ritual revolution" in the context of religious development. Most probably ritual transformation was related primarily to maintenance of the centralized political order rather than to changes in religious mentality. In a previous study I have suggested that towards the end of Western Zhou the religious scene seems to bifurcate in its development. The appearance of critical thought and writing that can be characterized as "intellectual," was represented by the *Ru* 儒 ("Confucians"), who began to engage in rational discussions of the Mandate of Heaven as well as concerning traditional religious concepts and practices. For the rest of the population, including the commoners and most of the ruling class, sacrificing to the deities, worshipping the ancestors and believing in ghosts and spirits remained widely practiced (Poo 1998: 66–68).

By the time of the Warring States period, Chinese society consisted of basically two camps regarding religious matters. First, there were those who did not hesitate to engage in all kinds of religious activity. They were the traditionalists, the majority of the people who followed the ancient lifestyle—as represented by a number of poems in the *Book of Poems*—and those who found that certain religious claims and concepts were beneficial to the ruling regime. Second, there were those who were more "rationalistic" and critical toward religious beliefs and activities, who felt the need to debate or discuss before making any commitment, religious or otherwise. These were the minority, the "intellectuals," whose ideas we encounter in the classical texts and in some of the newly excavated manuscripts. It is within this framework constructed by textual and archaeological evidence that the present study intends to probe the religious life of the Qin.

OFFICIAL CULT

According to the *Historical Records,* Lord Xiang 襄公 was the first Qin ruler to establish a cult worshipping the White Thearch (Baidi 白帝) in 770 (*Shiji* 14: 532; 28: 1358; see also Zhao, chapter 1, this volume). Sima Qian quotes from the "Qu li" 曲禮 chapter of the *Liji* 禮記, stating that the Son of Heaven should make sacrifice to Heaven and Earth, while the regional lords should make sacrifice to the mountains and rivers within their own borders. Thus he considers Lord Xiang's action an act of usurpation of the Zhou king's religious prerogatives (*Shiji* 15: 685). Clearly for Sima Qian the establishment of an official cult was a political statement, since the system of sacrifice as stated in the *Liji* was one that defined the hierarchical relationship between the Zhou king and his vassals, the regional lords. The goal of the sacrifice, moreover, was overtly political, as the *Zhouli* 周禮 account of the duty of the Grand Minister of Rites (Dazongbo 大宗伯) states: "The Grand Minister of Rites supervises the rituals of the state, overseeing the rites offered to heavenly spirits, human ghosts, and terrestrial divinities. He helps the king establish and protect the state."[3] The implicit assumption that sustains this statement is a correlative cosmology that sees a corresponding structure between the natural world and the human political structure. The sovereign needs to perform the correct ritual so as to place his regime in the proper cosmological position and thus to ensure his legitimacy both in the eyes of humans and the divine powers.

While we need not judge in haste how or when this correlative cosmology was developed or devised, it is clear that it was for the benefit of the ruling Zhou king. Thus it is also clear that when Lord Xiang established the worship of the White Thearch, or the Supreme Thearch, it was an act that attempted to assert his independent political status that put him on a par with the Zhou king. Moreover, such a measure was no doubt an imitation of the Zhou court practice. The willingness to adopt Zhou state ritual also indicates that the Qin were sufficiently familiar with the Zhou cultural logic, and understood clearly the implication of such ritual action. One example in this regard would be the inscription of the bronze bell of Lord Wu of Qin 秦武公 found in 1978 and dated to c. 697, in which the Qin ruler proclaims that "Our ancestors had received the Mandate of Heaven and were given our house and state" (Wang Hui 1990: 13). In terms of ruling ideology, therefore, it is clear that the Qin inherited the Zhou system. On another bronze vessel dated to 576 we find a similar inscription:

> Our august royal ancestors had received the Mandate of Heaven,
> and established our house at the old residence of Yu 禹. Twelve lords
> are now beside the Thearch (帝), reverently accepting the Mandate of
> Heaven and protecting the house of Qin. (Wang Hui 1990: 19)

In other words, the Qin did not have a different religious tradition, at least not in the officially practiced state cults.

That the Qin court ritual basically followed the Zhou example can be illustrated by the "Prayer Jade Tablet of Yin of Qin" 秦駰玉版 (hereafter the *Jade Tablet*) studied by many scholars.[4] In the text, in which a

Qin ruler[5] prays to the spirit of Mount Hua 華山 there is the following paragraph: "After the Zhou dynasty became defunct, its institutions and regulations were lost. I, a humble descendent, wished to serve Heaven and Earth, the Four Directions, the Three Luminaries, the deities of the mountains and rivers, the five domestic sacrifices, and the ancestors, yet could not find the proper method."[6] Whether or not the expression that "the Zhou dynasty became defunct" refers to a historical fact, the general sense of the text is that the Qin ruler wished to follow the Zhou ritual formality in carrying out his duty. The fact that he used animals (pigs, sheep, and cattle) and silk and jade as objects of sacrifice indicates that the ritual was carried out in the Zhou style of ritual paraphernalia. Moreover, the sacrifice directed at Mount Hua can be identified as a *wang* 望 sacrifice, a kind of ritual that was sometimes used to supplicate for the health of the ruler (Liu Zhaorui 2005: 46), and which was also a part of the broad Zhou system, as passages from the *Zuo zhuan* 左傳 demonstrate. For example: "When King Yi 夷王 was sick, regional lords all hurried to perform their *wang* sacrifice to pray for the health of the king." Elsewhere, a Jin 晉 dignitary says: "Our lord has been very sick for three months now. Even though he made sacrifices at the various mountains and rivers (*qunwang* 群望), the illness only aggravates."[7] However, by no means was the function of such sacrifice to the mountains and rivers limited to praying for the health of the ruler. Rather, the *Jade Tablet*, as well as the sayings in the *Zuo zhuan*, indicate that ritual sacrifices to Heaven and Earth and to terrestrial deities were effective for all purposes: they could be performed at the regular, seasonal festivals such as the *jiao* 郊 ritual, or at special occasions such as the *wang* sacrifice.

The establishment of the Chen Bao 陳寶 cult by Lord Wen 文公 in 747 (*Shiji* 14: 539) indicates that despite the imitation or adoption of the Zhou ritual tradition, there was no fixed policy at the Qin court regarding what the state should include in its official cult schedule. It seems that whatever was useful or extraordinary could become part of the official cult. The establishment of the Fu cult (伏祠) in 676 is another example (*Shiji* 14: 573). On the other hand, the addition of the cult of the Green Thearch (Qingdi, 青帝) in 672 and the cults of the Yellow Thearch (Huangdi, 黃帝) and Red Thearch (Yandi, 炎帝) in 422 (*Shiji* 14: 575, 15: 704; Wang Zijin 2005), should the record be trusted, speak of a gradual emergence of the idea of a correlative cosmology supported by the theory of Five Phases (*Wuxing* 五行). It was in the reign of the First Emperor that the theory of Five Phases began to gain official recognition, as the First Emperor decided that the color of Qin should be black, the sign of Water, which is the last color to appear in the record regarding the Qin official cult (*Shiji* 6: 237–238; 28: 1366; Poo 1988: 105). By this time the theory of Five Phases as reflected in the *Lüshi chunqiu*, among others, was already prevalent in society, probably representing a synthetic view of the late Warring States intellectuals and not an aspect of exclusively Qin ideology.

The culmination of the Qin's integration into Zhou ritual tradition is marked by the First Emperor's performance of the *fengshan* 封禪 cer-emony at Mount Tai 泰山.[8] Despite the somewhat erratic way in which the rite was performed (van Ess, chapter 7, this volume), this most exalted ceremony was firmly located in the ancient dynastic tradition that could legitimate the First Emperor's regime (Poo 1998: 104–105).

It should be made clear here that, although we tend to see those cults that carry certain political significance or grand cosmological implica-tions—such as the worship of the Five Thearchs or of Heaven-and-Earth—as "official cults," this concept in fact did not exist in early China, at least not in the Qin and Han periods. What distinguished an "official" from an "unofficial" cult was not the deities worshipped, but whether it was sup-ported by the court. For the First Emperor, all the cults that he supported were "official," and these cults served two clear and specific purposes: to prolong the rule of his dynasty, and to prolong his own life. Here is a common ground between the First Emperor and a commoner: the wor-ship of a deity was meant to enhance in a certain measure his personal welfare. The *fengshan* ceremony, for example, was a ceremony dedicated to Heaven and Earth for the welfare of the state. Yet for the First Emperor it was also a ceremony that he hoped could give him eternal life. When we read the description of the First Emperor's quest for immortality in the *Historical Records*, even though it is through Sima Qian's words, we can sense the strong desire of the First Emperor to ensure his personal well-being. For him, everything enjoyable in life could be and had been provided; the only thing lacking was the guarantee of immortality. For ordinary people, however, no *fengshan* ceremony could be expected, and as there was much to be desired in life, immortality was not their imme-diate concern—at least for the majority of them.

ARCHAEOLOGICAL INDICATIONS OF RELIGIOUS IDEAS OF THE QIN PEOPLE

Recent discussions on the subject of "Qin religion" have in general estab-lished the view that, in terms of burial customs, the Qin elite basically followed the Shang and Zhou style both in the construction of their tombs and their funerary assemblages (Feng Li 2006; Introduction to Part I, this volume). Towards the mid-fourth century, the increasing use of *mingqi* 明器 (miniature, usually pottery, vessels and figurines) in the composition of the funerary furnishings may have reflected a tendency to regard the tomb as a "microcosmos" (Falkenhausen 2004; cf. Wu Hung 2006). Other archaeological evidence could point to a similar tendency. The tomb no. 1 of Nanzhihui at Fengxiang, Shaanxi, possibly the tomb of Lord Jing 景公 (r. 577–537) of Qin, for example, shows interior corridors that resemble the dwelling of the living (Falkenhausen 2004: 118). These developments are not exceptional to Qin. In a roughly contemporaneous tomb found at Luoyang, symbolic doors are made for the wooden casket of the chariot pit (Luoyang bowuguan 1981). The tomb of Marquis Yi of Zeng 曾侯乙 (buried c. 433) is another good example that shows the idea of treating the tomb as the living quarters of the dead (Falkenhausen 2006: 306–312). The wooden casket of a late Warring States period Qin tomb is also equipped with two doors leading from the head compartment to the coffin chamber, as if to allow the deceased to pass through in the next life (Li Xueqin 1985: 32). Warring States period tombs in the Chu area again reveal a similar tendency to imitate the residence of the living not only by supplying various *mingqi* representing daily life, but also by supplying features such as windows, doors, and stairs to the wooden caskets so as to resemble houses (e.g., *Jiangling* 1984: 149; Poo 1993b: 193–198).

A novel development in the Qin area, however, is proliferation of the so-called catacomb tombs. The catacomb tomb, prevalent in the Qin area during the late Warring States period, is seen as a possible indication of an evolving concept of the netherworld, as it may originate from the cave dwellings of the vast area ranging from the Neolithic Majiayao 馬家窯 culture around the upper Yellow River to the upper Wei River region (Xie Duanju 1987; Falkenhausen 2006: 308–309). Excavations of a group of tombs dated from the late Warring States to the early Han period near Zhengzhou, Henan, indicate that there was a possible sequence of development of tomb styles, i.e., vertical pit–vertical pit with hollow brick casket–catacomb–catacomb with hollow brick casket. Subsequently, the hollow brick casket tombs gradually changed from "level top" (平頂) to "pointed-top" (人字頂), which finally culminated in the small brick chamber tombs of the early Han period, and which also undeniably imitated the houses of the living (Poo 1993b: 57–58; Huang Xiaofen 2003: 41–42; 90–95; Poo 2011). Again, it has to be pointed out that the development of the catacomb tomb is not exclusively a Qin phenomenon, but can be found more widely in the late Warring States period Central Plains area.

Another point in relation to Qin burial customs is the flexed burial style prevalent in the Qin region. Scholars have long been debating the meaning of the flexed burial without reaching a final consensus. Some hold that the position symbolizes the posture of the fetus in the womb; others see it as a natural position of sleeping, or an economic way of burial, or the position of a bound slave. Without textual support, none of these interpretations is convincing. Based on the exorcistic text found in the Qin bamboo text *Daybook* (*Rishu* 日書) from Shuihudi Tomb 11, it has been suggested that the flexed position might have been an apotropaic posture that was aimed at driving away evil spirits (Wang Zijin 1987). The text in question reads as follows: "What demons detest are namely: reclining in a crouch, sitting like a winnowing basket, linked movement, and the leaning stand."[9] This explanation, despite the support of textual evidence, still has to overcome the difficult fact that the flexed burial style is a very ancient practice for people to the west of China, and that if it was indeed an apotropaic posture, one would have difficulty explaining why there is only one reference to this practice amongst all the extant texts, and even this single reference in the *Daybook* is very late in time, appearing in a tomb with extended burial style from an area with mixed Chu and Qin customs, and it does not directly refer to "reclining in a crouch" as a burial style. Lastly, it is still uncertain if the "reclining in a crouch" position can be confidently explained as the flexed burial style (see more in Liu Junshe 2000). Thus it is best that we refrain from speculating on the religious significance of the flexed burial posture until further evidence appears.[10]

In the present state of knowledge, suffice it to say that archaeological evidence provides a general pattern of the emergence of a series of changes in burial customs that suggest a growing emphasis on treating the tomb as a residence for the deceased. Direct evidence that indicates the idea of the tomb as the place for the dead to live in is the resurrection story contained in a text found in a Qin tomb at Fangmatan, Tianshui (天水放馬灘) (*Tianshui Fangmatan* 2009: 59, 107; Li Xueqin 1990; Harper 1994). According to the narrative, the main character, Dan 丹, lived in his tomb for three years before he was resurrected.[11] Yet this idea should not be seen as an exclusively Qin phenomenon; and, more important, the trend observed in archaeological material does not mean that the mentality behind the material expressions did not exist in an earlier period. In other words, imagining the netherworld after that of the living, with different degrees of clarity, could have existed in society before any written or archaeological evidence substantiates it.

TEXTUAL EVIDENCE OF THE RELIGIOUS LIFE OF
THE QIN PEOPLE

Turning to textual evidence regarding the religious life of the Qin people, the immediate problem we face is the paucity of written evidence. As the available evidence is bound to be incomplete and piecemeal, it might be useful, first, to try to find the cosmological structure that underlies various expressions of religious piety. Here the daybooks excavated from Qin dynasty Tomb 1 at Fangmatan and similar ones found in Tomb 11, Shuihudi, may be the most important evidence we possess.[12] The Shuihudi daybooks have been extensively discussed during the past thirty years, and it seems that, although there may be certain aspects in the daybooks that reflect Chu customs, particularly the calendar system, the underlying mentality behind the Shuihudi and Fangmatan daybooks is basically identical. As more and more similar versions of daybooks dated to the early Han have been discovered in recent decades, there should be no doubt that the daybooks represent the religious mentality of the middle-lower social stratum of a wide area that covers Qin, Chu, and the Central Plains at least from the late Warring States onward (Li Ling 2000a: 43–47; 197–215). I shall therefore use the material from both the Fangmatan and Shuihudi daybooks to discuss the religious life of the common people at the beginning of the Qin Empire.

In contrast to the official ideology of the relationship between the ruler and the cosmological powers, the foremost concern of the common people was how to obtain a happy life. The daybooks are basically collections of various divinatory methods to predict the auspiciousness of days. These methods share some common assumptions about the relationships between the human world and certain cosmological patterns, such as the progression of time, astronomical phenomena, or the cardinal directions. These relationships could be formulated into various calculation methods that employ either the sexagesimal system (hemerology), or astronomical phenomena such as the positions of the constellations (uranomancy), or geographical concepts such as the cardinal directions and relative positions (geomancy).[13] These systems represent the underlying cosmological assumptions that people implicitly adhered to when they employed texts such as the daybook to guide them in their daily activities.

The first assumption is that the progress of time structures human destiny. As a number of "chapters" in the daybook clearly show, every day of the sexagesimal system would correspond to a certain auspicious or inauspicious quality regarding some specific subjects. For example, in the

"Qinchu" 秦除 chapter of the Shuihudi Tomb 11 *Daybook A*, the days in a year are defined in twelve categories (*Shuihudi* 2001: 183):

Jian-day: A good day. Suitable to work as a bailiff (*sefu*), suitable to make sacrifice. Auspicious for the morning; inauspicious for the evening. Suitable to hire people, to perform the capping ceremony, to ride a carriage. When engaging in activities, it will be auspicious.

建日,良日也。可以為嗇夫,可以祠。利棗(早)不利莫(暮)。可以入人、始寇(冠)、乘車。有為也,吉。

Chu-day: If servants and maids run off, they cannot be captured. If one contracts the illness of swelling, he shall not die. It is good for trade . . . , sweeping the ground, drinking and playing music, attacking bandits, but not capturing [them].

除日,臣妾亡,不得。有腫病,不死。利市責(積)、徵□□□除地、飲樂。攻盜,不可以執。

Ying-day: Suitable to build stables, suitable to give birth, suitable to build houses, to serve as a bailiff. If one is sick, he is unlikely to get well.

盈日,可以築閑牢,可以產,可以築宮室、為嗇夫。有疾,難起。

Ping-day: Suitable to take a wife, to hire people, to initiate business.

平日,可以取妻、入人、起事。

Ding-day: Suitable to store [food?], to build offices and houses, to perform sacrifices.

定日,可以臧(藏),為官府室,祠。

Zhi-day: Not suitable to travel. If one absconds, he is sure to be captured and taken in by government authorities and stopped.

摯(執)日,不可以行。以亡,必摯(執)而入公而止。

Po-day: One should not do anything.

柀(破)日,毋可以有為也。

Wei-day: Suitable to punish the captured and to attack [enemies?].

危日,可以責摯(執)攻(擊)。

Cheng-day: Suitable to plan projects, to gather people, and to commence important business.

成日,可以謀事、起□ (眾)、興大事。

Shou-day: Suitable to acquire servants, horses and cattle, grains, to take a wife and other things.

收日,可以入人民、馬牛、禾粟,入室取妻及它物。

Kai-day: Absconders will not be captured. If one asks to have interview (with a higher official), he will have it. If he reports a case of banditry, he shall succeed.

開日,亡者,不得。請謁,得。言盜,得。

Bi-day: Suitable to dig ponds, to acquire servants, horses, cattle, and other animals.

閉日,可以劈決池,入臣徒、馬牛、它生(牲)。

It is clear that the underlying assumption of this and similar systems is that the nature of the days is fixed and defined by the "weekly" system. Everyone using the text as guidance for daily activities must believe that the predictions of the auspiciousness of the days are the same for all. Thus, in a sense, whatever daily activities people considered important—which is why they are mentioned in the text—are predetermined by such systems.

The second assumption is that the varieties of the nature of days are confined to what is allowed by the calendrical system. The *Daybook* allowed only limited possibilities for the auspiciousness of the days. Depending upon different ways of calculation, the possibilities may recur every ten, twelve, or at most sixty days, because this is how the system works. The great mystery, however, is why people believed that time was related to human affairs, and in a cyclical manner. Yet clearly the calendrical structure of the *Daybook* must have resulted from a long divinatory tradition. Already in the Shang period people believed that the event of a certain date in the future was predetermined, and could be made known by divination before it happened. It is even possible that daybooks or similar texts existed already in the Shang period (Lian Shaoming 1997). The *Yijing* 易經, similarly, contains explanations to the meanings of the Hexagrams, which suggests an assumption that is similar to the *Daybook*, that is, that human affairs could be grouped into limited categories, and the significance of these categories is determined by the system defined by the Hexagrams.

In order to probe into the reality of religious life of the people that the *Daybooks* represent, we need to see in what ways the people's daily lives were affected by religious beliefs of one sort or another. We could examine other items in the daybooks. A logical approach is to divide daily activities into several categories and see how belief systems interacted with or intervened into the people's daily needs. For the basic needs of living, what people cared about usually consisted of food, clothes, housing, and traveling. For occupation-related activities, the majority of the common people would be concerned with farming. For a smaller number of people, trade and work with the government in various capacities could also be their choice. Events related to life course such as child birth, sickness, marriage, and death are also important in daily life. Finally, all these activities are often connected with the will of the spirits and gods; hence there was the need to deal with the extra-human world through various rituals. Proper dates needed to be selected for these activities to ensure successful execution of these rituals.

Here I do not intend to discuss the entire daybook, but to offer some preliminary observations on certain sections that could illustrate the religious mentality of the people using the text. Moreover, I am not concerned how or why certain dates were considered auspicious or not, but with the interests people might have had regarding certain kinds of activities. Take for example the making of garments. The Shuihudi daybooks provide a number of lists on the dates for making new garments. In addition, several paragraphs give some details regarding the meaning of "auspiciousness," such as the following (Liu Lexian 1994: 61–62):

> Clothes: Making clothes on *dingchou*, it will charm people; on *dinghai*, it will be fortunate; on *dingsi*, it will be comfortable; on *kuiyou*, there will be more clothes. Do not begin to wear new clothes on *jiwei* of the ninth month of Chu; if one does . . . will surely die.
>
> 衣, 袈(製)衣, 丁丑媚人,丁亥靈,丁巳安於身,癸酉多衣.毋以楚九月己未台(始)被新衣,衣手口必死. (*Shuihudi* 2001: 186)

> Making new clothes on *dingyou*, one will travel to the west and to the east, will sit and drink wine, and arrows and weapons shall not enter the body, the body will not be hurt.
>
> 丁酉製衣常(裳),以西有(又)以東行,以坐而飲酉(酒),矢兵不入于身,身不傷. (*Shuihudi* 2001: 224)

> Making clothes on *dingchou*, one will charm people. . . . Making clothes on *dingyou* of the eleventh month, one will wear silk for all his life. Making clothes on *dingyou* of the tenth month, one will wear silk before the year ends.
>
> 丁丑材(裁)衣,媚人, . . . 十一月丁酉材衣,終身衣絲,十月丁酉材衣,不卒歲必衣絲. (*Shuihudi* 2001: 224)

According to the text, people believed that when the correct date was chosen to make garments, the person who wore the new garments would charm others, have good fortune, wear the clothes safely or comfortably, or even have more clothes to wear. Or, one could sit and drink wine, without worrying about being shot by arrows, perhaps having some kind of magical power. The concerns are therefore partly on the effects of wearing new garments, that is, to charm others, to have good fortune, or to have magical power; and partly on the possessing of garments, that is, to be able to wear the clothes safely and comfortably, and to have more clothes, or even silk garments. However, if one attempts to make new garments on inauspicious days, the result could be catastrophic—death. (In fact, there are other cases where the result of not following the daybook's instructions is death.) We thus are confronted with the mentality of this severe punishment for not acting according to the prescribed dates: what kind of social constraint or cultural condition could have produced such serious concern with making new garments?

It seems that the concern with the ability to charm people or having certain kind of fortune and magical power points to a society that places important attention on the symbolic meaning of garments. In the daybook, due to the format of the text, no elaborate explanation is needed, neither is there space for such explanation. Yet if we look at the "Shi guan li" (士冠禮) chapter of the *Yili* 儀禮, we see that there is a clear emphasis on the symbolic importance of garments in various rituals. If we see the *Yili* as the culmination of the social etiquette of the Warring States society, we might have certain inkling of the connection between the taboos about making new garments in the daybook with a certain socially sanctioned idea of the propriety of dressing. Proper dressing at appropriate occasions is very much part of the expression of cultural values. This example shows that religious expressions regarding one aspect of social life could reveal the social value at its most basic level. It also suggests that, if our speculation is tenable, the high etiquette described in the *Yili* had already penetrated down to the life of the more ordinary folks who used the daybook for daily guidance.

More on the daily concerns of the people could be learned by examining the chapters in the daybooks that are related to the basic needs of living, occupations, and life courses. Yet, although these can no doubt add to our knowledge of the life of the people, they are not conceptually different. Since I have given an example of the day-selecting systems for making clothes and discussed their possible significance, I shall leave an analysis of the rest to another occasion, and concentrate on the relationship between the human world and the world of spirits and ghosts.

The Shuihudi *Daybook A* contains a by now famous "Demonography,"[14] which is practically a handbook for exorcism. The reason why it was inserted into the *Daybook* is not entirely clear, since it does not have anything to do with calendrical or day-selecting systems. Yet it is by far the longest chapter in the entire *Daybook A*. Since it is placed after the chapter on domestic geomancy, that is, a treatise on the relative position and size of domestic architecture and its connection with human fate, one suspects that this "Demonography," since it is mostly concerned with the exorcism of spirits and demons in a domestic environment, was inserted as a sort of a supplement to the chapter on domestic geomancy.

Most of the day selection systems in the *Daybook* speak of an orderly universe, because things that could happen to people's lives can be predicted and stated in the text. In such systems, there is no possibility for surprises, and no position for the extra-human powers—the spirits, ghosts, demons and even deities—to play. The "Demonography" chapter, however, provides an antithesis to the day-selection systems. It testifies to the fact that in the people's daily lives malicious spirits and demons could attack humans in various ways that were beyond people's expectations. They could appear and attack without any reason, in many different places, and completely unpredictably. The problem people faced then is this: since the day selection systems had already prescribed the auspiciousness of every date on the calendar in one way or another, what if a malicious spirit or demon happened to come and attack a person on an auspicious day? To ensure that the day selection systems would not fail, then, there had to be a way to deal with the spirits and demons—thus the "Demonography." By following the exorcistic methods provided by the text, people could neutralize the threat of the malicious spirits, and ensure the order prescribed by the day selection systems.

In the end, both the day selection systems and the "Demonography" share a basic mentality, that is: one's fate can be predicted and there is, or should be, nothing surprising in the world, since what will happen has already been given in the daybooks. Even the unpredictable attack of evil spirits can be effectively checked with proper exorcism. Given this situation, one might be inclined to say that the daybooks represent a popular mentality that believes in fate as the course of human life prescribed by whatever cosmic power that exists, and which cannot be changed. Indeed, one chapter in the *Daybook*, entitled "Childbirth," is a veritable prediction of the future life of a child according to the date that the child is born in the sexagisemal calendrical system. There seems no doubt that the text testifies to a belief in fate (Poo 2005).

However, further examination of the day selection systems shows that often the systems are mutually contradictory, that is, an auspicious day in one system could be inauspicious in another. For example, according to the "Qinchu" chapter, the *wei* 未-days of the first month are not good for traveling (*Shuihudi* 2001: 183). This, however, contradicts the "Travel" chapter, wherein the *wu* 午-days in the first month are inauspicious, thus the *wei* 未-days ought to be safe to travel (*Shuihudi* 2001: 200). Since all these systems are listed in the same daybook, one needs to ask whether or not people using the daybook knew about the contradiction. If they did know, what could be their reason to keep them together and thus endorsed their validity? It seems that not only people using the text knew this, but it is also stated clearly at least in one incidence in the daybook. In the "Travel" chapter, there is the following revealing instruction:

> Whenever one plans to do something [traveling], it is necessary to choose the leisure days within that month. As long as they are not the days for the descent of the Red Thearch, even if they may bear inauspicious names, there will be no great harm. (*Shuihudi* 2001: 200)[15]

This passage indicates that, for the purpose of travel, one could simply ignore predictions given in other texts and pay attention to the special days of the descent of the Red Thearch. A similar situation can be found in another daybook dated to the last days of the First Emperor:

> When one needs to travel in a hurry, and cannot wait for an auspicious day for travel, then one shall cross wood if traveling to the east, cross fire if traveling to the south, cross metal if traveling to the west, and cross water if traveling to the north. It will be fine even it is not an auspicious day for traveling. (*Guanju* 2001: 133)

The compilers might have realized that there were inconsistencies in the various texts, so that a particular day might be auspicious according to one text, yet inauspicious according to another. What can we make of this apparent inconsistency? Short of any sure answer, it seems that by keeping the inconsistency, it gave the user of the daybook an opportunity to find a way out and not be confined to one system. Although, ultimately, no matter if one followed one system or another, one could only operate in a prescribed web of auspicious dates to carry out his/her daily affairs. I would, however, hesitate to use the term fatalism to refer to the daybook mentality, since it is obvious that not everything in people's lives is mentioned in the daybook, and that we have yet to determine the degree to which people depended upon the daybook to guide their daily activities.

It seems that the daybooks of Shuihudi provide us with a twofold approach to the world: with the calendrical day selection systems the user could navigate through the many perils in life that were predestined to happen if one did not follow the instructions in the daybooks. With the exorcistic handbook "Demonography," on the other hand, people sought to confront and expel evil spirits that would attack without any forewarning. The relationship between the humans and the malicious ghosts, in this situation, appears to be that of power relations—so long as one possessed the correct and effective method of exorcism, there was no need to worry. Moreover, it seems that the activities of the spirits and ghosts were not regulated by the calendrical systems in the daybooks, since there is no prediction concerning which date the ghosts and spirits would likely come and harm people. It is also worth noticing that the exorcistic methods described in the text do not seem to need help from any deities, and no religious specialists are involved in the execution of the exorcistic acts.

However, regarding the relationship between the human and the divine, the picture that the daybooks reveal can only be a limited one. By the time of the Qin unification, it was common that in local societies people had to engage with various deities in daily affairs in the forms of divination, ritual, sacrifice, and prayer. In a text excavated from a Qin tomb in Hubei province, for example, one finds a case of toothache that requires ritual and prayer:

> The recipe for healing a tooth: Present oneself before the eastern wall;
> make three steps of Yu 禹步, and say: "Hao! I dare to implore the Lord
> of the Eastern Wall. So-and-so is ill because of a decayed tooth. If you
> can heal so-and-so, I promise to offer a cow and a calf: a fine pair." If
> you see a tile on the ground in front of you, take it; if you see a tile on
> the wall, perform the steps of Yu and stop. Take the tile on the wall
> and bury it under the eastern wall, place a "cow" on top of it, and use
> the tile you took [from the ground] to cover it, and bury it securely.
> The so-called cow is a large-head bug (?). (*Guanju* 2001: 129)

Here, a local deity (the Lord of the Eastern Wall) is implored to cure the illness, with the performance of ritual and prayer, and the offering of "substitute cattle." It seems that the status of the deity was not much higher than the ghosts in the "Demonography" since they are given similar treatment. All one needs to do is to take the correct measures and proper objects just as, when exorcising ghosts, one needs to use the correct instruments and bodily actions. They all originate from a similar mentality that sees illnesses and spirits as something coming from outside of the person and susceptible to expunging with precise techniques.

For the common farmers, in addition to what can be seen in the daybooks, sacrifice to the God of Agriculture (Xiannong 先農) seems to have been a widely established custom.[16] Texts found in a Qin tomb from Zhoujiatai indicate a cult to Xiannong:

> Xiannong: On the *la* 臘-day, order a female to the market to buy beef and wine. When passing the street, she should bow and pronounce: "People are all making sacrifice to the ancestors; I alone make sacrifice to Xiannong." When she reaches the barn, prepare a [sacrifice sheet], facing east, thrice making sacrifice of rice, pour the wine, and pray: "I use wine (*hulu*) and beef to cleanse the residence for Xiannong. Should Xiannong make my grain [harvest] the most abundant in the district, Xiannong should always be fed before the ancestors. When it comes the time to sow, one should huddle the richest in the district to sow together. When finished, make three steps of Yu, away from the place of plantation, and pronounce: "Your subject does not mean to be different, but this is for the business of farming." Then one should pronounce the name of the rich person, saying: "I could not hurt the rich, the farmer asks his helper to come and substitute him." Then one takes the rice and returns to the barn, and holds a piglet and prays before the barn saying: "I raise [this piglet?] for the farmer, if the farmer [has a good harvest?], [he shall] perform yearly sacrifice." Then he shall cut the ear of the piglet, and smear it together with the rice under the barn. One should always make sacrifice on the *la*-day as it used to be. (*Guanju* 2001: 132)

A recent find in Well 1, Liye, also produced similar evidence on the sacrifice dedicated to Xiannong. From the Liye slips, however, the sacrifice to Xiannong appears to be also part of the regular duties of the county government, since these slips document official fiscal transactions pertaining to the sacrificial items. (*Liye* 2007: 194–196; *Liye* 2012: 8-1091 [1093]; Chen Wei 2012: 259–260 see also Peng Hao 2007; Cao Lüning 2008a; Shi Zhilong 2009; Tian Xudong 2009).

The newly excavated texts in fact corroborate traditional texts such as the *Lüshi chunqiu* in describing social customs around the time of the unification of Qin. If we look at other areas at the end of the Warring States period, we find that the patterns are basically similar. The Baoshan 包山 Chu bamboo texts indicate that during a ritual for healing disease, the objects used in the offering ritual consisted of domestic animals such as dogs, pigs, and chickens and precious objects such as jade.[17] This is because the main benefactor of the ritual was a member of the Chu nobility. The spirits implored, consequently, are of a higher order and include cosmic deities such as Taiyi 太一 (the Great One) and the earth; functional deities such as Siming 司命 (the Director of Destiny) Sihuo 司

禍 (the Director of Calamity), and Dashui 大水 (the Great Water), in addition to local deities such as the two "Sons of Heaven" of the River Xiang (*er tianzi* 二天子) (Hu Yali 2002). The authors of the *Lüshi chunqiu* were critical of popular religious activities,[18] echoed in the newly discovered texts such as the ones quoted above, which provide concrete and contemporary evidence of how people's daily lives were affected by religious beliefs and practices with religious actions of various sorts.

CONCLUSION

The religious rituals practiced at the court by the rulers reflected at each historical stage the prevailing officially sanctioned cosmological interpretation of the relationship between the human world (represented by the ruling regime) and the divine world. This officially sanctioned cosmology, however, may not have been the only principle that the court followed when it came to decide whether to include certain cults in the officially recognized ritual schedule. Often personal or accidental factors might have prompted the establishment or abolition of cults in the official setting.

For religious activities in the common people's daily lives, on the other hand, newly found archaeological and epigraphic evidence provide us with two perspectives. Regarding the dead, the formation and a clearer expression of a concept of the world after death that bore some similarity to the world of the living seems to be one of the most prominent aspects of the development of religious beliefs at the end of the Warring States period. The imagination of a world after death can also be understood as a more practical way to deal with the unknown fate of the dead. The development of funerary equipment and the evolution of tomb styles are the physical manifestations of this conceptualization. The fundamental hope or belief was that death might not be the end of life for the dead, and when provided with funerary objects of daily life, whether real or surrogate, the dead might be able to continue his/her life in the netherworld. There is an unspoken assumption that the dead could somehow use the objects, just as the deities could somehow enjoy the offerings.

Regarding the life of the living, people sought to acquire all sorts of information that could help them to navigate through the perils of life, to fend off the attack of malicious spirits, and to implore the help of deities. The key is that there existed a belief in the possibility that such information could be acquired. This belief was based on several assumptions. First, the relationship between the human and the extra-human powers—including deities, ghosts, spirits and ancestors—was that of mutual give and take, i.e., *do-ut-des,* and the means of communication included offerings, rituals and prayers. In this relationship one can hardly detect any moral principle that any society would usually require. People could be attacked by malicious ghosts for no obvious reason; deities and ancestors could be expected to help the propitiators not because of they had done worthy deeds, but because of what they had to offer. Second, there existed a correlation between human affairs and the basic structure of the universe in terms of time, direction, and space. Such relationships could be expressed by numerical systems such as the sexagesimal system and the Five Phases system, as witnessed the various day selection and geomancy chapters in the daybooks. Third, there existed a belief in the efficaciousness of formality, as all religious activities have to conform to a certain formality in order to ensure their effectiveness. Personal emotions and moral sensibility did not have much to do with this formality.

What emerges from all these assumptions is a religious mentality that saw the world and human affairs as a fixed structure defined by the various numerical systems, and the life of a person could potentially be prearranged following the instructions of texts such as the daybook. In a sense, this mentality can be seen as rather optimistic, since there would be no hidden secrets for the future, as the future had already been written down in the daybooks. One can even say that the daybooks have eliminated the future since this future would be exactly the same as the past. Moreover, the use of daybooks implies an opportunist mentality, assuming that people would naturally tend to select the auspicious days for their own benefit. This opportunist and amoral mentality has remained the dominant religious mentality of the common people ever since the Qin Empire.

The religious expressions regarding the living and the dead, as we just described, point to a materialistic character of the religious mentality of the Qin, that is, there is little evidence of a transcendental element. People tried to solve all sorts of problems in life and in death neither by reflecting upon the meaning and goal of life, nor by connecting their personal piety with divine revelation, but by using practical methods to achieve a desired result, whether to enjoy life in the netherworld, or to charter a better life on earth.

6 The Changing Status of Slaves in the Qin-Han Transition

Robin D. S. Yates

It has been more than sixty years since Edwin Pulleyblank published his seminal article "The Origins and Nature of Chattel Slavery in China" in the inaugural issue of the *Journal of the Economic and Social History of the Orient* (1958), and almost seventy years since C. Martin Wilbur wrote his monograph *Slavery in China during the Former Han Dynasty, 206 B.C.–A.D. 25* (1943). Since that time, the topic of slavery has received an immense amount of attention from scholars worldwide. But only a handful of studies have explored the various aspects of slavery and forced bondage in China, the latest being those by Angela Schottenhammer (2003), on "Slaves and Forms of Slavery in Late Imperial China," and my own essay "Slavery in Early China: A Socio-Cultural Perspective" (Yates 2002). The result has been that the particular manifestations and forms of slavery and unfree labor in China have been all but ignored in world histories of slavery.[1] In China, however, as Pulleyblank pointed out, much effort was expended on analyzing slavery as an early stage in the Marxist conception of history before the establishment of the feudal mode of production, but very little was done to examine the nature of slavery in later times, presumably because slavery was thought to have been a mere remnant of the former mode.[2]

In my previous article, I adopted the sociocultural approach of Orlando Patterson to make a number of points about the status of slaves in Qin and Han times and I accepted his definition of the phenomenon, namely that "slavery is the permanent, violent domination of natally alienated and generally dishonored persons."[3] Thus I rejected the notion adopted by many Chinese scholars that the fundamental feature of early Chinese slaves was that they were property and treated like cattle or other objects that could be bought, sold, transferred, or killed and disposed of at the whim of the owner. I also noted, for example, that the Qin had several different terms for slaves and that slaves could not be legally married: a slave wife was always called a *qie* 妾 (concubine) in Qin legal parlance. Recent archaeological finds of statutes from such sites as Zhangjiashan 張家山 Tomb 247, probably buried in 186 BCE or slightly later, require a re-evaluation of my previous analysis. Although, in my opinion, the exact dating of each item of the statutes recovered from Tomb 247 remains unclear, it seems that the early Han made some significant alterations in the nomenclature and legal status of slaves, simplifying the complex and harsher Qin system. Indeed, the Qin system may have been more complex simply because Qin was rapidly conquering large tracts of territory from other states in different parts of the East Asian subcontinent, each of which may have had its own customs and practices and its own nomenclature for various types of permanent and semipermanent unfree labor. It is also clear from the new evidence that violence was not always a feature of slavery in early times.

In this chapter, I analyze some of the articles in the newly discovered Zhangjiashan Tomb 247 statutes relating to the status of slaves and argue that the Han made a conscious effort to assimilate slaves into the family system. Not only were slaves distinguished from movable and immovable property, such as houses and animals, but they were also included as persons on the official household registers. If an ordinary commoner lacked a viable heir, the longest-serving slave could be manumitted and made his or her heir. In punishments relating to a lack of filial piety, slaves were also treated similarly to male and female children. Thus the changing legal attitude toward slaves also transformed intrafamily relations.

Let me review the evidence from the Zhangjiashan Tomb 247 statutes and some of the cases preserved in the collection titled *Zouyan shu* 奏讞書, or transcripts of doubtful law cases that were submitted to the most senior legal authorities at the capital for review and decision. It goes without saying that my opinions and tentative conclusions are only preliminary and may need revision in the light of evidence to be found in other newly recovered texts that have not been, or are in the process of being, published. These include the legal texts from Zhangjiashan Tomb 336, to be published in the near future by Peng Hao 彭浩,[4] the 18,000 Liye 里 耶 Qin documents to be published in five volumes starting in 2012,[5] and the Qin legal texts recovered from the Hong Kong antiques market and repatriated in 2008 by the Yuelu Academy.[6] Of these, perhaps the most interesting document published in early 2012 is a board from the Liye hoard. It provides the first, and so far only, evidence for the price of slaves in the Qin Empire. It reads as follows:

Board 8-1287 (8-1282) (*Liye* 2012: 66; Chen Wei 2012: 306–307)

Line 1　卅一年十月乙酉朔 = (朔)日貳春鄉守
31st year (i.e., 216), tenth month, *yiyou* being the first day of the month, on the first day of the month, the Temporary [Bailiff] of Erchun Canton . . .

Line 2　大奴一人直錢四千三百
One adult male slave; value in cash, four thousand three hundred . . .

Line 3　小奴一人直錢二千五百
One non-adult male slave: value in cash two thousand five hundred . . .

Line 4　·凡直錢六千八百
In all, the value in cash six thousand eight hundred...

It is not clear whether the temporary bailiff of Erchun Canton, one of the three cantons below Qianling County, is buying or selling these slaves on the open market, or is merely recording a sale between private individuals. Unfortunately the board is broken and so this information is missing. And what the comparative value of one cash was in 216 also needs investigation (see also note 8 below). It goes without saying, however, that the Liye hoard, when published in full, may provide much more information on slaves and the slave market in the Qin Empire.

Before I start my analysis of the Zhangjiashan materials I would like to say a few words about the dating of the Zhangjiashan Tomb 247 slips. Some of them probably were holdovers from Qin statutory law, others promulgated in the Qin-Han interregnum, and others closer to the date when they were deposited in the grave, probably in or shortly after 186. It is to be noted, for example, that slips 201–202 of the "Statutes on Coins" 錢律 read:

盜鑄錢及佐者,棄市。同居不告,贖耐。正、典、⁷田典、伍人不告,罰金四兩。

Those who in a thievish fashion cast coins and their assistants are to be cast away in the market-place. Co-residents who do not denounce them are [sentenced to] redeemable shaving. If the Village Chief (*zheng, dian*), the Chief of the Fields (*tiandian*) and the five family members (*wuren*) do not denounce them, they are fined four *liang* of gold. (*Zhangjiashan* 2001: 161)

Here, the punishment to be levied on offenders is calculated in amounts of gold. This innovation appears to have taken place sometime during the

Qin Empire in comparison to the types of fines that are listed in the Qin statutes from Shuihudi 睡虎地 Tomb 11 that probably mostly date from preimperial times.[8] Since this item from the Zhangjiashan Han Statutes on Coins apparently refers to the village chief as both *(li)zheng* (里正) and as *(li)dian* (里典)—*dian* 典 being the word that replaced the word *zheng* 正, tabooed under the Qin because it was a homophone of the First Emperor's 秦始皇 given name Zheng 政[9]—I would suggest that these statutes were composed at a time when village chiefs who had been appointed by the Qin government authorities were still alive and these local officials had neither been relieved of their duties by the incoming Han government, nor had they been forced to be reappointed to their positions as *lizheng*.[10] Thus, I would conclude that the early Han government recognized the legitimacy of Qin legal and moral authority, something that was eventually repudiated later on under the influence of Confucian scholars and officials.

As a consequence, agreeing with Michael Loewe, I argue in a recent essay that it is unlikely that there was a legal code promulgated in either the Qin or Han. Most likely, the statutes found in Tomb 247, Zhangjiashan, were promulgated on different occasions by different rulers. Some may even have been Qin statutes that retained their legal force in the early Han:

> Since a calendar of the years 202–186 BC was found in the same Zhangjiashan tomb as the laws and the title "Statutes and Ordinances of the Second Year" was found on the back of one of the strips of bamboo on which the laws were copied, many scholars have assumed that these statutes and ordinances were also a "code" that was published in the "Second Year," generally agreed to be that of Liu Bang's Empress Lü, in other words, 186 BC. There is no guarantee, however, that the tomb was filled and closed in the same year or that the title was official, and, since there is no corroborating historical evidence, there is no reason to presume that a code was published in the "Second Year."
> (Yates 2009b: 413)

Furthermore, it is apparent that the laws and ordinances are incomplete and were probably copied for deposit in the tomb on the occasion of the death of the tomb occupant, whose given name was probably Xin 新. It seems, indeed, that at least one of the slips of bamboo was recycled (slip 81), for it contains the name of a copyist either surnamed Zheng 鄭 or deriving from the city of Zheng plus a given name written with a graph with a "woman" 女 radical which is otherwise unknown.[11] The editors have all assumed that this individual copied the laws (Peng Hao et al. 2007: 112n1), but the calligraphy of the graph is completely different from the way that "Zheng" is written elsewhere in the laws and cannot have been written by the same person. Thus I conclude that the Zhangjiashan Tomb 247 laws cannot have been copied by a female copyist named "Zheng X," but rather a slip was used which had her name on it, but which the actual copyist did not bother to erase (cf. Hsing's discussion of the nature of documents found in tombs in chapter 4 of this volume).

"STATUTES ON MALE AND FEMALE SLAVES"

In the Zhangjiashan Tomb 247 hoard, the titles of twenty-seven statutes have been preserved (Li Xueqin and Wen Xing 2001; Ōba Osamu 2001), and Li Junming 李均明 and Peng Hao have suggested that some items from another, the "Statutes on Prisons" ("Qiu lü" 囚律), have also survived, even though the slip with the title has been lost.[12] However, it appears that there may have been special statutes that were concerned with slaves, comparable to another set of "Statutes on Freedmen" ("Shuren lü" 庶人律), which is also alluded to in a fragmentary slip.[13] I say this because one of the "Statutes on Abscondence" ("Wang lü" 亡律) reads as follows:[14]

奴婢為善而主欲免者,許之,奴命曰私屬,婢為庶人,皆復使,及算事之如奴婢。主死若有罪,以私屬為庶人,刑者以為隱官。所免不善,身免者得復入奴婢之。其亡,有它罪,以奴婢律論之。

If a male or female slave is good and the master wishes to manumit (*mian*) [them], permit it, and male slave is [then] called a "private dependent" (*sishu*) and the female slave is made a freedman (*shuren*); in all cases they may again employ [them] as well as pay the poll tax (*suan*), and make them serve like male and female slaves. If the master commits a crime [that matches] death, make the "private dependent" a freedman, but if he is mutilated, make him a "Hidden Office" [artisan]. If those who have been manumitted are not good, the person who manumitted them is able to make them male or female slaves again. If they abscond, or commit other crimes, sentence them according to the Statutes on Male and Female Slaves.[15]

This statute contains other crucially important contents to which I will return below, but suffice it to say here that the Zhangjiashan Tomb 247 hoard apparently does not contain any items from these "Statutes on Male and Female Slaves," and it is not possible to determine whether Qin law also had "Statutes on Male and Female Slaves," or whether this was an innovation of the early Han.[16] However, given that Han terminology regarding slavery was different from that of the Qin (see below), it is my suspicion that these slave statutes were created after May–June 202 when the Han founder, Liu Bang 劉邦 (Han Gaozu 漢高祖, r. 202–195), after successfully defeating his rivals in the civil wars, moved his capital to Luoyang and issued his famous edict in which he ordered that refugees displaced in the disturbances following the fall of the Qin return to their homes to be registered by the newly constituted Han state authorities and "as to those people who because of famine or hunger have themselves sold their persons to be slaves or slave-girls, let them all be freed to become common people [freedmen]."[17] This edict was a clear signal that the Han had won and that peacetime activities should be resumed. It is possible that new discoveries of Qin and early Han laws will resolve the issue of whether or not the Qin had "Statutes on Male and Female Slaves" or whether they were an innovation of the early Han, and we will be able to find out what the contents of these statutes were, providing us with much more evidence for the nature of slavery and the legal status of slaves in the early empire. Without these statutes, we have to examine items in other, related statutes which refer to slaves.

THE NOMENCLATURE OF SLAVES IN THE EARLY HAN

In the Qin, there were a number of different terms that referred to slaves and other statuses below that of commoner or member of the rank and file without a degree of rank (*shiwu* 士五[伍]):[18] this was the legal "free" status in opposition to which all those in unfree status were compared.[19] These terms included, *rennu* 人奴, *renchen* 人臣, or *chen* 臣 for a man, and *renqie* 人妾 or *qie* 妾 for a woman (Wen Xia 2007). The former means a "male slave or servant," and the latter a "female slave or servant." The Han term for female slave (*bi* 婢) does not appear in the Qin laws discovered in Tomb 11 at Shuihudi in 1975;[20] however, it does appear in several documents published in volume one of the complete Liye documents, but not in the context of a statute or ordinance (e.g., *Liye* 2012: 5-18, p. 3; 8-404, p. 30). There were also other terms, such as "man-marmot" (*renhe* 人貉), a type of dependent laborer that does not appear in the transmitted historical sources (*Shuihudi* 2001: 140 slip 195; Hulsewé 1985: D174: 177). If the children of these latter types of individuals did not go to take care of their masters, they were to be enslaved by the government. However, if they served their master food, they were not to be seized by the Qin state authorities. More important, there appear to have been government slaves who were called "male and female bond servants" (*lichenqie* 隸臣妾). This term was also applied to three-year hard labor convicts, and there has been a vigorous academic debate as to the nature of their status, whether convicts or slaves. Indeed, scholars have debated whether convicts in the Qin were state slaves or not. Li Li 李力 has recently published a 776-page book in which he reviews all the arguments concerning this status, and concludes that there was great confusion in the use of the term: some "male and female bond servants" were indeed state slaves, but others were convicts (Li Li 2007a). There is no space here to repeat his arguments. However, it is clear that there was a definite distinction between private and state slaves in both the Qin and the Han, and that there was a clear difference between slaves and convicts, even though in some ways they were treated in a comparable fashion by the state and their owners: slave owners could even hand over to the government an ox, horse, or slave to work off a debt or fine for them, in which case the slave was forced to wear red clothing.[21] It is likely that the Liye documents, when fully published, will provide further evidence on this contested issue, for two as yet published documents on display in the Liye Museum state that in one case, 9-1369, the number of male and female bond servants accumulated by the Qianling County was 1400, and another, 9-227, states that in the first year of the Second Emperor of Qin (209) the number of such bond servants was two hundred persons. The first of these documents, 9-1369, is broken at both the beginning and end, so it is possible that the number is not complete, and the date is missing at the beginning of the first document.[22] It appears that such persons were under the control of the Bureau of Granaries (*Cang cao* 倉曹), which was responsible for grain, equipment, and various types of animals and other goods,[23] as well as under the Bureau of the Director of Works (*Sikong cao* 司空曹).[24] As I discuss below, the county government also bought and sold slaves known as *tuli* 徒隸 on the open market and had to report these transactions to higher authorities on a regular, monthly, basis.

In comparison with the Qin, however, we do not find in the early Han Zhangjiashan laws the terms *renchen/chen* and *renqie/qie*. We do find "male and female bond servants" (*lichenqie*), but these terms seem to refer to a type of convict.[25] In place of the former, we find *nu* 奴 and *bi* 婢. In the absence of other evidence, my tentative conclusion is, therefore, that the early Han changed or refined the legal nomenclature of slaves, possibly in 202, when the "Statutes on Male and Female Slaves" might have been enacted, as suggested above.

It is to be noted that there were statuses between slaves and free commoners, as indicated in the statute quoted above. Wang Aiqing (2007) has analyzed this statute and demonstrated that the term "private dependent" (*sishu*) was not another term for a slave and that Wang Mang's manumission of slaves at the end of the Western Han, where he proposed changing the status of slave to "private dependent," was rather different from what previous scholars had supposed. Here we see that "private dependents" were manumitted male slaves; manumitted female slaves became "freed-men" (*shuren*). The master was responsible for paying the poll tax to the state and could continue to employ them in a servile capacity and position. Only when the owner committed a crime that matched or war-ranted (*dang* 當) the death penalty were the "private dependents" to be released and categorized as "freedmen." However, if they were mutilated in some way, they were to be categorized as "hidden office" *yinguan* 隱官 (artisans). This statute has, therefore, solved another historical mys-tery regarding the nature of the term *yingong* 隱宮 in Sima Qian's 司馬遷 *Historical Records* 史記 and whether the infamous assistant of the Second Emperor of the Qin, Zhao Gao 趙高, was a eunuch. It now appears that the term *yingong* might be a scribal error for *yinguan* and that such individu-als were not necessarily castrated, but merely mutilated in some fashion. This is the conclusion of both Jiang Feifei (2004) and Liu Rui (2002).[26]

Finally, we should note that the freedom for these manumitted slaves was dependent on their continued good behavior. If the master did not consider that they had been "good" (*shan* 善), however that was defined in law, possibly that the dependents had shown a lack of filial piety and refused to work or to carry out orders, as a case in the Shuihudi *Forms for Sealing and Investigating* (*Fengzhen shi* 封診式) provides evidence,[27] he could request the state that they be re-enslaved. This situation in the early Han would appear to be similar to what seems to have been the case under the Qin. If an individual had committed a crime and there was an amnesty (*she* 赦), then, if he reoffended, he could be arrested and punished for his former crime.[28]

SLAVES AND THEIR FAMILIES

Another important difference between the Qin and the Han is that the Han recognized the legality of a slave's marriage. In the Qin, wives of male slaves were called *qie* 妾 (concubines). In the Zhangjiashan Han laws, however, we read:

奴有罪,毋收其妻子為奴婢者。有告劾未死遷,收之。匿收,與盜同法。

As for male slaves who commit a crime, do not impound their wives (*qi*) or children and make them male and female slaves. As for those who are denounced and are under investigation (*he*) [for a crime] that does not reach to [the punishment of] death [?], impound them. Those who fall into impoundment (*nishou*) share the same law as robbers [i.e., are treated as robbers are under the law].[29]

We also find the following law:

民為奴妻而有子,子畀奴主。主嬖奸,若為它家奴妻,有子,子畀嬖主,皆為奴婢。

When a member of the people (*min*) is made the wife (*qi*) of a slave and has children, the children are given to the slave's owner. When an owner and a female slave fornicate, if she is the wife of a slave of another family, and has children, the children are given to the owner of the slave woman; in every case they are to be made male and female slaves.[30]

On the surface these laws would appear to be contradictory. But in the first instance, I suspect that the marriage took place before the husband fell into slavery; the wife and children were not impounded on the first conviction and remained free. It is only when he commits (another?) very serious offence that his wife and children are to be "impounded" as state slaves. In the second case, the free commoner woman marries a man who is already a slave. Here, she is called a legal wife (*qi* 妻), but the children of the union are deemed slaves, following the status of their father, and are given to the slave's owner.

Conversely, if a slave merely had illicit sexual relations with a freed-woman, any resulting children were not to be considered slaves: they were to follow their mother's status, as in the following statute:

奴與庶人奸,有子,子為庶人。

If a male slave fornicates with a freedwoman (*shuren*) and has a child, the child is made a freedman (*shuren*).[31]

Given that the woman who marries a slave is called a "legal wife" (*qi*), and not a "concubine" (*qie* 妾), I believe that I have to revise my earlier (2002) conclusion: women who married slaves as wives were not "dishonored persons," as in Orlando Patterson's terminology.

SLAVES AS MEMBERS OF THEIR OWNERS' FAMILIES

Turning to the question of whether slaves were legally considered to be the same as commodities, like cattle and other objects that could be transferred from one free individual to another, or whether they were considered persons, albeit of a lower status than ordinary individuals, there has been a great amount of debate. Some scholars, such as Zeng Jia (2007; 2008, 116–131) have argued that slaves were not registered on their masters' household registers and that therefore they were not considered to be human, merely commodities. However, this view has been challenged and new evidence has come to light.[32] In particular, examples of Qin-time household registers from the hamlet of Nanyang 南陽, which record the statistics of members of the population who were former Chu residents, include the names of male slaves, designated as *chen* 臣, in a separate column at the end of some of the registers (Hsing, chapter 4 in this volume). There is no more than one slave registered per household. It is possible, in the light of this evidence, that the term *chen* (and possibly *qie*) for male and female slaves was the technical legal term in the state of Chu. More than four hundred years later, the names of slaves also appear in some of the household registers excavated from the wells at the site known as Zoumalou 走馬樓 in downtown Changsha, Hunan, dating from the Three Kingdoms period (220–280 CE) state of Wu 吳, Changsha 長沙 Commandery (Chen Shuang 2004). From this evidence it is clear that slaves were reckoned to be part of a head of household's family and were not separated off and treated merely as commodities.

Further startling evidence of the position of slaves in their masters' household comes from the Zhangjiashan Tomb 247 "Statutes on Appointing Heirs" (*Zhihou lü* 置後律), where we find the following rule:

死毋後而有奴婢者,免奴婢以為庶人,以[庶]人律□之[其]主田宅及餘財。
奴婢多,代戶者毋過一人,先用勞久、有□□子若主所言吏者。

If a person dies without an heir and they have a male or female slave, manumit the slave and make him/her a freedman. Use the Statutes on Freedmen to give him/her the owner's fields and house(s) and the remaining goods. If there are many male and female slaves, replace the household with not more than one person, and first use the person who has worked [for his/her owner] the longest. If there is . . . son or what the owner said to the officials.[33]

While the last part of the statute is fragmented and its meaning cannot be completely understood because of a probable lacuna, it is clear that the early Han officials were very anxious not to lose a household from the registers. If a man died without any heir at all and they searched very widely, as the following rule indicates, then the senior slave would be manumitted, made a freedman, and granted ownership of his master's goods and other slaves. The following statute indicates that women could be heads of households, and another item in the Zhangjiashan Tomb 247 laws states plainly, without any doubt, that a woman was considered to have the same rank as her husband.[34]

□□□□ 為縣官有為也,以其故死若傷二旬中死,皆為死事者,令子男襲其爵。毋爵者,其後為公士。毋子男以女,毋女以父,毋父以母,毋母以男同產,毋男同產以女同產。毋女同產以妻。諸死事當置後,毋父母、妻子、同產者以大父,毋大父以大母與同居數者。

. . . [35] those who are acting on state business, and for that reason die, or die within twenty days of an injury, are all considered to be "dying in service" (*sishi*). Order that the male offspring inherit his rank. As for those without rank, their heirs should be made *gongshi*. If there is no male offspring, take the daughter [as the heir]; if there is no daughter, take the father; if there is no father, take the mother; if there is no mother, take a male sibling (*nan tongchan*); if there is no male sibling, take a female sibling (*nütongchan*); if there is no female sibling, take the wife. For all those who die in service, an heir must be appointed; if there is no father or mother, wife, or child, or siblings, take the grandfather; if there is no grandfather, take the grandmother or those who are enumerated as co-residents.[36]

The legal position of women in the early Han dynasty as seen in the Zhangjiashan laws is also very surprising, but it derived from Qin legal practice, as is indicated in a Liye board 8-19 [8-17] (*Liye* 2012: 11; Chen Wei 2012: 32–33), which lists the number of households of various ranks, probably in a village (the top left-hand side of the board is missing), in order of precedence, starts with those of high rank and ends with an unspecified number of households led by "adult women" (*danüzi* 大女子). Given the numbers listed for the other households, and the total for the village, twenty-five households, the number of such households headed by adult women was approximately three, in other words, 12 percent of the total, a significant percentage.[37]

THE LEGAL STATUS OF SLAVES

In keeping with the slave's position as a member of the master's household, albeit at the lowest level, the Zhangjiashan statutes indicate that slaves were punished more severely than other commoners and were punished more severely if they committed a crime against their social betters than if their social betters committed a crime against them. In effect, slaves had a comparable status to children, who were likewise punished more severely if they committed crimes against seniors in their family. So, for example, slaves who beat freedmen or any other person higher in rank had their cheek-bones tattooed and were returned to their masters.[38] But if a slave attacked in a premeditated fashion his or her owner, then the punishment was the same as that meted out to children:

子賊殺傷父母,奴婢賊殺傷主、主父母妻子,皆臬其首市。

A child who maliciously kills or injures their father or mother, or a male or female slave who maliciously kills or injures their owner, or the father, mother, wife, or child of the owner, they are in every case to have their head cut off and have it exposed in the market place [i.e., executed].[39]

Similarly,

婦賊傷、毆詈夫之泰父母、父母、主母、後母,皆棄市。

Wives who maliciously injure, beat, or curse the grandfather or grandmother, father or mother, or principal mother or second mother of the husband, are in every case to be cast away in the marketplace.[40]

A master could petition the state to punish the slave for lack of filial piety and the state would mutilate the slave and return him/her to the master:

◇母妻子者,棄市。其悍主而謁殺之,亦棄市;謁斬若刑,為斬、刑之。其奧詢詈主、主父母妻□□□者,以賊論之。

[Slaves who] . . . the mothers, wives and children [of their masters] are cast away in the marketplace. Those who are scolds toward their owners, and [their masters] request[41] to kill them, are also cast away in the marketplace. When [their masters] request that they have the left foot cut off or that they be mutilated, carry out the cutting off and mutilate them. Those who scold, shame, or curse their masters, . . .[42] the fathers, mothers or wives of their masters, sentence them with malicious intent (*zei*).[43]

Given the evidence from the Qin *Forms for Sealing and Investigating* cited above, this statute most likely was also in force in Qin times.

Conversely, a son's attempt on his parents' lives could be one of the ways in which his own wife and children could be enslaved. It was considered such a heinous crime against filial piety that the offender's own wife and children could be enslaved by the state and he could not use his rank to diminish the penalty, as was the usual practice in crimes against non-family members or strangers:

賊殺傷父母,牧殺父母,歐〈毆〉詈父母,父母告子不孝,其妻子為收者,皆錮,令毋得以爵償、免除及贖。

[In cases of] maliciously killing or injuring a father or mother, or plotting to kill a father or mother, or beating or cursing a father or mother, and the father or mother denounces the child for lack of filial piety, and the wives and children are enslaved, in every case [the criminals] are to be kept in custody and it is ordered that they not be able to use their rank as an indemnity, or to be excused and released or pay off [the crime] with a fine.[44]

Similarly,

殺傷大父母、父母及奴婢殺傷主、主父母妻子,自告者皆不得減。告人不審, 所(告)者有它罪與告也罪等以上,告者不為不審。

In cases of killing a grandfather or grandmother, a father or mother, and of a male or female slave killing or injuring their master, or the father, mother, wife or children of their master, those who make a self-denunciation are in no case to be able to diminish [the crime].[45]

In short, heads of households had the same rights over slaves as they had over their own children. However, slaves were protected by the law to a certain extent against arbitrary punishment and death at the hands of their masters, because killing a slave was considered a crime, which was punished by the redeemable death penalty.

父母毆笞子及奴婢,子及奴婢以毆笞辜死,令贖死。

Fathers or mothers who beat or cane [with a bamboo rod] children or male and female slaves, and the children and male and female slaves die as a result of the beating or being hit by the rod, order that they redeem the death penalty.[46]

Slaves, like children and principal wives, who tried to make use of the law to redress their perceived wrongs against the seniors in their family had their cases summarily rejected and were executed:

子告父母,婦告威公,奴婢告主、主父母妻子,勿聽而棄告者市。

Do not hear[47] children who denounce their fathers and mothers, principal wives (*fu*) who denounce their mothers-in-law (*weigong*), male and female slaves who denounce their masters or master's father, mother, wife, or children. Rather, cast away the denouncer in the marketplace.[48]

And if they participated in a case and were found not to be speaking the truth, they were mutilated:

奴婢自訟不審,斬奴左止,黥婢 (顏)頯,畀其主。

As for male and female slaves who carelessly vindicate themselves [in a law case],[49] cut off the male slave's left foot and tattoo the female slave's face and cheekbones and return them to their master.[50]

The early Han state also tried to regulate the sexual relations between slaves and their masters and between children and the slaves of their immediate family members. The latter case was considered to be a form of incest:

奴取主、主之母及主妻、子以為妻,若與奸,棄市,而耐其女子以為隸妾。其强與奸,除所强。

If a male slave marries his owner, the mother of his owner or the wife or daughter of his owner and makes them his wife, or if they fornicate, he is to be cast away in the market place and shave the woman and make her a bond servant (*liqie*). If he fornicates by force, release those whom he has forced.[51]

復兄弟、孝〈季〉父、柏〈伯〉父妻、御婢皆黥為城旦舂。復男弟兄子、孝〈季〉父、柏〈伯〉父子之妻、御婢,皆完為城旦。

[All those who] have illicit sexual relations (*fu*) with the wife of their elder or younger brothers, or [the wife of] father's younger brothers or father's elder brothers, or female slaves with whom they sleep (*yubei*), are in every case to be tattooed and made wall builders or grain pounders. Those who have illicit sexual relations with the male children of their elder or younger brothers or the wives of the sons of their father's elder or younger brothers, or female slaves with whom they sleep,[52] are in every case to be made intact wall builders.[53]

A master, by contrast as in all slave-owning regimes, had sexual access to his female slaves. Should the slave have a child by him and he die, the Han manumitted her to become a freedwoman. Undoubtedly, the child would have been a commoner, following his father's status:

婢御其主而有子,主死,免其婢為庶人。

Should a female slave wait on her master and have a child, and the master die, manumit the slave and make her a freedwoman (*shuren*).[54]

This may have been one of the more common ways in which female slaves could gain manumission and the status of freedman, but there are no statistics to verify how common this eventuality was.

EVIDENCE FROM LEGAL CASES

From several law-cases preserved in the *Zouyan shu* in the Zhangjiashan hoard, it is apparent that in the period of political uncertainty during the civil war between the forces of Xiang Yu 項羽 (d. 202) and Liu Bang after the fall of the Qin, slaves tried to make use of the unsettled times and vacuum in duly constituted legal authority to free themselves from their bondage. By fleeing from the area controlled by Xiang Yu and submitting to legal authorities politically controlled by Liu Bang, they hoped to remove the stigma of their base status. However, the Han authorities only accepted the validity of their change of status if they registered themselves and their property and willingly subjected themselves to the tax impositions of the Han. If they failed to do so, and merely claimed to be free without having it verified and recorded, then, when their former masters pursued them and re-enslaved them, the Han officials acceded to their former masters' petitions and authorized their re-enslavement.

However, if they did register themselves as free individuals and the former slave master tried to re-enslave them, then the master was in the wrong. This is the situation in the complicated case of a thirty-seven-year-old former slave named Wu, an unranked commoner after his submission to the Han and his registration, whose former master, Jun, denounced him to a thief-catcher (a low-ranking official like a policeman responsible for security at the local level) for being a runaway slave.[55] This thief-catcher pursued Wu, who resisted arrest and struck the thief-catcher with a sword because, Wu later explained, he was angry that he was being accused of the crime of being a runaway slave. The thief-catcher drew his own sword and injured Wu and arrested him. This case was sent all the way up to Han Emperor Gaozu, who endorsed the decision that Wu should have explained the situation to the arresting official and should not have drawn his sword and injured him. Wu was sentenced for "wounding another person with malicious intent" and was sentenced to tattooing and five to six years of hard labor, the sentence of *chengdan* 城旦. Thus, although the former master admitted to the crime of "carelessly denouncing" another person, the thief-catcher was exonerated from any wrongdoing in making the arrest and injuring the former slave, and the former slave, although wrongly arrested, committed the most serious crime in an emotional outburst, for which he paid dearly.

In another case, the latest in the *Zouyan shu*, dated 196, a female slave named Mei 美 likewise tried to escape her bondage, but she failed to register her name as was required and was caught and re-enslaved by her former master. He then sold her to another individual, whereupon she absconded but was recaptured and denounced to the Han authorities. Although she claimed that she should never have been re-enslaved, the officials were suspicious of the reason why she had not properly registered herself and wondered whether she had committed some crime while on the run. The final disposition of the case is not provided in the source, with the officials divided over whether she should been freed to become a freedwoman, or whether she should be tattooed on her forehead and returned to her second master. Thus the second opinion was that, in conformity with the statute translated above, the slave Mei had tried to "carelessly vindicate herself" in a lawsuit. [56]

In a third case, a slave named Yi 宜 absconded and fled over the boundaries of Beidi Commandery 北地郡 in modern Gansu Province, quite probably to Xiongnu territory. Although both absconding and passing over the border without official authorization were crimes, the case concerns the punishment of those whose responsibility was to catch and arrest such an escapee, the official in charge of the border post and his men, not the slave Yi, whose fate is not recorded and who may never have been apprehended. According to the "Statutes on Levies" ("Xing lü" 興律), the penalty for the crime of an official failing to catch a runaway apparently was normally a fine. However, slip 404 in the Zhangjiashan statutes is broken halfway down the slip and it is not possible to determine the value of that fine. Nevertheless, this regulation was modified by the first item in the "Ordinance on Fords and Passes" ("Jinguan ling" 津關令), which specified that such frontier officials be sentenced to redeemable shaving of the facial whiskers, the punishment ordered by the senior legal official of the government, the Commandant of the Court (*tingwei* 廷尉), to whom the case was forwarded for final decision.[57]

A BRIEF CONCLUSION

Legal cases such as these shed precious light on the actual functioning of the laws involving slaves in the period of transition between the Qin and the Han, and how slaves tried to turn the laws to their own advantage: they were not merely pawns in the hands of their owners; they struggled to assert themselves and advance their personal interests. The cases also show how the Han managed to assert its authority over the vast population, many of whom were displaced, at the local level. The information provided by these cases, and the statutes that I have discussed in this chapter, have been lost for more than two thousand years. Now, finally, we are learning in extraordinary detail many aspects of daily life, and hearing the voices of slaves and ordinary commoners usually omitted in the transmitted historical sources, albeit mediated through the transcriptions of the legal scribes who reworded the plaintiffs' and defendants' oral statements into formal legal language fitting the form of the documents they were preparing for submission to their superiors. We also can see more clearly the various dimensions of slave status in the Qin and Han transition.

In short, it appears that the Han changed or refined the nomenclature of slaves they inherited from the Qin in 202 and enacted new legislation, the Statutes on Slaves and the Statutes on Freedmen. Although these laws are not extant, they are alluded to in the Zhangjiashan Tomb 247 legal documents. These may have been the first legal statutes that defined the legal obligations, rights, and punishments of slaves and freedmen in Chinese history. In the process, it would appear that the Han simplified the complex system of nomenclature of the Qin and gave freedmen a more defined legal status. Most particularly, the Han tried to assimilate slaves into the family system. However, at the same time as providing greater protection to slaves from abuse than seems to have been the case under the Qin (under the Han, a master who beat his slave to death was required to redeem the death penalty by paying the very heavy fine of two *jin* and eight *liang* of gold, among the highest fines specified in the Zhangjiashan laws, see Peng Hao et al. 2007: 140, slip 119), by treating them as family members, the Han inflicted a harsher punishment on a slave for acting in an "unfilial" fashion by denouncing master for a crime than was the case under the Qin: under the Qin such a denunciation was considered to be an "unofficial" or "non-public domain denunciation" (*fei gongshi gao* 非公室告) and the denunciation was not to be heard, but under the Han, the slave's denunciation was likewise not to be heard, but additionally the denouncer was to be publically executed.[58]

Similarly, the Han continued the harsh treatment of slaves that they had inherited from the Qin. Two Qin cases preserved in the *Forms for Sealing and Investigating* provide the evidence (Hulsewé 1985 E15-E16: 193–195; McLeod and Yates 1981). In one a male slave is denounced by his master for being a scold or obstreperous, and refusing to work in his master's fields and carry out orders. This was a crime and the master requests that his left foot be amputated, that he be made to serve a five- to six-year hard labor sentence, and that he be sold to the state. In the second, a female slave is similarly a scold toward her master, and the master requests that she be tattooed and have her nose cut off. In both cases, the Qin state authorities engage in an inquiry to determine whether the masters were speaking the truth, whether the denounced slave really had behaved in the way alleged, and whether they truly were who the master claimed them to be. The early Han statutes also permitted masters either to request that their slaves be mutilated in a similar fashion or even to be publically executed (Peng Hao et al. 2007: 107–108, slips 44–45). However, the statutes do not state whether a Qin-type investigation was to take place before the punishment was carried out.

Finally, there is another important issue that I have not discussed here. That is, despite the fact that the Qin state had very large numbers of hard labor convicts as well as regular corvée laborers at its disposal to work on its innumerable construction projects, it appears from the Liye documents that it still had to purchase slave labor to meet its needs in both ordinary and special circumstances. Document 8-154 (*Liye* 2012: 19; Chen Wei 2012: 93–94) quotes an ordinance which stated, "Always on the first day [of the month] report to higher authorities the number of *tuli* 徒隸 (bonded laborers) bought." Wang Huanlin (2007: 46) proposes that the term *tuli* generally refers to hard laborers serving long-term sentences, called *chengdan* for males and *chong* 舂 for females, and *guixin* 鬼薪 (males) and *baican* 白粲 (females), but since these could not be bought or sold, the phrase must refer to *lichenqie* 隸臣妾 (male and female bond servants). However, other scholars argue that the latter were three-year term hard laborers, serving a shorter sentence than the former two types of convicts.[59] Regardless of the identity of these workers, what is to be noted is that they were of such low slavelike status that the government could buy them on the open market, on the one hand, and, on the other, that Sima Qian uses this term *tuli* to identify many of the workers who constructed the First Emperor's mausoleum (cf. Shelach, chapter 3 in this volume). If *tuli* were really responsible for most of the hard labor for building that site, and the numbers mentioned by Sima Qian for that particular project, 700,000 workers all told, are close to being accurate, then there must have been a very large market for slavelike workers in the Qin.[60] It is clear that we still have a long way to go to understand the exact nature of the many statuses among the lower orders of the Qin and early Han and how they may have changed over time and political and military circumstances.

It is to be hoped that new evidence will come to light that reveals even more information about the legal status of slaves in the Qin and early Han and provide further evidence on how the treatment of slaves evolved in the early empires. Complete publication of the newly discovered administrative and legal documents is eagerly awaited.

PART III

Image and Impact of Qin

Introduction

The First Emperor and His Image

Yuri Pines

Of manifold controversial figures in Chinese history, the First Emperor of Qin occupies pride of place. He is depicted alternatively as a hero or a villain—the proud creator of an empire that lasted for two millennia or the savage destroyer of China's traditional civilization, a model universal ruler or a reviled tyrant. The controversy about his role and that of his short-lived dynasty in the history of Chinese civilization has continued unabated since the fall of the Qin, and it will no doubt continue for the foreseeable future, as it is fueled less by disagreement about basic facts of Qin imperial history than by conflicting moral and ideological evaluations of the First Emperor's grand enterprise. As such, the ongoing debate over the Qin Empire concerns not just the past, but, primarily, the present: it is the debate about how China is to be governed, how much autonomy is to be accorded to each of its parts, what role intellectuals should have in society, and what means are legitimate in restoring China's glorious position as a powerful and awe-inspiring polity.

Three major events from the history of the Qin Empire shaped its image in the eyes of subsequent generations. The first is its extraordinarily successful establishment. The First Emperor's campaigns of 233–221 succeeded in putting an end to the political fragmentation that had plagued the "Chinese" world for more than five centuries. Moreover, in the early years of his reign the Emperor and his aides established an effective system of centralized control over their huge realm; they took credit for unifying the written script, the weights and measures, coinage, laws and administrative regulations, and even the pantheon, laying thereby a solid foundation for the lasting unity of China proper. These achievements were a source of immense pride for the First Emperor, who duly used them in his self-propaganda: by claiming to have brought peace, stability and orderly rule, he could justify posing as the long-awaited savior who had realized the generations-long dreams of earlier statesmen and thinkers (Pines, chapter 8 in this volume). The magnitude of these achievements could not be ignored even by the Emperor's harshest critics.

The second event that influenced tremendously the posthumous image of the First Emperor was his assault on private learning. According to Sima Qian's *Historical Records*, in 213 a court discussion about the desirability of replacing a centralized administrative system of the Qin with the more dispersed model that had prevailed during the Western Zhou prompted a harsh reaction from the chief chancellor, Li Si 李斯 (d. 208). Accusing the proponents of the latter alternative of "using the past to reject the present," Li Si identified adherents of "private learning" (*si xue* 私學) as undesirable remnants of the bygone age of political fragmentation, whose divisiveness was undermining the recently won unity and who were threatening to subvert imperial power. He suggested to destroy historical writings of the vanquished Warring States, and to eliminate copies of the *Book of Poems*, the *Venerated Documents*, and *Speeches of the Hundred Schools* (*baijia yu* 百家語) from private collections, explicitly excluding, however, the possessions of the court erudites (*boshi* 博士). The Emperor approved Li Si's memorial, initiating thereby the infamous "biblioclasm" of 213.[1]

The biblioclasm became a turning point in the relations between the intellectuals and the throne in China's history. Until then, in the polycentric world of the Warring States, members of the educated elite had been able to choose their employer from among the competing courts, which allowed them a considerable degree of occupational and ideological autonomy (Pines 2009: 163–180). In the unified empire, however, new rules of engagement emerged, and Li Si did not hesitate to employ the coercive power of the imperial apparatus to subjugate the intellectuals. Leaving aside for the time being conflicting interpretations of this event (for which see below), it is clear that it caused deep enmity among segments of the educated elite toward the Qin. Indeed, soon thereafter several eminent followers of Confucius, including his descendant in the eighth generation, Kong Fu 孔鮒 (*style* Jia 甲), decided to throw their lot with the rebellious peasant Chen She 陳涉 (d. 208); Kong Fu eventually died in Chen's service (*Shiji* 121: 3116). This first-ever instance of members of the respected intellectual elite joining the ranks of rebels suggests a deep aversion on the part of at least some of the intellectuals toward the oppressive Qin regime. Eventually, the image of Qin was irreparably tarnished in the eyes of the overwhelming majority of the imperial literati.

The third event that shaped the later image of Qin was its rapid collapse. Sima Qian narrates in detail how the Second Emperor, who ascended the throne in a coup d'état in the immediate aftermath of the founder's death in 210, proved an intemperate and inept ruler, whose misrule, combined with the general oppressiveness of the Qin regime, led to an outburst of popular rebellions led by Chen She and his followers. Within two years, the formidable Qin armies, which less than one generation before had conquered the entire East Asian subcontinent, were crushed, and the first imperial dynasty was toppled. The success of Chen She, "a servant of peasants, an exile among exiles" (*Shiji* 48: 1964–1965; Watson 1993: 80), was an astounding event. For the first time in China's history, the warning by Xunzi 荀子 (c. 310–230) that the people could "capsize the [ruler's] boat" had materialized.[2] In a marked distinction from earlier dynastic polities, the lifespan of the imperial Qin was measured not in centuries but just in years. The dynasty had barely outlived its founder.

From the first generations in the aftermath of Qin's collapse, statesmen and scholars sought explanations to its peculiar trajectory, which seemingly defied the rules of history as they had been conceptualized by preimperial and early imperial thinkers. According to the traditional view, which can be traced back to the Western Zhou period, every major dynasty had to be founded by a virtuous leader, whose superb moral and intellectual qualities supposedly ensured him unequivocal support of both Heaven and men; while the leader under whom the dynasty collapsed was assumed to be either a monster or at least an extraordinarily benighted individual.[3] The latter depiction could fit well the Second Emperor, but how were historians to treat his father, the Qin's founder? Should he be lauded for his successful unification of the realm, or reviled for the oppressiveness of his rule and his inability to ensure the dynasty's survival? What was wrong with Qin, which had its life cut short so abruptly, in contrast to the Xia, Shang, and Zhou dynasties? And what lessons could be drawn from its failure?

The assessment of Qin's place in history was not just a matter of historical curiosity. The Han dynasty inherited the fundamental parameters of the Qin imperial polity, including the institution of emperorship, the basic administrative arrangements, the legal and ritual systems, and much of the imperial lexicon and imperial ideology. While the early Han leaders were less assertive and more prone to compromise than the Qin emperors, most notably by allowing establishment of autonomous princedoms in the eastern half of their realm, the overall impact of the Qin legacy on the Han is undeniable (see, e.g., Loewe 1987; Hsing and

Yates, chapters 4 and 6 in this volume, respectively). Yet the Han founder, Liu Bang 劉邦 (d. 195), came from the ranks of anti-Qin rebels, which precluded uncritical acceptance of the Qin legacy in toto. It was essential, therefore, for the very legitimacy of the Han dynastic enterprise to present a balanced evaluation of the Qin that would allow the continuation of the bulk of Qin policies, while also highlighting the faults that had justified the Qin's overthrow.

A masterfully balanced assessment of the Qin, which set the tone for many subsequent discussions, and which is widely cited throughout this volume, was presented by an influential early Han thinker, Jia Yi 賈誼 (200–168). In his *Faulting the Qin* (*Guo Qin lun* 過秦論), Jia Yi is careful to recognize Qin's achievements while criticizing the First Emperor for his excessive harshness and for his inability to seek advice from meritorious aides, as well as faulting the Second Emperor for his overall ineptitude. Jia Yi carefully distinguishes between a fundamentally positive assessment of the Qin dynastic enterprise—and by extension of the imperial polity—and a criticism of individual wrongdoings by the Qin leaders. Yet while these leaders are disparaged, they are not demonized in a same fashion as the paradigmatic tyrants of the past, such as the last Shang ruler Zhouxin 紂辛 (for whom see, e.g., Pines 2008b). A similarly careful synthesis of positive and negative assessments of the First Emperor is arguably evident also in Sima Qian's *Historical Records* (see Puett 2001: 188–191; for an alternative view, see van Ess, chapter 7 in this volume), and it may well reflect the dominant approach of the early Han thinkers.

Against this balanced view, from the early Han dynasty on we can distinguish a much more radical critique of the Qin. It is possible that the propagators of uncompromising anti-Qin views initially came from within the ranks of the aristocracy of the defeated Warring States, for whom the Qin unification had brought personal humiliation and a sharp decline in their fortunes;[4] and one can distinguish certain continuity in anti-Qin rhetoric of the Warring States period and that of the early Han age (see, e.g., Zang Zhifei 2002). Yet much more significant was the anti-Qin backlash which began about the middle of the Former Han dynasty. By then, those elite members who opposed the economic, administrative, and military activism initiated by Emperor Wu 漢武帝 (r. 141–87) began routinely to employ Qin as a foil against which the proper Han rule should be defined. Since the Han rulers consistently tried to distance themselves from the First Emperor, it was much safer for the opponents of imperial activism to focus on Qin's misdeeds than to criticize Emperor

Wu and his successors directly. Extremely negative views of Qin were fully vented, for example, during the famous "Salt and Iron" debates held in 81 BCE, shortly after Emperor Wu's death (e.g., *Yantie lun*, "Fei Yang" 非鞅 7: 93–97; "Zhou Qin" 周秦 57: 586); thereafter, the critics became increasingly vociferous. It was not incidentally under Emperor Wu that a leading Han thinker, Dong Zhongshu 董仲舒 (c. 195–115), proposed to expurgate the Qin from the sequence of legitimate dynasties (Arbuckle 1995). Countless literati from then on adopted a view of Qin as a disaster to civilization, an aberration in China's history, a "redundant" (*run* 潤) dynasty that had perpetrated heinous crimes and gained little if any merit worth remembering (for debates over Qin legitimacy, see, e.g., Rao Zongyi 1996).

The anti-Qin tide became stronger in the second century of the Former Han dynasty as opposition to government activism gained further momentum, paralleling the government's gradual abandonment of what Loewe (1974, 1987) dubs a "modernist" (i.e., Qin-inspired) model in favor of a looser one, which drew inspiration from the imagined Zhou past.[5] While influential statesmen and thinkers would at times endorse the Qin model, as was demonstrated by Sang Hongyang 桑弘羊 (152–80), one of the architects of Emperor Wu's economic policies, during the "Salt and Iron" debates, their voices were clearly outnumbered among the literati. By the time of Wang Mang 王莽 (r. 9–23 CE), the negative view of Qin became overwhelming: while historians continued to acknowledge the Han indebtedness to Qin precedents, in the mainstream political discourse the first imperial dynasty became associated primarily with misdeeds and failures rather than with the successful establishment of the imperial polity.[6]

Throughout the two millennia of imperial China, Qin became, to the majority of literati, an emblem of all those aspects of the imperial polity that they detested: a state ruled by a haughty and hyperactive monarch who would mistreat his aides and punish his critics; an intrusive bureaucracy that would disrupt the normal life of rural communities; excessive military activity and the proliferation of construction projects that depleted the people's resources; and, worst of all, the court's senseless and brutal suppression of (real or imagined) intellectual opposition. Qin was accused of a variety of crimes, sometimes real but more often imagined. It was blamed, for example, for having destroyed the semi-legendary "well-field system," which had supposedly ensured relative equality among peasants in the past; it was also alleged to have annihilated the so-called *fengjian* 封建 system, which late imperial theorists incorrectly imagined to have assured the autonomous self-rule of rural communities; moreover, it was accused of having committed woeful atrocities toward all social strata, with the First Emperor recast as the ultimate bloodthirsty villain, on a par with Zhouxin and similar legendary and semi-legendary monsters (Zhang Fentian 2005: 657–677).

One of the clearest examples of how the demonization of Qin proceeded is the story of the First Emperor's supposedly "burying Confucians alive" (keng ru 坑儒). Sima Qian tells of the First Emperor's decision, in 212 BCE, to execute 460 scholars (sheng 生) who were critical of him. In all likelihood this action was directed primarily or exclusively against the so-called technical masters (fang shi 方士), who were wasting precious state resources in attempts to procure the Emperor the pill of immortality, which of course they failed to deliver (Shiji 6: 258). Initially, this atrocity (which was not entirely unprecedented) was barely noticed by early critics of Qin such as Jia Yi, yet by the end of the Former Han it became linked with the biblioclasm that took place just a year before, and both events were interpreted as being directed against the followers of Confucius (Ru 儒). This allowed the literati in turn to interpret the First Emperor's assault on private learning—a step which had clear parallels in the attempts of later emperors, such as Emperor Wu, to ensure intellectuals' subservience to the throne (Ge Quan 2003, Pines 2012a: 85–89)—as an ideological suppression of Confucianism, an exceptional event that turned the First Emperor from a normal autocrat into a monster. The resultant "Legalist" and "anti-Confucian" image of Qin remains popular even today despite manifold indications that Qin culture was by no means "anti-Confucian" (Kern 2000), and despite numerous studies that expose the fallacy of the notion of an anti-Confucian oppression by the First Emperor (e.g., Zhang Shilong 1988; Zhang Zixia 1991; Zhou Fang 2013; cf. Neininger 1983).[7]

To be sure, not every traditional Chinese scholar subscribed to this anti-Qin propaganda. Sensitive historians, such as Zheng Qiao 鄭樵 (1104–1160 CE) and Gu Yanwu 顧炎武 (1613–1682 CE), pointed out obvious distortions; supporters of political centralization and of strong imperial power—from Liu Zongyuan 柳宗元 (773–819 CE) to Zhang Juzheng 張居正 (1525–1582 CE) and Wang Fuzhi 王夫之 (1619–1692 CE)—hailed Qin's lasting contribution to the empire's prowess; and we find even such unexpected personalities as the great Tang poet Li Bai 李白 (also known as Li Bo) (701–762 CE) and the controversial individualist Li Zhi 李贄 (1527–1602 CE) among the First Emperor's sympathizers.[8] But while the views of these individuals have proved important to modern scholars' quest to reassess the First Emperor, they were a minority opinion in their time. Insofar as Qin remained an emblem of oppressiveness and tyranny, and insofar as its founder was being portrayed as Confucius's antipode, negative views of the dynasty prevailed. Thus even the severely authoritarian-minded Ming founder, Zhu Yuanzhang 朱元璋 (1328–1398, r. 1368–1398), opted to distance himself from the Qin and to use it as an unequivocally negative historical example rather than seeking inspiration from it.[9] For a monarch eager to improve his image among the members of the educated elite, to denigrate, or at least to distance himself from, the First Emperor was as politically expedient as it was to extol Confucius.

China's entrance into the modern age was accompanied by a profound reassessment of the First Emperor's historical role. With the end of the intellectual hegemony of the imperial brand of "Confucianism," the supposedly "Legalist" inclinations of the empire's founder were no longer necessarily considered a fault. To the contrary, his ability to put an end to domestic turmoil and to turn "China" into a superpower was now hailed by many eminent thinkers, as was his perceived disdain of the Tradition and his preference of the "present" to the "past." That the fiercely nationalistic anti-Qing revolutionary Zhang Binglin 章炳麟 (1868–1936 CE) hailed the Qin emperor as one whose achievements had "almost" crowned those of the paragon rulers of antiquity is perhaps not very surprising.[10] More interestingly, even such a liberal thinker as Hu Shi 胡適 (1891–1962 CE) became fascinated with the Qin and went so far as to laud the biblioclasm of 213 BCE as an example of a liberation of the mind. Hu wrote:

> Political dictatorship is surely frightening, but the dictatorship of adoring the past is even more frightening . . . After two thousand years, having been fed up with two millennia of "narrating the past to harm the present and adorning empty words to harm the substance," we cannot but admit that Han Fei[zi] and Li Si were the greatest statesmen in Chinese history. Although we cannot completely endorse their methods, we should never let their brave spirit of opposing those who "do not make the present into their teacher but learn from the past" fall into oblivion: it deserves our utmost admiration![11]

Hu Shi's surprising endorsement of what hitherto had been considered the First Emperor's single most unforgivable anti-intellectual atrocity is revealing, but it should not be interpreted as representative of mainstream historical thought during the Republican era. On the contrary, soon enough the pendulum shifted again toward criticism of the Qin, as conservative thinkers, eager to restore the paramount position of Confucius as the national sage, decried Qin's cultural barbarism, while liberal and leftist scholars, most notably the eminent Marxist historian Guo Moruo 郭沫若 (1892–1978 CE) bitterly attacked the First Emperor's despotism, hinting thereby at the dictatorial tendencies of Chiang Kaishek's (Jiang Jieshi 蔣介石, 1887–1975 CE) rule.[12] In general, the negative image of the First Emperor continued to dominate historical discourse until the establishment of the People's Republic of China (PRC) in 1949.

In the first decades of the People's Republic the pendulum shifted again in the First Emperor's favor. While initially historians were hesitant about possibly endorsing a "representative of the exploitive classes," whose dynasty had been swept away by the first historically verifiable "peasant rebellion," soon enough the personal preferences of Chairman Mao (Mao Zedong 毛澤東, 1893–1976 CE) determined a new course. Mao's self-identification with the First Emperor can be traced already to the time of composition of his famous poem "Snow" (*Xue* 雪), in 1936; it became ever more pronounced as time passed, most notably during the last years of the Great Proletarian Cultural Revolution (1966–1976 CE). With Mao's blessing, the First Emperor was elevated to the position of an admirable historical figure, the representative of the "progressive feudal class" that put an end to the "reactionary slave-owner society."[13] Although this brief period of adoration ended shortly after Mao's death, it was indicative of the First Emperor's strong appeal after millennia of a predominantly negative image.

In the relaxed scholarly atmosphere of the post-Mao decades, the debates over the image of the First Emperor and his historical role have been renewed, and the divergence of opinion is now greater than ever. Especially in recent years, as the Internet has come to provide an additional forum for expressing individual opinions, one has been able to find a plethora of contrasting evaluations: for some he is the proud founder of the "Chinese nation," a glorious leader, "one in a thousand"; for others a reviled tyrant, a "fascist ruler," a person responsible for a "cultural Holocaust."[14] The dividing lines among the proponents of such opposite views are not clearly defined and surely cannot be reduced to two camps that might label one another as "nationalistic historians" or "petty Confucian doctrinaires," respectively. To complicate matters further, recently the First Emperor gained additional local popularity in his native Shaanxi province, which capitalizes on the tourist revenues from pilgrimages to his mausoleum. The multiplicity of assessments of this towering figure continues to bewilder scholars, textbook writers, and film directors alike and explains to a certain extent the avalanche of Qin-related publications and different media representations in recent years.[15]

Given the range of opinions regarding the historical role of the First Emperor, there are surprisingly few controversies about the factual basis of our evaluations. Indeed, in evaluating the history of the Qin Empire—especially that of its ruling elite—our dependence on the *Historical Records* remains overwhelming. Even when there are controversies on such issues as the degree of centralization under the Qin, the supposed execution of "Confucians," or the nature of the anti-Qin rebellions in 209–208, these revolve primarily around conflicting interpretations of Sima Qian's account.[16] While the amount of the new materials related to the history of the Qin empire is impressive (suffice it to mention the First Emperor's mausoleum, the Shuihudi slips, and the Liye Well 1 hoard, which rank among the major archaeological discoveries in China in recent decades), they are insufficient to verify, refute, or replace the bulk of Sima Qian's narrative insofar as the First Emperor's activities are concerned.

This overwhelming dependence on a single historical work in discussing one of the crucial periods and one of the most important personalities in Chinese history leaves many of us uncomfortable. It requires major efforts in assessing the reliability of the *Historical Records* and of the dominant interpretations of this work. In this respect, participants of the workshop took different positions. In chapter 7, Hans van Ess proposes a radically revisionist reading of the *Historical Records*. After meticulously comparing suspicious similarities between Sima Qian's accounts of the First Emperor and those that deal with Sima Qian's own imperial master, Emperor Wu, van Ess concludes that "it is quite plausible that the tale of the First Emperor of the Qin that we find in the *Shiji* was actually written as a warning to Emperor Wu of the Han." If this is correct, it follows that the entire foundation of our knowledge about the Qin is extremely shaky. While few of us would go as far as doubting the fundamental reliability of the *Historical Records,* van Ess's chapter cautions us against uncritical reliance on it, especially when it cannot be supported by additional independent sources.

In my treatment of the First Emperor in chapter 8, I adopt a different approach from van Ess. Following the lead of Martin Kern (2000), I accept the texts of the imperial steles, erected by the order of the First Emperor, as a major reliable source for the Emperor's ideology and his self-image. Analyzing Qin self-propaganda as seen in the stele inscriptions from the perspective of the Warring States period discourse, I demonstrate that far from being anti-traditional, the First Emperor actually synthesized and appropriated the legacy of the Warring States–period thinkers. I further argue that the notion of emperorship established by the First Emperor, and particularly the concept of the ruler as a reigning sage, became his major legacy for the Han and subsequent dynasties. At the same time, I suggest that the First Emperor himself was partly responsible for his subsequent image as a historical "aberration." Eager to bolster his power, he adopted a peculiar (I use the term "messianic") posture as an exceptional ruler, dwarfing the former paragons, declaring (as it were) the "end of history," and claiming to have realized utopia on earth. Thus, the First Emperor distinguished himself from both predecessors and successors, inadvertently contributing to the view that the Qin dynasty constituted a rupture in China's historical development.

Van Ess and I differ with regard to our understanding of details of the Qin imperial history and with regard of the degree to which we trust the sources; but beyond these disagreements, it is important to notice the common ground between us, and indeed among all the contributors. None of us subscribes to a view of the Qin dynasty as anti-traditional and anti-Confucian; none accepts the Han as the Qin antipode; and despite our differences, all of us agree that there was fundamental continuity from the Qin into the Han. As parts I and II have shown, the material and paleographic evidence overwhelmingly lend support to such a view. With regard to these points, we should emphasize the difference between the current scholarly consensus as crystallized here and the dominant narrative of the Qin as the Legalist other of Chinese civilization that still pervades popular accounts and, regrettably, some of the textbooks (e.g., Hardy and Kinney, 2005). We hope that our discussion here will contribute toward a major revision of this flawed narrative, based as it is on the uncritical acceptance of the Later Han and post-Han misreadings of the *Historical Records*.

Many other questions concerning Qin history await further research. What was the real degree of administrative centralization and uniformity in the unified empire given the little time the Qin had to impose its political agenda before it collapsed?[17] Which segments of the elites of the former Six Eastern States were incorporated into the Qin imperial government, and which were suppressed? Were there regional and temporal differences in the populace's acceptance of the Qin rule? How did different social strata react to the Qin conquest? While some of these questions may perhaps be answered after the publication of more of the

Liye and Yuelu Academy materials, others will have to wait until further discoveries and new approaches.

Qin history should not be treated as an isolated phenomenon. Rather, its peculiar historical trajectory from a minor polity to a superpower and then to a "universal" empire; its evolution from aristocratic to bureaucratic polity; its complex cultural interaction with members of the Zhou *oikoumenē* and with the non-Zhou periphery; and its administrative, intellectual, and cultural dynamics all call for comparison with similar developments elsewhere. Of particular interest would be analyzing similarities and differences between the Qin imperial enterprise and other early imperial polities. Why did the Chinese empire—at least insofar as its fundamental political structure is concerned—last longer than its counterparts elsewhere? How did the peculiar background of the empire's creation, in particular Qin's historical experience, contribute toward the empire's longevity? Which aspects of Qin's imperial polity are akin to those in other empires worldwide and which are peculiar to Qin?

Intriguing as they are, these questions remained by and large beyond the scope of the present volume. This was done not only because some of them had been already raised in several recent studies to which a few of us had contributed (Alcock 2001; Mutschler and Mittag 2008; Scheidel 2009), but primarily because we came to the conclusion that to allow a meaningful comparison, we should first present in a comprehensive and systematic form our understanding of Qin history proper.[18] And yet we did not want to sacrifice the comparative perspective altogether. Hence, as a suggestion for a possible line of future research, we decided to end our volume with an essay by Alexander Yakobson that focuses on the Roman Emperor Augustus rather than on the First Emperor of Qin (chapter 9).

Our selection of Augustus is not casual. Few figures in world history can be compared to the First Emperor as meaningfully as can Augustus. Both were exceptionally successful leaders who immensely influenced the historical course of their respective realms, both founded lasting empires, and both were well aware of the importance of public opinion—including the opinion of posterity—and did their best to project their desired image to their subjects. Yet these similarities aside, both leaders also differed tremendously. Augustus, even at the very end of his eventful life, tried to adopt the posture of protector of the Roman republican past, of magistrate rather than monarch, of a servant of the people and not just their leader. In contrast, the First Emperor emphasized his superhuman qualities as an absolute monarch, projecting himself as the one who was incomparably superior to the rest of the humankind. From the very inception, the Roman Empire appears to have been rooted deeply in its republican past, while the Chinese tends to further strengthen the monarchical foundation of Chinese political culture, which long predates the Qin unification (Liu Zehua 2000; Pines 2009).

These differences may have been highly significant in determining the future course of both empires. In Rome, as Yakobson observes, the concept of an emperor as a magistrate and not just the monarch eventually allowed the simultaneous establishment of two or more emperors—what would be as abnormal in the Chinese case as the simultaneous election of two popes for the Catholic Church. Does this mean that the stronger monarchic tendencies of the Chinese empire, which the First Emperor bequeathed on his successors, proved a more viable means of preserving the imperial enterprise intact? Did the more strongly pronounced super-human quality of the imperial office in China contribute to the empire's longevity? Or should the roots of China's imperial success be looked for elsewhere? To what extent was the greater longevity of the Chinese empire, as compared to Rome, a "success"? The answers to these questions will have to wait for future systematic comparative work, which the present volume hopes however modestly to inform.

7 Emperor Wu of the Han and the First August Emperor of Qin in Sima Qian's *Shiji*

Hans van Ess

The account of the First Qin Emperor in the *Historical Records* (*Shiji*), written by Sima Tan 司馬談 (died 110) and his son Sima Qian 司馬遷 (ca. 145–87), who succeeded Sima Tan in the position of court astronomer and scribe, has been a subject of debate in sinological literature for several decades. It has been pointed out by numerous scholars that this account was not a positive one. However, there have also been voices saying that Sima Qian actually criticized the Han, not so much the Qin, or better that he "pointed at Qin in order to criticize the Han" (*zhi Qin ma Han* 指秦罵漢).[1] This chapter explores this topic further by looking into several aspects which show that the Qin indeed served as a foil for Sima Qian's criticism of the Han, or, to be more precise, that the biography of the First Emperor of Qin served as a foil for Sima Qian's critique of Emperor Wu of the Han (漢武帝, r. 141–87).

At the outset, it may be interesting to note that the first section of the *Shiji*, which is the section of the basic annals devoted to the description of dynasties and individual rulers, consists of twelve chapters. Tang dynasty (唐, 618–907 CE) scholars explained this number as an allusion to the twelve months of the year, just as the number of chapters in other sections has been related to the calendar.[2] Interestingly, one may divide these twelve chapters into five chapters of early dynasties,[3] two chapters concerning reigns of rulers who ruled for a relatively short period so that their time might be understood as an interim period,[4] and five emperors of the Han. There is, of course, a problem with this interpretation, namely that this way of reckoning accords to the preimperial state of Qin (number five of the twelve annals chapters) the status of a fully legitimate dynasty. An elegant solution to this problem would be to divide the twelve annals sections into two halves. When doing this, the First

August Emperor of the Qin to whom the sixth annals chapter is devoted assumes the last position of the first half of this section.[5] According to this model the corresponding chapter 12, the last one of the second half, is devoted to Emperor Wu of the Han.[6]

This, of course, is just playing with numbers. Furthermore, it remains problematic that *Shiji* as it has come down to us today does contain a detailed account of the life and deeds of the First Emperor of Qin, whereas the Annals of Emperor Wu are missing and have been replaced by a large part of chapter 28 of the *Shiji*, the "Treatise on the *feng* 封 and *shan* 禪 sacrifices" at Mount Tai 泰山 and the other imperial sacrifices. As is well known, the *Xijing zaji* 西京雜記 contains a passage which says that Emperor Wu was angry after he had read the annals of his father, Emperor Jing 漢景帝 (r. 156–141), and had them deleted from the text of the *Shiji*.[7] Was it also the case with Emperor Wu's annals? Or were they just not written because Emperor Wu was still living when the *Shiji* was completed? Whatever the answer, it is amusing to see that one could construct a parallel between the First Emperor of Qin and Emperor Wu in the numerical system which the Sima adopted when they wrote their *Shiji*. And indeed it is not entirely out of place to speculate about the intention behind the relative positions of the rulers' accounts because a closer look reveals that the rulers are portrayed with many similar characteristics. Indeed, the text of the treatise on the *feng* and *shan* sacrifices, a second copy of which we can find in *Shiji* 12 instead of the Annals of Emperor Wu, is particularly important in this context.[8]

THE SO-CALLED TRIUMPH OF CONFUCIANISM

Emperor Wu of the Han is often credited with the introduction of Confucianism as a state orthodoxy. At first sight this ideological orientation therefore seems to have been in open contradiction to the one that the First Emperor, who supposedly "burned the canonical scriptures and buried Confucian scholars alive" (*fenshu kengru* 焚書坑儒), displayed throughout his life. However, a closer look reveals that Emperor Wu's actions were, according to the *Shiji*, much closer to the political measures of the First Emperor than one might first think. Although both emperors differed in concrete ideologies, their political intentions with respect to scholarship were the same. The First Emperor favored legal texts and texts on divination and the planting of trees, the second, Confucian texts. Yet both were against diversity.[9]

To understand the motivations of the First Emperor and Emperor Wu one should first look at the texts of the edicts that marked the beginning of the introduction of new strategies concerning intellectual matters. The First Emperor's edict against the Confucian scholars was a direct reaction to their opposition to his abolition of the so-called feudal system.[10] Right after the establishment of the centralized *junxian* (郡縣, "commanderies and counties") system, Qin statesmen and scholars began to scoff at the thearchs and kings of the past who had relied on feudal systems. They even scolded their gods and ghosts.[11] In Sima Qian's narrative, the First Emperor's famous erection of the stone inscriptions in which he praised his own achievements follows closely after this derogatory behavior toward past beliefs had become rampant. It seems obvious that the historian wanted his reader to understand the First Emperor's hubris (cf. Puett 2001: 190). During the court debates of 213, a supervisor 僕射 (probably the supervisor of the erudites 博士僕射)[12] flattered him:

> In former times, Qin's territory was no more than one-thousand *li* squared. Thanks to Your Majesty's perspicacity and sagacity, Qin has pacified the lands within the seas and expelled the uncivilized tribes. Wherever the sun and the moon shine, the people are submissive. The lands of the feudal lords are made into commanderies and counties, so that everyone is content and happy with his own life, and the calamity of war does not exist. [This] is to be handed down for ten-thousand generations. Since antiquity, none has attained the prestige and virtues of your Majesty. (*Shiji* 6: 254)

The text is a good example of what in Chinese is called *pai mapi* 拍馬屁 flattering.[13] As is well known, it raised the objection of an erudite who warned that regarding the feudal system, one should follow antiquity. This in turn provoked the chancellor Li Si 李斯 to submit his famous memorial in which he said that the rulers of the past had had different systems and could not be taken as a model. According to him the "stupid Confucians" 愚儒 were not able to understand the achievements of the First Emperor. Then he said:

> "In different times, the feudal lords struggled against each other, so that they attracted sojourning scholars with rich rewards. Now the world has been pacified and laws and ordinances come from one source. The common people, when managing their households, shall put efforts in agriculture and labor, and gentlemen [when managing their households] learn the laws, ordinances, and prohibitions. Now these masters do not learn from the modern but from the ancient, with which they criticize the present time and confuse the black haired.
> "The Chancellor, Your Subject, risks his life to say: Formerly the

world was divided and in disorder, and none was able to unify it, therefore the regional lords rose [to vie for hegemony] at the same time. In their words, they all talked about the ancient, thereby regarding the present [system] as harmful, and elaborated empty words to confuse reality . . . I would ask you burn all the records in the Scribes' offices which are not Qin's. If not needed by the Office of the Erudites, all *Poems, Documents,* and *Writings of the Hundred Schools,* which anyone in the world has ventured to keep, should be brought to the governors and commandants to be thrown together and burned. Anyone who ventures to discuss *Poems* and *Documents* will be executed in the marketplace. Those who use the ancient [system] to criticize the present will be executed together with their families. Officials who witness or know of this crime yet fail to prosecute it will have the same punishment as the criminals. Thirty days after the ordinance has been issued, anyone who has not burned his books will be tattooed and sentenced to hard labor. What are exempted are books of medicine, divination, and horticulture. *If one desires to learn laws and ordinances, he should make legal officials his teacher."*

The Emperor decreed: "We approve."[14]

The text is so famous that readers may wonder why it has been quoted here again. Our purpose is to enable the reader to compare. The memorial of the First Emperor's chancellor Li Si was submitted to criticize the Confucian practice of quoting from the *Poems* and the *Documents* in order to legitimate political opinions. However, Emperor Wu's chancellor,[15] Gongsun Hong (公孫弘, d. 121), wrote a strikingly similar text in order to promote literary scholars to official positions. According to the *Shiji* this memorial, not the activities of Dong Zhongshu 董仲舒 (c. 195–115), stood at the beginning of the introduction of Confucianism as a state orthodoxy.[16] Sima Qian tells us how Empress Dou 竇, the grandmother of the emperor, first blocked the erudites' way so that Confucian scholars could not get high positions because she liked the specialists of Huang-Lao doctrines. He then explains that after her death, when Tian Fen 田蚡 became chancellor, the situation changed:

"He rejected the doctrines of Huang-Lao [Daoism], of punishments and their names (*xing ming* 刑名, i.e., Legalism), and the theories of the *Hundred Schools,* inviting instead several hundred literary scholars and Confucians (*Ru*). Gongsun Hong because of his knowledge of the *Spring and Autumn Annals* advanced from the rank of commoner to that of one of the three excellencies of the Son of Heaven . . . "[17]

According to Sima Qian, Gongsun Hong obviously belonged to the group of Confucian and literary scholars who had not had their chance before the death of Empress-dowager Dou and who advanced after. His memorial, which was written in response to an edict in which Emperor Wu had asked for proposals for the advancement of men of outstanding moral worth and of wide learning, first praised the Emperor for his virtue. It then continued as follows:

> "We . . . beg that the ancient official system be utilized to increase the spread of instruction. In order to fill the offices of erudites we suggest that fifty additional students be selected and declared exempt from the usual labor services. The master of ritual shall be charged with the selection of students from among men of the people who are eighteen years of age or older and who are of good character and upright behavior in order to supply candidates for the quota of students of the erudites . . . *We have respectfully examined the edicts and laws which have been handed down to us by Your Majesty and we find that they distinguish clearly the provinces of heaven and man and combine the best principles of ancient and modern times* . . . [18] We request that men be selected from among those who have a rank of two hundred piculs or over, or those who have a rank of a hundred piculs and who have mastered at least one [canonical] discipline, to act as secretaries to the left and right prefects of the capital and the grand messenger; and that men be selected from among those who rank below a hundred piculs to act as secretaries to the governors of provinces, two for regular provinces and one for provinces on the border. In the selection, preference shall be given to those who can recite most . . . We request that an ordinance of merits be written. *The rest should be as with the rules and ordinances."*
>
> The Emperor decreed: "We approve."[19]

Although the purpose of Gongsun Hong's text at first seems to be the opposite of that of Li Si, namely the promotion of Confucian scholars, a closer look reveals that there are several corresponding elements. In both cases "the theories of the hundred schools,"[20] that is diverging opinions, are blocked off, and in both texts administrative rules are written that in the end serve to favor one school at the expense of others. Both texts in the final passage refer to laws and ordinances (法令) or to rules and ordinances (律令), and in both cases the emperor simply reacts with the words, "We approve."[21] This shows that while the leading ideology may have changed, the institutional framework for Emperor Wu's rule actually remained pretty much the one introduced by the First Emperor. Both emperors shared the same autocratic approach toward scholarship in general, although they favored divergent systems.[22]

It seems to me that Sima Qian intended to convey this impression.

There are a great many passages in the *Shiji* in which the historian calls into question the extent to which the empire under Emperor Wu's rule was actually subjected to the real ideas of Confucianism. This is probably most obvious in the biography of Gongsun Hong, the person who, according to Sima Qian, turned Confucianism from a philosophy into a tool for recruiting officials for the bureaucracy. In his characterization of Gongsun Hong, Sima Qian says that he was very eloquent, that he had memorized the affairs of functionaries and of written law (*wenfa* 文法), and that he was able to embellish the law by the "arts of the Confucians" (*Rushu* 儒術) (*Shiji* 112: 2950). He thus clearly wanted his reader to understand that Gongsun Hong did not live up to the actual ideals of Confucianism. For Gongsun Hong, Confucianism was more a public attitude that he displayed to make the naked requirements of the state look nicer than they really were. Sima Qian also mentions Gongsun Hong in connection with Zhang Tang 張湯, the chief minister of justice under whose guidance legalist practices were introduced into the government. In another article (van Ess 2004) I have pointed out that the "cruel officials," to whom chapter 122 of the *Shiji* is devoted, are characterized by the same lack of mercy that is the property of Legalists according to Sima Tan's treatise on the six schools. All in all it seems that according to Sima Qian the Confucianization of China at the time of Emperor Wu only took place on the surface. In reality, he went back to the politics that the First Emperor had introduced. According to many traditional readers of the *Shiji* it was obvious that Sima Qian disliked Gongsun Hong to the extreme.[23] Did this dislike extend only to Gongsun Hong and Emperor Wu or did it also apply to the First Emperor? To answer this question we have to look at other characteristics that the two emperors shared.

THE CHOICE OF DYNASTIC COLOR

One of the First Emperor's first measures upon the unification of the empire was to choose one of the five "elements," or "powers" (*de* 德), to dominate the rule of his dynasty:[24]

> The First Emperor reckoned the revolution of the cyclic Five Essences; he decided that Zhou was born with the power fire, and since Qin's power superseded the Zhou's, Qin's must conform to what Zhou's power could not overcome. To mark then the beginning of the water-power [era], he changed the beginning of the year: the New Year court ceremony always began on the first of the tenth month. For all official regalia, oxtail banners, and signal pennants, black was made

the most exalted . . . To him it had to be so in order to conform to the lot [determined] by the Five Powers.[25]

Interesting as this report may be it is still more relevant for us to know whether the historian who recorded this account approved of the emperor's changes. As is well known, most speculations concerning the cyclic five powers went back to Zou Yan 鄒衍, and Sima Qian's (or Tan's) account of this philosopher in *Shiji* 74 is very ambiguous. Although the description of Zou Yan's actions is partly positive the author certainly does not seem to be convinced by Zou's theories.[26] This interpretive ambiguity is important, since a man called Gongsun Chen 公孫臣[27] from Lu apparently accepted the First Emperor's choice when in 167 "he spread out the subject of the cyclic affairs of the five powers" and said that the element of the Han should be earth and its color yellow. He explicitly gave the Qin's choice of water as his reason, saying that the Han according to the cyclical theory had to adopt earth. However, the chancellor Zhang Cang 張蒼 believed that the element of the Han should be water, which the Qin had already chosen, and so the matter was suppressed until the next year,[28] when a yellow dragon, indicating the force of earth, appeared. Emperor Wen 文帝 (r. 180–157) summoned Gongsun Chen, employed him as erudite, and ordered him to deliberate with the other masters on a plan to change the calendar and the color of the uniforms. However, shortly thereafter a specialist in watching the ethers and making predictions was recognized as a charlatan, and so Emperor Wen dropped the idea and stopped performing sacrifices at newly established altars (*Shiji* 12: 452 and 28: 1383).

It is unclear what the historian thought of these speculations and of Emperor Wen's decision. Did Sima Qian think that Emperor Wen should have continued with his plan? Or was this just irony? An answer may be found some pages later in the treatise on the *feng* and *shan* sacrifices. Sima Qian there reminds his reader that after Emperor Wu ascended to the throne the Confucians were promoted. In this context he especially mentions the other Gongsun, namely Gongsun Hong, whom we met in the previous section (*Shiji* 12: 452 and 28: 1384). Sima Qian states that the officials all hoped that the emperor would perform the so-called *feng* and *shan* ceremonies at Mount Tai and that he would reform the institutions. It is well known that Emperor Wu, just like the First Emperor, liked to listen to magicians (*fang shi* 方士). And in this respect the emperor was most strongly influenced during the ensuing years by a third Gongsun, whose first name was Qing 卿.[29] The descriptions of the measures that

Emperor Wu took after consulting with Gongsun Qing are accompanied by the same statement that Sima Qian had already made to describe the Gongsun Hong's behavior: he used some Confucian decorum in order to disguise his real aims (*Shiji* 12: 473 and 28: 1397). If we follow Sima Qian's narrative, it must have been Gongsun Qing who was responsible for the reforms of 104, when the Han indeed changed the calendar and adopted yellow as their dynastic color (*Shiji* 12: 483 and 28: 1402). The language in which the relevant passage is couched suggests that Sima Qian must have strongly disapproved of these measures:

> In the summer [of 104] the calendar of the Han dynasty was changed so that the official year began with the first month. Yellow, the color of earth, was chosen as the color of the dynasty, and the titles of the officials were recarved on seals so that they all consisted of five characters, five being the number appropriate to the element earth. This year was designated as the first year of the era *tai-chu* 太初 or "Great beginning." This year the armies marched west to attack Ferghana. Swarms of locusts appeared. Ding Furen, Yu Chu of Luoyang, and others used their magical arts and sacrifices to put a curse upon the leaders of the Xiongnu and Ferghana.[30]

The change of the system thus provoked inauspicious omens. That the wars which followed immediately after the reform were a disaster does probably not need to be repeated here. For his institutional changes Emperor Wu apparently relied on the same system of knowledge as the First Emperor. Interestingly, Ban Gu tells us that it was actually Sima Qian himself who, together with Gongsun Qing and his own friend Hu Sui 壺遂, was the main advocate of the reforms (*Hanshu* 21A: 974). However, after having read the "Annals of Emperor Wu" in the *Shiji* and the treatise on the *feng* and *shan* sacrifices, one has to doubt whether Sima Qian would have been pleased had he known that 150 years later a historian would have put him into the company of a charlatan such as Gongsun Qing. Interestingly, Ban Gu also added Jia Yi 賈誼, whom Sima Qian respected very much, to Gongsun Chen when discussing those who suggested to Emperor Wen to change the dynastic color. He explicitly said that Sima Qian followed the ideas of Gongsun Chen and Jia Yi (*Hanshu* 25A: 1270 and 48: 2265; cf. Schaab-Hanke 2002).

Ban Gu's statement has been accepted as authoritative by many traditional readers and also by modern scholars. And yet I wonder whether Ban Gu got the facts wrong or even distorted them deliberately. Shortly after the account of the First Emperor's reform in Sima Qian's treatise on the *feng* and *shan* sacrifices, there is the following passage:

From the time of the Kings Wei (378–343) and Xuan (342–324) of Qi such masters as Zou Yan had propounded the theory of the cyclical succession of the five powers. When the ruler of Qin became emperor and a man from Qi submitted this, the First Emperor for this reason accepted and used it. But Song Wuji, Zhengbo Qiao, Chong Shang and Xianmen Gao in the end were all men from Yan who practiced magic and the way of the imortals, discarding their mortal forms and transforming themselves by relying on the affairs of demons and gods. Zou Yan had won fame among the regional lords for his ability to govern the succession [of the powers] by making use of *yin* and *yang*. Yet the magicians from the coast of Yan and Qi who transmitted his technique were not able to understand it. Thus from this time there appeared a host of men, too numerous to mention, who expounded all sorts of weird and fantastic theories and went to any lengths to flatter the rulers of the day and to carelessly seek agreement with them. (*Shiji* 28: 1368–1369, cf. Watson 1961 II: 25–26).

Here Sima Qian clearly says that the First Emperor adopted the water element because he believed in the authority of the men from Qi where Zou Yan had come from. Yet he also adds that unfortunately because of the influence of men from Yan, the magicians from Yan and Qi, who transmitted the theories of Zou Yan, did not understand them anymore and mixed them up with all kinds of things that were not effective but which they could use in order to flatter the emperor and to seek a "careless agreement" (苟合) with him. Sima Qian used exactly the same expression, "careless agreement," when, after having recounted the theories of Zou Yan, he wrote about the upright behavior of Confucius and Mencius, who certainly did not seek agreement at any price. Although Sima Qian inserted the statement about the "careless agreement" at this point in order to prepare the reader for what followed, namely the account of the First Emperor's desperate attempts to attain immortality which were soon followed by his death, it also throws a bad light on the choice of the element water: in Sima Qian's opinion, this suggestion obviously came from persons who did not understand Zou Yan's theories. On the one hand, it is possible that Sima Qian, as Ban Gu said, did not want to criticize the decision itself, but just the fact that magicians criminally mixed it with absurd theories on immortality. Indeed, it seems plausible that Sima Qian was one of the architects of the institutional reforms made in 104. On the other hand, given that he called Zou Yan's theories "irregular" 不軌 (*Shiji* 74: 2345), it would seem that he rejected five-element-speculations altogether.[31]

Thus, it seems to me that Sima Qian believed that the First Emperor and Emperor Wu committed the same mistake by trusting in a wrong system, namely Zou Yan's five elements speculations, which in addition to being dubious from the beginning were spoiled by the magicians. Both emperors trusted the same group of people. What is important is that the influence of the magicians, according to Sima Qian, had proven to be harmful or at least unhelpful in the first case. Nothing was obviously proven yet in Emperor Wu's case when Sima Qian was finishing his *Shiji*, but when reading the "Annals of the First Emperor" in this way it is easy to detect in them a warning for Emperor Wu. This topic is explored in more detail in the next section.

THE *FENG* AND *SHAN* SACRIFICES

An even more obvious parallel between the First Emperor and Emperor Wu of the Han is found in the discussions of the famous *feng* and *shan* sacrifices introduced by the First Emperor.[32] The relevant entry in the treatise states:

> Three years after he assumed the imperial title the First Emperor made a tour of the eastern commanderies and counties. He performed a sacrifice at Mount Yi 嶧山 in Zou 騶 and there set up a stone marker lauding the achievements of the Qin. He then summoned seventy Confucian scholars (儒生) from Qi and Lu to meet with him at the foot of Mount Tai, where the scholars began to debate the proper procedure for carrying out the *feng*- and *shan*-sacrifices. "In ancient times when the *feng*- and *shan*-sacrifices were performed," said some of them, "the wheels of the carriages were wrapped in rushes so as not to do any injury to the earth and grass of the mountain. The ground was swept clean and sacrifices performed, using rushes and peeled stalks of grain for mats. This means that it was easy to do." When the First Emperor heard that in these deliberations everybody expressed a different opinion which made it difficult to carry it out, he therefore dismissed the Confucian scholars. Eventually he had a carriage road opened up, ascending from the southern foot of the mountain to the summit, where he set up a stone marker praising his own virtue as First Emperor of the Qin. This he did to make clear that he had succeeded in performing the *feng*-sacrifice. From the summit he descended by a shadowy road and performed the *shan*-sacrifice at Mount Liangfu 梁父. In both of these ceremonies he on the whole followed those by the master of invocations in sacrificing to the Lord on High 上帝 at Yong, but the directions for the ritual were sealed and stored away, being kept strictly secret, so that none of the men of the time were able to record any description of the ceremonies.

When the First Emperor was ascending Mount Tai he encountered a violent wind and rain storm half way up the slope and had to stop for a while under a large tree. The Confucian scholars, who had been dismissed and were not allowed to take part in the ritual of the *feng*-sacrifice, hearing of the emperor's encounter with the storm, promptly used it as a basis to speak ill of him."[33]

This report is followed by a description of various gods and goddesses whom the First Emperor worshipped in the ensuing years and his various attempts to attain immortality, among them his sending out a number of youths and maidens to search for the island of Penglai 蓬萊 (*Shiji* 6: 247, 28: 1370). Our text explicitly says that the boats were crisscrossing the sea and that they blamed their failure to reach the island on the wind. Sima Qian speaks of "countless throngs of magicians." To this he adds that after climbing Mount Kuaiji 會稽, the First Emperor "followed along the coast on his way back, hoping to acquire some of the wonderful medicine of immortality brought from the three divine mountains in the sea. But his hopes were in vain. On his way back, as he had arrived at Sandy Hill 沙丘, he passed away" (*Shiji* 28: 1370; modifying Watson 1961 II: 26–27).

The message is clear: The First Emperor had been able to ascend Mount Tai and perform the *feng* and *shan* sacrifices in vain; he wasted huge amounts of resources but failed to attain immortality. This is important, since the part of the treatise on the *feng* and *shan* sacrifices, which is devoted to Emperor Wu, starts with the words, "When the present Emperor first ascended to the throne, he was particularly respectful of sacrifices to ghosts and spirits" (*Shiji* 12: 425 and 28: 1384; Nienhauser 1994 II: 220). Li Shaojun 李少君, the first among the countless magicians whom Emperor Wu invited, told him that by prolonging his life by means of Daoist alchemy he would be able to see the immortals of Penglai and that by seeing them he would attain immortality when performing the *feng* and *shan* sacrifices.[34] Interestingly, Sima Qian adds that Li Shaojun died after a while but that more and more "magicians from Yan and Qi with their weird and fantastic theories" 燕齊怪迂之方士 came to speak about godly affairs. By repeating the names of the states Yan and Qi and the words "weird and fantastic" which he had also used in the context of the discussions regarding the choice of the dynastic element (see above), Sima Qian thus makes clear that Emperor Wu's magicians belonged to exactly the same category as those who had misled the First Emperor. The topic recurs later in the treatise in the passage in which Gongsun Qing is introduced: Gongsun Qing produced a faked document[35] which he said to have received from Shen Gong 申公, the well-known specialist of the *Book* of *Poems* who had, however, passed away and could not speak up himself anymore. Gongsun Qing claimed that the document said that only the Yellow Emperor had been able to perform the *feng*-sacrifice at Mount Tai. Implicitly he thereby denied that the First Emperor had accomplished this task. He added that Shen Gong had said that the ruler of the Han should also ascend Mount Tai and perform the sacrifice and that the one who did that would become an immortal and ascend to Heaven.

There follows a description of the sacrifices Emperor Wu established during the next few years. This list is much more detailed than the one we know from Sima Qian's account of the First Emperor. When the subject of the *feng* and *shan* sacrifices reoccurs in the treatise, the historian again openly ridicules the magicians. He says that the emperor on his return from northern China performed a sacrifice at the tomb of the Yellow Emperor and then asked how it could be that there was a tumulus if the Yellow Emperor did not die.[36] What follows deserves complete quotation:

> From the time the precious tripod was obtained, the Sovereign together with the honorable officials, ministers and various scholars deliberated about [instituting] the *feng*- and *shan*-sacrifices. The *feng*- and *shan*-sacrifices had been rarely performed, and had been cut off for a long time; no one knew their ceremonies and rituals. The assembled Confucian scholars culled material selected from the *Venerated Documents* 尚書, the *Zhou Offices* 周官, and the "Royal Regulations" 王制 pertaining to the *wang* 望 sacrifice, and the [royal officiant's] shooting of the [sacrificial] ox. A man from Qi, Master Ding, who was over ninety years old, said: "The *feng* sacrifice is in accord with an immortal name. The [First] Emperor of Qin was unable to ascend [the mountain] and perform the *feng*-sacrifice. If Your Majesty insists on ascending [the mountain], go up a little and if there is not wind or rain, then make the ascent and perform the *feng*-sacrifice."
>
> At this, the Sovereign ordered the assembled Confucian scholars to practice shooting the [sacrificial] oxen and to draft the ceremonies for the *feng* and *shan* sacrifices. After several years, the time had come to carry out [these sacrifices]. The Son of Heaven had already paid heed to the words of Gongsun Qing and the practitioners of the [magical] methods about how the Yellow Emperor and earlier [rulers] had conducted the *feng* and *shan* sacrifices; they all had been able to summon strange creatures and commune with the spirits. The Emperor desired to imitate the Yellow Emperor's having been able to contact the spirits, immortals, and gentlemen of Penglai, to transcend the [mundane] world and compare in virtue to the Nine August Ones 九皇. Moreover, he selected from the methods of the Confucians to embellish them. The assembled Confucian scholars,

having been unable to discuss and clarify the affairs of the *feng* and *shan* rites, and furthermore constrained by rigid adherence to ancient documents like the *Poems* and the *Documents* dared not improvise. The Sovereign had ritual vessels for the *feng* sacrifice manufactured and showed them to the assembled Confucian scholars; one of the assembled Confucian scholars said, "These are not the same as in ancient times." Xu Yan further added, "The performance of the rites by the various scholars under the Grand Master of ceremonies is not as good as that of [the state of] Lu." Zhou Ba gathered together the [Confucian scholars] to plan the *feng* [and *shan*] affairs. At this, the Sovereign demoted [Xu] Yan and [Zhou] Ba, dismissed the assembled Confucian scholars, and did not employ them" (*Shiji* 12: 472, 28: 1397; modifying Nienhauser 1994 II: 241f).

Again, this text resembles the report on the First Emperor in many details. Especially interesting is the role of the Confucian scholars, who in both cases kick themselves out of the game with their pedantic adherence to old models. Once he has removed these obstacles, Emperor Wu, just like the First Emperor, has no problems actually performing the sacrifices. As with his predecessor, he erects a stone on its summit and "people from Qi who submitted memorials to the throne expounding on spirits, strange creatures, curiosities and [magical] methods numbered in the tens of thousands, but nothing could be verified." Like the First Emperor, Emperor Wu sent out numerous boats to seek out the spirit beings of Penglai. Even the wording with which Sima Qian describes these events is sometimes exactly the same as in the case of the First Emperor.[37]

In principle the Sima were in favor of the performance of the sacrifices.[38] And yet it is clear that they disapproved of the way it finally was achieved. As with the selection of the dynastic element and color, it is obvious that they disliked mixing up the search for immortality with the actual sacrifices.[39] What is not clear, however, at first sight is what the Sima thought of the role of the Confucians, which both the First Emperor and Emperor Wu had excluded because their opinions differed, because the rites they advocated "were difficult to perform," and because they always said that the ritual objects "were not the same as those of antiquity." In this context one sentence is especially important. Before narrating Sire Ding 丁公 from Qi's discussion of the relationship between the sacrifices and immortality, the historian says, "The *feng*- and *shan*-sacrifices had been rarely performed, and had been cut off for a long time; no one knew their ceremonies and rituals. The assembled Confucian scholars culled material selected from the *Venerated Documents*, the *Zhou*

Offices, and the "Royal Regulations" pertaining to the *wang* sacrifice . . . " In order to understand the relevance of these words the reader has to know that in the introductory passage of the treatise he said, "If rites are not performed for three years then these rites will certainly fall into disuse. If music is not performed for three years, this music will decay" (*Shiji* 28: 1355; Watson 1961 II: 13–14).

The meaning of this text is quite clear: for Sima Tan and Sima Qian it was obvious that any attempt to look for precedents for the *feng* and *shan* sacrifices in ancient texts was futile. After three years, unperformed rites were doomed to decay. As they frequently do, the Sima remind their readers of the introductory passage by using the same wording.[40] According to them it was inevitable that the Confucians had to fail: both at the time of the First Emperor and of Emperor Wu they did not understand that by definition it was impossible for rarely performed rituals to have precedents. It was a bitter irony that despite this insight, Sima Tan was lumped together with the stupid Confucians and could not participate in the ritual. Thus it seems obvious that the Sima were very displeased with the role played by the Confucian scholars during its preparation.

The question of what the Sima thought of the *feng* and *shan* sacrifices in general may not be important. Yet it is clear that the First Emperor's behavior was a model for the description of Emperor Wu. And while openly criticizing the magicians at the court of the First Emperor the Sima sent out a warning to their own emperor. Everybody knew what had happened after the First Emperor died: since he had been afraid of talking about death, his subjects had not dared raise the subject. And since he died without having written a last will, his succession could be manipulated by the unscrupulous attendant Zhao Gao 趙高. The heir apparent, as well as the successful general Meng Tian 蒙恬, was killed. Shortly after the dynasty fell.[41]

THE POLITICS OF EXPANSION

Interestingly, in *Shiji* 6, "The Annals of the First Emperor," the account of the beginning of the First Qin Emperor's wars against the Xiongnu 匈奴 is closely intertwined with the account of his quest for immortality. After returning from a seafaring voyage looking for demons and gods, a man from Yan, the place where most of the "bad" magicians came from, reported: "Those who will destroy the Qin will be the *hu* aliens" (亡秦者胡也, *Shiji* 6: 252). Thereupon the First Emperor sent out Meng Tian with 300,000 troops to attack the Xiongnu and annex the Ordos region. The entry which immediately follows adds the many territories which Qin integrated into the empire during the next two years to the south and north of its borders. The Xiongnu had to flee to the northern regions.

Yet after Meng Tian's execution (despite the victories he had secured) and the advent of the anti-Qin revolt, the "Xiongnu got some respite and some of them crossed the Yellow river and reestablished the border with the Middle States at the old frontier" (*Shiji* 110: 2887–2888). The story that follows is again well known: The founder of the Han lured Maodun 冒頓, the *chanyu* 單于, to start a war, yet he did not succeed but suffered instead a severe defeat and had to sign an humiliating peace treaty. It was only under Emperor Wu that the wars were resumed (Di Cosmo 2002).

It is unfortunate in this context that we do not possess a proper annals for Emperor Wu in the *Shiji*, because the treatise on the *feng* and *shan* ceremonies does not mention the beginning of the wars against the Xiongnu. This text does, however, contain a remark by Gongsun Qing, who, when he suggested that the *feng* sacrifice would lead to immortality, also said that the "Yellow Emperor led war at the same time as he studied the way of the immortals. He was distressed that the hundred families would reject his way and he therefore beheaded those who denied the existence of demons and gods" (*Shiji* 28: 1393). And the wars against Southern Yue 南越 are clearly related to the newly established sacrifices for the Goddess Taiyi 太一 (*Shiji* 28: 1395), just as those of the First Emperor against the Xiongnu were related to his quest for immortality. In a memorial which was handed in shortly before Emperor Wu performed the *feng* sacrifice for his first time, an official said: "Of old, the troops were brought back from their posts and temporarily disbanded before the *feng* and *shan* sacrifices were performed." Emperor Wu proceeded to make a tour of the northern border, calling up a force of over 100,000 troops to accompany him (*Shiji* 28: 1396). The text which follows mentions the wars against Chaoxian 朝鮮, and the entry on the change of dynastic color is directly followed by a sentence stating that Ferghana was attacked in this year in the West. Moreover, "Ding Furen, Yu Chu from Luoyang and others used their magical arts and sacrifices to put a curse upon the leaders of the Xiongnu and Ferghana" (*Shiji* 28: 1400 and 1402).

As far as the politics of expansion are concerned we do not have to wonder too much about Sima Qian's attitude. It is obvious that he was very much against the wars and that he was especially appalled by the fact that wars were led with the help of magicians. Yet it is most interesting to notice that once again Emperor Wu imitated closely the model set by the First Emperor.

THE ABOLISHMENT OF THE FIEFS

We have seen that the decision to ban the *Poems, Documents,* and *Speeches of the Hundred Schools* was taken because a Confucian had warned the First Emperor that it would be dangerous to destroy the kingdoms of old which had existed in the central states:

> "I have learned that Yin [Shang] and Zhou, ruling as kings for more than one-thousand years, enfeoffed their sons, brothers and meritorious ministers to branch out as support for the court itself. Now Your Majesty possesses all within the seas, yet your sons and brothers are all ordinary men. If there were suddenly [scheming] subjects like Tian Chang [of Qi] or the Six Ministers [of Jin], without support [from your branched-out vassals], who would come to your rescue? I have never heard that someone has been able to exist for long without following antiquity in this matter" (*Shiji* 6:254; modifying Nienhauser 1994 I: 146–147.)

The subject reoccurs several times in the biographies of men who lived at the beginning of the Han. Sima Qian never explicitly says what he thinks of the introduction of the *junxian* system and the abolishment of the feudal one. For example, in the biography of Gaozu's advisor Zhang Liang 張良 we find a proposal by Li Yiji 酈食其, who, when Xiang Yu succeeded in surrounding Liu Bang at Xingyang 滎陽, advised:

> "In ancient times when Tang overthrew Jie, he enfeoffed Jie's descendants in Qi 杞, and later when king Wu attacked Zhou[xin], he enfeoffed Zhou's heirs in Song 宋. Now Qin, abandoning virtue and disregarding righteousness, has overthrown the sacred altars of the regional lords and wiped out the descendants of the Six States, leaving them not enough territory to stick the point of an awl into. If you could only reestablish the descendants of the former kingdoms and present them with the seals of enfeoffment, then they, their ministers, and their people, being every one indebted to your virtue, would one and all turn in longing toward your righteousness and beg to become your subjects. With virtue and righteousness made manifest, you might face south and name yourself a hegemon, and Xiang Yu, gathering his sleeves together in respectful salute, would most certainly come to pay you homage."[42]

Li Yiji's proposal is sweepingly rejected by Zhang Liang immediately in eight steps. Yet Zhang Liang is not against it because he thinks it would be unwise to establish vassal kingdoms at all but because in his opinion it would be too dangerous to rely on the families of the former regional lords who could then become strong again.[43]

Related to this topic is an important passage which is often overlooked because it is only a short preface to the table covering the period of the passage of power from the Qin to Han, namely *Shiji* 16. There the historian himself speaks about the regional lords. He says that the First Emperor thought that the existence of regional lords was the reason for the wars of the Warring States period. Therefore, he did not give away even a foot of land as a fiefdom. Yet when the rebellion broke out, the new structure of the empire helped only the strong men who, contrary to the Qin, did not have many enemies but just one. "Therefore, when [just] giving vent to one's anger turns one into a hero of All-under-Heaven, how could it be true that 'without a territory one cannot become a king'?" (*Shiji* 16: 760).[44]

The topic is crucial for a correct understanding of why the *Shiji* was written. Sima Qian evidently supported those who thought it would be better not to copy the First Emperor's model but to establish vassal lords as helpers of a true lord. He seems to have seen the lack of a strong family as a reason for the initial weakness of the house of Liu. The Liu had to give out territories to its few members, and these territories were therefore necessarily much too large to be controlled by the central government in western China. This was the real reason for the revolt of the seven kingdoms in 154.[45] After this revolt, the size of these kingdoms was reduced. Yet when Emperor Wu came to the throne he went one step further: he began to destroy most of the kingdoms that had survived the rebellion and also wiped out most of the fiefs which belonged to the descendants of the loyal subjects of his predecessors. Again, these politics are only visible to their full extent when looking at the tables of the *Shiji* that give a convenient overview of these fiefs and of the dates of their final destruction.[46] Emperor Wu even abolished many of the fiefs that he himself had given out at the beginning of his reign. In the time when the *feng* and *shan* rites were first performed in 110 and the dynastic color changed and a new calendar introduced in 104, to a close observer the empire's structure therefore must have looked very similar to the one established by the First Emperor. There was an extremely powerful central government and only a very few influential men in the provinces.

CONCLUSION

The picture which Sima Qian draws of the emperor under whose reign he lived resembled in many aspects his depiction of the First Emperor of the Qin. And there are more aspects that have been left out here because of limitations of space.[47] When considering this similarity it seems only logical to ask whether it is indeed plausible that history repeated itself in such a glaring way. Indeed, one is tempted to ask whether what we read in *Shiji* is actually a factual account or whether it is not more plausible that Sima Qian deliberately modeled the image of Emperor Wu after that of his famous predecessor. It is even more tempting to ask whether the opposite was true. It would seem dangerous to believe in the facts that the *Shiji* reports about the life and times of the First Emperor because this account was written under the heavy influence of the experiences that Sima Qian had made with his own ruler. Indeed, it looks quite probable that Sima Qian made up facts about the First Emperor in order to make him look like an alter ego of Emperor Wu.[48] By doing this he implied a warning: As it was well known that the First Emperor had failed and that his dynasty had collapsed soon after his death, any reader who recognized the similarities between the First Emperor and Emperor Wu of the Han in the *Shiji* must have immediately felt the threat for the Han dynasty.

How many facts, then, can we actually accept from the *Shiji* for a reconstruction of the history of the end of the Qin? Of course, it does seem outrageous, at least at first sight, not to believe in the fact that the First Emperor, for example, abolished the feudal system. But many other so-called historical facts that today form some kind of a folklore attached to the figure of the First Emperor may have been made up deliberately by Sima Qian. To be sure, there must have been stories about the First Emperor at Sima Qian's time. And yet, a hundred years is a long time in an age which did not yet know the systematic writing of history.

In my opinion, one should, for example, also reconsider the famous stone inscriptions. As has been stated above, Emperor Wu, too, erected a stone on Mount Tai. Did the text of the inscriptions erected by the First Emperor look the same as the one preserved today? Other texts contained in the *Shiji* suggest that this must not necessarily be true.[49] How many contemporaries who read the *Shiji* had the chance to travel around and look up whether the text of the inscriptions was actually identical with the one contained in the *Shiji*?[50] And should they have discovered that it was not would there not have been many explanations for that fact? The reason why these questions should be asked is that there is no other text or group of texts in the *Shiji* that does so often speak of the "virtue" or "charisma" (*de* 德) of a ruler, and it seems most strange that the First Emperor should not have realized how ridiculous and, indeed, how repelling his drive to publicize his own achievements must have looked to any educated reader of the time. Twelve times does he speak of his own "virtue," and three times the historian says that the inscription was erected in order praise the "virtue" of the Qin (*Shiji* 6: 242–247, 249–252, 260–261). The hubris of these texts must have been obvious to every reader of the *Shiji*.[51] Their tune creates a stark contrast to other inscriptions which have been recovered by Chinese archaeology. Of course, it is possible that the rules of a polite style were not observed in the state of Qin. Yet it seems difficult for a modern reader to accept the wording as absolutely factual. It rather suggests that there are good reasons to doubt that the accuracy of texts contained in the *Shiji* should be taken for granted.

After all that has been discussed above it does not seem very plausible that the *Shiji* was just a patchwork of sources stitched together by a historian who refrained from adding his own opinions. Rather, this text is a conscious attempt by one historian or a small group of like-minded people to make the past correspond to their own ideas about the present. It would probably have been difficult in Sima Qian's time to present an account of the life of the ruling emperor that consisted of wrong data. To say things about the First Emperor that did not correspond exactly to the truth but that showed how similar his actions had been to those that contemporaries saw at Emperor Wu's time must have been easier. Numerous accounts in the Annals of the First Emperor of Qin have been called into question by modern authors. The explanation usually given is that later interpolators inserted passages into the text. As has been suggested above, we would do better to consider the possibility that Sima Qian himself wrote these details simply because they sounded plausible, since Emperor Wu had done similar things.

Which conclusions do we then have to draw about the account of the First Emperor and, indeed, about the reason why the *Shiji* was written at all? In my opinion it is quite plausible that the tale of the First Emperor of the Qin that we find in the *Shiji* was actually written as a warning to Emperor Wu of the Han. "Look," the historian said to Emperor Wu, "you are doing just the same as he did. What happened to him and his dynasty?"

8 The Messianic Emperor

A New Look at Qin's Place in China's History

Yuri Pines

Among many controversies concerning the short-lived Qin dynasty, few appear so difficult to resolve as the thorny issue of the Qin's place in the general course of Chinese history. Generations of traditional and modern scholars beginning with Dong Zhongshu 董仲舒 (c. 195–115) have tended to view it as a rupture or an aberration: an anti-"Confucian," anti-Traditionalist entity, which behaved violently and erratically and was duly eliminated from China's historical landscape. Others, most notably scholars of China's institutional history, by contrast, tended to emphasize Qin's role as an inseparable part of a historical continuum; Cai Yong 蔡邕 (133–192 CE) succinctly summarized: "Qin inherited [the system] of the last years of the Zhou, and was the forerunner of the Han" (秦承周末, 為漢驅除).[1]

While current research—including the chapters in this volume—tends to confirm the correctness of the latter approach, and the continuities between the Qin and its predecessors and successors appear to be self-evident, I think that the idea of Qin's exceptionality cannot be entirely discarded. While this notion does reflect the ideological biases of Han and later *Ru* (儒, "Confucians"), it also may be related to certain peculiarities of the Qin regime and its self-image. In what follows, I show that amid overall continuities, the Qin adopted a peculiar ideological posture—what I dub here the "Messianic posture"—which crucially distinguishes it from its Warring States period (453–221) predecessors and from its Han (206 BCE–220 CE) successors. To illustrate this point, I focus on the Qin notion of emperorship as reflected in the self-image of the First Emperor 秦始皇帝 (r. 246–221–210). My choice is not incidental. The institution and concept of emperorship was the single most important Qin innovation and its most significant contribution to subsequent dynasties; as such it serves as an ideal prism through which the Qin's place in Chinese history can be analyzed. Moreover, as we possess primary sources for the Qin emperor's self-image, namely the First Emperor's stele inscriptions, we can discuss this topic without being too dependent on potentially biased presentations in later historical sources.[2]

In the following discussion I demonstrate that the First Emperor's view of rulership is rooted in the monarchistic discourse of the preceding Warring States period, which he successfully appropriated, and that it had a lasting impact on his Han successors. Simultaneously, however, I argue that the First Emperor's presentation of his rule as "the end of history" distinguishes him critically from earlier and later monarchs, and may provide one explanation for the notion of the Qin's exceptionality in China's historical landscape. In addition, I hope that my discussion will contribute to a better understanding of the role of the monarchs in China's imperial polity and to the dialectical relationships between the Qin dynasty and its Han successor.

BACKGROUND: THE SEARCH FOR THE TRUE MONARCH

Qin's elimination of rival Warring States in 221 was a result of a series of brilliant military campaigns; but the empire established in its aftermath was not a purely military creature. Rather, the unification of the sub-celestial world was an idea envisioned and elaborated by generations of thinkers and statesmen long before it materialized under Qin rule. Two major concepts that emerged amid the ideological ferment of the Warring States era were particularly conducive to the future imperial enterprise: namely, that peace in All-under-Heaven would not prevail until the world was unified, and that political order in a single state and in the future unified realm was attainable only under the aegis of a powerful monarch. These ideas became the foundation upon which the Qin notion of emperorship was erected, and, more broadly, the basis of the imperial enterprise in general.

Elsewhere I have discussed in great detail the ideology of monarchism as it emerged in the preimperial period (Pines 2009, cf. Liu Zehua 1991; 2000); here, I only briefly outline its essential components. In the monarchistic discourse of the Warring States period we can identify three major threads: first, the idea of the ruler-centered universal polity as the only feasible way to ensure peace and stability; second, the concept of the sagacious True Monarch as the only person able to bring about perfect order in All-under-Heaven; and third, a subtle yet palpable bifurcation between that ideal future ruler and current, mediocre sovereigns, who were to retain nominal power but should be persuaded to delegate many of their everyday tasks to meritorious aides. Of these three threads, the most significant in terms of its impact on the First Emperor was the second, namely the ideal of the True Monarch, and in what follows I focus primarily on that ideal.

The ideology of monarchism in the Warring States period was formed as a reaction to the perennial weakness of the rulers' power during the preceding aristocratic Springs-and-Autumns period (770–453). Having identified the decline of the sovereign's position with the general deterioration of the sociopolitical order, thinkers of various intellectual inclinations proposed multiple arguments in favor of restoring monarchic power. Some promoted the idea of the exclusiveness of the ruler's position at the head of the ritual—and *mutatis mutandis*—sociopolitical pyramid; others provided moral, political, and metaphysical stipulations for the elevation of the monarch. While thinkers widely diverged as regards the ruler's conduct in his private and public life, there was a consensus that monarchic rule was the only proper and feasible political arrangement: a single ruler should serve as the only final decision maker, and there should be no institutional—as distinct from moral—limitations on his power. The ruler could—and, in the eyes of many, should—be admonished and criticized if necessary, but neither ministers nor advisers had the right to overturn his decisions; no group was independent of his will, and he was the single source of political (and religious) authority. These ideas served as the foundation of China's monarchic system for millennia to come (see Pines 2009: 25–53 and Pines 2012a: 44–75 for further details).

The staunch monarchism of preimperial ideologues does not mean, however, that they were insensible to the dangers of a wicked or inept ruler, or to the possibility of the monarch abusing his enormous power. On the contrary, rival thinkers overwhelmingly considered themselves intellectually and morally superior to contemporary sovereigns, whom they relentlessly criticized and whose mediocrity they lamented. It is as a foil to these mediocrities that thinkers proposed the ideal of the True Monarch. The True Monarch (usually identified as "one who acts as a monarch" 王者, a "sage monarch" 聖王, or "Heavenly monarch" 天王) was a morally and intellectually impeccable leader who would be able to fulfill the centuries-long aspirations of the multitudes and bring about political unity and perfect order.

Several major features crucially distinguished the True Monarch from contemporary, mediocre sovereigns. First, he was identified as a sage—an exceptional personality, whose morality and wisdom elevated him above the rest of humankind and, in the eyes of many thinkers, turned him into a semidivine (or fully divine) person (see more in Puett 2002). As such, the True Monarch was supposed to stand at the apex of the moral and intellectual—and not just sociopolitical—pyramid. Second, the True Monarch had to preside over the unified realm rather than over a single regional state. Third, his rule was to be marked by perfect sociopolitical order and by universal compliance. These were, in the eyes of most thinkers, the attainments of past paragons, such as the legendary Five Thearchs (*wu Di* 五帝) or the Three Monarchs (*san wang* 三王), that is, the founders of the Xia, Shang and Zhou dynasties. Yet most discussions of the True Monarch were directed not at the past but at the future: he was viewed as a savior-like figure, the one who arises "once in five hundred years" and whose arrival is long overdue.[3] These quasi-Messianic expectations of the True Monarch were duly emphasized by widespread utopian depictions of universal peace, prosperity, good order, and compliance, all generated by his rule.

To illustrate views of the True Monarch in the political thought of the Warring States period I briefly focus here on Xunzi 荀子 (c. 310–230), arguably the single most profound and influential thinker of his age.[4] Xunzi explains the essentials of the rule of the True Monarch as follows:

> To preserve the Way and virtue complete, to be the highest and the most esteemed, to enhance the principles of refined culture, to unify All-under-Heaven, to put in order even the smallest things, to cause everyone under Heaven to comply and follow him—this is the task of the Heavenly Monarch. . . . If All-under-Heaven is not unified, and the regional lords customarily rebel—then the Son of Heaven is not the [appropriate] man.[5]

Political unity, perfect order and universal compliance are the first cluster of features that distinguish the True Monarch from ordinary rulers. The second peculiarity of the True Monarch is his ability to imbue his subjects with superb morality and to put an end to moral and political deviancy:

> When the sage monarch is above, he apportions dutiful actions below. Then, *shi* 士 and the nobles do not behave wantonly; the hundred officials are not insolent in their affairs; the multitudes and the hundred clans are without odd and licentious habits; there are no crimes of theft and robbery; none dares to oppose his superiors.[6]

This perfect order in which every social group—from elite to commoners—is uniformly regulated by the True Monarch derives exclusively from the superb moral and intellectual qualities of the latter. This moral and intellectual superiority is the third feature which distinguishes the True Monarch from other sovereigns:

> The [True] Son of Heaven is the most respectable in terms of his power and position and has no rivals under Heaven. . . . His morality is pure; his knowledge and kindness are extremely clear. He faces southwards and makes All-under-Heaven obedient. Among all the people, there is none who does not politely hold his hands following him, thereby being compliantly transformed. There are no recluses under Heaven, the goodness of no one is neglected; the one who unites with him is right, the one who differs from him is wrong.[7]

The notion of unanimous obedience and absolute compliance with the True Monarch's will permeates the writings of Xunzi and of many of his contemporaries. Sometimes these panegyrics to the True Monarch are mistakenly interpreted as exemplifying Xunzi's "authoritarian" leanings, but this is not necessarily the case (Pines 2009: 82–97). Xunzi, like most contemporaneous thinkers, clearly distinguishes between the True Monarch and an average sovereign. The latter should enjoy absolute political and ritual authority, but in terms of morality and intellect he is tacitly understood to be inferior to his aides. It is the task of these aides, especially meritorious *Ru* such as Xunzi himself, to instruct the ruler and assist him in performing everyday tasks. In contrast, the True Monarch is perceived as morally and intellectually superior to his subjects and accordingly needs no consultations; rather, he simply "apportions dutiful actions below" and thereby orders every social stratum. Remarkably, even the intellectuals, the *shi*, whose abilities Xunzi frequently praises as being similar or even superior to those of the rulers, are expected to succumb to the will of the Sage Monarch. Insofar as the monarch's views are the sole criterion of goodness and badness, the intellectuals' moral autonomy appears significantly impaired.

These observations bring us to the last point. While the lionization of the True Monarch eventually contributed to bolstering the emperor's authority, in the short term it served a different goal. Many thinkers, Xunzi included, consistently employed the image of the True Monarch as a foil to contemporary rulers. By inflating the positive features of the True Monarch, thinkers emphasized his exceptionality. As long as reigning rulers fell short of that superhuman hero, they could not expect the same degree of obedience and submissiveness as the True Monarch should expect. Moreover, as their abilities could not match those of a sage on the throne, rulers of the Warring States were strongly advised to limit their involvement in everyday political matters and to delegate their power to meritorious aides (Pines 2009: 82–107).

Taken from this perspective, we can understand anew why Xunzi and his like displayed a willingness to yield their proud autonomous stance to the True Monarch. While promising unwavering obedience to a future, impeccable ruler, the thinkers preserved the right to criticize and occasionally to defy contemporary, inadequate sovereigns whose mediocrity was self-evident in comparison with the idealized sage unifier. What Xunzi could not possibly have anticipated is that one of his younger contemporaries, King Zheng of Qin, would be able not just to appropriate the discourse of the True Monarch but also to utilize it for an unprecedented assault on the political power and intellectual autonomy of the educated elite.

THE FIRST EMPEROR AS THE TRUE MONARCH

In 221, having successfully concluded a series of brilliant military campaigns that swept away the competing Warring States, King Zheng of Qin proclaimed himself emperor (*huangdi* 皇帝, literally "August Thearch"; hereafter I shall use both titles interchangeably), thereby inaugurating a new era in Chinese history. His was an exceptionally eventful decade in office as emperor, full of both great attainments and awful atrocities, which make him one of the most controversial figures in China's history. The complexity of this figure and the questionable reliability of many parts of the "Basic Annals of the First Emperor" in the *Historical Records* (*Shiji* 史記), our major source for Qin history (see van Ess, chapter 7 in this volume), turn the study of the First Emperor into a particularly challenging task. Luckily, the *Historical Records* and other sources preserved the texts of seven imperial stele inscriptions, which, as have been brilliantly shown by Martin Kern, may serve as a reliable source for the First Emperor's self-image and propaganda activities. These inscriptions, in addition to a few other historical and paleographic sources, allow us to reconstruct the ideology of the First Emperor with considerable precision (see Kern 2000; Liu Zehua 2000: 128–137).

Our discussion of the First Emperor may conveniently begin with the following pronouncement made by his entourage and inscribed on the stele erected on Mt. Yi 嶧山 shortly after unification had been achieved (Figure 8.1):

Figure 8.1. Mt. Yi Stele (Tenth-Century CE Reproduction). From Xi'an, "Forest of Steles" Museum

追念亂世, 分土建邦, 以開爭理. 攻戰日作, 流血於野, 自泰古始. 世無萬數, 阤及五帝, 莫能禁止. 迺今皇帝, 壹家天下, 兵不復起. 災害滅除, 黔首康定, 利澤長久.

They [the Qin ministers] recall and contemplate the times of chaos:
When [regional lords] apportioned the land, established their states,
And thus unfolded the pattern of struggle.
Attacks and campaigns were daily waged;
They shed their blood in the open countryside—
This had begun in highest antiquity.
Through untold generations,
One [rule] followed another down to the Five Thearchs,
And no one could prohibit or stop them.

Now today, the August Thearch
Has unified All-under-Heaven into one family—
Warfare will not arise again!
Disaster and harm are exterminated and erased,
The black-headed people live in peace and stability,
Benefits and blessings are lasting and enduring.[8]

This inscription is an excellent testimony to the mindset of Qin leaders in the aftermath of imperial unification. First, it identifies the past, including the age of the Five Thearchs, with persistent debilitating warfare. Second, it hails the First Emperor for bringing about unity, peace, and stability, dwarfing the achievements of his predecessors. Third, it promises that the emperor's achievements will be "lasting and enduring" and "warfare will never rise again." In a few sentences the inscription encapsulates the Qin vision of the past, present, and the future.

I analyze this particular concept of history expressed in the Mt. Yi inscription in the next section; here I focus on a single consequence of the Qin officials' bold proclamation that the achievements of their emperor dwarf those of the Five Thearchs. Insofar as these legendary sage rulers were routinely identified as "True Monarchs" of the past, by proclaiming his superiority over them the Qin Emperor clearly identified himself as the True Monarch of the present. This notion is duly present throughout the stele inscriptions. They consistently associate the reign of the First Emperor with each of the major features of the True Monarch: the universality of rule, his ability to attain perfect sociopolitical order, the emperor's moral and intellectual superiority, and, finally, his superhuman qualities. I now briefly survey these topoi which are ubiquitous in each of the seven inscriptions.

The first and most important theme that permeates the inscriptions is the notion of the universality of the emperor's rule and the peace and stability which results from it. Thus, in the Langye 瑯邪 inscription (219), the August Thearch proudly proclaims:

六合之內, 皇帝之土. 西涉流沙, 南盡北戶. 東有東海, 北過大夏. 人跡所至, 無不臣者. 功蓋五帝, 澤及牛馬.

Within the six combined [directions],
This is the land of the August Thearch:
To the west it ranges to the flowing sands,
To the south it completely takes in where the doors face north.
To the east it enfolds the Eastern Sea,
To the north, it goes beyond Daxia.

Wherever human traces reach,
There is none who does not declare himself [the Thearch's] subject.
His merits surpass those of the Five Thearchs,
His favor extends to oxen and horses.[9]

This statement is unequivocal: the emperor's rule is truly universal. While many of the geographical terms employed above are borrowed from earlier texts, most specifically from the "Yu gong" 禹貢 chapter of the *Venerated Documents* 尚書, the emperor is anxious to stress that his territorial attainments overshadow those of the Five Thearchs. His achievements are buttressed by the rhetoric of the absolute inclusiveness and comprehensiveness of imperial rule, which repeatedly refers to the emperor's possession of "All-under-Heaven," "the six directions" (六合), "four extremities" (四極), and the like (Kern 2000: 151–152).

Territorial expansion is closely associated in the inscriptions with the motif of universal peace. This topos was exceptionally important to the emperor, who propagated it even throughout the marketplaces. An identical pronouncement, inscribed on a series of newly standardized weights and measures, begins with the following words: "In his twenty-sixth year, the emperor completely annexed all the regional lords under Heaven; the black-haired people are greatly at peace."[10] This statement is further elaborated in stele inscriptions. The emperor repeatedly reminds his subjects that "warfare will never rise again," that he has "brought peace to All-under-Heaven," and that the "black-headed people are at peace, never needing to take up arms." "He has wiped out the powerful and unruly, rescuing the black-headed people, bringing stability to the four corners of the empire"; by "uniting All-under-Heaven, he put an end to harm and disaster, and then forever he put aside arms," the result of which is the "Great Peace" (*tai ping* 太平, a term which I discuss separately below).[11] By "unifying All-under-Heaven into one family," the emperor had fulfilled the imperative of the thinkers of the Warring States period, as summarized by Mengzi (孟子, c. 380–304): "stability is in unity."[12]

The second major topos of the inscriptions is the social and political order that the August Thearch brought. "The distinctions between noble and mean are clarified, men and women embody compliance"; the Thearch "unified and led in concord fathers and sons"; and henceforth "the honored and the humble, the noble and the mean will never exceed their position and rank." This social stability is matched by personal security: "six relatives guard each other, so that ultimately there are no bandits and robbers."[13] Political order under the "clear laws" (*ming fa* 明法) of the Qin has ensued: "Office holders respect their divisions, and each knows what to do"; "all respect measures and rules." The notion of universal compliance, which was so essential for the True Monarch in Xunzi's eyes, is duly emphasized: there is "none who is not respectful and submissive," "the hearts of the multitudes all became submissive," and "everybody is compliant with the orders."[14]

Universal peace and stability bring about universal prosperity. The latter ensues not automatically but due to the relentless efforts of the August Thearch, who emulates the sage thearch, Yu 禹, by ordering the terrestrial realm: he "tore down and destroyed inner and outer city walls; broke through and opened river embankments, leveled and removed dangerous obstacles, so that the topography is now fixed."[15] These efforts result in unprecedented affluence: "Men find joy in their fields; women cultivate their work." The Thearch "enriches the black-headed people," so that "all live their full life and there is none who does not achieve his ambitions."[16] As is noted in the Langye inscription cited above, even "horses and oxen" receive the emperor's favor.

It is useful to pause here for a moment and contextualize all these proud pronouncements within the intellectual discourse of the Warring States period. The emperor unmistakably indicates that the visions of a utopian future as presented in numerous texts of the Warring States are finally realized. This being so, the very magnitude of the First Emperor's merits qualifies him as True Monarch. Moreover, in the light of his achievements, the emperor is justified to proclaim himself a sage. It was, again, Xunzi who explained the intrinsic link between the monarch's sagacity and the scope of his success:

> The Son of Heaven is only he who is [a truly appropriate] person.
> All-under-Heaven is extremely heavy: only the strongest can bear it;
> it is extremely large: only the smartest can divide it; it is extremely
> populous: only the wisest can harmonize it. Hence, one who is not
> the sage cannot become a [True] Monarch. When a sage has internal-
> ized the Way, accomplishing its beauty, he will hold the scale and the
> weights of All-under-Heaven.[17]

Xunzi implies here that only a self-cultivated ruler could acquire universal rule. The First Emperor justifiably reverses this order: it is the attainment of the universal rule which testifies to the exceptional personal qualities of the ruler. This understanding is duly present in the inscriptions which repeatedly laud the emperor's virtue, sagacity, and his role as a moral leader of the society. The August Thearch proudly proclaims himself as "sage, knowledgeable, benevolent, and righteous," declaring that he "radiates and glorifies his teachings and instructions, so that his precepts and principles reach all around" and "prohibits and stops the lewd and licentious."[18] The people have been transformed accordingly: "None is not committed to honesty and goodness"; "men and women are pure and sincere." The emperor's "greatly orderly rule cleansed the customs, and All-under-Heaven received his influence."[19] The emperor leaves no doubt that he tops not just the sociopolitical pyramid, but the moral and intellectual pyramid as well.

Following Xunzi, and even exceeding his exaltation of the True Monarch, the First Emperor audaciously proclaims himself as immeasurably superior to other human beings, as a semidivine monarch. His "self-divinization" (Puett 2002) is expressed in a new title he adopted immediately upon the unification, the August Thearch, with its overt sacral connotation. Its second manifestation, fitting in with Xunzi's views cited above, is his self-proclamation as a sage, a title that had been applied in Warring States discourse to former paragons but never to a living ruler.[20] Thus, the emperor plainly declares that he "embodies sagehood" (*gong sheng* 躬聖),[21] and he enjoys the new title so much that he mentions it no less than ten times in seven imperial inscriptions.[22] As the first reigning sage, he adopts a series of measures to bolster his superhuman status: from reshaping the terrain of "All-under-Heaven" like the sage demiurge Yu, to a radical—and apparently entirely unprecedented—recasting of the imperial pantheon, and further to megalomaniacal construction projects, some of which are discussed by Shelach in chapter 3 of this volume. All of these dramatically distinguish the monarch from other mortals. Even the emperor's reported affronts to local deities, as in the case of Mt. Xiang 湘 mentioned in the *Historical Records*, may be indicative of his self-perception as a semidivine person.[23] While none of these provides unequivocal evidence to the effect that the August Thearch actually considered himself truly godlike, it is clear that at the very least he adopted a superhuman public status (cf. Yakobson, chapter 9, this volume).

One final observation with regard to the First Emperor's divine position is due here. It appears most remarkable that none of the imperial inscriptions, most of which were made on the holy sites of the conquered states, often after performing sacrifices to local deities, makes any reference to divine support for the First Emperor's political endeavor. In a marked distinction from all known rulers of China, preimperial and imperial alike, the First Emperor appears indifferent toward Heaven, the [Supreme] Thearch (Di 帝), or other deities, save the spirits of the former kings of Qin, whose support is duly recognized in the first inscription— that on Mt. Yi—and in a roughly simultaneous imperial declaration, recorded in the *Historical Records*.[24] The First Emperor's shunning the title of Son of Heaven (*tianzi* 天子) is yet another indication of his indifference toward Heaven. Is it possible that the Emperor believed—as his inscriptions repeatedly testify—that his achievements were due to his individual merits and had nothing to do with divine support? Did he fear that acknowledging the existence of a politically superior deity would endanger his—or his descendants'—position in the future? Or did he believe that as a true Sage Monarch he simply stood on an equal footing with (or above?) the divine forces and hence owed them no gratitude? We shall probably never have an answer to these questions. In any case, it is clear that the First Emperor's position vis-à-vis the divine powers was not of subservience but at the very least of equality, if not superiority. A man who saved humankind from centuries of warfare and turmoil was second to no one in either the mundane or celestial world.

A MESSIANIC MONARCH

In the above discussion, enough evidence had been marshaled to show that the First Emperor had firmly appropriated the posture of the True Monarch developed by the thinkers of the Warring States period. In what follows I analyze some of the peculiarities of this audacious appropriation of the centuries-old dream to show, first, that the First Emperor may well be identified as China's first and only quasi-Messianic ruler (prior to Mao Zedong, of course);[25] and, second, that his Messianic posture and the subsequent redefinition of the notion of rulership became a major source of tension between him and the intellectual elite—a tension which continued well after the First Emperor's death.

Describing the Qin as a "Messianic regime" may sound amiss: after all, there are clear distinctions between the intellectual atmosphere in China during the Warring States and Qin periods and that of the Messianic Middle East or Europe. Preimperial China witnessed neither millenarian movements nor prophecies about a forthcoming savior, and it lacked both apocalyptic literature and the idea of transcendent redemption. However, a brief look at the definition of Messianism in, for instance, the *Blackwell Dictionary of Modern Social Thought* shows numerous features which fit surprisingly well with the Chinese case. Among these, we may notice the perception of the current situation as unbearable, an active rather than contemplative attitude, a linear view of history (from current suffering to future redemption), and a visible and collective nature of redemption and its universal goals.[26] Some of these features are self-evident from the previous discussion (e.g., activism, the collective and universal nature of salvation) and I shall not address them here anew. What I focus on instead is the idea of a linear history going from the age of suffering into the final and irreversible redemption, an idea which is exemplified in Qin ideology and which is important for understanding both the First Emperor's perceived Messianism and Qin's place in Chinese history in general.

The Mt. Yi inscription cited at the beginning of the previous section is representative of the Qin view of its historical role as a savior of humankind from endless warfare. Qin propagandists did not invent the idea that the Warring States era caused unbearable suffering to the populace: this view was part and parcel of concurrent discourse. For instance, a passage from the *Lüshi chunqiu* 呂氏春秋, composed in the state of Qin two decades before the final unification, states:

> Our generation is extremely foul; nothing can be added to the misery of the black-headed people. The line of the Sons of Heaven has been exterminated, the worthies are cast to the ground; leaders of the age behave indulgently and have departed from the people. The black-headed people have nobody to whom they can complain.[27]

That the violence of the Warring States was considered intolerable is a common point; what distinguishes the Qin statements, however, is that this negative view of the past was radically expanded backward, including to the age of the paragon Five Thearchs. This persistent derision of the former sage rulers is puzzling: after all, it would be much easier to legitimate the Qin Empire by saying that its leaders had simply restored the ideal state of affairs of the age of the Five Thearchs and of other former paragons; yet Qin leaders opted not to do so. I believe this rejection of an efficient legitimating device was a well calculated gamble: it allowed the First Emperor and his entourage to present the empire as an entirely new entity, the final redemption of humankind and "the end of history."

The Qin leaders were extremely anxious to highlight the newness of their regime. Many of the symbolical steps they undertook in the immediate aftermath of the unification—such as the empirewide feast, enhancing everybody's rank of merit, and, most spectacularly, collecting bronze weapons and recasting them into bells and huge human statues—convey a strong feeling of a break from the past and the beginning of a new era (cf. Sanft, forthcoming). No regime in China's long history prior to the Communist Revolution was so consciously derisive of the past (*gu* 古), which was rendered infinitely inferior to "the present" (*jin* 今).[28] The very language of the imperial inscriptions, which abounds with terms such as *zuo* (作, to create, five times), *chu* (初, for the first time, four times) and *shi* (始, the beginning, four times), emphasizes the regime's determination to draw a clear line between what was and what is going to be.

The Qin leaders not only rejected the past but also firmly appropriated the future, boldly declaring that history had ended. Their propaganda lacks any reference to the possibility of their losing power in the future, a topos which figures so prominently in the supposedly early Zhou documents of the *Shang shu* and some of the *Shi jing* 詩經 odes.[29] Qin leaders perceived history not as a cyclical alteration of order and disorder as assumed by Mengzi ("Teng Wen Gong 滕文公 xia," 6.9: 154), but rather as a lengthy age of disorder under various dynasties, which ends with a new, eternal Qin era (Pines 2012c). This desire to conquer the future was expressed soon after the unification, when the emperor decided to abolish the tradition of giving posthumous names to the late monarchs, saying that henceforth his posterity would be numbered according to their generation: "the Second Generation [Emperor], the Third Generation [Emperor] and so on for myriad generations, being inherited endlessly" (*Shiji* 6: 236). This endlessness, eternity, and longevity is repeatedly mentioned in the Qin inscriptions, going much further than the traditional hopes of the lineage longevity expressed in the Zhou bronze texts.[30] For the Qin leaders, there could be no return to the past, with its fragmentation and disorder.

Some colleagues may contradict my assertion of the Qin's historical self-image by pointing at the Qin's adherence to the cyclical notion of historical development, as exemplified in its selection of water as its cosmic element, in accordance with the so-called five phases (*wu xing* 五行) theory associated with Zou Yan 鄒衍 (c. 305–240) and his followers (see more in van Ess, chapter 7 in this volume). This choice, however, does not mean that Qin expected to be replaced by a future ("earth") regime. Qin's acceptance of water should be considered in the context of the "Five Cycles" theory as presented in the "Ying tong" 應同 chapter of the *Lüshi chunqiu*. The "Ying tong" historical scheme might have been deliberately constructed so as to allow both cyclical and lineal explanation: by eliminating Yao 堯 and Shun 舜 from the list of the past rulers, the authors constructed the elements' changes of the past in such a way as to let the future element, water, become the final of the five, leaving a possibility that it would end the entire cycle once and forever. Michael Puett (2001: 143–144) may well be right, then, that by adopting water Qin leaders implied that the dynasty would never be replaced.

Finally, it is important to notice clear utopian motifs in the Qin's self-presentation, which again associate this regime with the concept of complete and final salvation. As noted above, the Qin firmly incorporated the utopian expectations of the Warring States thinkers into its self-image, presenting itself as the regime that allows every individual "to live their full life and to achieve their ambitions," that expands its munificence to "oxen and horses," and that attains universal and absolute compliance. Qin was the first regime in China's history to turn the long-anticipated utopia (literally: "no-place") of preimperial thinkers into what Alexander Martynov aptly names the emperors' "entopia" (literally: "in this place").[31] It is especially noteworthy that in his last inscription the emperor identified his reign as a manifestation of the Great Peace/Great Evenness (*tai ping* 太平). This term was marginal (or nonexistent) in the Warring States period, but became ubiquitous from the Han dynasty as the *terminus classicus* for utopia on earth.[32] It is not impossible that the association of this term with absolute tranquility and perfect order began with the First Emperor; if so it may be one of his most curious and heretofore neglected intellectual legacies.

The quasi-Messianic discourse adopted by the First Emperor, with its open disparagement of the past, and the emphasis on the regime's novelty, and its "entopian" features might have contributed decisively toward the subsequent identification of the Qin as an "aberration" or "rupture" in Chinese history. At the end of this chapter I return to this point; but first I want to explore why the emperor adopted his peculiar "Messianic" stance. An immediate answer would be that the emperor's hubris reflected to a certain degree the real magnitude of his truly unprecedented success. Yet I believe that there were also serious political considerations behind Qin's peculiar self-presentation. Politically, presenting the Qin regime as completely novel might have been conducive for the successful integration of the newly conquered population. Recall that the occupiers radically changed the lives of their new subjects, imposing on them the legal and administrative regulations of Qin, its weights and measures, script and coins, rites and laws, and even its specific administrative vocabulary. Qin altered the social system of the occupied states by decapitating local elites and by imposing the Qin system of twenty ranks of merit.[33] It might have been more expedient to present these measures not as subjugation to Qin rule but as a radical renovation of the lives of the new subjects, a renovation that would bring peace, tranquility and orderly rule under the Sage August Thearch.

In addition, and more important in terms of China's political history, the emperor's "self-Messianization" (rather than mere self-divinization) had immediate radical consequences for his political role. In any culture a Messiah is a charismatic leader, and Qin was no exception. Being a savior, a person who almost single-handedly changed history, the First Emperor buttressed his position as the True Monarch who had the right to rule and not just to reign. Practically, this meant introducing new rules to the political game, which bolstered the emperor's authority vis-à-vis his advisers and the intellectual elite in general.

As argued above, by inflating the image of the True Monarch, thinkers of the Warring States period did not intend to yield their intellectual autonomy or to hamper somehow their freedom of political action, which they enjoyed in the age of political division. Rather, by promising to acquiesce to the future sage ruler, they gained additional power against reigning sovereigns of average abilities, who were strongly encouraged not to meddle in routine administrative tasks, to delegate their everyday work to meritorious aides, and to remain satisfied with their unrivalled ritual prestige and position as the supreme arbiters in intrabureaucratic schisms. This arrangement allowed the thinkers to concentrate most government tasks in the hands of the qualified members of their stratum, while preserving the appearance of the ruler's omnipotence. This situation was supposed to change only in an unspecified future, under the sage True Monarch who would actively rule, while the officials would only "comply and follow him." Now, the First Emperor had proclaimed with the utmost clarity that the new age of the Sage Monarch had finally come.

Having asserted himself as the reigning sage, the First Emperor demanded—and acquired—effective administrative power that went far beyond what most statesmen would in all likelihood have wished to concede. While we should not accept uncritically accusations of senseless despotism of the August Thearch, as indicated in the *Historical Records*, there is little doubt that he did not accept the position of a ritual figurehead to which many preimperial thinkers would have eagerly relegated their sovereigns. Thus, his inscriptions proclaim that the August Thearch "is not remiss in rulership, rising early in the morning and resting late at night," that he "regulates and orders all within the universe, is not idle in inspecting and listening," and that he "uniformly listens to the myriad affairs."[34] We do not know whether the emperor was actually examining the documents he dealt with daily, not going to rest until a certain weight was reached, but the imperial proclamations and constant tours of inspection to the most remote corners of the new realm all present an image of an extraordinarily active ruler.[35] By skillfully appropriating the discourse of the Sage Monarch, the "Great Sage" of Qin created an entirely novel political situation, implementing those recipes of the "Hundred Schools" which were probably never meant to be implemented in real time.

The new position of an emperor as the embodiment of the True Monarch became the single most important contribution of Qin's August Thearch to posterity. Yet the First Emperor's radical attempt to actualize a centuries-old ideal met with considerable resentment. While the history of the Qin is too marred by later biased interpretations and accusations to permit us a reliable reconstruction of the contemporary court atmosphere (Kern 2000: 155–163; van Ess, chapter 7 in this volume), the extant evidence overwhelmingly points to the intellectuals' opposition to the emperor's policy. This opposition might have triggered the most notorious of the First Emperor's acts: the "biblioclasm" of 213 (for the discussion of which see Kern 2000: 188–191; cf. Pines 2009: 172–184), and it was not quelled thereafter. In particular, the decision of some eminent *Ru*—including Kong Jia 孔甲, a descendant of Confucius in the eighth generation—to join the rebellious peasant Chen She 陳涉 (d. 208), becoming Chen's erudite (*Shiji* 121: 3116), is noteworthy. Members of the educated elite were clearly dissatisfied with the rule of "Qin's Sage."[36]

The First Emperor's activist posture eventually became one of his major faults in the eyes of future generations. Jia Yi 賈誼 (200–168), the single most influential critic of the Qin, identified the emperor's overreliance on his abilities and mistrust of meritorious ministers as one of the prime reasons for the malfunctioning of his dynasty.[37] Jia Yi and other thinkers have further interpreted the disastrous collapse of the empire within a few months under an inept and intemperate Second Emperor as a proof of the wrongness of monarchical hyperactivity. In retrospect, the Qin emperor's creativity went too far. The Han rulers, faced with overwhelming criticism of their predecessor, had to modify the Qin model to meet the expectations of their courtiers for a more collegiate way of decision-making.

EPILOGUE: "TRUE MONARCHS" UNDER THE HAN

The collapse of the Qin endangered for a short while the imperial enterprise itself. In the wake of the disintegration of central authority, most of the extinguished Warring States were restored, and many other polities appeared on the map. The most powerful of rival potentates, Xiang Yu 項羽 (d. 202), even briefly abolished the imperial institution, choosing instead to rule under the name "overlord-king" (*ba wang* 霸王). Yet if he intended thereby to dismiss the Qin model, the result was exactly opposite to his expectations. The upsurge of woeful turmoil due to the void of legitimate authority may have convinced the major political actors of the advantages of the imperial system for ensuring political stability. Thus, when Xiang Yu was defeated in 202, his conqueror Liu Bang 劉邦 (d. 195) resumed the title August Thearch, which remained the designation of China's rulers for the next 2114 years.

As is well known, the Han adopted not just the Qin imperial title, but also most of the institutional and ritual arrangements of the preceding dynasty, its specific vocabulary and nomenclature, and many aspects of its imperial ideology and self-image (e.g., Loewe 1994: 124 ff). Certain topoi, characteristic of the Qin imperial inscriptions, became essential parts of the monarch's proclamations from the early Han period and throughout the imperial millennia. Thus, most emperors, unless under extreme duress, continued to hail the peace, stability and affluence that they presumably brought to their subjects; they pretended to rule the entire realm "within the seas," and also claimed the position of moral leaders of humankind (see, e.g., Kern 2000: 175–182). There are also obvious continuities in terms of the emperor's sacredness and sagacity, although these are less straightforward, as I explain below. In general, the Han's indebtedness to the Qin is undeniable.

Despite these continuities, a closer look at Han imperial rhetoric indicates significant departures from the Qin model. Most notably, the Messianic fervor is gone. Having internalized the lessons of their predecessors' astounding collapse, the Han emperors dared not claim that they had created a brave new world and ended history (although these notions occasionally resurfaced at the margins of Han political discourse). This "de-Messianization" of the emperors had profound consequences on the functioning of the imperial institution. Most notably, it allowed a bifurcation between the institution as such, which remained absolutely sacrosanct, and the reigning emperor, whose sagacity was not necessarily taken for granted. As a result, in a most curious development, the Han emperors became more sacred but less sagacious than their proud Qin predecessor (cf. Loewe 1994: 85–111; 121–122).

The sacred status of the Han (and subsequent) emperors was built on a reaffirmation of the emperor's links to the supreme deity, Heaven. The idea of Heaven's Decree (or Mandate, *Tian ming* 天命) was resurrected under Liu Bang, whose ritual hymns repeatedly thank Heaven's and the [Supreme] Thearch's (帝) support for the Han endeavor (Kern 1996); and eventually, this idea became the cornerstone of dynastic legitimacy throughout the imperial millennia. In their renewed capacity as "Sons of Heaven," the emperors acted as sole mediators between the supreme deity and the mundane realm, presiding over human and divine affairs, repeatedly reshaping the pantheon and managing manifold sacrificial activities. Moreover, the emperors were perceived as connected to Heaven in an additional way: through a system of resonance, meaning that Heaven sends down omens and portents to approve or disapprove of its "son's" conduct (Loewe 1994: 121–141). This notion added an additional sacral dimension to the imperial rule, making the emperor's body, and *mutatis mutandis* his kin, aides, ritual utensils, seals and other paraphernalia, sacrosanct. This sacral status was emphasized by the increasing usage of the *lèse majesté* clauses of penal law: any crime against the emperor's person was thereafter treated with the utmost harshness (Pines 2012a: 44–75).

Being firmly incorporated into state ideology and ritual practice, the concept of the emperor's divine status had become part and parcel of imperial political culture. However, its implications were quite equivocal. Reaffirming the existence of the supreme deity above the emperor, and the belief that this deity may express dissatisfaction with its human counterpart and even replace him, served as a powerful check against the monarch's atrocities. Not incidentally, the Han emperors from Emperor Wen 漢文帝 (r. 180–157) repeatedly issued "mea culpa edicts" (罪己詔), blaming themselves for natural disasters or unfavorable omens and promising to improve their ways, specifically by promoting upright officials (Liu Zehua 1996: 239–247). It seems then that the redefinition of the emperor's divine status under the Han bolstered the prestige of the emperorship in general, but somewhat reduced the power of individual monarchs.

The same bifurcation between the institutional and individual aspects of emperorship is evident in the concept of imperial sagacity under the Han. Ostensibly, the Han emperors rejected the First Emperor's hubris, and repeatedly asserted their weakness and inadequacy. This change is most evident in their posture vis-à-vis the sage rulers of the past, especially the Five Thearchs. From the Han on, these paragons were depicted in superhuman terms as generators of cosmic and not just sociopolitical harmony and order, while reigning monarchs modestly acknowledged their inability to match this ideal. This modesty is vivid, for instance, in an edict of young Emperor Wu 漢武帝 (r. 141–87), in which he called upon "the worthies" to arrive at court and help him in conducting government affairs:

> I heard that during the times of Tang [唐, i.e., Yao 堯] and Yu [虞, i.e., Shun 舜], they drew images [on the people's robes as the punishment], and the people did not transgress; wherever sun and moon shone everybody behaved humbly. At the times of Kings Cheng 成 and Kang 康 of the Zhou, mutilating punishments were not employed, virtue reached birds and beasts, instructions penetrated [all within] the four seas. Beyond the sea they expanded to Sujuan 肅眘; to the north developed Jusou 渠搜; Di 氐 and Qiang 羌 [tribesmen] came in submission. There were neither displacement of stars and constellations, nor eclipses of sun and moon; mountain ranges did not collapse, rivers and valleys were not blocked; unicorns and phoenixes lived in suburban marshes, the [Yellow] River and Luo River generated charts and documents. Wuhu, what should I do to approach this [state of affairs]?
>
> Now, as it has become my duty to protect the ancestral temples, I seek this when I get up at sunrise, and contemplate this at bed at night. [I am fearful] as if passing above the abyss and not knowing how to cross. How magnificent! How great! What should I do to manifest the splendid enterprise and munificent virtue of the former emperors, above to stay in trinity with Yao and Shun, below to match the Three Dynasties? I am lacking perspicacity, and cannot sustain virtue for long. (*Hanshu* 6: 160–161)

Emperor Wu's edict contrasts sharply with the First Emperor's statements (and most possibly it was consciously designed to be so). The past is superb; the current ruler cannot match its attainments; it is only with the help of worthy aides that he may approach the splendor of the past. Yet we should not be misled by the humble rhetoric of the Han emperor: the rules of the game in the Han era were different, and it was the task of the ministers to flatter their ruler and to extol his supposed sagacity. Thus, while Emperor Wu did not claim to be a sage and used this epithet exclusively for his ancestors, his ministers, conversely, routinely identified him as a sage. A new court *bon ton* was for the emperor to humbly proclaim inadequacy and even blame himself for multiple malfunctions, while it was up to the ministers to hail the sovereign. Eventually, the ministerial voice prevailed; the term "sage" (*sheng* 聖) became firmly incorporated into the emperors' image, becoming a synonym of the adjective "imperial" (Hsing 1988; Liu Zehua 1998).

So, does this mean that any Han emperor was supposed to be a sage just like the Qin First Emperor? Not necessarily. At a closer look, we may notice that in the Han, sagacity became more a feature of the imperial office than of its occupant. Technically, the emperor had to be considered a sage, much like he had to be considered sacred: after all, in his capacity as the supreme administrator he had to make among others decisions on purely ideological issues, for example, approving or dismissing a certain exegetical tradition or canonical work as worthy of incorporation into the court education system. Since his judgments were final and supposedly infallible, it had to be assumed for preserving the dynasty's face that the monarch was intellectually superior to his subjects. Simultaneously, however, it was well known that the throne was more frequently than not occupied by mediocre persons, and even by child emperors manipulated by their kin or, most notoriously, by court eunuchs. To believe in the sagacity of these individuals required too great a leap of faith for most literati.

If my analysis is correct and the major impact of Qin's "Messianic revolution" was turning the emperor into a divine and sage person, then, again, echoing Martynov (1987: 29), we may notice that the Han retained the "yardstick" of the utopia and not its content. The imperial position was continuously regarded as divine and sagacious; its occupant—less so. Eventually, this dichotomy between image and reality proved to be a much more viable pattern than the Qin model of a charismatic "Messianic" monarch. The latter was unsustainable, especially due to the inevitability of the eventual accession of an incapable monarch under the principle of lineal succession, as the case of the notorious Second Emperor proves.[38] The Han system was much more flexible. The sacrosanct position of the imperial institution as such allowed it to retain the major function as the symbol of universal unity and of political order with the "single esteemed" at the top. Simultaneously, subtle reaffirmation of the possibility that an individual monarch might be mediocre and inept encouraged the formation of bureaucratic system of "checks and balances" which allowed for preserving the empire intact even under inadequate rulers, including, most remarkably, under a sequence of child monarchs in the Later Han. Although a few Han and later emperors took their sagacity literally and tried to impose their will on all imaginable spheres of human activity (Wang Mang 王莽 [45 BCE-23 CE] immediately comes to mind), most were coached to understand their personal limitations and to consult their aides, adopting a much more collegiate way of government than the Qin idea of imperial sagacity would allow (see Pines 2012a: 63–69, for further details).

Finally, allow me two concluding remarks. First, I believe that adding the "Messianic" angle to an analysis of the Qin provides a possible solution to the riddle of its historical place. The Qin's exceptional position in Chinese history derives neither from its culture nor from its institutions but from the very peculiar mindset of its leaders, most notably the First Emperor, who claimed to end history and demanded the literal realization of his theoretical omnipotence. This mindset, which is not attested to in either the preimperial or later imperial period, significantly distinguishes the Qin from its predecessors and successors. Qin's exceptionality was in the final account a matter of its self-presentation; and this self-presentation, rather than the post-factum manipulation of Qin's enemies, is largely responsible for the later view of Qin as a historical "aberration."

Second, I believe that my interpretation sheds additional light on the problem of the Qin's collapse, discussed by Shelach in chapter 3 of this volume. As is well known, Jia Yi in his seminal discussion on the reasons for the Qin's collapse noticed its inability to change and modify its ways as the major malady of its rule (*Shiji* 6: 283). Yet this is exactly the common malady of Messianic regimes worldwide, most notably Communist regimes in the USSR and in Mao's China among others. Having promised to bring utopia here and now and end history, these regimes find it difficult to deviate from the patterns established at the moment of their foundation, and are commonly very rigid in terms of their structure. Facing the difficulty of fulfilling their promises, they often radicalize and escalate their "Messianic" rhetoric to conceal the growing divergence between image and reality, and overburden the society with multiple unreasonable projects. This, apparently, was the case with the Qin which, as Shelach shows, entered into a spiral of ever escalating projects aimed, among other things, at projecting its unrivalled power amid increasing strains on its rule. Although it is not impossible that had the Qin continued for a longer period it would have adapted itself to a more "normal" mode of conduct, I believe that the quasi-Messianic mindset of its rulers substantially hindered this possibility. It was only after the utopia was abandoned that what Shelach aptly calls the "fuzzy" empire, modeled after the Han, acquired its true immortality—or, at least, the most remarkable longevity in the political history of humankind.

9 The First Emperors

Image and Memory

Alexander Yakobson

TWO FIRST EMPERORS

This chapter examines the image and posthumous reputation of Augustus, the first Roman emperor, with an eye to a comparison with the First Emperor of Qin. A systematic comparison is precluded by the author's lamentably limited knowledge of Chinese history. Nevertheless, some basic facts in this field are nowadays sufficiently known even to a nonexpert to enable certain useful parallels and comparisons. The differences between the two cases and their two cultural and political backgrounds are deep and manifold—so much so, indeed, that it may legitimately be asked whether comparing them promises more than just a satisfaction of intellectual curiosity (not that this motivation is to be altogether dismissed). But it is precisely because the differences are so great that it is so instructive that some parallels emerge nevertheless. These parallels may point to certain fundamental patterns of empire and imperial rule that transcend not just personality and political context but the divide between civilizations.

One fundamental difference between the two cases needs to be stressed from the outset: the two men cannot be defined as "founders of empire" in the same sense. In the Chinese case, the First Emperor's achievement was the creation of the unified empire, whereas his mode of government—absolute monarchy—was, despite the highly personal characteristics of his rule, the traditional one in the Chinese world. Augustus, in contrast, was the founder of the emperorship rather than of the empire—in a culture in which autocracy was, traditionally, vehemently rejected. He was by no means the founder of the Roman Empire—though he certainly took great pride in its far-reaching expansion under his rule. The empire had existed for generations before him, under a republican form of government characteristic of the Greco-Roman world, the city-state. Although this political system was, in principle, ill-suited for running an empire, its Roman version was flexible and successful enough to perform this feat for a long time; but it is widely accepted that in the end, the tensions between the empire and the republican form of government contributed decisively to the republic's fall.[1]

When Augustus started his career, one-man rule was still a moral and cultural taboo in Rome. The failure of the brief experiment in autocracy carried by his adoptive father, Julius Caesar the dictator, which ended in the latter's assassination by senators in the Senate house (44 BCE), only emphasized the potency of the taboo and the dangers facing anyone inclined to defy it. By the time Augustus died in 14 CE, after decades of peaceful sole rule (in this he was luckier than his Chinese counterpart), this mode of government had become well established and rooted enough to ensure smooth hereditary succession. The hereditary nature of the succession was thinly disguised—or, rather, balanced, as a nod to tradition—by the ritual of the Senate and people formally conferring his powers on Tiberius, his adopted son and successor, as they had done for Augustus and would continue to do for succeeding emperors. In the past, the Roman people chose those who governed their state in competitive elections. From now on the voting—confirming the powers of a predetermined sole ruler—would be turned into a ceremony and a ritual; an empty ritual, as many Roman historians would say—though a Chinese audience might perhaps be less quick to dismiss "mere" rituals.

Restoring the republic, at any rate, would never again be a serious political option. It can be said that Augustus succeeded in turning the sole rule not just into a political reality but into a new ancestral tradition (without wholly obliterating the older one). His own posthumous reputation would be much better than could be expected, in a traditionally minded society, for someone who went against centuries-old tradition. Whereas the great change carried out by the First Emperor of Qin—the unification of "all-under-Heaven" under a sole ruler—enjoyed strong legitimacy both in the tradition preceding the deed itself and in the later Chinese tradition (see, e.g., Pines 2012a), the change brought by Augustus—providing the Roman state with an autocrat—had, under the republic, been considered as perhaps the worst imaginable crime that could be committed by a Roman citizen. Later tradition accepted it as the only way to put an end to the civil wars that had ravaged the late republic—similarly to the way in which the chaos and bloodshed of the period of the Warring States generated a longing for unification. Both "first emperors" could thus base their legitimacy in large measure on having brought internal peace.

Nevertheless, republican sentiment in Rome was far from extinguished even after the republic itself had been dead and buried. Many—especially in the still-powerful senatorial elite—accepted the imperial regime only grudgingly, as the lesser of two evils compared with the prospect of anarchy and civil war. Augustus had to tread carefully. He removed the Roman taboo against monarchy by continuously undermining it rather than openly defying it, and by the sheer length of his rule (which might not have lasted so long had he been less careful in this respect). By the end of his reign, as the historian Tacitus wrote, very few Romans could personally remember how the republic really looked (*Annales*, 1.3).

Augustus's own rule was, thus, much less openly autocratic and despotic than that of his Chinese counterpart. He appears never to have admitted in public that he was the sole ruler of the Roman state—though others, as we shall see, were not at all shy in admitting this for him. In fact, the "cult of personality" surrounding Augustus was so blatant that it has been doubted that any kind of a "republican façade" could have co-existed with it.[2] But this view, I believe, is mistaken: the propagandistic flexibilities available to a successful autocrat who is also a master of propaganda should not be underestimated. Augustus's prestige was enhanced both by the unprecedented powers and honors he took and by those he turned down, despite the people's urgent pleas, thus proving his civic moderation. However, in the days of his immediate successors, the Julio-Claudian emperors, any attempt to disguise imperial absolutism quickly disappeared. While a good emperor would always be expected to respect certain sensitivities that had originated in the republican past, under some of Augustus's immediate successors the potential for despotism and cruelty intrinsic in an absolutist regime was fully realized. In this respect it is they, rather than Augustus, that perhaps should be compared to the First Emperor of Qin—also in the sense that their undoubted cruelties may have been exaggerated by a hostile later tradition.

Augustus's posthumous reputation greatly benefited from flattering comparisons with his successors, while at the same time he was credited with having put an end to civil wars by establishing a regime that would succeed—mostly, though not invariably—in preserving internal peace for many generations. Of course, as the founder of the new order of things

Augustus was no less responsible for the long-term costs of autocracy than for its benefits. As regards his image and reputation among posterity, Augustus was certainly luckier that the First Emperor of China—at least until modern times, when more favorable assessments of the latter appeared in China, while in the Western world today, and for some time, no autocrat (at least no Western one) can receive wholehearted praise. But their respective polities display, despite the obvious great differences, certain fundamental similarities that seem to be characteristic of empire as such. As for the rituals, characteristic of the Roman imperial regime, of unanimous votes conferring popular legitimacy on autocrats—these had to wait until modern times in order to find worthy analogies.

THE MESSAGE OF THE *RES GESTAE*

Both rulers left detailed documents reflecting the way they wished to be perceived by their subjects and by posterity: the imperial steles of the First Emperor of Qin and the *Res Gestae Divi Augusti* (The Achievements of the Divine Augustus)—an account of his life and achievements published after his death and set originally on two bronze tablets before his mausoleum in Rome.[3] The two documents are very different in tone—though not lacking in significant similarities as to the content of the message. The First Emperor of China speaks through his servants and indulges in open self-glorification, as befits an absolute ruler and founder of a huge empire, impressing on the reader the superhuman magnitude of his achievements and his own superhuman stature (see Pines, chapter 8 in this volume). Augustus speaks in the first person from beyond the grave—from the skies, actually, since he has been deified after his death. His purpose is, naturally, none other than self-glorification, and the overall image projected is no less than superhuman—even in life, not to mention the fact that for the reader, facing the mausoleum with the huge bronze statue of Augustus on top of it, he had already become a god. At the same time, Augustus is careful to pay proper respect to republican tradition. In fact, had we not possessed this text, we would hardly have guessed how strong this tradition still was—or at least could be, when the emperor so chose—to the very end of Augustus's long reign. I am quoting its opening paragraph and its two final ones[4]:

> (1) At the age of nineteen [44 BCE] on my own responsibility and at my own expense I raised an army, with which I successfully championed the liberty of the republic when it was oppressed by the tyranny of a faction. 2 On that account the Senate passed decrees in my honor

enrolling me in its order in the consulship of Gaius Pansa and Aulus Hirtius [43 BCE]. . . . 4 In the same year, when both consuls had fallen in battle, the People appointed me consul and triumvir for the organization of the republic.

(34) In my sixth and seventh consulships [28–27 BCE], after I had extinguished civil wars, and at a time when with universal consent I was in complete control of affairs, I transferred the republic from my power to the dominion of the senate and people of Rome. 2 For this service of mine I was named Augustus by decree of the Senate, and the door-posts of my house were publicly wreathed with bay leaves and a civic crown was fixed over my door and a golden shield was set in the Curia Julia [Senate house], which, as attested by the inscription thereon, was given me by the Senate and People of Rome on account of my courage, clemency, justice and piety. 3 After this time I excelled all in influence [*auctoritas*], although I possessed no more official power [*potestas*] than others who were my colleagues in the several magistracies.

(35) In my thirteenth consulship [2 BCE] the Senate, the equestrian order and the whole People of Rome gave me the title of Father of my Country, and resolved that this should be inscribed in the porch of my house and in the Curia Julia and in the Forum Augustum below the chariot which had been set there in my honor by decree of the Senate. 2 At the time of writing I am in my seventy-sixth year.

This, as Augustus would have it, is the story of his life: he started his career as a liberator of the republic (from a rival who was naturally "oppressing" it). He went on to defeat all his enemies in a series of civil wars, inevitably amassing "emergency" powers in the process, but fighting for the republic, and not for personal domination; his final victory (in 30 BCE) left him the sole master of the Roman world. In 28–27 BCE, as promised, he surrendered all his extraordinary powers and restored the republican form of government. There followed the long decades of his established peaceful rule—the principate, as it was commonly described—the rule of the *princeps*, the First Citizen.[5] As *princeps*, he was, legally, no more that a magistrate—an elected official on whom various special powers had been conferred, who enjoyed, indeed, unique influence (*auctoritas*) but possessed no more power than was allowed by republican tradition. For his manifold services to the state (always referred to as *res publica*—the commonwealth), notably, for having handed it over from his personal power to the rightful dominion of the Senate and people of Rome—he received from them many honors which he proudly parades throughout the document, culminating in the supreme honor of being proclaimed "Father of His Country" (the solemn final accord of the *Res Gestae*). The people, naturally, were eager to heap on him additional honors and powers, but he checked their zeal and refused to accept any untraditional powers since the "restoration of the republic" in 27 BCE. "I would not accept any office inconsistent with the custom of our ancestors" (6). "The dictatorship was offered to me by both Senate and People in my absence and when I was at Rome [22 BCE] . . . , but I refused it" (5).

The refusal of the dictatorship which the populace, harassed by famine and believing that only Augustus's personal intervention would put an end to the crisis, was urging him to assume in 22 BCE was staged in grand style. The Roman dictatorship had once been a legitimate office assumed in grave emergencies for no more than six months; in the later republic and finally by Julius Caesar it became something similar to dictatorship the modern sense of the term. Augustus would have none of it: "When the people did their best to force the dictatorship upon him, he knelt down, threw off his toga from his shoulders and with bare breast begged them not to insist" (Suetonius, *Augustus*, 52).

It is, needless to say, impossible to image the First Emperor, or any other emperor, of China in this posture—any more than it is possible to imagine them, or indeed any other premodern autocrat, taking part in the following ceremony: "Whenever Augustus took part in the election of magistrates, he went the round of the tribes with his candidates and entreated [*supplicabat*] for them in the traditional manner. He also cast his own vote in his tribe, as one of the people" (Suetonius, *Augustus*, 51).

One wonders if he also stood in line before voting "as one of the people." Perhaps not: modern heads of state, after all, are exempt from this. But we may be quite sure that Augustus's participation in elections, whatever the technicalities surrounding it, was in itself turned into one of the many public rituals reaffirming the people's boundless love, loyalty, and devotion to their leader. The ostensibly civic and pseudo-republican aspects of the emperor's public image, carefully cultivated by the regime, served, no less than the blatantly monarchical and quasidivine ones, like- wise carefully cultivated, the same overall propagandistic aim. And the aim was to project, for contemporaries as well as for posterity, the image of an all-powerful and superhuman ruler of a world empire—a benefactor of the human race (and not just of the Roman people) who has opened a new era of peace and prosperity. The analogy with the steles of the First Emperor of China does not seem artificial after all.

REPUBLICAN SCRUPLES AND MONARCHIST ADULATION

One of the honors heaped on the First Citizen by the grateful Senate in 27 BCE, in recognition of his generosity in "restoring the republic," was the name-*cum*-title of Augustus (as related in *Res Gestae* 34, quoted above). The name has clear religious connotations—somewhere between "revered" and "worshipped," denoting a status of more than a mere mortal, though falling short of full divinization.[6] Since his adoptive father was officially deified after his death, Augustus was designated as *divi filius*—son of the divine (Julius); it was openly predicted (by others, naturally) that he would become a god after the end of his mortal life.[7] In the provinces of the empire where there existed a tradition of paying divine honors to rulers, Augustus was worshipped as a god in temples dedicated to him and to the goddess Roma who symbolized the Roman state; he made his acceptance of this cult conditional on the association of Roma with it. This is regarded by Suetonius, the biographer of the emperors, as a sign of modesty; meanwhile, "in the city itself [i.e., in Rome] he refused this honor most emphatically" (*Augustus*, 52). If he had occasion to refuse it emphatically, it must have been emphatically offered to him. This is remarkable, and a measure of Augustus's extraordinary position, for the deification of a living man was unheard of in Rome. Posthumous deification, too, was exceptional: the first case was that of Romulus, Rome's legendary founder and first king; that of Julius Caesar only the second. Nevertheless, despite Augustus's refusal, various forms of quasidivine worship of the emperor crept into Rome and Italy.

Furthermore, a month was named after him (the month of August in which I am now, appropriately, writing this chapter); his birthday was publicly celebrated; his name was added to the official hymns to the gods (as he records in *Res Gestae*; probably by asking the gods to bless and protect him personally, alongside the Roman people as a whole). Augustus's statutes filled the city, Italy, and the Roman world; one of them was a statue of him as a victorious commander riding a carriage with four horses that was placed at the center of the new Forum bearing his name; it is there that the inscription bearing witness that he had been proclaimed Father of his Country (a hugely powerful image in a strictly patriarchal society) was placed in 2 BCE, as he mentions in the last paragraph of the *Res Gestae*. His returns to Rome from prolonged inspection tours in the different parts of the empire (a feature common to both first emperors) were turned into major public celebrations, with monuments to preserve the memory of the happy occasion; one of them, the Altar of Peace (*Ara*

Pacis), can still be seen (after considerable reconstruction) in Rome. The emperor's image appeared regularly on state coins. Beyond a certain point in his reign, virtually all military victories—traditionally the highest source of glory and prestige in the state—were attributed personally to him as commander-in-chief.

Whereas the message coming from Augustus itself, in the *Res Gestae* or conveyed officially on various occasions, as to the emperor's standing in the state was in a sense ambiguous—combining (quasi-)republican and monarchic elements—there was nothing ambiguous about the image of Caesar Augustus projected by the way he was addressed in public by others. He was regularly and clearly portrayed—by people who knew better than to say something the emperor would be unhappy with—as an all-powerful and quasidivine ruler of a world empire who had brought peace and prosperity to the human race, as well as the founder of a dynasty that was destined to rule Rome after him. A few examples to convey the tone that makes the music:

> When your divine mind and power, Imperator Caesar, put the whole world under its command, your citizens[8] glorified in your triumph and victory; for all their enemies were crushed by your invincible courage and all mankind obeyed your bidding. The Roman people and Senate, liberated from fear, have been guided by your bountiful thoughts and counsels . . . Since . . . it was the heavenly counsel to commit him [Julius Caesar] to the regions of immortality and transfer imperial control to your power. (Vitruvius, *De architectura*, preface)

> O father and guardian of the human race [Jupiter, the supreme god of the Roman pantheon], to thee by fate has been entrusted the charge of mighty Caesar [Augustus]; mayst thou be lord of all, with Caesar next in power. . . . Second to thee alone shall he with justice rule the broad earth. (Horace, *Odes*, 1.12.49–52, 58).

> In the line of Augustus the guardianship of the fatherland shall abide; it is decreed that his house shall hold the reins of Empire. (Ovid, *Fasti*, 1.531–32)

> All that exists beneath the canopy of Jove [Jupiter] is Caesar's own. (Ovid, *Fasti*, 2.138; "All under Heaven" seems a reasonable rendering)

> Caesar is the *res publica*. (Ovid, *Tristia*, 4.4.15)

This kind of rhetoric has been adduced as proof that Augustus never tried to disguise the autocratic nature of his rule.[9] But it is precisely one of the privileges of autocracy to convey contradictory propagandistic messages when it suits the regime. That a leader can be presented to the people simultaneously as a fellow citizen and as an all-powerful ruler of more than human stature should not surprise anyone acquainted with the history of the twentieth century.

The obvious modern parallels should not, however, be pushed too far. The republican tradition to which Augustus was paying largely symbolic homage was still potent enough to produce practical results that might surprise a modern reader—and certainly caused the next generations of Romans, living under the successors of Augustus, to marvel. An absolute ruler who votes as "one of the people," and who receives his powers by popular suffrage, may not particularly surprise us; it is less easy to envisage an autocrat of a world empire who, "when he gave testimony in court, was most patient in submitting to questions and even to contradiction,"[10] or who, "when he was assailed with scurrilous or spiteful jests by certain men, made reply in a public proclamation [without punishing the offenders]; yet vetoed a law to check freedom of speech in wills" (Suetonius, *Augustus*, 56.1). The elections in which Augustus took part had not yet become a purely ceremonial occasion. Those recommended by him were chosen as a matter of course, but most magistrates were still elected by free (within reason) and, at any rate, competitive elections—so much so that we still hear of measures taken against electoral bribery and violence (a sure sign of political freedom). It was only after a change carried out by his successor, Tiberius (who claimed to be acting according to instructions left by Augustus),[11] that the popular assemblies assumed the far more natural role, befitting the true nature of the regime, of unanimously rubber-stamping a list of candidates submitted to them.

The Senate under Augustus was still a forum where genuine debates could take place and real decisions be made—though not, naturally, on issues of the highest importance. Even the emperor himself might be openly contradicted—though there could never be any doubt that he would have his way whenever he chose to insist. Suetonius would relate the wonders of senatorial freedom under the founder of the principate: "As he was speaking in the Senate someone said to him, 'I did not understand,' and another: 'I would contradict you if I had the opportunity.' Several times when he was rushing from the House in anger at the excessive bickering of the disputants, some shouted after him: 'Senators ought to have the right of speaking their mind on public affairs'" (*Augustus*, 54).

Suetonius's contemporary readers are clearly expected to marvel at what was still possible under the first emperor. Such scenes were inconceivable in the Senate of their own time, though this was a relatively nondespotic period of "the enlightened emperors," early second century. These emperors were generally on good terms with the Senate and, among other things, allowed criticism of previous emperors who were considered as tyrants by high-class (mostly senatorial) public opinion—thereby signaling that they shared the outlook and the values of the senatorial order to which the emperor, too—as a public official— belonged. Augustus's forbearance in the face of verbal attacks could, to some extent, be understandable to his biographer's contemporaries: the enlightened emperors made a point of not enforcing the law of treason in such cases, unlike some of Augustus successors under whom an incautious word about the emperor could spell a man's ruin. "Treason" here is a rather imprecise rendering of the Roman term (*laesa*) *maiestas*—the offense of injuring the majesty of the Roman people (as in was originally formulated, under the republic) and hence, under the imperial regime— of its chief elected representative, the *princeps*. Under Augustus, both the law and the death penalty were enforced without hesitation when it came to actual conspiracies, and at least in one case—against a dangerous rabble-rouser who may well not have been—despite his conviction—an actual conspirator.[12] Toward mere words, where no serious danger was perceived, the first Roman emperor showed remarkable tolerance.[13] He summed up his attitude—not exactly typical of an autocrat—in a letter to his future successor, Tiberius: "My dear Tiberius, do not be carried away by the ardour of youth in this matter, or take it too much to heart that anyone speak evil of me; we must be content if we can stop anyone from doing evil to us" (Suetonius, *Augustus*, 52).

It was under Tiberius, the second emperor, that the Roman notion of *laesa maiestas*—injured majesty—was first unambiguously turned into an offense, punishable by death, of showing disrespect to the person of the ruler—a characteristic feature of autocratic monarchies widely known by the French *lèse majesté*. Under the republic, according to Tacitus, "deeds were called into question, words remained unpunished"; the first widening of the scope of the law of *maiestas* took place already under Augustus,[14] but the logic of monarchy was not yet, as we have seen, fully applied by him in this field. However, it was in the nature of things, under the regime that he created, for verbal offenses against the ruler to be treated as grave crimes against the state, and this potential was fully realized under his immediate successor. Thereafter, applying the law in this way or forbearing to apply it depended wholly on the emperor's pleasure.

THE LOGIC OF IMPERIAL MONARCHY

The monarchical "nature of things" was destined to prevail in this field over Augustus's personal inclination. This was only natural: an autocratic ruler is indeed "the state," and an autocratic state is indeed undermined when its ruler is brought into disrespect.[15] And so it was with numerous other aspects of the regime established by Augustus: the full potential of the imperial autocracy would be realized only after—sometimes, long after—the reign of the first Roman emperor, but the foundations were laid by him, and the process set firmly on its course. The Senate was destined—though this took time—to lose its deliberative and decision-making functions and become, under the later empire, an assembly whose chief function was to applaud and acclaim imperial proclamations. The latter were openly declared the highest law of the land, and the emperor himself was explicitly placed—in the writings of Roman jurists—above the law. In form, none of this was true during Augustus's reign (which should not even be formally defined as a reign); in substance, his will was always bound to prevail on any issue which he regarded as sufficiently important. It was natural that an empire ruled by an autocrat would need a highly developed and increasingly intrusive bureaucracy, encroaching on both central and local traditional foci of power and often replacing them. This process started under Augustus and developed—relatively slowly, but inexorably—after him. All civil and military appointments were destined to be concentrated, officially, in the emperor's hands (with the inevitable emergence of the patronage networks that controlled appointments in practice). The bureaucratic imperial despotism of the later empire, however different in form and style from the Augustan principate, was its natural and easily predictable outgrowth.

An almighty ruler of a world empire had to reside, in the nature of things, remote from his subjects, in an imperial palace, with all the pomp and circumstance of imperial monarchy, his person surrounded with an aura of divinity, and those approaching him prostrating themselves before him. All these things would come—though no imperial palace ever dominated Rome (or even Constantinople, the "second Rome" of the later empire) in the same way that the Forbidden City dominated Beijing. Augustus, so far from receiving a palace from the state, turned his private house (on the Palatine hill—hence the word *palace* in European languages) over to the state, making it public property. This, of course, turned it precisely into a palace. In this house of his, not particularly grand or luxurious by contemporary Roman standards but protected by the newly established imperial ("praetorian") guard, he would receive his guests in the manner of a Roman senator:

> His morning receptions were open to all, including common people, and he met the requests of those who approached him with great affability, jocosely reproving one man because he presented a petition to him with as much hesitation "as he would a penny to an elephant."
>
> [As for senators,] he exchanged social calls with many of them, and did not cease to attend all their anniversaries, until he was well on in years and was once incommoded by the crowd on the day of a betrothal. (Suetonius, *Augustus*, 53)

His policy was, clearly, to hold fast to the substance of monarchic power while avoiding many (though not all) of its external trappings. Paradoxically, he came closest to his openly despotic successors precisely as regards the most unrepublican and un-Roman symbolic aspect of absolute monarchy, which was, however, also the most politically important one—the divinization of the ruler. How could an autocrat at the head of a world empire, many of whose peoples had a tradition of ruler-worship, fail to be accorded divine honors? Open divinization in the provinces, where emperor-worship served as a powerful symbol of imperial unity and loyalty; honors bordering on full divinization but not quite attaining it in Rome and Italy, with official deification reserved for "good rulers" after their death (and the title of "son of the divine"—to their successors)—this was the norm established already by Augustus, and not much could be added to it thereafter.

Why did Augustus decide to import this outrageously un-Roman form of adulation, seemingly incompatible with any republican façade, into Rome and Italy? He may well have concluded that the cult of the emperor (in its "light" version reserved for citizens) was politically useful and important as regards the lower classes of Rome and Italy, as well the soldiers, for reasons not dissimilar to those that applied to the empire's subjects in the provinces. It should be borne in mind that the city populace included a large foreign element (consisting of both immigrants and manumitted slaves).[16] The soldiers, whose loyalty, focused on the person of their supreme commander, was naturally of paramount importance, hailed mainly from the rural poor of Italy, largely unaffected by republican sensitivities (more so than the urban plebs).[17] Moreover, the legions, with their citizen-soldiers, were stationed in the provinces, where the emperor was openly worshipped; as far as devotion to the emperor was concerned, they could hardly lag far behind the soldiers from the auxiliary forces that consisted of noncitizens. By contrast, the Roman elite, where old sensitivities were the strongest, could be placated by his steadfast refusal of full divinization. At any rate, its members did not have to suffer to the tiresome un-Roman ceremonial surrounding of an absolute monarch with claims to divinity. Most of the senators must have had no difficulty grasping the facts of life: they fostered the imperial cult with all due diligence as governors in the provinces, while hosting Augustus at their family celebrations in the capital, and even allowing themselves occasionally to argue with him (on issues of less than fateful importance) in the Senate.

The cult of the emperor, in its various forms, was thus required by reasons of state—above all, by reasons of empire, with its hugely diverse population that had to be provided with a visible and personal symbol of loyalty and devotion that united all, and of the imperial army which sustained both the empire and the regime. Adulation was functional; Augustus did not let it go to his head, or at least avoided this danger to a degree highly unusual among autocrats. The First Emperor of China could not reconcile himself to his own mortality; this had serious consequences. Augustus alluded, in a letter to Tiberius, to his future deification (and perhaps to the entire "cult of personality" around him) in a tone of self-deprecating humor: "My magnanimity will exalt me to heavenly glory" (Suetonius, *Augustus*, 71.4; he had spent time gambling with his friends and boasts of his generosity to fellow gamblers). He would be a god, as far as political necessity demanded; however, allowing himself to be addressed as *dominus* (master, lord) seemed wholly unnecessary and uncalled-for: "He always shrank from the title of *dominus* as reproachful and insulting" (Suetonius, *Augustus*, 53.1). In reality, of course, he was a master of the Roman state and of the Roman world; as regards his divinity he apparently harbored no illusions.

THE EMPEROR AND THE EMPIRE

The nature of the empire itself, and the relations between the Roman people and the subject peoples, is a pivotal issue on which Augustus cuts a paradoxical figure. Successful empires, while they arise as a result of one ethnocultural group conquering many others, have, for a variety of reasons, a propensity for blurring the boundaries between the conquerors and the conquered. It makes obvious sense from the imperial point of view to make the conquered feel that they are part of the imperial enterprise—if only to be able to enlist them and tap their resources against external enemies rather than having to guard against them constantly as (potential) internal ones. For an autocrat ruling an empire it is natural to wish to enjoy the loyalty (and loyal active service, wherever appropriate)

of all his subjects, of whatever origin. This "universal" potential of imperial rule often competes (with divergent degrees of success) with another
powerful force: the ruler's commitment to his own ethnocultural group—
the usual original core of an empire. The more absolute the ruler, the
stronger is his ability to overcome such constraints, unifying his empire
and towering equally high above all its components.

The most famous imperial ruler in the Greco-Roman world who
adopted—hard on the heels of the conquest—a radical policy of erasing the
distinctions between the conquerors and the conquered was Alexander
the Great. This policy was closely connected with his determination to
break loose from the traditional constraints of Macedonian kingship, appropriating both the substance of "Oriental" absolute monarchy and its
external trappings, including the ruler cult. The Chinese First Emperor
is famous for his policy of imposing uniformity throughout his newly
conquered empire; however Qin-inspired this uniformity inevitably was,
he presented himself—notably, in the steles—as a universal ruler and unifier, avoiding any emphasis on Qin particularity.

The word *empire* comes from the Latin *imperium*, meaning (the power
to) command. The Roman Empire, *imperium populi Romani*, was precisely
the rule of the Roman people over the peoples it had conquered. However,
the Roman people, the community of Roman citizens, was by no means
a closed club. Rome was exceptional among the city-states of antiquity in
its readiness to confer citizenship on the conquered, who would integrate
culturally and fight Rome's next wars alongside the "original" Romans.
This was undoubtedly one of the main reasons why the city grew into a
world empire. Roman tradition ascribed the first instances of this policy
to Romulus, the city's legendary founder. The Roman conquest of Italy
was a long-drawn process during which the Romans conferred citizenship on some and avoided, as a rule, prolonged direct rule over populations whom they were unwilling to enfranchise. These were turned into
"allies" subject to Roman hegemony but enjoying substantial self-rule; the
allies, too, contributed to Rome's military power by sending "auxiliary"
forces who fought alongside the legions under Roman command. Thus,
Rome conquered the whole of Italy without reducing large populations
for a long time to the status of conquered subjects. By the last decades
of the republic, first century BCE, the whole of Italy, with its millions of
free inhabitants, had received Roman citizenship. Italy was thoroughly
Romanized culturally; "Roman" and "Italian" became virtual synonyms.
Historians of the ancient world (who are much less hesitant than modern
ones about applying national terminology to premodern phenomena)

sometimes describe the late-republican Roman Italy as (something similar to) a "nation-state."[18]

Outside Italy, however, in the provinces of the empire, the Roman people (now comprising the millions of Italians) were ruling the subject peoples. Some of them were regarded by the Romans as barbarians (mostly those living in the North and the West); toward the Greek culture predominant in the East the Romans had great respect; but the spread of Roman citizenship in the provinces did not start as long as the republic stood. It was Julius Caesar the dictator who first started conferring Roman citizenship on communities in the provinces (mostly as a reward for supporting him during the Roman civil wars that were fought in the provinces in the 40s BCE). This process also signified the loss of the republican political significance traditionally attached to Roman citizenship. The complicated voting system of the republic made it worthwhile for people from the local elites throughout Italy to come to Rome on some important occasions in order to cast their vote (something that was only possible there, as in every city-state). Roman citizenship granted to people in Gaul or in Spain had naturally nothing to do with the possibility of voting: it was an autocrat's reward for loyalty conferring legal and fiscal privileges and opening the gates of military service in the legions and of an official career. It is thus Caesar, rather than Augustus—much less concerned than the latter to preserve republican appearances—that should be regarded as the harbinger of a wholly new concept of Roman *imperium*, one that was more in tune with its character as a world empire: no longer the Roman people ruling other peoples, but a huge and heterogeneous, yet increasingly Romanized, population ruled from Rome by an autocrat.

The long and gradual process of conferring citizenship on the subject peoples in the provinces was finally concluded in 212 CE, when all the free population of the empire was granted citizen status. The distinction between citizens and subjects disappeared; all the free inhabitants of the Roman world were henceforward, legally, the Roman people. The Latin language and culture became predominant in the Western part of the empire (with far-reaching consequences that are still felt today), while the East remained Greek speaking. The local elites throughout the empire (West and East) were fully integrated in the Roman governing elite; every position of power, including that of emperor, was open to people of diverse ethnic and geographical origins.

Augustus was the founder of the regime which led to all this. His own attitude in this field, however, was conservative, Roman in the (relatively) restricted republican sense. His declared policy on citizenship was the opposite of Caesar's. "He was most chary of conferring Roman citizenship"; Suetonius gives two examples of Augustus refusing to accede to requests for such a grant coming from his wife, Livia, and her son from her previous marriage, his future successor, Tiberius, on behalf of their personal protégés. In the former case he offered instead to grant an exemption from taxes, saying that the loss of revenue was preferable to "vulgarizing" the honor of Roman citizenship. The biographer's explanation is that Augustus "considered it of great importance to keep the people pure and unsullied by any taint of foreign blood" (*Augustus*, 40, 3). This sounds awkward, considering how ethnically "impure" the Roman people already were by that stage, but it probably reflects Augustus's officially stated policy in the field—and perhaps the style of his rhetoric. It was probably popular, whereas Caesar's excessive generosity to foreigners had been much resented (Suetonius, *Deified Julius*, 80.2).

We may safely call this attitude backward-looking in a nonjudgmental sense, for it reversed a tendency that had started under Augustus's predecessor and was destined to be renewed with new vigor by his successors, clearly acting according to the logic of empire. This attitude dovetailed well with the first emperor's republican and traditionalist posture, as well as, perhaps, with his well-attested conservative taste in several fields. He cultivated his image as a champion of old Roman customs, of traditional religion, of traditional morality and family values; he revived ancient rites and rebuilt temples; he insisted on full traditional Roman dress, the toga, rather than the less formal Greek one in the Forum and its vicinity (Suetonius, *Augustus*, 40.5—clearly, a conservative and "nationalist" gesture rather than a real policy). "He highly commended his grandson Gaius for not offering prayers at Jerusalem as he passed by Judaea" (Suetonius, *Augustus*, 93)—not out of any hostility to this particular tribe and its idiosyncratic religion (which was given full official protection), but presumably because he thought that excessive honors to foreign gods should be avoided. Augustus's insistence on preserving the distinction between the Roman people and the empire's subjects was probably much more genuine and heartfelt that his show of deference to the traditional political rights of the Roman people. But both these things were, to a large extent, two sides of the same coin; both were fundamentally out of tune with the imperial monarchy established by Augustus; both were destined to disappear.

In the *Res Gestae*, the "nationalistic" theme—one insisting on a strict distinction between the ruling Roman people and the conquered ones (that had, in traditional terms, to be treated fairly as long as they knew their place) is rather stronger than the republican one which is usually more commented on. The whole document is entitled (in the inscription in Ankara, probably following literarily the Roman title) "The achievements [*res gestae*] of the divine Augustus, by which he brought the world under the *imperium* of the Roman people, and the expenses that he bore for the republic and the people of Rome."

> (3.1–2) I undertook many civil and foreign wars. . . , and as victor I spared the lives of all citizens who asked for mercy. When foreign peoples could safely be pardoned I preferred to preserve rather than to exterminate them.

The first sentence exaggerates his clemency to Roman citizens during the early and rather sanguinary stages of his career, during the civil wars. This is one of the very few places in the document—possibly the only one—where Augustus deviates from his usual policy of misleading rather than actually lying on strictly factual matters. The second sentence, by contrast, gives the impression that exterminating whole peoples was much more of a routine Roman practice than it actually was. The Roman people liked and in fact expected to hear that Rome was merciful to defeated (and compliant) foes, and fair to (loyal) subjects, bringing the blessings of peace to all under its rule;[19] however, maintaining the proper distinction between "us" and 'them" was even more important. It was only because the claim of having shown mercy to non-Romans is placed right after a similar claim as regards Roman citizens, creating the danger of allowing this distinction to be blurred, that it had to be couched in such strikingly genocidal terms.

The emperor's generosity (including a vast program of public works and building), to which, alongside the chapters dealing with victories and conquests, most of the document is dedicated, is generosity to the Roman people—above all, to the inhabitants of the city of Rome. The provinces are not mentioned in this context.[20] The reader—who is presumed to be the one standing before the Mausoleum of Augustus in Rome—is assumed to be a Romano-centric citizen who appreciated a Romano-centric leader. The true picture of Augustus's imperial policy, however, was very different. He was far from neglecting the provinces. He spent much of his reign in inspection tours; in this he was not unlike his Chinese counterpart, who had a very different officially proclaimed vision of empire. Beyond military matters and securing Roman rule, he certainly attended to the welfare of the provincials. The granting of Roman citizenship (or the "Latin rights," a lesser privilege which was the first step to full Romanization) was found to be an effective instrument of imperial governance that could not be readily dispensed with, despite Augustus's rhetoric and possibly despite his personal predilections. "He relieved some cities [in the provinces] that were overwhelmed with debt, rebuilt some which had been destroyed by earthquakes, and gave Latin rights or full citizenship to such that could point to services rendered to the Roman people" (Suetonius, *Augustus*, 47, cf. Dio 54.30.3). [21] It was probably already under Augustus that non–citizen soldiers serving in the empire's auxiliary forces (some 150,000 at a time) started receiving Roman citizenship as of right upon completing their twenty-five years of service. Thus, while bickering with Livia and Tiberius about individual requests, Augustus apparently established an institutionalized channel through which great masses of people and their descendants would, over time, enter the citizen body—or at any rate, he created the auxiliary forces that were most logically maintained with the help of offering this reward to their veterans.

The logic of empire strongly favored the continued spread and eventual universalization of Roman citizenship. This was the Roman version of a unified empire ruled by an autocrat unfettered by an excessive commitment to a particular ethnocultural group and its traditions, privileges, and prejudices. Nothing Augustus said in public ever implied that this was his aim—quite to the contrary. Moreover, it does not at all seem likely that he himself could conceive of such a thing. Nevertheless, this was the natural consequence of his life's work. Thus, in the second century, when Roman citizenship was not yet universal but had already become widespread and open in principle to all those who merited it, an educated Greek from the East hails the empire for making "no distinction between Europe and Asia" and developing "a single, harmonious, all-embracing union" (Aristides, *To Rome*, 58–66). A century earlier, the Emperor Claudius, who contributed greatly to the Romanization of the provinces, is described by Tacitus as attributing this policy to the founder of the principate: "The day of stable peace at home and victory abroad came" when "we added [to the veterans of the legions settled in the provinces] the stoutest of the provincials, and succored a weary Empire" (*Annales*, 11.24). There was more truth in this statement than Augustus himself would perhaps have admitted.

CONCLUSION

"Make haste slowly" (Suetonius, *Augustus*, 25.4)—this was, appropriately, a favorite saying of a man who was one of history's great revolutionaries while presenting himself as a champion of tradition. A daring and ruthless revolutionary with a conservative posture, and in some ways, perhaps, a genuine conservative bent in his character, was probably the ideal candidate for successfully revolutionizing a society deeply committed to tradition and ancestral customs but ripe for a revolutionary change.

There can be little doubt that the conservative public image carefully projected and cultivated by Augustus—which, in the "constitutional" sphere, meant a show of deference to republican institutions and sensitivities—was one of the secrets of his success. He always studiously avoided giving unnecessary offense to traditional sensitivities and prejudices (with an emphasis on "unnecessary"—see below). Roman historians usually stress that in this Augustus was different from Julius Caesar. When one compares him with the First Emperor of China—who also acted within a culture that sanctified tradition—the difference is even more striking.

But this is not the whole story. The public image of the ruler and his rule, cultivated by the regime, included highly untraditional elements alongside traditional ones. This was not a case of blind adherence to tradition—even outwardly. The "cult of personality" of the emperor, including his divinization or quasi-divinization, the celebration of the imperial family and of the presumptive heirs—indicating that the new regime was not merely a lifelong dictatorship but in fact a hereditary monarchy—all these were revolutionary innovations. In fact, the hereditary element made Augustus's rule more clearly untraditional than even that of Caesar the dictator. Augustus was ready, and powerful and self-confident enough, to break with tradition when this appeared necessary. By the same token, he was ready to execute his rivals when necessary—not just in the turbulent period of the civil wars, when he displayed great ruthlessness with little evidence of hesitation, but also during the peaceful decades of his settled rule, when he was, as a rule, anxious to make a show of clemency. The image projected by the regime involved a skillful combination of the traditional and the untraditional, the civic and the autocratic—equally designed to glorify the ruler and enhance his rule.[22] One of the advantages of autocracy—even a relatively "soft" one, as practiced by Augustus—was that nobody dared point out the contradiction.

One of the main spheres in which Augustus displayed his fidelity to Roman tradition was in the notion of empire as expressed, among other things, in the *Res Gestae*. It stressed military glory and conquest (following "just wars," as the tradition demanded) and the Roman People's firm and fair rule over the peoples it had conquered; this rule was beneficent to the subjects chiefly because it brought them the "Roman peace," but preserved a strict distinction between the conquerors and the conquered. This traditional Roman attitude Augustus may well have genuinely shared. However, successfully managing a world empire ruled by monarch required, in the long run, a very different policy. In the end— though it took a lot of time—the logic of empire won decisively. Though Augustus could hardly have imagined this end result, his own policy in this field appears to have been less narrow and restrictive than his (no doubt, highly popular) public posture.

Roman historical memory was generally kind to Augustus. He was held up as an example of a benevolent and beneficial ruler—often as a rebuke to other rulers who fell short of this ideal. The brutality of his early days, when he was fighting his way to the top in the civil wars, was not forgotten,[23] but it was contrasted with, and overshadowed by, his later moderation as *princeps*. He was given credit for acting in the spirit of the rule that the First Emperor of China was blamed for ignoring: that the proper way to maintain power differs from the way to obtain it.[24] Post-Roman Western tradition also viewed him favorably—until modern times, when autocracy itself, however "enlightened," went out of favor. The Chinese First Emperor was less lucky in this respect: his dynasty was overthrown shortly after his death, and his memory was subjected to bitter assaults. But his main legacy—the unified empire—proved more enduring.

Trying to explain why this was so would go well beyond the scope of this paper. Various explanations can presumably be offered. One of them is probably the powerful legitimacy which the unity of "All-under-Heaven" and the unity of the imperial office (the latter guaranteeing the former) continued to enjoy in China. The feeling that splitting the empire is fundamentally illegitimate was, apparently, strong enough to help explain why such splits were eventually overcome (Pines 2012a). The Roman Empire, on the other hand, was split—for the first time toward the end of the third century, and finally toward the end of the fourth—into the Western (Latin-speaking) and Eastern (Greek-speaking) empires. The fall of the Western Empire to its Germanic conquerors in the late fifth century is considered as the fall of Rome, whereas the Eastern Empire, which continued to exist for a thousand years until the Ottoman conquest, is usually known as the Byzantine Empire. Formally, the Western and Eastern emperors were, until the fall of the West, considered as co-rulers of a unified Roman Empire; in practice, however, and for various reasons, the two parts were moving apart, and the theoretical unity of the Roman Empire had become a fiction. It is by no means certain that without the split, the West would have been able to survive; thus its fall should not be "blamed" on it. But it is interesting that the idea of splitting the imperial office did not, apparently, seem outrageous to Romans—despite its divinization. In fact, the same emperor, Diocletian (244–311, r. 284–305 CE), both turned the emperorship more than ever into a sacral absolute monarchy with all its ceremonial trappings, and split it. The first, short-lived experiment in having two emperors with equal powers (without a territorial split) had taken place already in the second century, under the "philosopher-emperor" Marcus Aurelius (121–180, r. 161–180 CE). Perhaps it is the ostensibly republican origins of the Roman emperorship, the fact that the Roman emperor was, despite his absolute powers, conceived as an elected public official, that helps explain how this was possible.

Notes

1. As noted in the front matter, hereafter all dates are Before the Common Era (BCE) unless indicated otherwise.

2. For a listing of all recently discovered paleographic sources, see the compilations by Wang Hui and collaborators (n13 below); for a general overview of Qin documents written on bamboo and wooden boards and slips, see Chen Wei 2009.

3. For Chinese secondary scholarship on the Qin, see the annual bibliography published (until 2008) in the series of collected essays dedicated to Qin studies, *Qin wenhua luncong*.

4. For the *Zuo zhuan* prediction, see *Chunqiu Zuozhuan,* Wen 6: 549; it is clear that it was made prior to Qin's resurrection as a major military power in the 360s. For Mozi's list of major regional powers, from which Qin is omitted, see *Mozi,* "Fei gong zhong" 非攻中 V.18: 203–204. Notably, a recently published fourth-century BCE historical text from the bamboo manuscript collection of Qinghua (Tsinghua) University, named by its editors *Xinian* 繫年, which was probably composed in the state of Chu, pays more attention to Qin than any of the early received texts; yet even in *Xinian* it is clear that by the fifth century BCE Qin's impact on political life of the Zhou world declined. For further discussion of Qin coverage in early sources, including the *Xinian,* see Pines 2013.

5. Duyvendak 1928 remains heretofore the single most detailed—even if fairly outdated—study of *The Book of Lord Shang* in English (recently supplemented with Pines 2012b); for other studies, see, e.g. Kroker 1953; Zheng Liangshu 1989; Yoshinami 1992; Perelomov 1993; Tong Weimin 2013; Zhang Linxiang 2008; cf. the French translation by Levi (2005).

6. The ideological impact of the *Lüshi chunqiu* on Qin and later imperial ideology (see, e.g., Sellmann 2002) is debatable.

7. See *Zhanguo ce,* "Wei ce 魏策 3" 24.8: 907; see more in Pines 2002b and Pines 2005/6.

8. For Xiao He saving Qin documents from the burning, see *Shiji* 53: 2014; for detailed studies of the Qin records, see Yoshimoto 1995; Fujita 1997: 227–278. It is possible that the term *Qin Records* is a generic term for Qin historical texts and not the name of a single text.

9. The only general survey of Qin archaeology in English can be found in Li Xueqin 1985: 222–262, which is now outdated. For a relatively recent survey in Chinese, see Wang Xueli and Liang Yun 2001. Much is being published annually in archaeological journals and in excavation reports. See the annual bibliography of archaeological publications in *Qin wenhua luncong* and note 13 below.

10. For two of the reports of the excavations of Yong, see Shaanxi Sheng Shehuikexueyuan Kaogu Yanjiusuo Fengxiang Dui 1963 and Shaanxi Sheng Yongcheng Kaogudui 1985; for Yueyang, see Zhongguo Shehuikexueyuan Kaogu Yanjiusuo Yueyang Fajuedui 1985; for Xianyang, see Shaanxi Sheng Kaogu Yanjiusuo 2004 and the review of this publication by Wang Xueli (2009); see also Zhao Huacheng and Gao Chongwen 2002 for a general overview.

11. For the stone drums, see Mattos 1988; for major Qin bronze inscriptions, including those known since the Song dynasty, see Kern 2000; for the Song rubbings of the Qin stone inscriptions of *Imprecations against Chu* (*Zu Chu wen* 詛楚文), see Kern 2000: 51n8 (q.v. for further references). For an early example of a chime-stone inscription, see Li Xueqin 2001.

12. For a sample of English-language discussions of the slips from Tomb 11 at Shuihudi, see McLeod and Yates (1981); Yates (1985/7); (1987); (1995); Harper (1985); Hulsewé (1985); Loewe (1988); in Chinese and Japanese the number of relevant publications well exceeds one thousand (see a partial list in Li Jing 2009).

13. The best introduction to the majority of these sources is Wang Hui and Cheng Xuehua 1999; Wang Hui 2000 and 2002; Wang Hui and Wang Wei 2006; Wang Hui and Yang Zongbing 2007; Wang Hui and Wang Wei 2008. Altogether 3,493 items of Qin-related inscriptions were published up to 2008; for English-language studies of selected inscriptions, see Kern 2000; Pines 2004: 4–12; Sanft, forthcoming. For an impressive, albeit incomplete, bibliography of studies of many of these sources, see Li Jing 2009. The entire corpus of Qin paleographic materials is due to be published by the team led by Chen Wei 陳偉 as a project supported by the Chinese Academy of Social Sciences (Chen Wei 2009).

14. It is quite possible that Sima Qian had at his disposal a separate, more detailed account of Lord Mu's exploits than was found in the *Qin Records*.

15. Relevant Qin inscriptions are fully translated and studied in Kern 2000; for the political analysis of their content, see Pines 2005/6: 18–24; see more in the introduction to part I of this volume.

16. New paleographic evidence indicates that the unification process might have gone less smoothly than the textual sources suggest; even the

rebellions that toppled the Qin in 209–207 may have been a reappearance of earlier resistance (see n33 below). More research should be done on this topic.

17. The *Book of Lord Shang* suggests that only the impossibility of escaping the punishment for absconding will turn the people into courageous soldiers (*Shangjun shu*, "Hua ce" 畫策 IV.18: 108).

18. There are no absolute figures for pre-imperial China's population (see chapter 3 in this volume), yet there are manifold indications—both archaeological and textual—that the population of all of the competing Warring States and of Qin in particular was expanding at a relatively quick pace. The most recently published census data from one Qin county (Qianling 遷陵), established in the recently conquered Chu territory circa 222, provide an amazingly high figure of 55,534 households (i.e., 250,000–300,000 inhabitants); see Zhang Chunlong 2009: 188; *Liye* 2012, 8-552 [553]; Yates 2012. While these data require further analysis, they do indicate that at the time of the imperial unification the population numbers could have been considerably higher than is usually estimated.

19. Archaeologists have discovered the remains of a major dam that was constructed out of rammed earth during Zheng Guo's irrigation project (Qin Jianming et al. 2006).

20. On the sophistication of Qin hydraulic engineering, see also chapter 3 in this volume.

21. It should be noticed here that Qin's development trajectory does not support Wittfogel's theory of inevitable growth of "hydraulic despotism" in arid areas: prior to the Warring States period, Qin—like other Zhou states—was much more "polycentric" than suggested by Wittfogel. Moreover, in Qin's case it seems that its ability to construct large-scale hydraulic projects was a by-product of its agro-managerial and centralistic political system rather than vice versa.

22. We borrow the term "right of alienation" from Oi 1999: 18–19. Absence of a market land in Qin is noticed by the editors of Liye documents (*Liye* 2012: 4), among others; for the possibility that it was introduced by the end of the Qin dynasty, see Yuan Lin 2000; cf. Zhang Jinguang 2013: 91–167.

23. Publishers of the *Liye* 2012 volume confusingly used different numbers for the transcribed slips from those used in the archaeological report; and Chen Wei (2012) followed the transcribed numbers only. We refer to the transcribed number, adding the archaeological number in square brackets if it was employed in earlier publications to which we refer. This applies throughout our volume.

24. It is most likely that the Qin regulated by legal statute the size of burial and the tomb furnishings of each rank in the social hierarchy. The recently discovered tomb M77 at the Shuihudi cemetery contains the fragmentary remains of the early Han "Statutes on Burial." These, Peng Hao (2009b) suggests, were based on Qin precedent.

25. A few Qin burials from the late Warring States period do yield ritual

vessels, either bronze or ceramic imitations; but it is widely asserted that these come from the tombs of migrants from eastern states who settled in the Qin core area (e.g., Lu Qingsong 2010: 41).

26. The passport says: "Zeng[?]: fair-colored; two *chi* five *cun* tall (i.e., 57.75 cm or 22.74 inches); five months old; registered by the [Village] Chief Si (or He)." *Liye* 2012: 8–550 (552); Chen Wei 2012: 178. As the graph of the child's personal name bears a "woman" (*nü* 女) radical, it is quite possible that the child was a girl (Yates 2012).

27. It is still impossible to assess fully the degree of absconding as reflected in the Liye documents; sometimes it appears that the absconding population was simply erased from the registries (*Liye* 2012: 8-1716 [1726]), but elsewhere we have an (incomplete) report of just two people who absconded from a group of 15,030 households (i.e., of approximately 75,000 people!) (*Liye* 2012: 8-927 [934]). A wooden board on display in the Liye Museum mentions that, of 4,376 bondservants employed by the Bureau of Granaries, "90 men" had absconded (Yates 2012).

28. The problematic of dividing Chinese thinkers into putative "schools of thought" has been raised several times in the past (e.g., Kern 2000: 164–175; Csikszentmihalyi and Nylan 2003; cf. Pines 2009: 4–5); specifically, the fallacy of the "Legalist" label was recently demonstrated by Goldin (2011). We do employ—rarely—these labels for heuristic reasons, but clearly they are inadequate for analyzing the ideological landscape of the Warring States world.

29. We now have several fairly similar Qin manuals for the education (or training) of officials. The first to be published was *Wei li zhi dao* (為吏之道, "The Way of Being an Official") from Shuihudi Tomb 11 (*Shuihudi* 2001: 167–173; Liu Hainian 2006: 364–377). It was followed by the publication of (an)other related text(s), from the Yuelu Academy collection, titled *Wei li zhi guan ji qianshou* 為吏之官及黔首 ("Being an Official and the Black-Headed People"; the title is on the basis of the phrase found using infrared photography on the verso side of slip no. 1531 [Chen Songchang 2010; *Yuelu shuyuan* 2011)]. Both of these texts are discussed by Giele (2011). The third text, named by its editors *Cong zheng zhi jing* 從政之經 ("The Canon of Being Engaged in Government") is a part of Peking University collection; for its preliminary publication, see Zhu Fenghan 2012. The last of the similar texts has been reported but not published in its entirety: it is *Zhengshi zhi chang* 政事之常 ("Constants of Political Affairs") from Wangjiatai (Wang Mingqin 2004: 42). The precise nature of these manuals requires further exploration. For the seals of Qin officials, see Wang Hui and Cheng Xuehua 1999: 299–309.

30. For the dictum to "love" 慈 the people below, see, e.g., *Shuihudi* 2001: 167, slip 15(1) and ibid: 170, slips 50(2)–51(2); *Yuelu shuyuan* 2011: 60, slip 1562(2). The Qin officials were punished for failing to report the person's seniority, because this would prevent reduction of his tax burden (Hulsewé 1985: C20: 115; see also Goldin 2012: 8–9).

31. The provisions to supervise a temple appear in a document

reconstructed by Chen Wei (2012: 78–80) from the following slips: *Liye* 2012: 8-138 (137) + 8-174 (175) + 8-522 (525) + 8-523 (526). See more in Yates 2012/13.

32. For a few interesting departures in dealing with some of these questions, see Korolkov 2010.

33. For instance, an archaeological survey conducted along the southeastern coast of the Shandong peninsula suggests "dramatic effects on both the local economy and the settlement history" in the immediate aftermath of the Qin conquest (Feinman et al., 2010). The Liye documents testify to the swift incorporation of the area into the Qin administration immediately after its conquest: Qin rulers conducted a new census and imposed their rank system on the conquered population (Hsing, chapter 4, this volume); they ordered sweeping modification of the language used by local officials (introduction to part II of this volume); and, as mentioned above in the text, even an appointment of a hamlet head and a postman required the approval of the county authorities.

34. One of the texts from the collection of doubtful legal cases, *Zouyan shu* 奏讞書, from Tomb 247 at Zhangjiashan, testifies to large-scale armed resistance to Qin rule among the "new black-haired people" 新黔首 (i.e., new subjects of Qin) in the newly acquired Chu territories (Zhangjiashan 2006, slips 124–161; Barbieri-Low and Yates, forthcoming).

INTRODUCTION TO PART I

1. As examples, one might mention the east-west orientation of Qin tombs and the flexed body posture of Qin tomb occupants, which contrast with the prevalent Zhou-wide practice of north-south orientation and extended body posture. Rather than as ethnic markers, these cultural attributes are probably best explained as reflections of certain religious beliefs prevalent in the Qin territory, but by no means exclusive to it (Falkenhausen 2004; 2006: 213–223 *et passim*; 2008c).

2. We would like to signal possible disagreement with Zhao's claim, based on unprovenanced bronzes said to have come from Dabuzishan, that the two large tombs at that site are those of a ruler of Qin (Qin *gong* 秦公) and his son (Qin *zi* 秦子) (cf. Li Feng 2011). A Zhou-wide comparison reveals that normally at rulers' cemeteries from this period, paired tombs are those of a ruler and his principal consort (Li Boqian 1999; Falkenhausen 2006: 74–98 *et passim*), and this seems likely to be the case here as well. Even if the "Qin zi" bronzes did come from one of these tombs (which we cannot know for certain, since they were looted), their donor might not have been identical to the tomb occupant. To insist on such an interpretation would be tantamount to flagging the joint burial of rulers and princes as a Qin idiosyncrasy, which seems risky given the state of the evidence. Interpreting the situation as an example of Qin adherence to the customs of the Shang, whose rulers did not practice joint husband-and-wife burial, seems equally risky given the murkiness of all other alleged Shang elements in Qin élite culture (*pace* Han Wei 1986).

3. Another piece of indirect evidence for the presence of a Zhou princess in Qin is the inscription on the so-called Huaihou 懷后 chime stones, preserved in the Song rubbings; see Li Xueqin 2001.

4. The sometimes-encountered verbal rendering of *ji* 及 in this phrase, in the sense of "the ruler of Qin addressed the royal princess, proclaiming . . . ," is incompatible with the usage of *ji* 及 as a particle meaning "and," which is especially prominent in the recently excavated Qin manuscripts (see Zhang Yujin 2011: 275).

5. For other instances of unusual proximity between the Qin and the Zhou rulers throughout the Eastern Zhou period, see Pines 2004: 4–23.

6. It is worth mentioning here that some of the works associated with the so-called Confucian canon were in all likelihood produced by the imperial Qin court erudites. Among these, the most notable is probably the *Zhouli* 周禮, that quintessential evocation of an ideal Zhou régime (Jin Chunfeng 1993; Lewis 1999b: 42–48; Schaberg 2010; cf. Zhang Quanmin 2004), and several other texts, including, possibly, the famous *Doctrine of the Mean* (*Zhongyong* 中庸) (Kanaya 1981: 353–374; cf. Kern 2000: 183–196). Of course, these texts do not necessarily reflect the mainstream Qin imperial ideology; actually they—like the slightly earlier *Lüshi chunqiu* 呂氏春秋 (composed ca. 239)— might have been produced to subvert or criticize certain draconian aspects of the régime associated with Shang Yang and his legacy.

7. Robin D. S. Yates (personal communication, 2010) urges caution in accepting the common consensus that the Qin armies were fully equipped with iron weaponry, insisting on the continued importance of bronze as a material used in warfare. We tend to think that bronze weapons by the third century were restricted mostly to élite circles, but we look forward to future studies of this issue. Wagner (2008: 146–147) interestingly ascribes Qin's superiority over such rivals as Chu to the more efficient organization of its iron industry.

8. An example for this is an inscribed tablet from Liye spelling out a new administrative and religious vocabulary to replace the old one (*Liye* 2012 8-461 [455]; Zhang Chunlong 2009; Hu Pingsheng 2009; see also the introduction to part II of this volume).

CHAPTER 1

1. [For debates about the "eastern" or "western" origins of the Qin people, see more in the general introduction to this volume.—*Eds.*]

2. [As noted in the front-matter note on conventions, we refrain from applying European aristocratic designations for the rulers of regional states of the Zhou era. The author, in his conclusion, identifies the *zi* of Qin as a prince who did not actually succeed the throne and was granted posthumously a lord's title. For an alternative interpretation see n2 in the introduction to part I and n4 below.—*Eds.*]

3. The survey primarily targeted areas along the rivers and did not cover upland areas far away from the main rivers.

4. [For a possibility of an alternative interpretation of the Qin *zi* vessel's owner, see n2 in the introduction to part I; Li Feng (2011) suggests that the tomb occupants are, respectively, Lord Zhuang 莊公 (r. 821–778) and Lord Xiang.—*Eds.*]

5. [Zhao Huacheng refers here to the recently published *Xinian* text from the Tsinghua (Qinghua) University collection. See more in the general introduction to this volume.—*Eds.*]

CHAPTER 2

1. The term here rendered as "vassal-states system" (*fengjian zhi* 封建制) is different from "feudal society" (*fengjian shehui* 封建社會), which is commonly used in research on the chronology of ancient Chinese history. Hereafter "vassal-states system" refers to the system of establishing vassal states that was implemented during the Western Zhou period to facilitate effective Zhou rule. [Most of the editors and contributors to this volume prefer the term "regional state" to avoid implications of vassal relations between regional lords, such as Qin leaders, and the Zhou royal house.—*Eds.*]

2. [This burial ground has not yet been identified. —*Eds.*]

3. [For our translation of this term see the front-matter note on conventions.—*Eds.*]

4. Although scholars have not arrived at consensus on the nature of northern-style straight-blade short daggers found in Qin tombs, they have not ruled out the appearance of this type of short dagger was related directly to ancient cultures from the north. Thus it can be said they are either a northern cultural element or can be attributed to influences from the north.

5. No ceramic imitations of bronze ritual vessels were found in tombs M26 at Xigoudao in Fengxiang or M202 at Keshengzhuang in Chang'an. Tomb CM9 at Baqitun in Fengxiang was looted previously, with only one ceramic imitation of a *hú* being found, rendering the task of reconstructing the original assemblage of the vessels difficult. *Guǐ, hú, dòu, pán,* and *yí* were found in tombs M10 and M49 at Gaozhuang in Fengxiang. However, the most important status-defining vessel, the *dǐng*, was missing in both tombs.

6. [As the Zhou royal domain had split into two tiny principalities after 510, while the state of Jin was divided among three of its former components in 453, Chinese archaeologists conventionally refer to the region under their rule as the "three Jin and two Zhou" (三晉兩周); hereafter this term is consistently rendered as "north-central China."—*Eds.*] Burial goods such as the bronze *zhōu* and *guàn* from tomb M10 at Gaozhuang in Fengxiang, the covered bronze *dǐng* from M26 at Xigoudao in Fengxiang, and the *lì*-shaped bronze *dǐng* from CM9 at Baqitun in Fengxiang were all vessels commonly found in the "three Jin and two Zhou" area and belong to the same period. There were also bronze weapons originating from the Wu-Yue 吳越 region

in the lower Yangzi River delta. For example, a bronze *gē* dagger was buried in tomb M10 at Gaozhuang in Fengxiang. A bronze sword excavated from tomb M26 at Xigoudao in Fengxiang could possibly have originated from the southeastern Wu-Yue region as well.

CHAPTER 3

I am grateful to Yitzhak Jaffe for his help in calculating workload estimates and in drawing the figures for this chapter. I benefited immensely from the comments of Norman Yoffee on the chapter's theoretical aspects as well as from suggestions by Hsing I-tien and Robin Yates on Han sources relevant to my workload calculations. I am always in debt to my colleague and friend Yuri Pines for comments, references, and constructive criticism.

1. See, for example, Jared Diamond's popular book *Collapse* (Diamond 2005).

2. *Shiji* 6; Nienhauser 1994 I: 162. All translations of *Shiji* 6 ("The Basic Annals of the First Emperor of Qin") are taken from Nienhauser 1994 I: 127–177. "East of the Mount" refers to the territory to the east of either Mount Hua 華山 or Mount Xiao 崤山, i.e., to the east of Qin.

3. Jia Yi seems to regard the construction of the Great Wall favorably and does not criticize the excessive use of manpower needed for the project (Nienhauser 1994 I: 167).

4. Jia Yi's reluctance to discuss local anti-Qin sentiments may reflect his fear that similar sentiments could be employed against the Han in the same way as they were against the Qin.

5. Flannery (1972: 409) describes social complexity in two dimensions: *Segregation* (the amount of differentiation between and specialization of subsystems) and *centralization* (the degree of linkage between the various subsystems and the highest-order controls in society). Therefore, society becomes more complex if it has more hierarchical steps and control units, or if the number of specialized subsystems increases.

6. Whether the Classic Maya society actually collapsed is a question beyond the scope of this chapter. What interests me in the Maya example are models that explain collapse rather than the collapse itself. For a recent and advanced discussion of the collapse of the Classic Maya, see Webster 2002, esp. pp. 327–348.

7. A recent study by McAnany and Negrón (2009), published after the research for this chapter was completed, provides a new assessment of the evidence for the "collapse" of the Maya. While the authors reject some earlier notions and popular depictions of the alleged Maya collapse, as an outsider to the field of Mayan archaeology I think that even in their discussion the main characteristics of the Mayan trajectory are not substantially different from what is presented here. As mentioned in the previous note, whether or not it can be seen to represent a systemic collapse is an issue beyond the scope of this chapter.

8. For a comprehensive discussion on the meaning of *tuxing* 徒刑, see Cao Lüning 2008b.

9. The official site of the Institute of Archaeology of the Chinese Academy of Social Sciences (http://www.kaogu.cn/) places under the heading of 直道 several recent reports on the excavations of Qin roads.

10. See especially the map in Waldron 1990: 20, where virtually all of the line of the wall is assigned to preunification construction.

11. Not included in this calculation and in the workload estimate is the wall's foundation, which is not mentioned in the excavation reports. It is possible, though, that terrain and geology concerns required preparation of foundation trenches at some parts of the wall.

12. The calculations of the *Jiuzhang suanshu* for pounded-earth wall construction are perhaps more costly because they take into account the fact that each m³ of excavated earth produce only 0.75 m³ of wall and because the pounding work is more time consuming (Shen Kangshen et al. 1999: 254–260).

13. A more conservative estimate suggests an area of some 35 km² (Ciarla 2005: 133), as the area was not completely filled with monuments and underground pits. However, as research continues, new such sites continue to be found. Duan Qingbo (2011: 2) assesses the territory to be "approximately 60 square km."

14. Epigraphic evidence further supports this observation. The nineteen epitaphs on the tombs of the mausoleum's workers from the Zhaojia Beihucun 趙家背戶村 cemetery, discovered in 1979, provide information of the workers' origins; all came from the newly conquered eastern territories (Yuan Zhongyi 2008: 31–32).

15. Qin policy makers were aware of the danger of overburdening the conscripts, and they clearly preferred to use convicts for a variety of routine public works (see Liye document J1[16]5; Wang Huanlin 2007: 104–105). Yet with the increasing workload on the population this regulation could not possibly be maintained. Either the state had to mobilize conscripts for longer periods of time than usual, or it had to expand the number of convicts, which could be attained only by increasing the harshness of the law enforcement and further alienating the empire's subjects.

16. The higher number of 40 million derives from the work of Ge Jianxiong (2002: 300–312). However, this does not fit well with Ge's estimate that the population at the beginning of the Han was around 15–18 million (ibid: 312). It is hard to believe that the population might have declined some 60 percent in a single decade, even taking into account the devastating civil war that followed the fall of the Qin. Further research on Qin population figures may be prompted by the recently published census data from the Qianling County (Zhang Chunlong 2009; see n18 to the general introduction to this volume).

17. Barbieri-Low (2007: 8–9) suggests that some of the private artisans conscripted to work on the ceramic statues of the "terracotta army" were

female. It is probable that other women took part in the large projects (ibid: 393), and women are specifically mentioned in the *Hanshu* in relation to the construction of the walls of Chang'an (*Hanshu* 2: 89–90), but the bulk of the manual labor must have been carried out by young and healthy men. This is reflected, for example, in the composition of Chen She's conscript team (*Shiji* 48; Watson 1993: 217–226) and the fact that the Qin general Zhang Han 章邯 was able to mobilize the builders of the First Emperor's mausoleum to fight against the rebels (Nienhauser 1994 I: 158–159). Even if some of the fighters were females, their proportion was surely minuscule.

18. Lu Yu and Teng Zezhi (1999: 74) estimate that the workforce constructing those monuments and imperial projects comprised 2.5 million people. When the size of the Qin's army is added, they reach the estimate of 4 million. Such high estimates imply that as much as 60 percent of the male workforce of the Qin's population was taken out of the production of food and basic commodities.

19. Bodde (1986: 62n62) argues that "it is self-evident that its [the Great Wall's] construction must have required a far longer period." However, the sequence of events described in *Shiji* 6, where Meng Tian first fights the tribes on the empire's northern and western borders, and then builds the wall inside their territory, makes sense and lends support to a relatively late start of construction. See also Di Cosmo 2002: 127–158.

20. It is possible that Qin's campaign against Southern Yue started in 218, while 214 is the year of its ultimate success (Cao Lüning 2011). In this case, the canal construction might have started before 214.

21. See Hulsewé 1985: A7: 26; D130: 162–163; A8: 27; Liye documents J1(9) 1-J1(9) 12; Zhang Junmin, 2003; Sanft, in progress. I thank Yuri Pines for bringing these references to my attention, as well as for informing me of Korolkov's study (2010).

22. Compare, for example, the total area of Yangling, which is estimated at 12 km² (Yan Xinzhi et al. 2009), to the 54 km² of the First Emperor's burial monument (Zhao Huacheng and Gao Chongwen 2002: 16–17).

INTRODUCTION TO PART II

1. In particular, the ongoing publication of the documents from the Imperial Qin Qianling County 遷陵縣, modern Liye 里耶, Hunan Province, will make a major contribution to our understanding of the workings of a lower-level administrative unit in the Qin Empire (Yates 2012 and the general introduction to this volume).

2. The major exceptions to this rule are Qin documents from Tomb 50 at Haojiaping, Qingchuan (Sichuan), and from Tomb 1 at Fangmatan, Tianshui (Gansu). Significant discoveries from the northwestern frontier and from elsewhere date only from the Han period. In eastern China, so far only two major finds of texts have been made, those at Yinqueshan, Lin'yi 臨沂銀雀山 (Shandong), and at Yinwan, Lianyungang 連雲港尹灣 (Jiangsu). The former

tomb dates from the 130s BCE, the era of Emperor Wu of Han, and the latter from the very late Western Han period.

3. Yates 2011; cf. Ye Shan 2008. Some of the material discussed in Hsing's chapter originated in tombs belonging to county level officials later in the Han dynasty.

4. *Liye* 2007; Zhongguo Shehuikexueyuan Kaogu Yanjiusuo 2009; *Juyan* 1987; *Juyan xinjian* 1994; Wang Mingqin 2004.

5. *Shuihudi* 2001; *Guanju* 2001; *Longgang* 2001; *Suizhou Kongjiapo* 2006; *Juyan xinjian* 1994; cf. Chen Wei 2009.

6. For a general introduction to the Qin materials retrieved from Hong Kong and now held in the Yuelu Academy, Hunan University, see Chen Songchang 2009; for the new collection acquired by Peking University, see Beijing Daxue 2012.

7. For example, *Shiji* 127: 3215–3222, and *Lun heng* 論衡 by Wang Chong 王充 (27–100 CE): see Alfred Forke 1962: I: 525–531, II: 376–409.

8. For the responsibility of scribes for writing such documents, see Giele 2005.

9. No less than four texts directed at the officials' training have been discovered and their nature is still under discussion (see e.g., Giele 2011). For a brief summary of these manuscripts see n29 to the general introduction to this volume.

10. Fangmatan Tomb No. 1, Tianshui, contained the earliest known "supernatural" story of a man who died and came back to life, framed as a legal case, perhaps a predecessor of the genre of literary fiction later known as *zhiguai* 志怪 (see Harper 1994). For a recently published similar story from the Peking University collection of Qin manuscripts, see Li Ling 2012.

11. Many of the problems described in the mathematics texts derive their examples from administrative matters. For example, how much different types of unhulled grain yielded in hulled grain, the price of salt, how much cloth could be woven by women of different capabilities within a given time period, and the amount of different types of fodder horses in the postal system would consume. See Peng Hao 2001; Cullen 2007.

12. The most extensive annotations are found in the calendars of Scribe Xi 喜, the occupant of Tomb 11, Shuihudi, and of the occupant of Tomb 30, Zhoujiatai. It is not clear whether these calendars were a type of diary kept by the tomb occupant during his lifetime, or whether they were composed postmortem by his colleagues or relatives on the basis of their own knowledge of the tomb occupant's career. Xi's calendar, which starts several decades before his birth, may belong to some other type of annalistic record of major events of Qin political and military history interspersed with significant events in Xi's own family history. The Yuelu hoard contains what may well be two or even three calendars by different, possibly related scribes (*Yuelu shuyuan* 2011: colored photographs and transcription, 3–24; infrared photographs, transcription and notes, 47–106), but their nature requires further investigation. The Liye archive contains at least one document, not yet published but

on display in the Liye Museum of Qin Slips, which may be an example of the official record of the travels of one or some of the Qianling scribes on the basis of which the type of calendar deposited in the tombs of scribes might have been later compiled.

13. See Hulsewé 1985, A101: 87. The head instructor appears to have born the title *xue'er* 學佴, according to some of the Liye documents, such as nos. 14–18, 15–146, and 15–154. See Zhang Chunlong 2010.

14. Several scholars suggested from their analysis of the Liye and the Han period Juyan 居延 materials that most documents were prepared by scribes and their assistants, while senior officials only applied their seals to the documents to verify that they had read them or had them read to them—in other words, they had listened to them, read out by their scribes—and authenticated them and had assumed legal responsibility for them (Giele 2005; Hsing 2006). It is likely then that higher officials were not uniformly highly literate. This makes perfect sense in a society that allowed considerable social advancement due to military merits (see the general introduction to this volume).

15. Surprisingly, the newly published Liye documents reveal that some families were headed by women (Yates, chapter 6 in this volume).

16. Likewise, the Qin developed similar complex and detailed rules for assigning responsibility for official misdemeanors or crimes. See Yates 1995.

17. See An Zuozhang and Xiong Tieji 2007 for a detailed description of Qin and Han state organization, and Yu Zhenbo 2005 and Cao Lüning 2002 for "metropolitan offices." Qianling was composed of three cantons (*xiang* 鄉), Duxiang 都鄉, Erchun 貳春, and Qiling 啟陵.

18. *Shiji* 68: 2230; Duyvendak 1928: 15.

19. See, respectively *Shuihudi* 2001: 137, slip 185; Hulsewé 1985, D164: 174; and "Zhi hou lü" 置後律, slips 367–368; *Zhangjiashan* 2001: 182–183; *Zhangjiashan* 2006: 59.

20. Why this placard was distributed to administrative offices throughout the realm and why scribes at such a relatively small county as Qianling, deep in the countryside in recently conquered Chu territory, would have needed such information remains to be determined. One possibility is that it was thought that, sometime in the course of their duties, they might need to use the new terminology in their reports to their superiors and the central administration. A second possibility is that *all* edicts and pronouncements having legal force had to be circulated to all levels of the Qin bureaucratic hierarchy, no matter what their direct relevance for daily administration might be. In other words, it was another way to assist in the integration of the empire and to ensure that officials realized that they were working for a huge imperial system, not just for their own special interests at the local level.

21. *Zhangjiashan* 2001, slip 478; Peng Hao et al. 2007: 299–301.

22. Perhaps an individual who as a teenager did not show a proclivity toward or competency in writing, but showed promise in memorization, was directed into the occupational stream of "prayer-maker."

23. For example, in the Shuihudi Tomb 11 hoard, two types of systems are represented: those of the state of Qin and those of the state of Chu. Even though the area in which the tomb occupant, Xi, was active had been conquered and administered for at least fifty years, it would appear that some of the locals were still using Chu almanac systems. However, after the unification and the establishment of the empire, Chu systems seem to have disappeared. Only Qin systems survived, some of them down to contemporary times, for example, the system of reckoning auspicious and inauspicious days by the *Jian-Chu* 建除 system and the years by the twelve-animal cycle, starting with the Rat (Loewe 1988; Poo 1998; cf. Kalinowski 1986).

24. For the contents of scribes' tombs, see, for example, *Yunmeng Shuihudi Qin mu* 1981, and Hubei Sheng Wenwu Kaogu Yanjiusuo and Yunmeng Xian Bowuguan 2008. For the possibility that the Qin had "Statutes on Burial" ("Zang lü" 葬律) that specified the sumptuary regulations depending on rank that were to be followed in burials, see n24 to the general introduction to this volume.

25. Items from the "Statutes on Households" have been found in Tomb No. 247, Zhangjiashan, dating from the early Han, and these may well have derived ultimately from the Qin. On first capturing the Qin capital, all of Liu Bang's generals rushed to loot the storehouses and treasuries of their precious contents; Xiao He alone went and gathered up and preserved the maps and official records from the Qin archives, so that later on, "because of the maps and registries of Qin which Xiao He had in his possession, the King of Han (Liu Bang) was able to inform himself of all the strategic defense points of the empire, the population and relative strength of the various districts, and the ills and grievances of the people" (Watson 1961, I:126, modifying his translation to *Hanyu pinyin; Shiji* 53:2014).

26. See Yates 2012. I am grateful to Brian Lander and Maxim Korolkov for sharing their photographs of the exhibition of Liye materials with me.

27. See Wang Huanlin 2007: 115–118, for a slightly different transcription than the one Hsing uses.

28. *Suizhou Kongjiapo* 2006, slips 196–202, pp. 153–55; Shuihudi Tomb 11 "Book A" calls this system "Good Days for Entering Office" (*Ruguan liangri* 入官良日) (slips 157 *zheng* 6 to 166 *zheng* 6) (*Shuihudi* 2001: 208; Liu Lexian 1994: 203–204; Wu Xiaoqiang 2000: 246–247; Wang Zijin 2003: 308–309).

CHAPTER 4

1. *Li* has also been translated as "village" and "ward," as authorities did not distinguish between urban and rural communities at the lowest level of administration. See the discussion in the conclusion of this chapter.

2. See *Liye* 2007: 203–211, plates 36–39; Tianchang 2006; Yinwan 1997. Some scholars maintain that there are household registries among documents from the age of Han Emperor Wu, excavated at Zoumalou 走馬樓. Based on the published slips, however, the documents are too fragmented to

yield enough evidence for verification. Regarding the Eastern Han household registries excavated from Well 7 of the Dongpailou 東牌樓 site, see *Changsha Dongpailou* 2006: 107–108.

3. Since the discovery of the Wu (吳, 222–280 CE) documents at the Zoumalou site, household registration of the Wu state is understood and can be used for comparison. See Wang Xiaoxuan 2004, the first section, "Household Registration," in Li Junming and Song Shaohua 2007 and relevant parts of Zhang Rongqiang 2010.

4. Table I appended to *Liye* 2007 states that fifty-two slips were excavated (p. 690); but the text says there are fifty-one slips (p. 203). According to Zhang Chunlong (2009: 195n2) the latter number is correct.

5. For detailed discussion of the standards for the lengths of bamboo and wooden slips, see Wang Guowei 2004: 10–34.

6. For this translation, see Hulsewé 1985 A9n22: 30; Kudō Motoo 1981: 275–307.

7. In the case of male children the sex is not given but is indicated by a merit rank, which females did not hold. See discussion below in the text for "minor ranks."

8. The meaning of 隸 here is uncertain. Since 隸大女子 appears in the same column as 妻, wife, perhaps she is some sort of concubine or a female slave to serve in the inner chamber. Since this is the only case, it is difficult to determine.

9. Note in the original: "The first line in Column 2 should be the name of Song Wu's wife. The graphs were scraped off" (*Liye* 2007: 205).

10. There is an excellent treatment of this topic in Wang Guihai 1999: 227–232.

11. 年籍 or 年細籍. I suspect this was concerned with recording such information as age, dates of birth and death, bestowal of merit rank, and so forth.

12. The Chinese for the latter is 田命籍; here the word *ming* 命 is probably an allograph for 名. The purpose of this registry may have been to record the change of field ownership due to land grant, inheritance, or commercial transaction.

13. [Some of us doubt that this passage from the *Book of Lord Shang* accurately represents actual Qin practice.—Eds.]

14. For some additional examples of household registration and other documents from Liye, see Zhang Chunlong 2009 and Chen Wei 2012.

15. The term 初產, here rendered as "births," is the same as 初生. This use of 產 is seen from the *Annals* 編年記 from Shuihudi Tomb 11, which use the term 產 for records of individual births.

16. [In the lacuna, probably the official of Qiling is citing the relevant ordinance about submitting reports to higher authority.—Eds.]

17. According to the personal explanation of Prof. Ma Yi 馬怡 to the author, the tenth unit time of the eleven-unit clepsydra refers to the time around the sunset.

18. [For a rare instance in which minors were recorded as household heads, see slip 8-19 (8-17) (*Liye* 2012: 11; Chen Wei 2012: 32–33).—*Eds.*]

19. [These do, in fact, appear in the newly published Liye documents (Chen Wei 2012).—*Eds.*]

20. Suzuki Naomi (2008: 10) speculates that squad leaders were associated with the organization of *wu* squads.

21. Regarding slip no. K30/45, which reads: "Nanyang, household head, fourth merit rank *bugeng*, Peng Yan" 南陽戶人不更彭奄, the *Liye Excavation Report* maintains that the prefix "Jing" was omitted (*Liye* 2007: 208). It seems more likely, however, that this was not an intentional omission but a scribal error.

22. 不更至上造子為公卒. *Zhangjiashan* 2001, "Fu lü" 傅律, slip 360: 182. The precise meaning of *gongzu* is not clear: it may refer either to an unranked commoner or to a holder of lowest rank of merit—a rank that is not attested to in extant documents (cf. Loewe 2010: 299).

23. Yin Zaishuo 2003; Liu Min 2004. Suzuki Naomi (2008: 8) argues that the word *xiao* 小 in the term *xiaoshangzao* means "minor," as in the term *xiaonüzi*.

24. During the Warring States period, the governor of Shangdang 上黨 Commandery of the state of Han 韓, Feng Ting 馮亭, sent a messenger to the state of Zhao 趙 expressing his willingness to cede seventeen (or seventy?) walled cities in Shangdang and surrender to Zhao. Zhao replied that if Feng Ting and the people of Shangdang surrendered, the governor and all county magistrates would be granted high appointments, and "all officials will be promoted by three ranks" 吏皆益爵三級. See *Zhanguo ce*, "Zhao ce 1," 18.11: 638; cf. a slightly different account in *Shiji* 43: 1826. This is a good example of using "the promotion by three ranks" to win over subjects of neighboring states.

25. Servants were also recorded in the household registries of Wu 吳 Kingdom (222–280 CE) (Chen Shuang 2004).

26. For example, *Juyan* 1987 15.2; *Juyan xinjian* 1994, EPT 56:68.

27. Similarly, an inscription on a horizontal scale beam from Tomb 168 at Fenghuangshan reads "Shiyang, household head, Ying Jia" 市陽戶人嬰家. That "Shiyang" means "Shiyang hamlet" as corroborated by other slips (Li Junming and He Shuangquan 1990, 70–72; 77). Additionally, in the Xuanquan 懸泉 documents from Dunhuang we find the phrase, "Lijian, Wudu hamlet, household head, female adult, Gao Zhejun" (驪軒武都里戶人大女高者君, *Dunhuang Xuanquan* 2001, slip 63: 61-62).

28. In translating the term 服約 as "waterway merchants' covenant," we follow Xu Zhuoyun (Hsu Cho-yun) 1980.

29. [In 2012 the content of the slips from Tombs 8, 9, and 10, as well as from Tombs 167, 168 and 169, which were excavated slightly later, were published in *Jiangling Fenghuangshan* 2012.—*Eds.*]

30. For references to distribution of seed grain, see *Hanshu* 4: 117, 7: 220,

8: 249, 9: 279, 12: 353, 99C: 4152; *Hou Hanshu* 4: 188, 192, 193, 44: 1498; Dubs 1938/55 I: 242–243, II: 1 57, 227, 304, III: 374.

31. These population figures are for 2 CE. Figures for households and individuals are given for each commandery, with empirewide totals at *Hanshu* 28B: 1640. For earlier studies using these data, see Bielenstein 1947 and 1987.

32. The graph *qing* 卿, which is placed at a lower part of the wooden board, is omitted in the transcription in Tianchang 2006.

33. The graph *nan* 南 is transcribed in the excavation summary report as *dong* 東. Based on the form of this graph and the same graph in the accounting record, this graph should be *nan*.

34. The excavation summary report transcribes the graph *ju* 掬 as *ju* 鞠 (?). Based on the form, this graph should be transcribed as *ju* 掬 with the hand radical on the left side, or *xiang* 翔. A good reference is the *xiang* 翔 graph in the Juyan slip 503.15, plate 443 (Lao Gan 1977).

35. The excavation summary report wrongly transcribes the graph *nan* 南 as *dong* 東.

36. The excavation summary report inserts an extra word *hu* 戶 after the graph *xiang* 鄉.

37. The excavation summary report mistakenly transcribes *nan* 南 as *dong* 東.

38. It seems that there is a graph on the left side of the slip, but it is too obscure to be identifiable. Yang Yiping and Qiao Guorong (2008: 196) believe that the graph is *qing* 卿. They argue that this word testifies that "this household record was not for submission to superior officials, but the verification copy for the head official at this government level to validate the information and then store in the archive as data sets of the annual household statistics report." Based on the general government formula of wooden-slip documents, I speculate that this graph *qing* 卿 should refer to a scribe's name.

39. Zhang Rongqiang 2004; Hu Pingsheng 2005; Meng Yanhong 2006; Yu Zhenbo 2007: 129–152.

40. Yuan Yansheng's (2008) understanding of *suan* 算 simply as poll taxes is doubtful. Yuan explains the meaning of *shisuan* 事算 in the Tianchang taxation records: "*Shi* and *suan* form one term, which refers to *suanfu* 算賦 (poll taxes). Although the word *shi* connotes 'corvée taxation,' it does not carry a separate meaning. It is a modifier in the term *shisuan*, qualifying the word *suan*" (p. 109). In other words, Yuan reads *shi* and *suan* as denoting poll taxes. I believe that *shi* and *suan* refer to two separate levies and should not be conflated. The Tianchang taxation records are summary documents, listing annual amounts of *shi* and *suan* for each canton. Furthermore, the household records total the numbers of households and population in each canton. The population figures apparently include the entire household, such as the elderly and children, and not just the adults between the ages of fifteen and fifty-six who were liable for taxation. The word *suan* in the Tianchang taxation records should refer not only to poll taxes, but also to other Western Han taxes levied in the form of *suan*, such as *suanminqian* 算緡錢 (property

taxes), *suanchechuan* 算車船 (vehicle taxes), and *suanniumayang* 算牛馬羊 (livestock taxes).

41. I agree with Qiu Xigui (1974: 58). For additional opinions, see Liu Zenggui 1998; Yamada 1993: 188, and 2007: 5.

42. Ying Shao states that merchants and slaves paid double. This suggests that the Han Statutes he cites date from the period when Emperor Wu was taking measures against the powerful and the wealthy merchants and was raising money for his military ventures (Qiu Xigui 1974: 59). Emperor Wu fixed the amount of the poll tax, and subsequently the poll tax and service became combined. For the fixing of the amount of the *suan*, see Yue Qingping 1985.

43. In the Tianchang slips, the totals for the service capitation and exemption differ slightly between the eighth and ninth months (20,009 – 19,988 = 21; 2,065 – 2,045 = 20). Some believe that is a difference between calculated and verified numbers. I think all the total figures are of the same type. The actual levy and the exempted population size could change for various reasons (change of tax status or population fluctuations, etc.); this can be inferred from the tax totals for different months in the Fenghuangshan documents. See Yang Yiping and Qiao Guorong 2008: 197.

44. [Later publications confirmed the author's insights. For the new research of the dating of Tianchang Tomb 19, which suggest that the tomb was sealed shortly after 54 BCE, see Wang Xiaoguang 2012. For further analysis of the differences between *suan* and *shi* and the changes from the Han to the Three Kingdoms period, see Yang Zhenhong 2011.—*Eds.*]

45. [Of course, some texts reveal from the form of their calligraphy that they were copied earlier than the death of the tomb occupant.—*Ed. (Robin Yates).*]

46. In a recent article, Peng Hao (2009a) mentions that Zhou Yan served as the bailiff of Xi Canton, but his highest career assignment was as commandant 尉 in Nanping. Unfortunately, the original document has not yet been published.

47. [The newly published data from the Songbocun registries suggests that reports of population situation in the local communities were severely skewed so as to lessen the service burden on the community (Yang Zhenhong 2010; this situation resembles the one which we observe in Yinwan documents, discussed below in the text). If so, then Zhou Yan might have discovered those who falsely claimed inability to serve and added them to the service list, for which reasons he had the right to be proud of himself.—*Eds.*]

48. For an attempt to explore this question, see, e.g., Su Weiguo 2010.

49. "Recovered refugees" 獲流 were persons who had left their homes usually because of natural disaster and thus had fallen off the census and tax rolls but who were now re-registered.

50. Current studies rarely focus on the population age structure in ancient China. For the demographic structure in the prehistoric period, see Wang Jianhua 2007. According to Wang's analysis on human skeletons from tombs

in the middle and lower Yellow River valley, the most common age of death was between thirty-six and fifty. Only a few people were over fifty. Although this analysis cannot be applied to the Han times, it can be instructive.

51. Huang Jinyan (1988) has shown that the age for poll tax liability in the Han times varied. It was three in the reign of Emperor Wu and seven under Emperor Yuan. In the Eastern Han, population in some areas was levied at age one. Huang further argues that "Levying poll tax from age seven probably became standard practice from reign of Emperor Yuan" (p. 218). Huang was very wise to add "probably" here. After the discovery of the taxation documents from Tomb 10 of Fenghuangshan, we can almost be certain that the taxation system in the Han times was far more complex than portrayed in the received texts and may have gone through several changes over time. As the Yinwan "Collected Registries" enumerate the population under age six and not age seven, we are reminded that even in between the reigns of Emperors Yuan and Cheng many previously unknown changes may have occurred.

52. Family planning has become common practice in Taiwan, and therefore the birth rate and child population have declined. In Han times birth was encouraged. As the number of children in a household must have been relatively higher, it seems probable that larger percentage of the Donghai population was under age six. Nevertheless, if we look at individual household size for Donghai Commandery, we find the average population per household was 5.24 members. This number is very close to the average household size recorded in the "Treatise on Geography." With father, mother, and a few senior members of the family such as grandparents, there were unlikely many minors in each household.

53. 務為欺謾,以避其課 (*Hanshu* 8: 273). Dubs (1938/55 II: 263) has misunderstood the meaning of 課 here.

54. "People who have sons born to them should be exempted from public service for two years" (*Hanshu* 1B: 63; Dubs 1938/55 I: 118). For an analysis of Han population policy, see Ge Jianxong 1986: 33–34.

55. [The above passage was added by Yuri Pines and approved by the author.—*Eds.*]

CHAPTER 5

1. Keightley 1999: 251–268; idem 2004: 3–63; Eno 2009. A still useful monograph on Shang religion in general is Chang 1970; see also Thorp 2006: 172–213.

2. The small Shang tombs are stylistically the same as the larger, "elite" tombs. The only difference is in the richness of the funerary equipment. See Poo (Pu Muzhou) 1993b: 41–45.

3. 大宗伯之職,掌建邦之天神人鬼地示之禮,以佐王建保邦國 (*Zhouli zhushu* 18: 757; translation follows Sommer 1995: 29, with minor changes).

4. Li Ling 1999; for a full bibliography, see Hou Naifeng 2005; Liu Zhaorui 2005.

5. The identity of the owner of the *Jade Tablet* has been identified as King Huiwen 秦惠文王 (r. 337–311). See Hou Naifeng 2005. For different opinions, see Pines 2004: 9–10.

6. 周室既没,典灋薜(散)亡。惴惴小子,欲事天地,四亟(極),三光,山川神示(祇),五祀,先祖,而不得厥方。 Translation by the author. Cf. Pines 2004: 6.

7. *Chunqiu Zuozhuan*, Zhao 25.9: 1475–1476; Zhao 7.7: 1289; cf. Ai 6.4: 1636.

8. That the sacrifice on Mount Tai was part of the Zhou state ritual is suggested by *Historical Records*: "When King Wen received the Mandate of Heaven, his policy did not touch Mount Tai [issue]. . . . When King Cheng inherited the virtue of Zhou and its harmony, he performed *feng* and *shan* sacrifices at Mount Tai, which was close [to proper norms]. Later when the subjects' subjects began to control the government, the head of the Ji lineage performed the *lü* 旅 sacrifice at Mount Tai, and it was criticized by Confucius" (*Shiji* 28: 1364).

9. 鬼之所惡,彼窋卧,箕坐,連行,奇立 (*Yunmeng* 1981: slip 871 verso–870 verso; translation follows Lopez 1996: 244).

10. See further discussion in Falkenhausen 2004: 135–138.

11. For a similar resurrection story, which belongs to a hoard of bamboo and wooden manuscripts that apparently were looted from another Qin tomb and subsequently purchased by Peking [Beijing] University, see Li Ling 2012.

12. *Yunmeng* 1981; *Shuihudi* 2001; *Tianshui Fangmatan* 2009; He Shuangquan 1989; Liu Lexian 1994.

13. For various later examples, see Kalinowski 2003.

14. *Shuihudi* 2001: 212–16; Harper 1985; translated by Harper in Lopez 1996: 241–250.

15. For a study of travel rituals, see Liu Zenggui 2001.

16. It is believed that Xiannong is to be identified as the legendary Shennong 神農 (Tian Xudong 2009).

17. For details, see *Baoshan* 1991; *Xincai* 2003; Yan Changgui 2005; Hu Yali 2002.

18. "Our generation elevates crack-making and milfoil divination and prayers for averting evil; hence illnesses and maladies are increasingly prevalent" (今世上卜筮禱祠,故疾病愈來). *Lüshi chunqiu*, "Jin shu" 盡數 3.2: 137.

CHAPTER 6

Support for the research for this paper has been generously provided by the National Endowment for the Humanities and the Chiang Ching-kuo Foundation for International Scholarly Exchange.

1. For example, Chinese slavery barely features in Milton Meltzer's magisterial survey (1993).

2. See, for example, Liao Meiyun 1995; Wei Qingyuan 1982; and Zheng Zhimin 1997.

3. Patterson 1982: 13. The definition of slavery is much debated. For recent discussions, see, inter alia, Miers 2003 and Campbell 2003.

4. The only substantive publication to date on this find is Cao Lüning and Zhang Rongfang 2007.

5. The bibliography on the hundred or so Liye documents that were published up through 2011 is extensive and too large to cite here; for a partial list see Li Jing 2009: 115–120. For more see *Liye* 2007; Wang Huanlin 2007; cf. Hsing, chapter 4 in this volume.

6. Chen Songchang 2009; Cao Lüning 2009; *Yuelu shuyuan* 2011, 2012.

7. I follow the punctuation of two of the Japanese research teams who have translated the Zhangjiashan laws into Japanese in reading *zheng* and *dian* as two names for the same office, that of village chief *lizheng/dian* 里 正/典. See Peng Hao et al. 2007: 170n1 to slip 201. For the identification and activities of the *lidian* as evidenced in the published Liye documents, see Bu Xianqun 2009: 106–107.

8. In the Qin state (i.e., prior to 221), fines were calculated for the most part in shields and suits of armor (cf. *Shuihudi* 2001), while debts were calculated in cash (round coins with a square hole in the middle): see *Liye* 2007; Wang Huanlin 2007. Fujita Takao 2001 argues that one shield was calculated at 5,000 cash and, if one was poor and could not pay the fine, one could pay it off by working for the government at six cash per day if you received food, or at eight if you did not (cf. Cao Lüning 2001; Zhang Weixing 2004). However, already in the Liye documents dating from the Qin Empire, fines were being calculated in cash. See Song Yanping 2004. Yu Zhenbo 2010 cites and comments on two slips from the looted hoard of Qin documents repatriated by the Yuelu Academy:

> 訾一甲, 直錢千三百卅四, 直金二兩一垂. 一盾直金二垂. 贖耐, 馬甲四, 錢一 (? = 七)千六百八十馬甲一, 金三兩一垂, 直千□(六/九)百廿. 金一朱(銖) 直 錢廿四. 贖入馬甲十二, 錢二萬三千卅

> The fine of one set of armor is worth 1,344 cash and is worth 2 *liang* and 1 *chui* of gold. One shield is worth two *chui* of gold. Redeemable shaving is four sets of horse armor, 7,680 cash. One set of horse armor is 3 *liang* 1 *chui* and worth 1920 [cash]. One *zhu* of gold is worth 24 cash. When redeeming and submitting/entering twelve sets of horse armor, the cash is 23,040.

It appears that rates of exchange between gold and cash were different from commandery to commandery and fluctuated from year to year. Thus, without knowing the exact date of the Yuelu hoard (or hoards—the documents may have come one or more tombs), it is not possible to determine the value of a fine in any given location and at any given point during the Qin state and empire. See also Yates 2012/13 for further discussion of the question of the value of fines in the Qin.

9. This is a phenomenon also seen in the Zhangjiashan Tomb 247, "Stat-

utes on Households" ("Hu lü" 戶律), slips 328–330, and in the "Statutes on Appointing Heirs" ("Zhihou lü" 置後律), slip 390.

10. All the village chiefs mentioned in the first volume of the complete Liye documents (*Liye* 2012; Chen Wei 2012) appear to be called *dian*.

11. The text reads "Zheng X wrote [this]" (鄭X書).

12. See Peng Hao 2004; Li Junming 2002; *Zhangjiashan* 2006: 211–214.

13. In the initial two transcriptions, this fragment was placed at the beginning of slip 318; Peng et al. (2007: 325) renumber it as X1. For the status of *shuren* as "freedman," see Cao Lüning 2007.

14. For a full analysis of the crime of "abscondence," abandoning one's home district and failing to fulfill state tax and corvée obligations, in the Qin and Han, see Zhang Gong 2006.

15. *Zhangjiashan* 2001: 155; 2006: 30; Peng Hao et al. 2007: 155–156; Zhu Honglin 2005: 116–117. For an interpretation of this statute, see Wang Yanhui 2004. See also Cao Lüning 2005: 142–152, for an analysis of the set of "Statutes on Abscondence" as a whole.

16. There is another possibility for interpreting the last phrase in the statute quoted above, that the phrase "male and female slaves" comprised the initial words of another statute.

17. Dubs 1938/55 I: 104; Wilbur 1943: 268, item 9.

18. For the status of commoner in the Qin, see, inter alia, Yates 1987; Liu Hainian 2006; Shi Weiqing 2004b.

19. As Miers (2003: 2) states, "No definition of slavery can be separated from the definition of its antithesis—freedom."

20. Yates 2002; cf. *Shuihudi* 2001; Hulsewé 1985.

21. *Shuihudi* 2001, slip 140: 51; Hulsewé 1985: A68: 69.

22. The complete set of documents found in level 9 of Well 1, Liye, is scheduled for publication in the second volume of the Liye hoard.

23. I am grateful to Brian Lander for sharing his photographs of these documents with me.

24. See Yates 2012 for a detailed discussion of the responsibilities of these and other bureaus in the Qianling County government.

25. See Li Li's most recent discussion of the problem of the status of *lichenqie* in the Zhangjiashan Tomb 247 laws (Li Li 2009: 405–424).

26. See Michael Loewe's careful assessment of the terms and of Zhao Gao's status (Loewe 2005).

27. This case indicates that it was a crime in the Qin for a slave to refuse to carry out his master's orders, as the slave is made a *chengdan* forced laborer and sold to the state on his master's denunciation. The state inspects whether or not the slave is sick and determines whether or not the slave had ever been manumitted. Presumably the slave's treatment would have been different if he had been so freed. See *Shuihudi* 2001: 154–155, slip 37–41; Hulsewé 1985: E15–E16: 193–195; McLeod and Yates 1981: 146–148.

28. McLeod and Yates 1981: 136n67; Hulsewé 1955: 225.

29. *Zhangjiashan* 2001: 157; 2006: 32–33; Peng Hao et al. 2007: 160; Zhu Honglin 2005: 123. Note that the term *he* 劾 is usually understood as the technical term for the denunciation of one official by another. This cannot be true in the present case.

30. *Zhangjiashan* 2001: 158; 2006: 34; Peng Hao et al. 2007: 166; Zhu Honglin 2005: 129.

31. *Zhangjiashan* 2001: 158; 2006: 34; Peng Hao et al. 2007: 166; Zhu Honglin 2005: 129.

32. See, inter alia, Cai Yijing 2002; Li Junming 2002b; Shi Weiqing 2004a; Yang Zuolong 1985; Zhang Jinguang 2002. For recent studies of Qin and Han household registers, see Gao Min 1998; Wang Weihai 2006; Du Zhengsheng 1990; Li Mingzhao 2009; and Hsing, chapter 4 in this volume.

33. *Zhangjiashan* 2001: 184; 2006: 61; Peng Hao et al. 2007: 239; Zhu Honglin 2005: 231. The wording of this slip is comparable to that on the fragment attached to slip 318. The obscure graphs have been retrieved using infrared technology, but there is still probably a lacuna at the end of the item, at the beginning of the second slip, slip 383.

34. Slip 372, *Zhangjiashan* 2001: 183; 2006: 59; Peng Hao et al. 2007: 239; Zhu Honglin 2005: 228: "A woman is comparable (*bi*) to her husband's rank" 女子比其夫爵.

35. Four graphs are missing at the top of the slip.

36. *Zhangjiashan* 2001:183; 2006: 59; Peng Hao et al 2007: 236; Zhu Honglin 2005: 227–28.

37. I will examine the legal status of women in the early empires on another occasion.

38. Slip 30; *Zhangjiashan* 2001: 138; 2006: 13; Peng Hao et al. 2007: 102; Zhu Honglin 2005: 36: "As for male and female slaves who beat a freedman (*shuren*) on up: tattoo their cheekbones and return them to their masters."

39. *Zhangjiashan* 2001: 139; 2006: 13; Peng Hao et al. 2007: 103; Zhu Honglin 2005: 38–39.

40. *Zhangjiashan* 2001: 140; 2006: 14; Peng Hao et al. 2007: 106; Zhu Honglin 2005: 45.

41. The term *ye* appears in the "Denouncing a Slave" (*Gao chen* 告臣) in the Shuihudi Tomb 11 legal texts *Forms for Sealing and Guarding,* and refers to an individual petitioning the authorities to inflict a punishment. See *Shuihudi* 2001: 154; McLeod and Yates 1981: 146; 5.14. Hulsewé (1985, E15: 193), translates *ye* as "wishes," an unattested meaning.

42. Three graphs indecipherable at the top of slip 45.

43. *Zhangjiashan* 2001: 140; 2006, 14–15; Peng Hao et al. 2007: 107–108; Zhu Honglin 2005: 46–48.

44. *Zhangjiashan* 2001: 139; 2006: 14; Peng Hao et al. 2007: 105–106; Zhu Honglin 2005: 43–44.

45. *Zhangjiashan* 2001: 151; 2006: 26–27; Peng Hao et al. 2007: 145–146; Zhu Honglin 2005: 99–100.

46. *Zhangjiashan* 2001: 139; 2006: 14; Peng Hao et al. 2007: 108; Zhu Honglin 2005: 44–45.

47. These are instructions to officials. In other words, "Do not hear [the cases of] children who denounce their fathers and mothers. . ."

48. *Zhangjiashan* 2001: 151; 2006: 27; Peng Hao et al. 2007: 146; Zhu Honglin 2005: 102.

49. In other words, their arguments in a law case are not held to be valid.

50. *Zhangjiashan* 2001: 152; 2006: 27; Zhu Honglin 2005: 103–104.

51. *Zhangjiashan* 2001: 158; 2006: 34; Peng Hao et al. 2007: 166; Zhu Honglin 2005: 129–130.

52. Zhang Xiaofeng (2004), on the basis of this statute and evidence in Han historical sources, argues that these women had a higher status than ordinary slaves, as they had a particular close and intimate relationship with their masters.

53. *Zhangjiashan* 2001: 159; 2006: 34–35; Peng Hao et al. 2007: 207; Zhu Honglin 2005: 131–132.

54. *Zhangjiashan* 2001: 185; 2006: 61; Peng Hao et al. 2007: 240; Zhu Honglin 2005: 233.

55. Peng Hao et al 2007: 343–344, case 5.

56. Peng Hao et al. 2007: 337–338, case 2; Yates 2002.

57. Peng Hao et al. 2007: 347, case 8.

58. Of course, the punishment was the same for a child who committed the same crime. For the Qin, see *Shuihudi* 2001: 118; Hulsewé 1985: 148–149 D 87; for the Han, see Peng Hao et al. 2007: 146 slip 133. Cf. Wen Xia 2009.

59. Cf. Li Li's 2007b analysis of the different interpretations of the term *tuli;* cf. Chen Wei 2012: 20.

60. Luo Kaiyu (2009) suggests that the largest slave market in Qin and Han times was based in the city of Chengdu, Sichuan province, because so many slaves came from minority tribes, being either captured by or sold to the Qin and Han governments or to wealthy private individuals. He may well be right; but he does not have concrete figures to back up his claims. Slaves in the Qin and Han had a number of different origins, some being born into slavery, others being the family members of criminals, others debtors, and so on. See Yates 2002.

INTRODUCTION TO PART III

1. See *Shiji* 6: 254–255, and 87: 2546; Watson 1993: 54–55, 185. Li Si's memorial is cited by van Ess in chapter 7 of this volume. The extent to which the order for the destruction of banned material was actually carried out, is, of course, debatable; in any case, later scholars interpreted the event in an extremely negative light. See more about the biblioclasm in Petersen 1995; Kern 2000: 183–196; Pines 2009: 180–183.

2. "The ruler is a boat; commoners are the water. The water can carry the boat; the water can capsize the boat." (*Xunzi,* "Wang zhi" 王制 V.9: 152).

3. See, for example, *Shang shu*, "Duo shi" 多士, "Duo fang" 多方; for a slightly different angle, see also *Shang shu*,"Wu yi" 無逸.

4. In November 2009, Peking University announced of its possession of several Han manuscripts that apparently had been plundered from the mainland and sold in Hong Kong. One of these texts, titled *Zhao Zheng's Book* (趙正 〈政〉書), narrates the story of the fall of the Qin. The text, which might have been used later by Sima Qian, rejects the legitimacy of Qin, refusing to call the First Emperor by his title, and naming him derisively "Zheng born in [the state of] Zhao." Zhao Huacheng (2011), the author of the preliminary report about the text, assessed that it might have been composed by "aristocrats from one of the six states" destroyed by Qin.

5. This gradual change in the view of Qin was outlined by Michael Nylan in her paper presented at the Jerusalem workshop that preceded the development of this volume.

6. To demonstrate how widespread the negative image of Qin became by the Later Han dynasty 後漢 (25-220 CE), suffice it to mention Cui Shi 崔寔 (ca. 103-170 CE), an important thinker who is sometimes identified as "Legalist" (Balazs 1964: 205-213), and whose overt support of harsh and resolute government could have turned him into a natural admirer of Qin. Yet, contrary to these expectations, Cui Shi's views of Qin are derisive to the extreme: thus, whenever he mentions the Han indebtedness to Qin's institutions, he does it so as to identify the Qin as the source of Han's manifold maladies. Curiously, he even attributes Han's abuse of amnesties and resultant laxity of the Han law to the Qin legacy, an assessment which is clearly counter-factual (*Zheng lun* 8: 157).

7. For the recent exchange of opinions about the historicity of "burying Confucians alive," see Li Kaiyuan 2010; Dai Guoxi 2012. Significantly, their disagreements aside, both scholars dismiss as untenable the traditional interpretation of this event as related to the ideological oppression of "Confucians".

8. For Zheng Qiao, see *Tongzhi* 71/1a–2a; for Gu Yanwu, see "Qin ji Kuaijishan ke shi" 秦紀會稽山刻石, in *Rizhilu*, 13: 468–469; for Liu Zongyuan, see his "Fengjian lun" 封建論, in *Liu Hedong ji* 3: 6–7. Zhang Juzheng is cited from Huang Zhongye 2001:161; for Wang Fuzhi, see his *Du 'Tongjian' lun* 1: 1–2. Li Bai portrays the First Emperor sympathetically in his poem "Qin Wang sao liu he" 秦王掃六合 (*Li Taibai jizhu* 2: 5a), albeit ridiculing the emperor's quest for immortality, possibly criticizing thereby Li Bai's patron, Emperor Xuanzong (唐玄宗, r. 712–756 CE), who was similarly fascinated with immortality. For Li Zhi's note that the First Emperor was a "hero in one thousand generations," see Li's self-annotation in *Cang shu*, p. 3 (藏書世紀列傳總目).

9. Zhu Yuanzhang faulted the First Emperor for abolishing the system of hereditary ranks (*Ming Taizu wenji* 4: 78–79), but, curiously, also for insufficient centralization of power in the monarch's hands, as is manifested in the relegation of powers to the chancellor (ibid, 10: 4–5). To recall: Zhu Yuanzhang abolished the chancellor's position to further strengthen his power.

10. Zhang opined that had the First Emperor been properly succeeded by his capable son, Fusu 扶蘇, then "even the fourth of the Three August and the sixth of the Five Thearchs would not be as thriving as him, not to mention the politicians of later generations, who knew only how to multiply writings and adorn rituals" ("Qin zheng ji" 秦政記, in Zhang Binglin 1977: 500–501).

11. See Hu Shi 1930: 480–481.

12. For the complex background of Guo Moruo's assault against the First Emperor, see a brief discussion in Chen Kangheng 2009: 57.

13. In 1958, at a Party meeting, Mao lauded the First Emperor as "an expert in strengthening the modern and weakening the ancient" and proudly proclaimed that since the Communist Party buried "46,000 counter-revolutionaries" and not just "460 Confucians," it surpasses the First Emperor "a hundred times" (Mao Zedong 1958). In 1973 Mao Zedong identified himself as "Marx + the First Emperor" and a secret order was made to the academic circles to refrain from criticizing the First Emperor even in a mild form (Liu Zehua 劉澤華, personal communication to Yuri Pines, 2012; see also Pines, forthcoming [a]). For more about Mao's reevaluation of the First Emperor, see Goldman 1975; cf. Li Yu-ning 1977; Chen Kangheng 2009.

14. The most radical views appear, expectedly, in a variety of blogs. In scholarly publications, for identification of the First Emperor as a "fascist ruler," see Lin Shifang 1998; for "cultural Holocaust," see Meng Xiangcai and Wang Keqi 2004: 66–73; see also the next note.

15. For some of the debates, see, e.g., Zhang Fentian 2005; Huang Zhongye 2001; Chen Kangheng 2009 (who exposes the difficulties of current textbook writers); see also Du Bin and Gao Qun 2009. Among major movies that deal with the controversial figure of the First Emperor, one could mention *The Emperor and the Assassin*, by Chen Kaige 陳凱歌 and *Hero*, by Zhang Yimou 張藝謀. Both movies are analyzed by Marinelli 2005 (q.v. his references); cf. Pines 2008c: 32–33. For an example of a fierce media debate over the assessment of the First Emperor, see, for instance, Zhou Fang 2013: 41–42.

16. For debates over the empire's centralization, see the next note; for the so-called burying alive of Confucians, see the discussion above in the text. For the debates about whether or not the anti-Qin uprising can be classified as peasant rebellion, see Dull 1983; cf. Yuan Zhongyi 1983. This latter question was not addressed at our workshop.

17. This issue was raised recently by Griet Vankeerberghen (2007: 97–100), who questioned the historicity of the universal abolition of enfeoffment system under the Qin (cf. van Ess, chapter 7 in this volume), and it was a source of considerable controversy during the Jerusalem workshop. As Vankeerberghen admits, extant textual and archaeological evidence "does not allow us to conclude that there were *zhuhou* [regional lords] in Qin after 221 BC, and thus that the *Shiji* report is false . . . [However,] there might have been more tolerance for the institution of *zhuhou* at the Qin court than the dismissive account in the *Shiji* lets us assume" (2007: 99–100).

18. A major recent comparative study of early empires (Morris and Scheidel 2009) notably omits the Qin case—and China in general—from its discussion (aside from a few references in an insightful introduction by Goldstone and Haldon [2009]). We hope that our volume will help our colleagues engaged in comparative studies of early empires to fill in the extant gap.

CHAPTER 7

1. The most important contribution in Western literature is arguably Bodde 1986; for more literature, see Durrant 1994: 46nn1–10. See especially pp. 29–30 of the latter, in which Durrant argues that the real target of Sima Qian's criticism was not the First Emperor of Qin but Emperor Wu of the Han. Puett (2001: 187) shows that Sima Qian offers a very balanced assessment of the Qin but that the presentation of the First Emperor "is not flattering" (191).

2. Hardy has briefly discussed this point (1999: 50–51, 232n51).

3. These are the chapters of the earliest rulers of China, namely the "Five Thearchs" 五帝, the chapters on the "Three Dynasties" (Xia, Shang, and Zhou), and the chapter on predynastic Qin, which nominally did not rule but took over from the Zhou in the middle of the third century.

4. This applies to the First Emperor of the Qin and to the anti-Qin rebel Xiang Yu (項羽, d. 202).

5. Interestingly, the Qin adopted a system exalting the number six under the First Emperor (*Shiji* 28: 1366).

6. The chapter structure of the *Shiji* is a subject that until today has not received the attention it deserves in Western scholarship. This chapter, too, can not go into much detail about this important topic.

7. *Xijing zaji*, 6: 43, anecdote 136. In *Shiji* 130: 3321, commentary 16, this story is quoted from Wei Hong's 衛宏 (fl. 25 CE) *Hanshu jiuyi zhu* 漢書舊儀注.

8. Li Changzhi (2007: 101) argues that there are no lost chapters of the *Shiji*. He speculates that the double inclusion of the treatise on the *feng* and *shan* ceremonies might be irony on Sima Qian's part.

9. Michael Nylan (1999) has questioned the so-called triumph of Confucianism under Emperor Wu.

10. Whether the term "feudal" is an accurate translation of *fengjian* 封建, which presumed delegation of the monarch's power to local potentates, is debatable (see, e.g., Li Feng 2003); I adopt this term for heuristic convenience.

11. *Shiji* 6: 246 and 6: 248. The First Emperor cut off the trees of Xiang 湘 Mountain when there was a tempest at his arrival and after an erudite had told him that the Goddess of Xiang was the daughter of Thearch Yao 堯 and the wife of Thearch Shun 舜.

12. In Han times there were several positions for "supervisors." The *boshi puye* 博士僕射 headed the erudites at the imperial academy from 136 on (hence Nienhauser 1994 I: 146 translates "their supervisor"). *Hanshu* 19A.728 says that the *puye* 僕射 dated back to Qin times and that among other positions there had also been a *puye* for the erudites. As *Shiji* speaks of the

erudites first and the *puye* after, it would seem logical that the *puye* of the erudites is implied.

13. There is another good and very similar example for *pai mapi* in *Shiji* 6: 246–247.

14. *Shiji* 6: 254–255, modifying Nienhauser, 1994 I: 147–148 (italics mine). Compare the somewhat shorter and slightly different version in *Shiji* 87: 2546. Yuri Pines has discussed the memorial recently (Pines 2009: 180–183).

15. Gongsun Hong was still imperial secretary when he wrote the memorial, but he was to become chancellor shortly after.

16. It was Ban Gu (班固, 32–92 CE) who credited Dong Zhongshu with this achievement. In the *Shiji*, Dong Zhongshu is depicted as a petty scholar who "did not look into his garden for three years" because he was so concentrated—and so little interested in the affairs of daily life (*Shiji* 121: 3127).

17. *Shiji* 121: 3118; cf. the translation by Watson (1961 II: 398–399).

18. Note that the wording of this passage reminds us of Sima Qian's motives for writing the *Shiji* (130: 3304, 3319).

19. *Shiji* 121: 3119; cf. the translation by Watson (1961 II: 400–401). Italics are mine.

20. For a debate about the meaning of "the hundred schools" 百家, see, e.g., Petersen 1995.

21. This concluding formula is to be found at several places in the *Shiji* and it shows above all that there was a high degree of continuity between the Qin and the Han as far as the administrative system was concerned. Yet one should not overlook the possibility that it may have been the historiographer who intended that his reader recognized this continuity.

22. One may also add to this the third memorial submitted by Dong Zhongshu to Emperor Wu, which is similar to Gongsun Hong's text in argument but different in style. See *Hanshu* 56: 2523.

23. This is the opinion of Fang Bao 方苞 (1668–1749 CE) as found in his commentary on the *Shiji*, the *Shiji zhu buzheng* 51b. Some Westerners have differing opinions; see, e.g., Zufferey 2003.

24. On this and the next topic, see also Schaab-Hanke 2002.

25. *Shiji* 6: 237–238; Nienhauser 1994 I: 136. I have rendered *de* as "power," rather than use Nienhauser's "essence." For a slightly different version of the story, see *Shiji* 28: 1366 (Watson 1961 II: 22–23).

26. *Shiji* 74: 2345. Sima Qian ends his description with the words, "As for Zou Yan, although his teachings were not reliable, perhaps he too had the same intentions as the men with cows and cauldrons" (Nienhauser 1994 VII: 182). By "men with cows and cauldrons," he refers to lowly upstarts who succeeded in ascending to the top of the political pyramid: Yi Yin 伊尹, who "made himself a betrothal servant . . . carrying a cauldron" and "persuaded Tang [the founder of the Shang dynasty] to realize the way of the king" (Nienhauser 1994 VII: 182, note 38; Sterckx 2011: 65-76), and Baili Xi 百里奚 who made himself acquainted with Lord Mu of Qin (秦穆公, r. 659–621) (Thatcher 1988).

27. This, of course, simply means "Gongsun the Subject." I do not imply

that "Chen" was not used as a personal name in Han times and before, but I do think it is necessary to pay attention to names in the *Shiji*.

28. *Shiji* 10: 429–430. In *Shiji* 28: 1381 this is said to have taken place three years later. Compare also *Shiji* 96: 2681–2682.

29. First mentioned in *Shiji* 12: 467 and 28: 1393. Thus, this was "Gongsun the Minister," which contrasts nicely with the aforementioned "Gongsun the Subject." As with the name Chen, there can be no doubt that Qing was used as a personal name—but again it is interesting to note that only the magicians used these names.

30. *Shiji* 12: 483, 28: 1402; translation by Watson 1961 II: 66–67.

31. This does not mean that he was against the change of the element and the adoption of yellow as the dynastic color. Rather, he may have come to this conclusion by means other than five-element speculations.

32. This is how we have to read the introductory passage in which Sima Qian says that there had been *feng* and *shan* sacrifices in the remote past—but not in the one which was documented.

33. *Shiji* 28: 1366–1367, modifying Watson 1961 II: 23–24. The ceremonies are only briefly mentioned in *Shiji* 6: 242–244, where, however, the text of the stone inscription at mount Liangfu is given.

34. *Shiji* 12: 455 (Nienhauser 1994 II: 223); *Shiji* 28: 1385. For further attempts to reach Penglai under the reign of Emperor Wu, see *Shiji* 28: 1393.

35. *Shiji* 28: 1393 explicitly says that the text was not canonical (*bu jing*) and adds that Suo Zhong, a man who is otherwise known as a confidante of Sima Xiangru, thought it was a forgery. On Suo Zhong and his potential relationship to the Sima, see Schaab-Hanke 2002.

36. *Shiji* 12: 472, 28: 1396. The answer was that only his clothes and cap were buried there.

37. Cf. *Shiji* 28: 1366, 28: 1398 [Nienhauser 1994 Vol 2: 243]: "The sovereign reflected [on the fact that] the words of the assembled Confucian scholars and practitioners of [magical] methods in discussing the *feng* and the *shan* [sacrifices] differed from one man to the other, were inconsistent, and [were] difficult to put into effect." Cf. the account about the First Emperor: "But as the First Emperor listened to the debates of the scholars, he found that each of them expressed a different opinion and their recommendations were difficult to carry out, and with this he dismissed the whole lot" (*Shiji* 28:1366; Watson 1961, vol 2: 23).

38. It is well known that Sima Qian's father, Sima Tan, on his deathbed lamented that he, as the official who should have been responsible for the sacrifices, had been excluded from the performance.

39. Again, Fang Bao has argued in favor of that reading in his two essays on the treatise on the *feng* and *shan* sacrifices (*Fang Bao ji:* 46–48).

40. 即事用希 in the opening paragraph, 封禪用希 in the discussion of the *feng* and *shan* sacrifices

41. Summary in *Shiji* 6: 264, details in the biography of Li Si (*Shiji* 87).

42. *Shiji* 55: 2040, modifying Watson 1963, I: 140: for *ba* 霸 I have replaced the anachronistic word "dictator" with "hegemon."

43. Compare also *Shiji* 97: 2695, 89: 2573. In the last passage, Zhang Er 張耳 and Chen Yu 陳餘 recommend to Chen She 陳涉 that he establish the descendants of the ruling houses of the six kingdoms in order to establish a faction which would increase the number of the enemies of the Qin. Chen She does not listen to the proposal, however. One wonders whether Sima Qian sees this as a reason for his downfall shortly thereafter.

44. Meaning that rebellion can endanger the supreme ruler even if it is instigated by a mere commoner: one should not be afraid of enfeoffed nobles only and there is no point in excessively oppressing them.

45. [Given that the *wang* 王-led units under the Han were of clearly subordinate nature—unlike in the Warring States period—most of us prefer to translate them as "princedoms" and not "kingdoms"—*Eds.*]

46. See especially Tables 6 and 7 (*Shiji* 18 and 19), and more in Schaab-Hanke 2012: 117–123.

47. For example, the hunting park Shanglin 上林 established by the First Emperor and used by Emperor Wu would be a topic worthy of further exploration.

48. This may be true, for example, for the account of the First Emperor's choice of the water element, which is so remarkably similar to the one of Emperor Wu and his predecessors' choice of earth. Bodde (1986: 96–97) has cautioned against this challenge to the *Shiji* brought up by Japanese scholars. Yet his reasons for discounting it are weak: he thinks it is unlikely that an interpolator could have been able to recount the same fact in several places, yet if that interpolator were Sima Qian himself this problem would not exist.

49. In van Ess 2005/6: 62, I show that the reading of a sacrificial hymn of Emperor Wu as contained in *Shiji* does not throw a very positive light on the emperor, whereas the slightly different version contained in *the History of the Former Han Dynasty* (*Hanshu*) is much more reverential. When I published the article I suggested that the *Hanshu* may have been a rewritten version, but of course the hymn in *Shiji* may also have been slightly altered by Sima Qian (or by whoever authored the relevant passage) in the beginning in order to shed a negative light on the emperor.

50. It is interesting to note that there are two early references which state that the last of the inscriptions, the one on Mount Kuaiji 會稽 (simply called Ji 稽 in the earlier text, namely *Shuijing zhu*), was actually there. Li Daoyuan 酈道元 (469–527 CE) says in his *Shuijing zhu* 水經注 (40: 3310) that the inscription "is still preserved at the side of the mountain" 尚存山側. Zhang Shoujie 張守節 (fl. 725–735 CE) says in his *Shiji zhengyi* 史記正義 that "this inscription is to be seen on top of Mount Kuaiji" 其碑見在會稽山 (*Shiji* 6: 261). Martin Kern (2000: 1–2, nn3, 14), provides a useful list of relevant references. We cannot know, however, whether the inscription was indeed the one erected by the First Emperor or whether it was carved on the basis of the text of the *Shiji*

at a later time. Strangely, to my knowledge there are no records confirming the existence of the other inscriptions.

51. Just take one example: "As for the Five Emperors and the Three Kings of the past: Their knowledge and teachings were different from ours, and their laws and regulations not as clear. By utilizing the awesome influence of ghosts and gods to oppress the people of the remote regions, their actual deeds did not live up to their fame. Thus they did not last long" (*Shiji* 6: 246; Nienhauser 1994 I: 142; cf. the earlier translation by Chavannes 1967 II: 150–151, 1893: 500–502). Martin Kern (2000: 34) does not translate this part of the inscription. See his discussion on p. 25n42.

CHAPTER 8

This research was supported by the Israel Science Foundation (Grant 1217/07) and by the Michael William Lipson Chair in Chinese Studies of the Hebrew University of Jerusalem.

1. Dong Zhongshu's expurgation of Qin from the line of legitimate dynasties can be deduced from his peculiar construction of dynastic cycles of the past, for which see Arbuckle 1995; for Cai Yong's views, see his *Du duan* 1: 1. For a brief summary of divergent views of Qin's place in history, see, e.g., Wang Yundu and Zhang Liwen 1997, 263–277.

2. See an excellent discussion of the Qin stele inscriptions in Kern 2000. Kern's study served as an inspiration for my research. In chapter 7 in this volume, Hans van Ess warns that the reproduction of the stele inscriptions by Sima Qian may be unreliable. I am unconvinced: as Kern (2000: 6) shows, not a single rubbing of the steles presents a picture that is "fundamentally different" from Sima Qian's reproduction; moreover, the first of the stele inscriptions, that on Mt. Yi 嶧山, which was not reproduced by Sima Qian, does not differ ideologically from other six steles.

3. *Mengzi*, "Gongsun Chou 公孫丑 xia," 4.13: 109.

4. For studies of Xunzi, see, e.g., Goldin 1999; Sato 2003; cf. Pines 2009, *passim*.

5. *Xunzi*, "Wang zhi" 王制, V.9: 171.

6. *Xunzi*, "Junzi" 君子, XVII.24: 450.

7. *Xunzi*, "Zheng lun" 正論, XII.18: 331.

8. Cited with minor modifications from Kern 2000: 13–14.

9. *Shiji* 6: 245; Kern 2000: 32–33. Those "whose doors face north" are dwellers of the areas to the south of the Tropic of Cancer, where people reportedly "open their door north to face the sun" (Kern 2000: 33n76); see Kern's notes for other geographical identifications.

10. See Wang and Cheng 1999: 63–69; these inscriptions were insightfully discussed by Charles Sanft in a paper presented at the Jerusalem workshop; see also Sanft, forthcoming.

11. The citations are from, respectively, the Mt. Yi inscription (221); the Taishan 泰山 inscription (219); the Langye inscription (219); the western and

eastern vista of the Zhifu 之罘 inscription (218); and the Kuaiji 會稽 inscription (c. 211). See *Shiji* 6: 243, 245, 249, 250, 261; Kern 2000: 14, 21, 32, 36, 39, 49.

12. See the Mt. Yi inscription (Kern 2000: 13); for "stability is in unity," see *Mengzi*, "Liang Hui Wang 梁惠王 shang," 1.6: 17–18; cf. Pines 2000.

13. Cited from the Taishan and Langye inscriptions (*Shiji* 6: 243, 245; Kern 2000: 22, 26, 30, 32).

14. See the Taishan, Jieshi 碣石 (215), and Kuaiji inscriptions (*Shiji* 6: 243, 249, 262; Kern 2000: 18, 36, 49).

15. See the Jieshi inscription (*Shiji* 6: 252; Kern 2000: 43).

16. See, respectively, the Jieshi and Langye inscriptions (*Shiji* 6: 252, 245; Kern 2000: 43, 28).

17. *Xunzi*, "Zheng lun," XII.18: 324–325.

18. See, respectively, the Langye, Taishan, and Kuaiji inscriptions (*Shiji* 6: 245, 243, 261; Kern 2000: 26, 22–23, 48).

19. See, respectively, the Langye and Kuaiji inscriptions (*Shiji* 6: 245, 261; Kern 2000: 31, 48).

20. For the importance of the titles appropriated by the August Thearch, see Liu Zehua 2000: 131–136.

21. Taishan inscription (*Shiji* 6: 243; Kern 2000: 21).

22. More precisely, the epithet "sage" appears in only five inscriptions: it is notably lacking in the first, Mt. Yi inscription, which is somewhat more modest in its tone than the latter ones, and it is absent from the incomplete Jieshi inscription (on the incompleteness of which, see the discussion in Kern 2000: 41n117).

23. For the radical modification of the imperial pantheon under the Qin, see *Shiji* 28: 1366–1367; for the punishment of the Mt. Xiang deities, see *Shiji* 6: 248.

24. See Kern 2000: 12–13 for the first; *Shiji* 6: 236 for the second. While the emperor duly performed manifold sacrifices, he might have focused on seeking personal gains from the deities (e.g., immortality, see Poo, chapter 5 in this volume) rather than support for his political endeavor.

25. It should be remembered that eschatological religions and the related phenomenon of religious messianism have existed in China since the turn of the Common Era (see, e.g., Zürcher 1982), and a few emperors, most notably Zhu Yuanzhang 朱元璋 (1328–1398 CE, r. 1368–1398), adopted what may be dubbed a messianic posture; yet not a single ruler between the First Emperor and Mao Zedong was so eager to present his rule not as a restoration of past glory but as a new beginning.

26. My adoption of the term "messianic" in the political rather than religious context is influenced by J. L. Talmon's concept of "political Messianism" (see, e.g., Talmon 1960).

27. *Lüshi chunqiu*, "Zhen luan" 振亂, 7.3: 393–394.

28. See for instance the Mt. Yi inscription cited above in the text; or the Zhifu eastern vista inscription, which summarizes: "Viewed against the old, [our times] are definitely superior" (*Shiji* 6:250; Kern 2000: 39). See also Li

Si's memorial, which initiated book burning of 213, in which Li Si accused his opponents of "speaking about the past to harm the present" (道古以害今. *Shiji* 6: 255).

29. The fear of the potential loss of the mandate is evident in many supposedly early Western Zhou texts, such as the "Kang gao" 康誥 and "Duo fang" 多方 documents or the "Wen wang" 文王 ode.

30. See such terms as "for a long time" (*chang* 長, 5 times) and "forever" (*yong* 永, 3 times); similar references to longevity for "myriad generations" (*wanshi* 萬世) are scattered in the speeches cited in the "Basic Annals of the First Emperor." For the quest for the lineage longevity in the Zhou bronze inscriptions, see Xu Zhongshu 1936.

31. Martynov (1987: 25–30) discusses early Han texts, but his observation can easily be applied to the Qin steles as well.

32. The term *tai ping* appears in pre-Qin texts only twice: in the *Lüshi chunqiu* and in *Han Feizi*, both of which mention it just in passing. The only significant reference to *tai ping* in a preimperial text appears in a controversial (in terms of dating and authorship) "Tian Dao" 天道 chapter of the *Zhuangzi* 莊子, where this term is explicitly associated with the "utmost of orderly rule" (治之至也) attained by the "enlightened" (*ming* 明) rulers of antiquity. For its usages in the Han, see Loewe 1995: 313–314. A possible predecessor of the term *tai ping* is the compound "utmost peace/evenness" (*zhi ping* 至平), employed by Xunzi (*Xunzi*, "Jun dao" 君道, VIII.12: 232).

33. For Qin unification measures, see *Shiji* 6: 239–241; for an analysis of these measures as imposition of Qin's institutions on the conquered population, see the introduction to part 1 of this volume; for the imposition of the new vocabulary, see Hu Pingsheng 2009 and the introduction to part 2 of this volume; for the imposition of Qin ranks, see Hsing, chapter 4 in this volume.

34. Taishan, Zhifu east, and Kuaiji inscriptions (*Shiji* 6: 243, 250, 261; Kern 2000: 21, 39, 47, modified).

35. On the emperor's examination of documents, this claim was reportedly made by "technical specialists" (*fang shi* 方士) at Qin's court as an excuse for their failure to teach the emperor the art of immortality. See *Shiji* 6: 258. According to Li Rui and Wu Hongqi 2003: 132, the First Emperor visited thirty-eight out of forty-six commanderies of Qin, this in addition to his departures into the sea. Only very few rulers in China's long imperial history could match the scope of his tours. For the connection between the emperor's peregrinations and imperial activism in general, see Pines, forthcoming (b).

36. "Qin's Sage" (秦聖, which probably should be read as "Great Sage" 泰聖) is the First Emperor's self-appellation in the Kuaiji stele (*Shiji* 6: 261; Kern 2000: 45). Kong Jia's activities at the court of Chen She and his reasons for joining the rebel are summarized in chapters 19–21 of *Kong congzi* 孔叢子 (*Kong Congzi*, 409–435). While the book itself is almost certainly spurious (Ariel 1989), it is likely that it incorporated earlier materials which may well be reliable insofar as activities of Kong Jia (a.k.a. Kong Fu 孔鮒) are concerned.

37. See *Shiji* 6: 283; for Jia Yi's impact on later assessments of Qin, see

Shelach, chapter 3 in this volume. For a somewhat similar argument against Qin's hyperactive rule as the source of its misfortune, see Lu Jia's (陸賈, c. 240–170 BCE) *Xin yu*, "Wu wei" 無爲, 4: 62.

38. Huhai 胡亥, the Qin second emperor, was blackened beyond imagination in the *Historical Records*, our only significant source for his rule. Yet even if many anecdotes about him are wrong, the very fact that during two years of his rule the huge empire collapsed, not in small measure due to the defection of its major army, proves his inadequacy beyond doubt.

CHAPTER 9

1. The best explanation connecting imperial realities to the fall of the republic is still, in my opinion, Brunt 1962. According to Brunt, the military needs of the empire changed the character of the Roman military by turning it from a citizen militia loyal to the republic into a semiprofessional army whose various legions were loyal to rival generals who were, under the republican system, also rival politicians—an obvious recipe for civil war.

2. See below, n9.

3. On the *Res Gestae*, see Witschel 2008; on the Qin imperial steles, see Kern 2000.

4. For translation and commentary, see Brunt and Moore 1967.

5. Calling Augustus Emperor as a designation of his official position is historically true but formally inaccurate. Under the republic, *imperator* had been an honorific title bestowed on victorious commanders by the army. Augustus took it as his personal name, and also received numerous "imperial salutations" after military victories. *Imperator* would become one of the appellations designating the supreme ruler of the Roman state, but the most widely used term was *princeps* (hence *prince* in European languages). But there was never a single imperial office which Augustus received at some point in time—he was voted various powers and honors, accumulating them throughout his rule, and all of them made up his position as First Citizen.

6. See Suetonius, *Augustus*, 7.2.

7. E.g., Virgil, *Georgica*, 4.562.

8. Note that Roman citizens are still citizens, rather than subjects, but they are "your citizens." The examples of flattery to Augustus are taken from Millar 1973.

9. See Millar 1973: 65–67; contra Cotton and Yakobson 2002: 205–209.

10. Cf. Dio 55.4.2–3; cf. 54.30.4: a somewhat less "republican," but still far from despotic, behavior in court.

11. Tacitus, *Annales*, 1.15; *Velleius Paterculus*, 2.126.

12. The case of Egnatius Rufus in 19 BCE—see Dio, 53.24.4–6; *Velleius Paterculus*, 2.91.3–4.

13. "He thought it enough to punish with a mild form of banishment [without confiscation of property] a plebeian . . . who had openly declared at

a large dinner party that he lacked neither the earnest desire nor the courage to kill him" (Suetonius, *Augustus*, 52).

14. Tacitus, *Annales*, 1.72; 3.24.2–3.

15. The law also came to be applied, already under Tiberius, though not without delays and hesitation, to offenses against the dignity of members of the imperial family. This was fully in accordance with the logic of hereditary monarchy, though harder to reconcile with the letter of the law than the punishment of those who insulted the emperor himself, who stood for the "majesty of the people" because of his official publicly conferred powers. On this (and with reference to the development of the law of *maiestas* under the early principate), see Yakobson 2003.

16. On the state-sanctioned cult of the genius of Augustus among the urban plebs in Rome, see Price 1996: 823–824.

17. On this, see Brunt 1962.

18. See, e.g., Sherwin-White 1973: 159; cf. Mendels 1992: 13–33.

19. See Virgil's famous rendering of the Roman ethos in this respect in *Aeneis*, 6.851–853.

20. See Brunt and Moore 1967: 66 for a minor exception which is clearly meant to demonstrate Augustus's piety to gods rather than his beneficence to provincials. "The empire as a functioning body and its numerous inhabitants are of no real interest to the author of the RG. Instead, Augustus presented a very traditional picture of Roman imperialism which was based on victory and conquest. In this scenario there was no doubt that Rome was the center of the orbis terrarum and nearly the only place a good emperor had to care for intensively" (Witschel 2008: 256–257).

21. On Augustus and the extension of Roman citizenship, see now Eck 2007: 108–111.

22. Cf. Wallace-Hadrill 1982: 32–48.

23. Even by admirers, not to mention skeptics like Tacitus; see *Annales*, 1.9–10; Seneca, *De Clementia*, 1.11.1–2.

24. Jia Yi cited from Watson 1993: 81. I am grateful to Yuri Pines for this reference.

Bibliography

Abrams, Elliot M. 1994. *How the Maya Built Their World: Energetics and Ancient Architecture*. Austin: University of Texas Press.

Abrams, Elliot M., and Thomas W. Bolland. 1999. "Architectural Energetics, Ancient Monuments, and Operations Management." *Journal of Archaeological Method and Theory* 6.4: 263–291.

Alcock, Susan E., et al., eds. 2001. *Empires: Perspectives from Archaeology and History*. Cambridge: Cambridge University Press.

An Zuozhang 安作璋 and Xiong Tieji 熊鐵基. 2007. *Qin Han guanzhi shigao* 秦漢官制史稿. Ji'nan: Qilu shushe.

Arbuckle, Gary. 1995. "Inevitable Treason: Dong Zhongshu's Theory of Historical Cycles and Early Attempts to Invalidate the Han Mandate." *Journal of the American Oriental Society* 115.4: 585–597.

Ariel, Yoav. 1989. *K'ung-Ts'ung-tzu: The Kung Family Masters' Anthology*. Princeton, NJ: Princeton University Press.

Balazs, Etienne. 1964. "Political Philosophy and Social Crisis at the End of the Han Dynasty." In Etienne Balazs, *Chinese Civilization and Bureaucracy: Variations on a Theme*. Translated by H. M. Wright, edited by Arthur F. Wright. New Haven: Yale University Press, 187-225.

Barbieri-Low, Anthony J. 2007. *Artisans in Early Imperial China*. Seattle and London: University of Washington Press.

Barbieri-Low, Anthony, and Robin D. S. Yates. Forthcoming. *Law, State, and Society in Early Imperial China: Study and Translation of the Zhangjiashan Legal Texts*. Seattle: University of Washington Press.

Baoji Shi Bowuguan 寶雞市博物館 and Baoji Xian Tuboguan 寶雞縣圖博館. 1980. "Baoji Xian Xigaoquancun Chunqiu Qin mu fajue ji" 寶雞縣西高泉村春秋秦墓發掘記. *Wenwu* 文物 9: 1–9.

Baoji Shi Kaogu Gongzuodui 寶雞市考古工作隊 and Baoji Xian Bowuguan 寶雞縣博物館. 2001. "Shaanxi Baoji Xian Nanyangcun Chunqiu Qin mu de qingli" 陝西寶雞縣南陽村春秋秦墓的清理. *Kaogu* 考古 7: 21-29.

335

Baoshan Chumu 包山楚墓. 1991. Published by Hubei Sheng Jingsha tielu kaogudui 湖北省荊沙鐵路考古隊. Beijing: Wenwu chubanshe.

Beijing Daxue Chutuwenxian Yanjiusuo 北京大學出土文獻研究所. 2012. "Beijing Daxue cang Qin jiandu gaishu" 北京大學藏秦簡牘概述. *Wenwu* 6: 65–73.

Bielenstein, Hans. 1947. "The Census of China during the Period A.D. 2–742." *Bulletin of the Museum of Far Eastern Antiquities* 19: 125–163.

———. 1987. "Chinese Historical Demography, A.D. 2–1982." *Bulletin of the Museum of Far Eastern Antiquities* 59: 1–288.

Bodde, Derk. 1938. *China's First Unifier: A Study of the Ch'in Dynasty as Seen in the Life of Li Ssu* 李斯 *280–208 B.C.* Leiden: Brill.

———. 1986. "The State and Empire of Ch'in." In Denis Twitchett and Michael Loewe, eds., *The Cambridge History of China. Vol. 1: The Ch'in and Han Empires, 221 BCE–220 A.D.* Cambridge: Cambridge University Press, 20–102.

Brunt, Peter A. 1962. "The Army and the Land in the Roman Revolution." *Journal of Roman Studies* 52: 69–84.

Brunt, Peter A., and John M. Moore, eds. 1967. *Res Gestae Divi Augusti: The Achievements of the Divine Augustus.* Oxford: Oxford University Press.

Bu Xianqun 卜憲群. 2009. "Cong jiandu kan Qin dai xiangli de liyuan shezhi yu xingzheng gongneng" 從簡牘看秦代鄉里的吏員設置與行政功能. In Zhongguo Shehuikexueyuan Kaogu Yanjiusuo 中國社會科學院考古研究所 et al., eds., *Liye gucheng: Qin jian yu Qin wenhua yanjiu* 里耶古城·秦簡與秦文化研究. Beijing: Kexue chubanshe, 103–113.

Cai Wanjin 蔡萬進. 2006. *Zhangjiashan Han jian Zouyan shu yanjiu* 張家山漢簡奏讞書研究. Guilin: Guangxi shifan daxue chubanshe.

Cai Yijing 蔡宜靜. 2002. "Zhanguo shiqi Qin guo zhi huji zhidu" 戰國時期秦國之戶籍制度. *Zhongguo shanggushi yanjiu zhuankan* 中國上古史研究專刊 2: 105–124.

Campbell, Gwyn. 2003. "Introduction: Slavery and Other Forms of Unfree Labour in the Indian Ocean World." *Slavery and Abolition* 24.2: ix–xxxii.

Cao Lüning 曹旅寧. 2001. "Qin lü zhong suojian zhi zi jiadun wenti" 秦律中所見之貲甲盾問題. *Qiusuo* 求索 6: 136–138.

———. 2002. "Qin lü duguan xintan" 秦律都官新探. *Qin wenhua luncong* 秦文化論叢 9: 233–243.

———. 2005. *Zhangjiashan Han lü yanjiu* 張家山漢律研究. Beijing: Zhonghua shuju.

———. 2007. "Qin Han falü jiandu zhong de 'shuren' shenfen ji falü diwei wenti" 秦漢法律簡牘中的"庶人"身份及法律地位問題. *Xianyang shifan xueyuan bao* 咸陽師範學院報 6 (22.3): 12–14.

———. 2008a. "Liye Qin jian 'cilü' kaoshu" 里耶秦簡"祠律"考述. *Shixue yuekan* 史學月刊 8: 37–42.

———. 2008b. "Shi 'tuli' jianlun Qin xingtu de shenfen ji xingqi wenti" 釋"徒隸"兼論秦刑徒的身份及刑期問題. *Shanghai shifan daxue xuebao (zhexue shehuikexue ban)* 上海示範大學學報(哲學社會科學版) 5: 61–65.

———. 2009. "Yuelu shuyuan xincang Qin jian congkao" 岳麓書院新藏秦簡叢考. *Huadong zhengfa daxue xuebao* 華東政法大學學報 6: 93–102.

———. 2011. "Cong chutu jiandu kaozheng Qin Shi gong Nan Yue zhi niandai" 從出土簡牘考證秦始攻南越之年代. http://www.bsm.org.cn/show_article.php?id=1535.

Cao Lüning 曹旅寧 and Zhang Rongfang 張榮芳. 2007. "Zhangjiashan 336 hao Han mu *Chao lü* de jige wenti" 張家山336 號漢墓《朝律》的幾個問題. In Benshu bianwei hui 本書編委會, ed., *An Zuozhang xiansheng shixue yanjiu: Liushi zhounian jinian wenji* 安作璋先生史學研究：六十周年紀念文集. Ji'nan: Qi Lu shushe, 348–356. Republished as Cao Lüning 曹旅寧, "Zhangjiashan 336 hao Han mu 'Chao lü' de jige wenti" 張家山336 號漢墓《朝律》的幾個問題, *Guizhou shifan daxue xuebao (shehuikexue ban)* 貴州師範大學學報(社會科學版) 2008.1: 14–18.

Cao Ying 曹英. 2004. "Zhiduxing fubai: Qin diguo huwang de yuanyin fenxi" 制度性腐敗：秦帝國忽亡的原因分析. *Jiangsu shehuikexue* 江蘇社會科學 2: 127–133.

Chang, Tsung-tung. 1970. *Der Kult der Shang-Dynastie im Spiegel der Orake-linschriften*. Wiesbaden: Otto Harrassowitz.

Changsha Dongpailou Donghan jiandu 長沙東牌樓東漢簡牘. 2006. Published by Changsha Shi wenwu kaogu Yanjiusuo 長沙市文物考古研究所. Beijing: Wenwu chubanshe.

Chavannes, Édouard. 1893. "Les inscriptions des Ts'in." *Journal Asiatique*, n.s., 1: 473–521.

———, trans. 1967 [1895]. *Les Mémoires historiques de Se-ma Ts'ien*. Paris, Librairie d'Amérique et d'Orient, 6 vols.

Chen Kangheng 陳康衡. 2009. "Shen yong Mao Zedong 'wenge' shiju pinglun 'fenshu kengru'" 慎用毛澤東"文革"詩句評論"焚書坑儒". *Lishi jiaoxue* 歷史教學 5: 56–58.

Chen Ping 陳平. 1984. "Shilun Guanzhong Qin mu qingtong rongqi de fenqi wenti" 試論關中秦墓青銅器的分期問題. *Kaogu yu wenwu* 考古與文物 3: 58–73, 4: 63–73. Rpt. in Chen Ping (2003): 176–200.

———. 1987. "Shilun Zhanguo xing Qin bing de niandai ji youguan wenti" 試論戰國型秦兵的年代及有關問題. In *Zhongguo kaoguxue yanjiu lunji* 《中國考古學研究論集》 editorial board, eds., *Zhongguo kaoguxue yanjiu lunji: Jinian Xia Nai xiansheng kaogu wushi zhounian* 中國考古學研究論集：紀念夏鼐先生考古五十週年. Xi'an: San Qin chubanshe, 310–335. Rpt. in Chen Ping (2003): 222–243.

———. 2003. *Yan Qin wenhua yanjiu: Chen Ping xueshu wenji* 燕秦文化研究：陳平學術文集. Beijing: Beijing Yanshan chubanshe.

———. 2004. *Guanlong wenhua yu Ying Qin wenming* 關隴文化與嬴秦文明. Nanjing: Fenghuang chubanshe.

Chen Shuang 陳爽. 2004. "Zoumalou Wu jian suojian nubi huji ji xiangguan wenti" 走馬樓吳簡所見奴婢戶籍及相關問題. In Beijing Wujian yantaoban 北京吳簡研討班, ed., *Wujian yanjiu* 吳簡研究, vol. 1. Wuhan: Chongwen shuju, 160–166.

Chen Songchang 陳松長. 2009. "Yuelu shuyuan suo cang Qin jian zongshu" 嶽麓書院所藏秦簡綜述. *Wenwu* 文物 3: 75–84.

———. 2010. "Yuelu shuyuan cang Qin jian 'Wei li zhi guan ji qianshou' lue-shuo" 嶽麓書院藏秦簡《為吏之官及黔首》略說. *Chutu wenxian yanjiu* 出土文獻研究 9: 30–36.

Chen Wei 陳偉. 2009. "Guanyu Qin jiandu zonghe zhengli yu yanjiu de ji dian sikao" 關於秦簡牘綜合整理研究的幾點思考. *Jianbo* 簡帛 4: 1–10.

———, ed. 2012. *Liye Qin jiandu jiaoshi (di yi juan)* 里耶秦簡牘校釋(第一卷). Wuhan: Wuhan daxue chubanshe.

Chunqiu Zuozhuan zhu 春秋左傳注. 1981. Annotated by Yang Bojun 楊伯峻. Beijing: Zhonghua shuju.

Ciarla, Roberto. 2005. *The Eternal Army: The Terracotta Army of the First Chinese Emperor.* White Star: Vercelli.

Connerton, Paul. 1989. *How Societies Remember.* Cambridge: Cambridge University Press.

Cook, Constance A. 1999. "The Ideology of the Chu Ruling Class: Ritual Rhetoric and Bronze Inscriptions." In Constance A. Cook and John S. Major, eds., *Defining Chu: Image and Reality in Ancient China.* Honolulu: University of Hawai'i Press, 67–76.

Cotton, Hanna M., and Alexander Yakobson. 2002. "Arcanum Imperii: The Powers of Augustus." In Gillian Clark and Tessa Rajak, eds., *Philosophy and Power in the Graeco-Roman World.* Oxford: Oxford University Press, 193–209.

Csikszentmihalyi, Mark, and Michael Nylan. 2003. "Constructing Lineages and Inventing Traditions through Exemplary Figures in Early China." *T'oung Pao* 89.1–3: 59–99.

Cullen, Christopher. 2007. "The *Suàn shù shū* 算數書, 'Writings on Reckoning': Rewriting the History of Early Chinese Mathematics in the Light of an Excavated Manuscript." *Historia Mathematica* 34: 10–44.

Dai Chunyang 戴春陽. 2000. "Lixian Dabuzishan Qingong mudi ji youguan wenti" 禮縣大堡子山秦公墓地及有關問題. *Wenwu* 文物 5: 74–80.

Dai Guoxi 代國璽. 2012. "Keng ru yi shi zhenwei bian—yu Li Kaiyuan xian-sheng shangque" 坑儒一事真偽辨—與李開元先生商榷. *Shixue jikan* 史學集刊 1: 105–112.

Diamond, Jared M. 2005. *Collapse: How Societies Choose to Fail or Succeed.* New York: Viking.

Di Cosmo, Nicola. 2002. *Ancient China and Its Enemies.* Cambridge: Cambridge University Press.

Ding Nan 丁楠. 2008. "Qianxi Qin chao miewang de yuanyin—jianyi Qin chao zhidu goujian ji shishi queshi" 淺析秦朝滅亡的原因—兼議秦朝制度構建及實施的缺失. *Jiaoyu wenhua* 教育文化 5: 217–218.

Du Bin 堵斌 *and Gao Qun* 高群. 2009. "Jindai yilai 'Fenshu kengru' yanjiu zongshu" 近代以來"焚書坑儒"研究綜述. *Wulumuqi zhiye daxue xuebao* 烏魯木齊職業大學學報 1: 59–62.

Du Zhengsheng 杜正勝. 1990. *Bianhu qimin: chuantong zhengzhi shehui jiegou zhi xingcheng* 編戶齊民: 傳統政治社會結構之形成. Taibei: Lianjing.

Duan Qingbo 段清波. 2011. *Qin Shihuangdi lingyuan kaogu yanjiu* 秦始皇帝陵園考古研究. Beijing daxue chubanshe.

Dubs, Homer H., trans. 1938/1955. *History of the Former Han Dynasty*. 3 vols. Baltimore: Waverly Press.

Du duan 獨斷. By Cai Yong 蔡邕 (133–192 CE). Electronic *Siku quanshu* 四庫全書 (e-Siku) edition.

Dull, Jack L. 1983. "Anti-Qin Rebels: No Peasant Leaders Here." *Modern China* 9.3: 285–318.

Dunhuang Xuanquan Han jian shicui 敦煌懸泉漢簡釋粹. 2001. Edited by Hu Pingsheng 胡平生 and Zhang Defang 張德芳. Shanghai: Shanghai guji chubanshe.

Durrant, Stephen. 1994. "Ssu-ma Ch'ien's Portrayal of the First Ch'in Emperor." In Frederick P. Brandauer and Chun-chieh Huang, eds., *Imperial Rulership and Cultural Change in Traditional China*. Seattle and London: University of Washington Press, 28–50.

Du 'Tongjian' lun 讀《通鑑》論. 1998. By Wang Fuzhi 王夫之 (1619–1692). Beijing: Zhonghua shuju.

Duyvendak, J. J. L., trans. 1928. *The Book of Lord Shang: A Classic of the Chinese School of Law*. London: Probsthain.

Ebrey, Patricia, B., Anne Walthall, and James B. Palais. 2006. *Pre-Modern East Asia to 1800: A Cultural, Social, and Political History*. Boston: Houghton Mifflin.

Eck, Werner. 2007. *The Age of Augustus*. 2nd ed. Oxford: Wiley-Blackwell.

Eno, Robert. 2009. "Shang State Religion and the Pantheon of the Oracle Texts." In John Lagerwey and Marc Kalinowski, eds., *Early Chinese Religion: Part One: Shang through Han (1250 BC–220 AD)*. Leiden: Brill, 1: 41–101.

Erasmus, Charles. 1965. "Monument Building: Some Field Experiments." *Southwestern Journal of Anthropology* 21: 277–301.

Ess, Hans van. 2004. "Éducation classique, éducation légiste sous le Han." In Christine Nguyen Tri and Catherine Despeux, eds., *Éducation et Instruction en Chine III. Aux marges de l'orthodoxie*. Paris: Bibliothèque de l'INALCO 6, 23–43.

———. 2005/6. "Some Preliminary Notes on the Authenticity of the Treatise on Music in *Shiji* 24." *Oriens Extremus* 45: 48–67.

Falkenhausen, Lothar von. 1991. "Chu Ritual Music." In Thomas Lawton, ed., *New Perspectives on Chu Culture During the Eastern Zhou Period*. Washington, DC: Smithsonian Institution, Arthur M. Sackler Gallery, and Princeton University Press, 47–106.

———. 1992. "On the Early Development of Chinese Musical Theory: The Rise of Pitch Standards." *Journal of the American Oriental Society* 112.3: 433–439.

——. 1999. "The Waning of the Bronze Age: Material Culture and Social Developments 770–481 BC." In Michael Loewe and Edward L. Shaughnessy, eds., *The Cambridge History of Ancient China*. Cambridge: Cambridge University Press, 352–544.

——. 2004. "Mortuary Behavior in Pre-imperial Qin: A Religious Interpretation." In John Lagerwey, ed., *Religion and Chinese Society. Volume 1: Ancient and Medieval China*. Hong Kong: Chinese University of Hong Kong Press, 109–172.

——. 2006. *Chinese Society in the Age of Confucius (1050–250 BC): The Archeological Evidence*. Los Angeles: Cotsen Institute of Archaeology, UCLA.

——. 2008a. "Archaeological Perspectives on the Philosophicization of Royal Zhou Ritual." In Dieter Kuhn and Helga Stahl, eds., *Perceptions of Antiquity in Chinese Civilization*. Heidelberg: Edition Forum, 135–175.

——. 2008b. "Le culte des ancêtres et le culte du tombeau à Qin: Repères archéologiques et interprétation religieuse." In Alain Thote and Lothar von Falkenhausen, eds., *Les Soldats de l'éternité: L'armée de Xi'an*. Paris: Pinacothèque de Paris, 33–45.

——. 2008c. "Les origines ethniques des Qin: Perspectives historiques et archéologiques." In Alain Thote and Lothar von Falkenhausen, eds., *Les Soldats de l'éternité: L'armée de Xi'an*. Paris: Pinacothèque de Paris, 47–54.

——. 2009. "The Xinzheng Bronzes and Their Funerary Contexts." *Zhongguo Wenhua Yanjiusuo xuebao tekan* 中國文化研究所學報特刊 2: 1–130. Hong Kong: Chinese University of Hong Kong.

Fang Bao 方苞 (1668–1749). 1964. *Shiji zhu buzheng* 史記注補正. Baibu congshu 百部叢書集成 edition. Taibei: Yiwen.

Fang Bao ji 方苞集. 1983. By Fang Bao 方苞 (1668–1749). Collated by Liu Jigao 劉季高. Shanghai: Shanghai guji chubanshe.

Feinman, Gary M., Linda M. Nicholas, and Fang Hui. 2010. "The Imprint of China's First Emperor on the Distant Realm of Eastern Shandong." *Proceedings of the National Academy of Sciences* 107.11: 4851–4856.

Feng Li 馮莉. 2006. "Li yu Qin ren sangzang xisu" 禮與秦人喪葬習俗. *Wenbo* 文博 3: 31–33.

Flannery, Kent V. 1968. "Archaeological Systems Theory and Early Mesoamerica." In Betty J. Meggers, ed., *Anthropological Archaeology in the Americas*. Washington, DC: Archaeological Society of Washington, 67–87.

——. 1972. "The Cultural Evolution of Civilizations." *Annual Review of Ecology and Systematics* 3: 399–426.

Forke, Alfred. 1962 [1907]. *Lun-hêng: Philosophical Essays of Wang Ch'ung*. 2 vols. Rpt. ed. New York: Paragon Book Gallery.

Fujita Katsuhisa 藤田勝久. 1997. *Shiki Sengoku shiryō no kenkyū* 史記戰國史料の研究. Tōkyō: Tōkyō University Press.

——. 2010. "Liye Qin jian yu Qin dai zhengfu de yunzuo" 里耶秦簡與秦代政府的運作. In Qin Shihuang Bingmayong Bowuguan 秦始皇兵馬俑博物館, ed., *Qin yong Bowuguan kaiguan sanshi zhounian,Qinyongxue di qi jie nianhui, Guoji xueshu yantaohui lunwenji* 秦俑博物館開館三十周年,秦俑學第七屆年會, 國際學術研討會論文集. Xi'an: San Qin chubanshe, 449–459.

Fujita Takao 藤田高夫. 2001. "Qin Han fajin kao" 秦漢罰金考. Translated by Yang Zhenhong 楊振紅. *Jianbo yanjiu 2001* 簡帛研究 2001: 602–613.

Gansu Sheng Wenwu Gongzuodui 甘肅省文物工作隊 and Beijing Daxue Kaoguxuexi 北京大學考古學系. 1987. "Gansu Gangu Maojiaping yizhi fajue baogao" 甘肅甘谷毛家坪遺址發掘報告. *Kaogu xuebao* 考古學報 3: 359–396.

Gansu Sheng Wenwu Kaogu Yanjiusuo 甘肅省文物考古研究所. 1997. "Gansu Qin'an Shangyuanjia Qin Han muzang fajue" 甘肅秦安上袁家秦漢墓葬發掘. *Kaogu xuebao* 考古學報 1: 57–77.

Gansu Sheng Wenwu Kaogu Yanjiusuo 甘肅省文物考古研究所 and Lixian Bowuguan 禮縣博物館. 2002. "Lixian Yuandingshan chunqiu Qin mu" 禮縣圓頂山春秋秦墓. *Wenwu* 文物 2: 4–30.

———. 2005. "Gansu Lixian Yuandingshan 98LDM2. 2000LD4 Chunqiu Qin mu" 甘肅禮縣圓頂山98LDM2. 2000LDM4春秋秦墓. *Wenwu* 文物 2: 4–27.

Gansu Sheng Wenwu Kaogu Yanjiusuo 甘肅省文物考古研究所, Zhongguo Guojia Bowuguan 中國國家博物館, Beijing Daxue Kaogu Wenbo Xueyuan 北京大學考古文博學院, et al. 2008. *Xihanshui shangyou kaogu diaocha baogao* 西漢水上游考古調查報告. Beijing: Wenwu chubanshe.

Gao Dalun 高大倫. 1998. "Yinwan Han mu mudu jibu zong hukou tongji ziliao yanjiu尹灣漢墓木牘集簿中戶口統計資料研究." *Lishi yanjiu* 歷史研究 5: 110–123.

Gao Min 高敏. 1998. "Qin Han de huji zhidu" 秦漢的戶籍制度. In Gao Min, *Qin Han shi tantao* 秦漢史探討. Zhengzhou: Zhongzhou guji chubanshe, 156–173.

Ge Jianxiong 葛劍雄. 1986. *Liang Han renkou dili* 兩漢人口地理. Beijing: Renmin chubanshe.

———. 2002. *Zhongguo renkou shi* 中國人口史. Shanghai: Fudan daxue chubanshe.

Ge Quan 葛荃. 2003. *Quanli zaizhi lixing: shiren, chuantong zhengzhi wenhua yu Zhongguo shehui* 權力宰制理性—士人、傳統政治文化與中國社會. Tianjin: Nankai daxue chubanshe.

Giele, Enno. 2005. "Signatures of 'Scribes' in Early Imperial China." *Asiatische Studien/Études Asiatiques* 59.1: 353–387.

Goldin, Paul R. 1999. *Rituals of the Way: The Philosophy of Xunzi*. Chicago: Open Court.

———. 2011. "Persistent Misconceptions about Chinese 'Legalism,'" *Journal of Chinese Philosophy* 38.1: 64–80.

———. 2012. "Han Law and the Regulation of Interpersonal Relations: 'The Confucianization of the Law' Revisited." *Asia Major* 25.1: 1–31.

Goldman, Merle. 1975. "China's Anti-Confucian Campaign. 1973–74." *The China Quarterly* 63: 435–462.

Goldstone, Jack A., and John F. Haldon. 2009. "Ancient States, Empires and Exploitation: Problems and Perspectives." In Ian Morris and Walter

Scheidel, eds., *The Dynamics of Ancient Empires: State Power from Assyria to Byzantium*. Oxford: Oxford University Press, 3–29.

Graham, Angus C. 1989. *Disputers of the Tao: Philosophical Argument in Ancient China*. Chicago and La Salle, IL: Open Court.

Guan Donggui 管東貴. 1998. "Qin Han fengjian yu jun xian you xiaochang dao tonghe guocheng zhong de xueyuan qingjie" 秦漢封建與郡縣由消長到統合過程中的血緣情結. *Yanjing xuebao* 燕京學报, n.s. 5: 1–31.

Guanju Qin Han mu jiandu 關沮秦漢墓簡牘. 2001. Published by Hubei Sheng Jingzhoushi Zhouliangyuqiao yizhi Bowuguan 湖北省荆州市周梁玉橋遺址博物館. Beijing: Wenwu chubanshe.

Guojia Wenwuju 國家文物局. 2007. *2006 Zhongguo zhongyao kaogu faxian* 2006 中國重要考古發現. Beijing: Wenwu chubanshe.

Han Wei 韓偉. 1986. "Guanyu Qin ren zushu wenhua yuanyuan guanjian" 關於秦人族屬文化淵源管見. *Wenwu* 文物 4: 23–28. Rpt. in Han Wei 韓偉, *Moyan shugao: Han Wei kaogu wenji* 磨硯書稿: 韓偉考古文集, Beijing: Kexue chubanshe: 2001, 20–26.

———. 2007. "Jiekai Chang'an Shenheyuan damu zhuren zhi mi" 揭開長安神禾塬大墓主人之謎. *Shaanxi Lishi Bowugun guankan* 陝西歷史博物館館刊 14: 31–33.

Han Wei 韓偉 and Jiao Nanfeng 焦南峰. 1988. "Qin du Yongcheng kaogu zongshu" 秦都雍城考古綜述. *Kaogu yu wenwu* 5/6: 111–127.

Hansen, Valerie. 2000. *The Open Empire: A History of China to 1600*. New York: Norton.

Hanshu 漢書. 1997. By Ban Gu 班固 (32–92 CE) et al. Annotated by Yan Shigu 顏師古. Beijing: Zhonghua shuju.

Hardy, Grant. 1999. *Worlds of Bronze and Bamboo: Sima Qian's Conquest of History*. New York: Columbia University Press.

Hardy, Grant, and Anne B. Kinney. 2005. *The Establishment of the Han Empire and Imperial China*. Westport, CT: Greenwood Press.

Harper, Donald. 1985. "A Chinese Demonography of the Third Century B.C." *Harvard Journal of Asiatic Studies* 45: 459–498.

———. 1994. "Resurrection in Warring States Popular Religion." *Taoist Resources* 5.2: 13–28.

He Huaihong 何懷宏. 1996. *Shixi shehui ji qi jieti: Zhongguo lishi shang de Chunqiu shidai* 世襲社會及其解體: 中国歷史上的春秋時代. Beijing: San-lian shudian.

He Shuangquan 何雙全. 1989. "Tianshui Fangmatan Qin jian zongshu" 天水放馬灘秦簡綜述. *Wenwu* 文物 2: 23–31.

Heather, Peter. 2010. *Empires and Barbarians: The Fall of Rome and the Birth of Europe*. Oxford: Oxford University Press.

Hobsbawm, Eric J. 1992. *Nations and Nationalism since 1780: Programme, Myth, Reality*. 2nd ed. Cambridge: Cambridge University Press.

Hobsbawm, Eric J., and Terence Ranger, eds. 1983. *The Invention of Tradition*. Cambridge: Cambridge University Press.

Hosier, Dorothy, with Jeremy A. Sabloff and Dale Runge. 1977. "Simulation

Model Development: A Case Study of the Classic Maya Collapse." In Norman Hammond, ed., *Social Process in Maya Prehistory*. London: Academic Press, 553–590.

Hou Naifeng 侯乃峰. 2005. "Qin Yin daobing yuban mingwen jijie" 秦駰禱病玉版銘文集解. *Wenbo* 文博 6: 69–75.

Hsing I-t'ien (Xing Yitian 邢義田). 1988. "Qin Han huangdi yu 'shengren'" 秦漢皇帝與"聖人". In Yang Liansheng 楊聯陞, Quan Hansheng 全漢昇, and Liu Guangjing 劉廣京, eds., *Guoshi shilun—Tao Xisheng xiansheng jiuzhi rongqing zhushou lunwenji* 國史釋論—陶希聖先生九秩榮慶祝壽論文集. Taibei: Shihuo chubanshe, 389–406.

——. 1993. "Han dai biansai lizu de junzhong jiaoyu" 漢代邊塞吏卒的軍中教育. *Dalu zazhi* 大陸雜誌 87.3: 1–3.

——. 2002. "Shinian shumu, bainian shuren—Cong Yinwan chutu jiandu kan Han dai de 'zhongshu' yu 'yanglao'" 十年樹木, 百年樹人—從尹灣出土簡牘看漢代的"種樹"與"養老". In Song Wenxun 宋文薰, Li Yiyuan 李亦園, and Zhang Guangzhi 張光直, eds., *Shi Zhangru yuanshi baisui zhushou lunwenji—Kaogu, lishi, wenhua* 石璋如院士百歲祝壽論文集—考古、歷史、文化. Taibei: Nantian shuju, 531–551.

——. 2006. "Hunan Longshan Liye J1(8)157 he J1(9)1–12 hao Qin du de wenshu goucheng, biji he yuandang cunfang xingshi" 湖南龍山里耶J1(8)157 和J1(9)1–12 號秦牘的文書構成、筆跡和原檔存放形式. *Jianbo* 簡帛 1: 275–295.

——. 2007a. "Lun Mawangdui Han mu zhujuntu ying zhengming wei jiandao fengyutu" 論馬王堆漢墓駐軍圖應正名為箭道封域圖. *Hunan daxue xuebao (shehuikexue ban)* 湖南大學學報(社會科學版)5: 12–19. Expanded version: http://www.bsm.org.cn/show_article.php?id=772.

——. 2007b. "Han dai jiandu de tiji, zhongliang he shiyong—yi Zhongyanyuan Shiyusuo cang Juyan Han jian wei li" 漢代簡牘的體積、重量和使用—以中研院史語所藏居延漢簡為例. *Gujin lunheng* 古今論衡 17: 66–101.

——. 2009. "Xi Han huji shenfen chengwei cong 'daxiao nannüzi' bianwei 'daxiao nannü' de shijian" 西漢戶籍身份稱謂從"大小男女子"變為"大小男女"的時間. In http://www.bsm.org.cn/show_article.php?id=1171.

——. 2011. "Han dai *Cangjie*, *Jijiu*, bati he 'shishu' wenti—zailun Qin Han guanli ruhe xuexi wenzi" 漢代《蒼頡》、《急就》、八體和"史書"問題—再論秦漢官吏如何學習文字. In Hsing I-tien (Xing Yitian) 邢義田, *Zhi guo an bang: fazhi, xingzheng yu junshi* 治國安邦:法制、行政與軍事. Beijing: Zhonghua shuju, 595–654.

Hu Pingsheng 胡平生. 2005. "'Changsha Zoumalou sanguo Wu jian' di er juan shiwen jiaozheng" 《長沙走馬樓三國吳簡》第二卷釋文校證. *Chutu wenxian yanjiu* 出土文獻研究 7: 123–125.

——. 2009. "Liye Qin jian 8–455 hao mufang xingzhi chuyi" 里耶秦簡8–455 號木方性制芻議. *Jianbo* 簡帛 4: 17–25.

Hu Shi 胡適 1930. *Zhongguo zhonggu sixiang shi changpian* 中國中古思想史長篇. Rpt. in Ouyang Zhesheng 歐陽哲, ed., *Hu Shi wen ji* 胡適文集. Vol. 6: 423–668. Beijing: Beijing Daxue chubanshe, 1998.

Hu Yali 胡雅麗. 2002. "Churen bushi gaishu" 楚人卜筮概述. *Jianghan kaogu* 江漢考古 4: 70–74.

Huainanzi 淮南子, see *Huainan honglie jijie* 淮南鴻烈集解 (ca. 140 BCE). 1997. Compiled by Liu Wendian 劉文典, collated by Feng Yi 馮逸 and Qiao Hua 喬華. Beijing: Zhonghua shuju.

Huang Jinyan 黃今言. 1988. *Qin Han fuyi zhidu yanjiu* 秦漢賦役制度研究. Nanchang: Jiangxi jiaoyu chubanshe.

Huang Liuzhu 黃留珠. 2002. *Qin Han lishi wenhua lungao* 秦漢歷史文化論稿. Xi'an: San Qin chubanshe.

Huang, Ray. 1997. *China: A Macro History*. Armonk, NY: M. E. Sharpe.

Huang Shengzhang 黃盛璋. 1980. "Yunmeng Qin mu liangfeng jiaxin zhong youguan lishi dili de wenti" 雲夢秦墓兩封家信中有關歷史地理的問題. *Wenwu* 文物 8: 74–77.

Huang Xiaofen 黃曉芬. 1991. "Shin no bosei to sono kigen" 秦の墓制とその起源. *Shirin* 史林 74.6: 109–144.

———. 2003. *Han mu de kaoguxue yanjiu* 漢墓的考古學研究. Changsha: Yuelu shushe.

Huang Zhanyue 黃展岳. 2000. *Xian Qin Liang Han kaogu yu wenhua* 先秦兩漢考古與文化. Taibei: Yunchen wenhua.

———. 2004. *Gudai renxing renxun tonglun* 古代人牲人殉通論. Beijing: Wenwu chubanshe.

Huang Zhongye 黃中業. 2001. "Chongping Qin Shihuangdi" 重評秦始皇帝. *Shehuikexue zhanxian* 社會科學戰線 5: 159–165.

Hubei Sheng Wenwu Kaogu Yanjiusuo 湖北省文物考古研究所 and Yunmeng Xian Bowuguan 雲夢縣博物館. 2008. "Hubei Yunmeng Shuihudi M77 fajue jianbao" 湖北雲夢睡虎地M77發掘簡報. *Jianghan kaogu* 4: 31–37.

Hulsewé, A. F. P. 1955. *Remnants of Han Law, Vol. 1: Introductory Studies and Annotated Translation of Chapters 22 and 23 of the History of the Former Han Dynasty*. Leiden: Brill.

———. 1985. *Remnants of Ch'in Law: An Annotated Translation of the Ch'in Legal and Administrative Rules of the 3rd Century B.C. Discovered in Yünmeng Prefecture, Hu-pei Province, in 1975*. Leiden: Brill.

———. 1988. "The Wide Scope of Tao 盜 "Theft" in Ch'in-Han Law." *Early China* 13: 166–200.

Jiang Feifei 蔣非非. 2004. "*Shiji* zhong 'yingong tuxing' ying wei 'yinguan tuxing' ji 'yinguan' yuanyi bian" 史記中隱宮徒刑應為隱官徒刑及隱官原義辨. *Chutu wenxian yanjiu* 出土文獻研究 6: 136–139.

———. 2011. "Jiandu shiliao yu zaoqi Zhonghua diguo lixing xingzheng—yi Liye Qin jian 'Si Xiannong' jian weili" 簡牘史料與早期中華帝國理性行政—以里耶秦簡"祀先農"簡為例. Paper presented at the Second International Gansu Conference on Bamboo Slips, August 2011.

Jiangling Fenghuangshan Xi Han jiandu 江陵鳳凰山西漢簡牘. 2012. Edited by Hubei Sheng Wenwu Kaogu Yanjiusuo 湖北省文物考古研究所. Beijing: Zhonghua shuju.

Jiangling Yutaishan Chumu 江陵雨台山楚墓. 1984. Edited by Hubei Sheng

Jingzhou diqu Bowuguan 湖北省荊州地區博物館. Beijing: Wenwu chubanshe.

Jin Chunfeng 金春峯. 1993. *Zhouguan zhi chengshu ji qi fanying de wenhua yu shidai xinkao* 周官之成書及其反映的文化與時代新考. Taibei: Dongda Tushu Gongsi.

Jingzhou Bowuguan 荊州博物館. 2008. "Hubei Jingzhou Ji'nan Songbo Han mu fajue jianbao" 湖北荊州紀南松柏漢墓發掘簡報. *Wenwu* 文物 4: 24–32.

Juyan Han jian shiwen hejiao 居延漢簡釋文合校. 1987. Edited by Xie Guihua 謝桂華, Li Junming 李均明, and Zhu Guozhao 朱國炤. Beijing: Wenwu chubanshe, 2 vols.

Juyan xinjian 居延新簡. 1994. Published by Gansu Sheng Wenwu Kaogu Yanjiusuo 甘肅省文物考古研究所. Beijing: Zhonghua shuju.

Kalinowski, Marc. 1986. "Les Traités de Shuihudi et l'Hémérologie chinoise à la fin des Royaumes-combattants." *T'oung Pao* 72: 175–228.

———, ed. 2003. *Divination et société dans la Chine médiévale*. Paris: Bibliothèque nationale de France.

Kanaya Osamu 金谷治. 1981. *Shin Kan shisō shi kenkyū* 秦漢思想史研究. Tokyo: Nihon Gakujutsu Shinkōkai.

Keightley, David N. 1999. "The Shang: China's First Historical Dynasty." In: Michael Loewe and Edward L. Shaughnessy, eds., *The Cambridge History of Ancient China*. Cambridge: Cambridge University Press, 232–291.

Keightley, David. 2004. "The Making of the Ancestors: Late Shang Religion and Legacy." In John Lagerwey, ed., *Religion and Chinese Society, vol. 1: Ancient and Medieval China*. Hong Kong: Chinese University of Hong Kong Press, 3–63.

Kern, Martin. 1996. "In Praise of Political Legitimacy: The *miao* and *jiao* Hymns of the Western Han." *Oriens Extremus* 39.1: 29–67.

———. 2000. *The Stele Inscriptions of Ch'in Shih-huang: Text and Ritual in Early Chinese Imperial Representation*. New Haven: American Oriental Society.

Khayutina, Maria, ed. 2013. *Qin: The Eternal Emperor and His Terracotta Warriors*. Zürich: NZZ Libro.

Kim Yop (Jin Ye) 金燁. 1994. "'Qin jian' suojian zhi 'fei gongshi gao' yu 'jiazui'" 秦簡所見之非公室告與家罪. *Qin Han shi luncong* 秦漢史論叢 6: 156–166.

Kiser, Edgar, and Yong Cai. 2003. "War and Bureaucratization in Qin China: Exploring an Anomalous Case." *American Sociological Review* 68.4: 511–539.

Knoblock, John, and Jeffrey Riegel, trans. 2000. *The Annals of Lü Buwei: A Complete Translation and Study*. Stanford: Stanford University Press.

Kong Congzi jiaoshi 孔叢子校釋 (ca. 230 CE?). 2011. Collated by Fu Yashu 傅亞庶. Beijing: Zhonghua shuju.

Korolkov, Maxim. 2010. "Zemel'noe zakonodatel'stvo i kontrol' gosudarstva nad zemlej v epokhu Chzhan'go i v nachale ranneimperskoj epokhi (po dannym vnov' obnaruzhennykh zakonodatel'nykh tekstov)." Ph.D. thesis, Russian Academy of Sciences, Institute of Oriental Studies.

———. Forthcoming. "K voprosu ob interpretatsii tsin'skogo ukaza o poliakh 309 g. do n.e.: Zemel'naia reforma v Tsin' i formirovanie drevnekitajskoj imperii." *Vestnik drevnej istorii.*

Kroker, Eduard Josef. 1953. *Der Gedanke der Macht im Shang-kün-shu: Betrachtungen eines alten chinesischen Philosophen.* St. Gabrieler Studien 12. Vienna and Mödling: St. Gabriel-Verlag.

Lao Gan 勞榦. 1977. *Juyan Han jian—Tuban zhi bu* 居延漢簡—圖版之部. Taibei: Academia Sinica, Institute of History and Philology.

Lévi, Jean, trans. 2005. *Le livre du prince Shang.* Paris: Flammarion.

Lewis, Mark E. 1990. *Sanctioned Violence in Early China.* Albany: State University of New York Press.

———. 1999a. "Warring States: Political History." In Michael Loewe and Edward L. Shaughnessy, eds., *The Cambridge History of Ancient China.* Cambridge: Cambridge University Press, 587–650.

———. 1999b. *Writing and Authority in Early China.* Albany: State University of New York Press.

———. 2006. *The Construction of Space in Early China.* Albany: State University of New York Press.

———. 2007. *The Early Chinese Empires: Qin and Han.* Cambridge, MA: Harvard University Press.

Li Boqian. 1999. "The Sumptuary System Governing Western Zhou Rulers' Cemeteries, Viewed from a Jin Ruler's Cemetery." Trans. by Lothar von Falkenhausen. *Journal of East Asian Archaeology* 1.1–4: 251–276.

Li Changzhi 李長之. 2007. *Sima Qian zhi renge yu fengge* 司馬遷之人格與風格. Tianjin: Tianjin renmin chubanshe. (1st ed.: Kaiming shudian 開明書店, 1948.)

Li Feng. 2003. "'Feudalism' in Western Zhou China: A Criticism." *Harvard Journal of Asiatic Studies* 63.1: 115–144.

———. 2006. *Landscape and Power in Early China: The Crisis and Fall of the Western Zhou. 1045–771 BC.* Cambridge: Cambridge University Press.

———. 2008a. *Bureaucracy and the State in Early China: Governing the Western Zhou.* Cambridge: Cambridge University Press.

———. 2008b. "Transmitting Antiquity: The Origin and Paradigmization of the 'Five Ranks.'" In Dieter Kuhn and Helga Stahl, eds., *Perceptions of Antiquity in Chinese Civilization.* Würzburger Sinologische Schriften. Heidelberg: Edition forum, 103–134.

———. 2011. "Li Xian chutu Qinguo zaoqi tongqi ji jisi yizhi lungang" 禮縣出土秦國早期銅器及祭祀遺址論綱. *Wenwu* 文物 5: 55–67.

Li Jing 李靜. 2009. "Qin jiandu yanjiu lunzhu mulu" 秦簡牘研究論著目錄. *Jianbo* 簡帛 4: 73–122.

Li Junming 李均明. 2002a. "*Ernian lüling—Jülü zhong ying fenchu Qiulü tiaokuan*" 二年律令—具律中應分出囚律條款. *Zhengzhou daxue xuebao* 鄭州大學學報 3: 8–10.

———. 2002b. "Zhangjiashan Han jian nubi kao" 張家山漢簡奴婢考. *Guoji jiandu xuehui huikan* 國際簡牘學會會刊 2002.4: 1–11.

Li Junming 李均明 and He Shuangquan 何雙全, eds. 1990. *Sanjian jiandu heji* 散見簡牘合輯. Beijing: Wenwu chubanshe.

Li Junming 李均明 and Song Shaohua 宋少華. 2007. "'Changsha Zoumalou Sanguo Wu jian' zhujian 'si' neirong jiexi ba ze"《長沙走馬樓三國吳簡》竹簡[四]內容解析八則. *Chutu wenxian yanjiu* 出土文獻研究 8: 182–195.

Li Kaiyuan李開元, 2010. "Fenshu kengru de zhenwei xushi—bazhuang wei-zao de lishi" 焚書坑儒的真偽虛實—半椿偽造的歷史. *Shixue jikan* 史學集刊 6: 36–47.

Li Li 李力. 2007a. *"Li chenqie" shenfen zai yanjiu* "隸臣妾"身份再研究. Beijing: Zhongguo fazhi chubanshe.

———. 2007b. "Lun 'tuli' de shenfen—cong xinchu Liye Qin jian rushou" 論"徒隸"的身份—從新出土里耶秦簡入手. *Chutu wenxian yanjiu* 出土文獻研究 8: 33–42.

———. 2009. *Zhangjiashan 247 hao mu Han jian falü wenxian yanjiu ji qi shuping (1985.1-2008.12)* 張家山 247 號墓漢簡法律文獻研究及其述評 (1985.1-2008.12). Tokyo: Tōkyō Gaikoku daigaku Ajia Afurika gengo bunka kenkyūjo.

Li Ling 李零. 1999. "Qin Yin daobing yuban de yanjiu" 秦駰禱病玉版的研究. *Guoxue yanjiu* 國學研究 6: 525–547.

———. 2000a. *Zhongguo fangshu kao* 中國方術考. 2nd ed. Beijing: Dongfang chubanshe.

———. 2000b. "Qin Han cizhi tongkao" 秦漢祠時通考. In Li Ling, *Zhongguo fangshu xukao* 中國方術續考. Beijing: Dongfang chubanshe, 187–203.

———. 2008. "Shiri, rishu he yeshu—sanzhong jianbo wenxian de qubie he dingming" 視日, 日書和葉書—三種簡帛文獻的區別和定名. *Wenwu* 文物 12: 73–80.

———. 2012. "Beida Qindu *Qin yuan you sizhe* jianjie" 北大秦牘《秦原有死者》簡介. *Wenwu* 6: 81–84.

Li Mingzhao 黎明釗. 2009. "Liye Qin jian: huji dang'an de tantao" 里耶秦簡: 戶籍檔案的探討. *Zhongguo shi yanjiu* 中國史研究 2: 5–23.

Li Rui 李瑞 and Wu Hongqi 吳宏岐. 2003. "Qin Shihuang xunyou de shikong tezheng ji qi yuanyin fenxi" 秦始皇巡遊的時空特徵及其原因分析. *Zhong-guo lishi dili luncong* 中國歷史地理論叢 18.3: 130–138.

Li Taibai jizhu 李太白集注. By Li Bai 李白 (701–762); compiled by Qian Tang 錢塘 and Wang Qi 王琦. Electronic *Siku quanshu* 四庫全書 (e-Siku) edition.

Li, Xiuzhen Janice, Marcos Martinón-Torres, Nigel D. Meeks, Yin Xia, and Kun Zhao. 2011. "Inscriptions, Filing, Grinding and Polishing Marks on the Bronze Weapons from the Qin Terracotta Army in China." *Journal of Archaeological Science* 38.3: 492–501.

Li Xixing 李西興. 1994. *Shaanxi qingtongqi* 陝西青銅器. Xi'an: Shaanxi ren-min meishu chubanshe.

Li Xueqin. 1985. *Eastern Zhou and Qin Civilizations*. New Haven / London: Yale University Press.

———. 1990. "Fangmatan jian zhong de zhiguai gushi" 放馬灘簡中的志怪故事. *Wenwu* 文物 4: 43–47.

———. 2001. "Qin Huaihou qing yanjiu" 秦懷后磬研究. *Wenwu* 文物 1: 53–55.

———. 2011. "Tan Qin ren chu ju 'Zhuwu' de dili weizhi" 談秦人初居"邾吾"的地理位置. *Chutu wenxian* 出土文獻 2: 1–5.

Li Xueqin and Wen Xing. 2001. "New Light on the Early-Han Code: A Reappraisal of the Zhangjiashan Bamboo-Slip Legal Texts." *Asia Major,* 3rd series, 14.1: 125–146.

Li Yiyou 李逸友. 2001. "Zhongguo beifang changcheng kaoshu" 中國北方長城考述. *Neimenggu wenwu kaogu* 內蒙古文物考古 1: 1–51.

Li Yu-ning, ed. 1977. *Shang Yang's Reforms and State Control in China.* White Plans, NY: M. E. Sharpe.

Li Zhi 李贄 (1527–1602). 1974. *Cang shu* 藏書. Rpt. Beijing: Zhonghua shuju.

Lian Shaoming 連劭名. 1997. "Shangdai de rishu yu buri" 商代的日書與卜日. *Jianghan kaogu* 江漢考古 4: 56–63.

Liao Meiyun 廖美雲. 1995. *Tang ji yanjiu* 唐伎研究. Taibei: Taiwan xuesheng shuju.

Lin, Fu-shih. 2009. "The Image and Status of Shamans in Ancient China." In John Lagerwey and Marc Kalinowski, eds., *Early Chinese Religion, Part One: Shang through Han (1250 BC–220 AD),* vol. 1. Leiden: Brill, 397–458.

Lin Jianming 林劍鳴. 1981. *Qin shi gao* 秦史稿. Shanghai: Shanghai renmin chubanshe.

Lin Shifang 林世芳. 1998. "Qin Shihuang bu shi Zhongguo lishi shang di yi ge fengjian huangdi" 秦始皇不是中國歷史上第一個封建皇帝. *Fujian shida Fuqing fenxiao xuebao* 福建師大福清分校學報 1: 40–45.

Liu Cuirong 劉翠溶. 1998. "Qing dai laonian renkou yu yanglao zhidu chutan" 清代老年人口與養老制度初探. In Hao Yanping 郝延平 and Wei Xiumei 魏秀梅, eds., *Jindai Zhongguo zhi chuantong yu tuibian—Liu Guangjing yuanshi qishiwusui zhushou lunwenji* 近代中國之傳統與蛻變—劉廣京院士七十五歲祝壽論文集. Taibei: Zhongyang jindaishi yanjiusuo, 259–281.

Liu Dezhen 劉得楨 and Zhu Jiantang 朱建唐. 1981. "Gansu Lingtai Jingjiazhuang Chunqiu mu" 甘肅靈台景家莊春秋墓. *Kaogu* 考古 4: 298–301.

Liu Hainian 劉海年. 2006. *Zhanguo Qin dai fazhi guankui* 戰國秦代法制管窺. Beijing: Falü chubanshe.

Liu Hedong ji 柳河東集. By Liu Zongyuan 柳宗元 (773–819). Electronic *Siku quanshu* 四庫全書 (e-Siku) edition.

Liu Junshe 劉軍社. 1994. "Yijiabao leixing wenhua yu zaoqi Qin wenhua" 壹家堡類型文化與早期秦文化. *Qin wenhua luncong* 秦文化論叢 3: 396–409.

———. 2000. "Guanyu Chunqiu shiqi Qinguo tongqimu de zangshi wenti" 關於春秋時期秦國銅器墓的葬式問題. *Wenbo* 文博 2: 37–42.

Liu Lexian 劉樂賢. 1994. *Shuihudi Qin jian rishu yanjiu* 睡虎地秦簡日書研究. Taibei: Wenjin chubanshe.

Liu Min 劉敏. 2004. "Zhangjiashan Han jian 'xiaojue' yishi" 張家山漢簡"小爵"臆釋. *Zhongguoshi yanjiu* 中國史研究 3: 19–26.

Liu Rui 劉瑞. 2002. "Qin dai de 'yinguan' 'yingong' kao" 秦代的"隱官""隱宮"考. *Qin wenhua luncong* 秦文化論叢 9: 298–312.

Liu Tseng-kuei (Liu Zenggui). 2009. "Taboos: An Aspect of Belief in the Qin and Han." In John Lagerwey and Marc Kalinowski, eds., *Early Chinese Religion, Part One: Shang through Han (1250 BC–220 AD)*, vol. 2. Leiden: Brill, 881–948.

Liu Weimin 劉偉民. 1975. *Zhongguo gudai nubi zhidu shi (you Yin dai zhi Liang Jin Nanbeichao)* 中國古代奴婢制度史(由殷代至兩晉南北朝). Taibei: Longmen.

Liu Xinning 劉欣寧. 2008. "Liye huji jiandu yu 'xiao shangzao' zaitan" 里耶戶籍簡牘與"小上造"再探. http://www.bsm.org.cn/show_article.php?id=751.

Liu Zehua 劉澤華. 1991. *Zhongguo chuantong zhengzhi siwei* 中國傳統政治思維. Changchun: Jilin jiaoyu.

———. 1996. *Zhongguo zhengzhi sixiang shi (Qin Han Wei Jin Nanbeichao juan)* 中國政治思想史(秦漢魏晉南北朝卷). Hangzhou: Zhejiang renmin chubanshe.

———. 1998. "Wang, sheng xiangdang er fen yu he er wei yi–Zhongguo chuantong shehui yu sixiang tedian de kaocha zhi yi" 王、聖相當二分與合而為一中國傳統社會與思想特点的考察之一. *Tianjin shehui kexue* 天津社会科学 5: 66–74. (The Monarch and the Sage: Between Bifurcation and Unification of the Two" forthcoming in *Contemporary Chinese Thought*.)

———. 2000. *Zhongguo de Wangquanzhuyi* 中國的王權主義. Shanghai: Renmin chubanshe.

Liu Zenggui 劉增貴. 1998. "'Juyan Han jian bubian' de yixie wenti" 《居延漢簡補編》的一些問題. In Zhongyang yanjiuyuan lishi yuyan yanjiusuo 中央研究院歷史語言研究所, ed., *Juyan Han jian bubian* 居延漢簡補編. Taibei: Wenyuan.

———. 2001. "Qin jian rishu zhong chuxing lisu yu xingyang" 秦簡日書中出行禮俗與信仰. *Lishi yuyan yanjiu suo jikan* 歷史語言研究所集刊 72.3: 503–539.

Liu Zhaorui 劉昭瑞. 2005. "Qin Yin daobing yujian, wangji yu daojiao toulong yi" 秦駰禱病玉簡、望祭與道教投龍儀. *Sichuan wenwu* 四川文物 2: 44–47, 69.

Lixian Bowuguan 禮縣博物館 and Lixian Qin Xichui wenhua Yanjiuhui 禮縣秦西垂文化研究會. 2004. *Qin Xichui lingqu* 秦西垂陵區, ed. Zhu Zhongxi 祝中熹, Zhang Kuijie 張奎杰, and Wang Gang 王剛. Beijing: Wenwu chubanshe.

Liye fajue baogao 里耶發掘報告. 2007. Published by Hunan sheng wenwu kaogu yanjiusuo 湖南省文物考古研究所. Changsha: Yuelu shushe.

Liye Qin jian (yi) 里耶秦簡(壹). 2012. Published by Hunan sheng wenwu kaogu yanjiusuo 湖南省文物考古研究所. Beijing: Wenwu chubanshe.

Loewe, Michael. 1960. "The Orders of Aristocratic Rank of Han China." *T'oung Pao* 48.1–3: 97–174.

———. 1967. *Records of Han Administration. Volume II: Documents.* Cambridge: Cambridge University Press.

——. 1974. *Crisis and Conflict in Han China, 104 BC to AD 9*. London: George Allen and Unwin Ltd.

——. 1987. "The Religious and Intellectual Background." In Denis Twitchett and Michael Loewe, eds., *The Cambridge History of China. Vol 1: The Ch'in and Han Empires, 221 B.C. to A.D. 220*. Cambridge: Cambridge University Press, 649–725.

——. 1988. "The Almanacs (*Jih-shu*) from Shui-hu-ti: A Preliminary Survey." *Asia Major*, 3rd series, 1.2: 1–27. Rpt. in Loewe (1994): 214–235.

——. 1994. *Divination, Mythology, and Monarchy in Han China*. Cambridge: Cambridge University Press.

——. 1995. "The Cycle of Cathay: Concepts of Time in Han China and Their Problem." In Chun-chieh Huang and Erik Zürcher, eds., *Time and Space in Chinese Culture*. Leiden: Brill, 305–328.

——. 2001. *A Biographical Dictionary of the Qin, Former Han and Xin Periods (221 BC–AD 24)*. Leiden: Brill.

——. 2005. "On the Terms *bao zi, yin gong, yin guan, huan*, and *shou*: Was Zhao Gao a Eunuch?" *T'oung Pao* 91.4–5: 301–319.

——. 2010. "Social Distinctions, Groups and Privileges." In Michael Nylan and Michael Loewe, eds., *China's Early Empires: A Re-appraisal*. Cambridge: Cambridge University Press, 296–307.

Longgang Qin jian 龍崗秦簡. 2001. Published by Zhongguo Wenwu Yanjiusuo 中國文物研究所 and Hubei Sheng Wenwu Kaogu Yanjiusuo 湖北省文物考古研究所. Beijing: Zhonghua shuju.

Lopez, Donald S. Jr., ed. 1996. *Religions of China in Practice*. Princeton, NJ: Princeton University Press.

Lu Qingsong 陸青松. 2010. "Cong lizhi biange kan Qin guo de junzhu zhengzhi" 從禮制變革看秦國的君主政治. *Wenbo* 文博 1: 39–43.

Lu Yu 路遇 and Teng Zezhi 滕澤之. 1999. *Zhongguo renkou tongshi* 中國人口通史. Ji'nan: Shandong renmin chubanshe.

Luo Kaiyu 羅開玉. 2009. "Qin Han Sanguo shiqi de nuli—yi Chengdu weili" 秦漢三國時期的奴隸—以成都為例. *Chengdu daxue xuebao (Sheke ban)* 成都大學學報(社科版) 6: 9–18.

Luoyang Bowuguan 洛陽博物館. 1981. "Henan Luoyang Chunqiu mu" 河南洛陽春秋墓. *Kaogu* 考古 1: 24–47.

Lü Simian 呂思勉. 1969. *Qin Han shi* 秦漢史. Rpt. Taibei: Kaiming shudian, 2 vols.

Lüshi chunqiu jiaoshi 呂氏春秋校釋. 1990. Compiled and annotated by Chen Qiyou 陳奇猷. Shanghai: Xuelin chubanshe.

Mao Zedong 毛澤東, 1958. "Speeches at the Second Session of the Eighth Party Congress. The First Speech at the Eighth Party Congress." http://www.marxists.org/reference/archive/mao/selected-works/volume-8/mswv8_10.htm.

Marinelli, Maurizio. 2005. "Heroism/Terrorism: Empire Building in Contemporary Chinese Films." *Journal of Asian Cinema* 16.2: 183–209.

Martynov, Aleksandr S. 1987. "Konfutsianskaia Utopiia v Drevnosti i

Srednevekov'e." In Lev P. Deliusin and L. N. Borokh, eds., *Kitajskie Sotsial'nye Utopii*. Moscow: Nauka, 10–57.

Matsumaru Michio 松丸道雄. 1992. "Sei Shū jidai no jūryō tan'i" 西周時代の重量単位. *Tōkyō Daigaku Tōyō Bunka Kenkyūjo kiyō* 東京大學東洋文化研究所紀要 117 (Sōritsu gojūshūnen kinen ronshū 創立五十周年記念論集, vol. 2): 1–59. Translated by Cao Wei 曹瑋 as "Xi Zhou shidai de zhongliang danwei" 西周時代的重量單位. In Cao Wei 曹瑋, *Zhouyuan yizhi yu Xi Zhou tongqi yanjiu* 周原遺址與西周銅器研究. Beijing: Kexue chubanshe, 2004, 203–230.

Mattos, Gilbert L. 1988. *The Stone Drums of Ch'in*. Nettetal: Steyer Verlag.

McAnany, Patricia A., and Tomás Gallareta Negrón. 2009. "Bellicose Rulers and Climatological Peril? Retrofitting 21st Century Woes on 8th Century Maya Society." In Patricia A. McAnany and Norman Yoffee, eds., *Questioning Collapse: Human Resilience, Ecological Vulnerability, and the Aftermath of Empire*. Cambridge: Cambridge University Press, 142–175.

McKnight, Brian E., trans. 1981. Song Ci (Sung Tz'u), *Xiyuan Jilu: The Washing Away of Wrongs*. Ann Arbor: Center of Chinese Studies, University of Michigan Press.

McLeod, Katrina C. D., and Robin D. S. Yates. 1981. "Forms of Ch'in Law: An Annotated Translation of the *Feng-chen shih*." *Harvard Journal of Asiatic Studies* 41.1: 111–163.

Meltzer, Milton. 1993. *Slavery: A World History*. New York: Da Capo Press.

Mendels, Doron. 1992. *The Rise and Fall of Jewish Nationalism: Jewish and Christian Ethnicity in Ancient Palestine*. New York: Anchor Bible Reference Library.

———. 2004. *Memory in Jewish, Pagan and Christian Societies of the Graeco-Roman World*. London and New York: T. & T. Clark International.

Meng Yanhong 孟彥弘. 2006. "Wujian suojian 'shi' yi yishuo—cong 'shi' dao 'ke'" 吳簡所見"事"義臆說—從"事"到"課". *Wujian yanjiu* 吳簡研究 2: 201–213. Wuhan: Chongwen shuju.

Meng Xiangcai 孟祥才 and Wang Keqi 王克奇. 2004. *Qi Lu wenhua tongshi: Qin Han juan* 齊魯文化通史: 秦漢卷. Beijing: Zhonghua shuju.

Mengzi yizhu 孟子譯注. 1992. Annotated by Yang Bojun 楊伯峻. Beijing: Zhonghua shuju.

Miers, Suzanne. 2003. "Slavery: A Question of Definition." *Slavery and Abolition* 24.2: 1–16.

Millar, Fergus. 1973. "Triumvirate and Principate." *Journal of Roman Studies* 63: 50–67.

Ming Taizu wenji 明太祖文集, by Zhu Yuanzhang 朱元璋 (1328–1398). Electronic *Siku quanshu* 四庫全書 (e-Siku) edition.

Moriya Kazuki 森谷一樹. 2001. "Senkoku Shin no sōhō ni tsuite" 戰國秦の相邦について. *Tōyōshi kenkyū* 東洋史研究 60.1: 1–29.

Morris, Ian, and Walter Scheidel. 2009. *The Dynamics of Ancient Empires: State Power from Assyria to Byzantium*. Oxford: Oxford University Press.

Mozi jiaozhu 墨子校注. 1994. Compiled and annotated by Wu Yujiang 吳毓江. Beijing: Zhonghua shuju.

Mutschler, Fritz-Heiner, and Achim Mittag, eds. 2008. *Conceiving the Empire: China and Rome Compared.* Oxford: Oxford University Press.

Neininger, Ulrich. 1983. "Burying the Scholars Alive: On the Origin of a Confucian Martyrs' Legend." In Wolfram Eberhard, Krzysztof Galikowski, and Carl-Albrecht Seyschab, eds., *East Asian Civilizations: New Attempts at Understanding Traditions.* Vol. 2: *Nation and Mythology.* München: Simon and Magiera, 121–137.

Nienhauser, William. 1994-. *The Grand Scribe's Records,* vols. 1–8. Bloomington: Indiana University Press.

Nylan, Michael. 1999. "A Problematic Model: The Han 'Orthodox Synthesis,' Then and Now." In Kai-wing Chow, On-cho Ng, and John B. Henderson, eds., *Imagining Boundaries: Changing Confucian Doctrines, Texts, and Hermeneutics.* Albany: State University of New York Press, 17–56.

Ōba Osamu. 2001. "The Ordinances on Fords and Passes Excavated from Han Tomb #247, Zhangjiashan." Translated by David Spafford, Robin D. S. Yates, and Enno Giele, with Michael Nylan. *Asia Major,* 3rd series, 14.2: 119–141.

Oi, Jean C. 1999. *Rural China Takes Off: Institutional Foundations of Economic Reform.* Berkeley: University of California Press.

Okamura Hidenori 岡村秀典. 1985. "Shin bunka no hennen" 秦文化の編年. *Koshi shunjū* 古史春秋 2: 53–74.

———. 1991. "Sengoku kara Shin Kan he no monyō no tenkai" 戦国から秦漢への文様の展開. *Sen'oku Hakkokan kiyō* 泉屋博古館紀要 7: 48–69.

Patterson, Orlando. 1982. *Slavery and Social Death: A Comparative Study.* Cambridge, MA: Harvard University Press.

Peng Hao 彭浩. 2001. *Zhangjiashan Han jian* Suanshu shu *zhushi* 張家山漢簡《算數書》註釋. Beijing: Kexue chubanshe.

———. 2004. "Tan Ernian lüling zhong jizhong lü de fenlei yu bianlian" 談二年律令中幾種律的分類與編連. *Chutu wenxian yanjiu* 出土文獻研究 6: 61–69.

———. 2007. "Du Liye 'Ci Xiannong' jian" 讀里耶"祠先農"簡. *Chutu wenxian yanjiu* 出土文獻研究 8: 18–24.

———. 2009a. "Du Songbo chutu de Xi Han mudu (4)" 讀松柏出土的西漢木牘(四). http://www.bsm.org.cn/show_article.php?id=1019.

———. 2009b. "Du Yunmeng Shuihudi M77 Han jian Zang lü" 讀雲夢睡虎地 M77漢簡《葬律》. *Jianghan kaogu* 江漢考古 4: 130–134.

Peng Hao 彭浩, Chen Wei 陳偉, and Kudō Motoo 工藤元男, eds. 2007. *Ernian lüling yu Zouyan shu: Zhangjiashan ersiqi hao Han mu chutu falü wenxian shidu* 二年律令與奏讞書: 張家山二四七號漢墓出土法律文獻釋讀. Shanghai: Shanghai guji.

Perelomov, Leonard S. 1993. *Kniga Pravitelia Oblasti Shan (Shang jun shu).* Moscow: Ladomir.

Petersen, Jens Østergård. 1995. "Which Books Did the First Emperor of Ch'in

Burn? On the Meaning of *Pai Chia* in Early Chinese Sources." *Monumenta Serica* 43: 1–52.

Pines, Yuri. 2000. "'The One That Pervades All' in Ancient Chinese Political Thought: Origins of the 'Great Unity' Paradigm." *T'oung Pao* 86.4–5: 280–324.

———. 2002a. *Foundations of Confucian Thought: Intellectual Life in the Chunqiu Period, 722–453 AD.* Honolulu: University of Hawai'i Press.

———. 2002b. "Changing Views of *tianxia* in Pre-imperial Discourse." *Oriens Extremus* 43.1–2: 101–116.

———. 2004. "The Question of Interpretation: Qin History in Light of New Epigraphic Sources." *Early China* 29: 1–44.

———. 2005/6. "Biases and Their Sources: Qin History in the *Shiji*." *Oriens Extremus* 45: 10–34.

———. 2008a. "Imagining the Empire? Concepts of 'Primeval Unity' in Pre-imperial Historiographic Tradition." In Fritz-Heiner Mutschler and Achim Mittag, eds., *Conceiving the Empire: China and Rome Compared.* Oxford: Oxford University Press, 67–90.

———. 2008b. "To Rebel Is Justified? The Image of Zhouxin and Legitimacy of Rebellion in Chinese Political Tradition." *Oriens Extremus* 47: 1–24.

———. 2008c. "A Hero Terrorist: Adoration of Jing Ke Revisited." *Asia Major,* 3rd series, 21.2: 1–34.

———. 2009. *Envisioning Eternal Empire: Chinese Political Thought of the Warring States Era.* Honolulu: University of Hawai'i Press.

———. 2012a. *The Everlasting Empire: Traditional Chinese Political Culture and Its Enduring Legacy.* Princeton, NJ: Princeton University Press.

———. 2012b. "Alienating Rhetoric in the *Book of Lord Shang* and Its Moderation." *Extrême-Orient, Extrême-Occident* 34: 79–110.

———. 2012c. "From Historical Evolution to the End of History: Past, Present and Future from Shang Yang to the First Emperor." In Paul R. Goldin, ed., *Dao Companion to the Philosophy of Han Fei.* Berlin: Springer Verlag, 25–45.

———. 2013. "Reassessing Textual Sources for Pre-Imperial Qin History." In Maxim Korolkov and Sergej Dmitriev, eds., *Drevnij Kitaj: Istoria, Arkheologia, Kul'tura: Sbornik Statej v chest' 85-letiia S.R. Kuchery.* Moscow: Vostochnaia Literatura.

———. Forthcoming (a). "Introduction: Liu Zehua and Studies of China's Monarchism." In *Contemporary Chinese Thought,* special issue dedicated to Liu Zehua, ed. Yuri Pines and Carine Defoort.

———. Forthcoming (b). "Immobilized Emperor: 'Dynastic Cycles' Revisited."

Poo Mu-chou (Pu Muzhou) 蒲慕州. 1993a. "Shuihudi Qin jian *Ri shu* de shijie" 睡虎地秦簡《日書》的世界. *Zhongyang yanjiuyuan lishi yuyan yanjiusuo jikan* 中央研究院歷史語言研究所集刊 62.4: 623–675.

———. 1993b. *Muzang yu shengsi: Zhongguo gudai zongjiao zhi xingsi* 墓葬與生死:中國古代宗教之省思. Taibei: Lianjing. 2nd ed. Beijing: Zhonghua shuju, 2008.

——. 1998. *In Search of Personal Welfare: A View of Ancient Chinese Religion*. Albany: State University of New York Press.

——. 2005. "How to Steer through Life: Negotiating Fate in the *Daybook*." In Christopher Lupke, ed., *The Magnitude of Ming: Command, Allotment, and Fate in Chinese Culture*. Honolulu: University of Hawai'i Press, 107–125.

——. 2011. "Preparation for the Afterlife in Ancient China." In Philip J. Ivanhoe and Amy Olberding, eds., *Mortality in Traditional Chinese Thought*. Albany: State University of New York Press, 13–36.

Portal, Jane, ed. 2007. *The First Emperor*. Cambridge, MA: Harvard University Press / London: Trustees of the British Museum.

Powers, Martin J. 2006. *Pattern and Person: Ornament and Social Thought in Classical China*. Cambridge, MA: Harvard University Press East Asian Series.

Price, Simon R. F. 1996. "The Place of Religion: Rome in the Early Empire." In Alan K. Bowman, Edward Champlin, and Andrew Lintott, eds., *The Cambridge Ancient History*, vol. 10: *The Augustan Empire, 43 B.C.–A.D. 69*. Cambridge: Cambridge University Press, 812–847.

Puett, Michael J. 2001. *The Ambivalence of Creation: Debates concerning Innovation and Artifice in Early China*. Stanford: Stanford University Press.

——. 2002. *To Become a God: Cosmology, Sacrifice, and Self-Divinization in Early China*. Cambridge and London: Cambridge University Press.

Pulleyblank, Edwin G. 1958. "The Origins and Nature of Chattel Slavery in China." *Journal of the Economic and Social History of the Orient* 1: 185–220.

Qin Jianming 秦建明, Yang Zheng 楊政, and Zhao Rong 趙榮. 2006. "Shaanxi Jingyangxian Qin Zheng Guo qu shoulan heba gongcheng yizhi diaocha" 陝西涇陽縣秦鄭國渠首攔河壩工程遺址調查. *Kaogu* 考古 4: 12–21.

Qinghua daxue cang Zhanguo zhujian 清華大學藏戰國竹簡. 2011. Edited by Li Xueqin 李學勤. Vol. 2. Shanghai: Shanghai Wenyi chubanshe.

Qinyong Kaogudui 秦俑考古隊. 1980. "Lintong Shangjiaocun Qin mu qingli jianbao" 臨潼上焦村秦墓清理簡報. *Kaogu yu wenwu* 考古與文物 2: 42–50.

Qiu Xigui 裘錫圭. 1974. "Hubei Jiangling Fenghuangshan shihao Han mu chutu jiandu kaoshi" 湖北江陵鳳凰山十號漢墓出土簡牘考釋. *Wenwu* 文物 7: 49–63.

——. 2000. *Chinese Writing*. Translated by Gilbert L. Mattos and Jerry Norman. Berkeley: The Society for the Study of Early China.

Qu Yingjie 曲英杰. 1991. *Xian-Qin ducheng fuyuan yanjiu* 先秦都城復原研究. Harbin: Heilongjiang renmin chubanshe.

Rao Zongyi 饒宗頤. 1996. *Zhongguo shixue shang zhi zhengtong lun* 中國史學上之正統論. Shanghai: Yuandong.

Rawson, Jessica. 1990. *Western Zhou Ritual Bronzes from the Arthur M. Sackler Collections*. 2 parts. Ancient Chinese Ritual Bronzes in the Arthur M. Sackler Collections, vol. 2. Cambridge, MA: Harvard University Press.

——. 1999. "Western Zhou Archaeology." In Michael Loewe and Edward L. Shaughnessy, eds., *The Cambridge History of Ancient China*. Cambridge: Cambridge University Press, 352–449.

Ren Jianku 任建庫. 2007. "'Fusi' zakao" "伏祠""雜考. *Qin wenhua luncong* 秦文化論叢 15: 209–225.

Renfrew, Colin, and Paul Bahn. 1996. *Archaeology: Theories, Methods, and Practice.* 2nd ed. London: Thames and Hudson.

Rizhilu jishi 日志錄集釋. 1990. By Gu Yanwu 顧炎武 (1613–1682); annotated by Huang Rucheng 黃如成. Changsha: Yuelu shushe.

Rodin, Miriam, Karen Michaelson, and Gerald M. Britain. 1978. "System Theory in Anthropology." *Current Anthropology* 19.4: 747–762.

Sage, Steven F. 1992. *Ancient Sichuan and the Unification of China.* Albany: State University of New York Press.

Sanft, Charles. 2008. "The Construction and Deconstruction of Epanggong: Notes from the Crossroads of History and Poetry." *Oriens Extremus* 47: 160–176.

———. 2011. "Debating the Route of the Qin Direct Road (Zhidao): Text and Excavation." *Frontiers of History in China* 6.3: 323–346.

———. Forthcoming. *Communication and Cooperation in Early Imperial China: The Qin Dynasty and Publicity.* Albany: State University of New York Press.

———. In progress. "Population Records from Liye: Ideology in Practice." In Yuri Pines, Paul R. Goldin and Martin Kern, eds., *Ideology of Power and Power of Ideology in Early China.*

Sanfu Huangtu jiaozhu 三輔黃圖校注 (6th century CE?). 1998. Annotated by He Qinggu 何清谷, edited by Shaanxi Sheng Guji Zhengli Bangongshi 陝西省古籍整理辦公室. Xi'an: San Qin chubanshe.

Sato, Masayuki. 2003. *The Confucian Quest for Order: The Origin and Formation of the Political Thought of Xun Zi.* Leiden: Brill.

Schaab-Hanke, Dorothee. 2002. "The Power of an Alleged Tradition: A Prophecy Flattering Han Emperor Wu and Its Relation to the Sima Clan." *Bulletin of the Museum of Far Eastern Antiquities* 74: 243–290.

———. 2012. "'Waiting for the Sages of Later Generations': Is There a Rhetoric of Treason in the *Shiji?*" *Extrême-Orient, Extrême-Occident* 34: 111–140.

Schaberg, David. 2010. "The *Zhouli* as Constitutional Text." In Benjamin A. Elman and Martin Kern, eds., *Statecraft and Classical Learning:* The Rituals of Zhou *in East Asian History.* Leiden: Brill.

Scheidel, Walter, ed. 2009. *Rome and China: Comparative Perspectives on Ancient World Empires.* Oxford: Oxford University Press.

Schottenhammer, Angela. 2003. "Slaves and Forms of Slavery in Late Imperial China (Seventeenth to Early Twentieth Centuries)." *Slavery and Abolition* 24.2: 143–154.

Scott, James. C. 1998. *Seeing Like a State: How Certain Schemes to Improve the Human Condition Have Failed.* New Haven: Yale University Press.

Sellman, James D. 2002. *Timing and Rulership in Master Lü's Spring and Autumn Annals (Lüshi chunqiu).* Albany: State University of New York Press.

Shaanxi Sheng Kaogu Yanjiusuo 陝西省考古研究所. 2004. *Qin du Xianyang kaogu baogao* 秦都咸陽考古報告. Beijing: Kexue chubanshe.

Shaanxi Sheng Kaogu Yanjiusuo 陝西省考古研究所 and Lintong Xian Wenguanhui 臨潼縣文管會. 1987. "Qin Dongling yihao lingyuan kanchaji" 秦東陵一號陵園勘察記. *Kaogu yu wenwu* 考古與文物 4: 19–28.

Shaanxi Sheng Kaogu Yanjiusuo 陝西省考古研究所 and Lintong Xian Wenwu Guanli Weiyuanhui 臨潼縣文物管理委員會. 1990. "Qin Dongling di'erhao lingyuan diaocha zuantan jianbao" 秦東陵第二號陵園調查鑽探簡報. *Kaogu yu wenwu* 考古與文物 4: 22–30.

Shaanxi Sheng Kaogu Yanjiusuo Baoji Gongzuozhan 陝西省考古研究所寶雞工作站 and Baoji Shi Kaogu Gongzuodui 寶雞市考古工作隊. 1988. "Shaanxi Long Xian Bianjiazhuang wuhao Chunqiu mu fajue jianbao" 陝西隴縣邊家莊五號春秋墓發掘簡報. *Wenwu* 文物 11: 14–23.

Shaanxi Sheng Kaogu Yanjiusuo Yongcheng Gongzuozhan 陝西省考古研究所雍城工作站. 1991. "Fengxiang Dengjiaya Qin mu fajue jianbao" 鳳翔鄧家崖秦墓發掘簡報. *Kaogu yu wenwu* 考古與文物 2: 14–19.

Shaanxi Sheng Shehuikexueyuan Kaogu Yanjiusuo Fengxiang Dui 陝西省社會科學院考古研究所鳳翔隊. 1963. "Qin du Yong cheng yizhi kancha" 秦都雍城遺址勘查. *Kaogu* 考古 8: 419–422.

Shaanxi Sheng Wenguanhui 陝西省文管會 and Dali Xian Wenhuaguan 大荔縣文化館. 1978. "Chaoyi Zhanguo muzang fajue jianbao" 朝邑戰國墓葬發掘簡報. *Wenwu ziliao congkan* 文物資料叢刊 2: 75–91.

Shaanxi Sheng Wenwu Guanli Weiyuanhui 陝西省文物管理委員會. 1965. "Shaanxi Baoji Yangpingzhen Qinjiagou Qin mu fajue ji" 陝西寶雞陽平鎮秦家沟秦墓發掘記. *Kaogu* 考古 7: 339–346.

Shaanxi Sheng Yongcheng Kaogudui 陝西省雍城考古隊. 1985. "Qin du Yong cheng zuantan shijue jianbao" 秦都雍城鑽探試掘簡報. *Kaogu yu wenwu* 考古與文物 2: 7–20.

——. 1986a. "Shaanxi Fengxiang Baqitun Xigoudao Qin mu fajue jianbao" 陝西鳳翔八旗屯西沟道秦墓發掘簡報. *Wenbo* 文博 3: 1–31.

——. 1986b. "Yijiubayi nian Fengxiang Baqitun mudi fajue jianbao" 一九八一年鳳翔八旗屯墓地發掘簡報. *Kaogu yu wenwu* 考古與文物 5: 23–36.

Shang jun shu zhuizhi 商君書錐指. 1996. Annotated by Jiang Lihong 蔣禮鴻. Beijing: Zhonghua shuju.

Shang shu zhengyi 尚書正義. 1991. Annotated by Kong Yingda 孔穎達. In Ruan Yuan 阮元, comp., *Shisanjing zhushu* 十三經注疏. Beijing: Zhonghua shuju, 1:109–258.

Shaughnessy, Edward L. 1996. "Military Histories of Early China: A Review Article." *Early China* 21: 159–182.

Shelach, Gideon. 2009. *Prehistoric Societies on the Northern Frontiers of China: Archaeological Perspectives on Identity Formation and Economic Change during the First Millennium* BCE. Approaches to Anthropological Archaeology Series. London: Equinox.

Shelach, Gideon, and Yuri Pines. 2005. "Power, Identity and Ideology: Reflections on the Formation of the State of Qin (770–221 BCE)." In Miriam Stark, ed., *An Archaeology of Asia*. Oxford: Blackwell Publishers, 202–230.

Shen Kangshen, John N. Crossley, and Anthony W.-C. Lun. 1999. *The Nine Chapters on Mathematical Arts*. Oxford: Oxford University Press.

Sherwin-White, Adrian. N. 1973. *Roman Citizenship*. Oxford: Clarendon Press.

Shi Weiqing 施偉青. 2004a. "Qin Han shiqi de sijia nubi xintan" 秦漢時期的私家奴婢新探. In Shi Weiqing, *Zhongguo gudai shi luncong* 中國古代史論叢: 171–182. Changsha: Yuelu shushe.

———. 2004b. "Yelun Qin 'Shiwu' de shenfen" 也論"士伍"的身份. In Shi Weiqing, *Zhongguo gudai shi luncong* 中國古代史論叢. Changsha: Yuelu shushe, 43–63.

———. 2004c. "Lun Qin zi Shang Yang bianfa hou de taowang xianxiang" 論秦自商鞅變法後的逃亡現象. *Zhongguo shehui jingji shi yanjiu* 中國社會經濟史研究 2: 39–46.

Shi Zhilong 史志龍 2009. "Qin 'Ci Xiannong' jian zaitan" 秦"祠先農"簡再探. http://www.bsm.org.cn/show_article.php?id=1081.

Shiji 史記. 1997. By Sima Qian 司馬遷 (ca. 145–90 BCE) et al. Annotated by Zhang Shoujie 張守節, Sima Zhen 司馬貞, and Pei Yin 裴駰. Beijing: Zhonghua shuju.

Shuihudi Qin mu zhujian 睡虎地秦墓竹簡. 2001 [1990]. Published by Shuihudi Qin mu zhujian zhengli xiaozu 睡虎地秦墓竹簡整理小組. Beijing: Wenwu chubanshe.

Shuijing zhu jiao 水經注校. 1984. Annotated by Li Daoyuan 酈道元 (ca. 470–527), collated by Wang Guowei 王國維. Shanghai: Shanghai renmin chubanshe.

Sommer, Deborah. 1995. *Chinese Religion: An Anthology of Sources*. Oxford: Oxford University Press.

Song Liheng 宋立恒. 2007. "Dui tongyi hou de Qin wangchao suwang yuanyin de zai fenxi" 對統一後的秦王朝速亡原因的再分析. *Neimenggu minzu daxue xuebao* 內蒙古民族大學學報 33.5: 5–8.

Song Yanping 宋艷萍. 2004. "Cong *Ernian lüling* zhong de 'zi' kan Qin-Han jingji chufa xingshi de zhuanbian" 從二年律令中的訾看秦漢經濟處罰形式的轉變. *Chutu wenxian yanjiu* 出土文獻研究 6: 147–149.

Song Zhimin 宋治民. 1993. *Zhanguo Qin Han kaogu* 戰國秦漢考古. Chengdu: Sichuan daxue chubanshe.

Sterckx, Roel. 2011. *Food, Sacrifice, and Sagehood in Early China*. Cambridge: Cambridge University Press.

Su Weiguo 蘇衛國. 2010. "Xi Han Jiangxia jun yange lue kao—cong Ji'nan Songbo Han mu jiandu shuo qi" 西漢江夏郡沿革略考—從紀南松柏漢墓簡牘說起. *Xueshu jiaoliu* 學術交流 5: 184–188.

Suizhou Kongjiapo Han jiandu 隨州孔家坡漢墓簡牘. 2006. Published by Hubei Sheng Wenwu Kaogu Yanjiusuo 湖北省文物考古研究所 and Suizhou Shi Kaogudui 隨州市考古隊. Beijing: Wenwu chubanshe.

Sun Weizu 孫慰祖. 1994. *Gu fengni jicheng* 古封泥集成. Shanghai: Shanghai shudian chubanshe.

Suzuki Naomi 鈴木直美. 2008. "Riya Shinkan ni miru Shin no kokō haaku-dōkyo shitsujin saikō" 里耶秦簡にみる秦の戸口把握—同居,室人再考. *Tōyō gakuhō* 東方學報 89.4: 1–31.

Swann, Nancy Lee. 1950. *Food and Money in Ancient China*. Princeton, NJ: Princeton University.

Talmon, Jacob L. 1960. *Political Messianism: The Romantic Phase*. London: Secker & Warburg.

Tan Qixiang 譚其驤, ed., 1991. *Zhongguo lishi ditu ji* 中國歷史地圖集. Hong Kong: Sanlian shudian.

Teng Mingyu 滕銘予. 1993. "Lun Guanzhong Qin mu zhong dongshimu de niandai" 論關中秦墓中洞室墓的年代. *Huaxia kaogu* 華夏考古 2: 90–97.

———. 1999. *Lun Dongzhou shiqi Qin wenhua de fazhan yu kuozhang: Zhong-guo kaoguxue de kuashiji fansi* 論東周時期秦文化的發展與擴張: 中國考古學的跨世紀反思. Hong Kong: Shangwu yinshuguan.

———. 2002. "Dianzi mudi de xingcheng yu fazhan ji xiangguan wenti taolun" 店子墓地的形成與發展及相關問題討論. *Kaogu yu wenwu* 考古與文物 supplement, 286–298.

———. 2003. *Qin wenhua: cong fengguo dao diguo de kaoguxue guancha* 秦文化: 從封國到帝國的考古學觀察. Beijing: Xueyuan chubanshe.

———. 2004. "Xianyang Ta'erpo Qin mudi zai tantao" 咸陽塔兒坡秦墓地再探討. *Beifang wenwu* 北方文物 4: 7–14.

———. 2009. "Renjiazui Qin mudi xiangguan wenti yanjiu" 任家咀秦墓地相關問題研究. In Jilin Daxue bianjiang kaogu yanjiu zhongxin 吉林大學邊疆考古研究中心, ed., *Xin guoji: Qingzhu Lin Yun xiansheng qishi huadan lunwenji* 新果集:慶祝林沄先生七十華誕論文集. Beijing: Kexue chubanshe, 389–411.

Thatcher, Melvin P. 1985. "Central Government of the State of Ch'in in the Spring and Autumn Period." *Journal of Oriental Studies* 23.1: 29–53.

———. 1988. "The Case of the Five Sheepskins Grandee." *Journal of the American Oriental Society* 108.1: 27–49.

Thierry, François. 2008. "L'unification monétaire de Qin Shihuangdi: Abou-tissement d'un processus ou rupture radicale?" In Alain Thote and Lothar von Falkenhausen, eds., *Les Soldats de l'éternité: L'armée de Xi'an*. Paris: Pinacothèque de Paris, 217–221.

Thorp, Robert L. 2006. *China in the Early Bronze Age: Shang Civilization*. Philadelphia: University of Pennsylvania Press.

Thote, Alain. 2009. "Shang and Zhou Burial Practices: Interpretation of Material Vestiges." In John Lagerwey and Marc Kalinowski, eds., *Early Chinese Religion, Part One, Shang through Han (1250 BC–AD 220)*. Volume 1. Leiden: Brill, 103–142.

Thote, Alain, and Lothar von Falkenhausen, eds. 2008. *Les soldats de l'éter-nité: L'armée de Xi'an*. Paris, Éditions de la Pinacothèque de Paris.

Tian Changwu 田昌五 and Zang Zhifei 臧知非. 1996. *Zhou Qin shehui jiegou yanjiu* 周秦社會結構研究. Xi'an: Xibei daxue chubanshe.

Tian Xudong 田旭東 2009. "Cong Liye Qin jian 'ci Xiannong' kan Qin de jici huodong" 從里耶秦簡"祠先農"看秦的祭祠活動. In Zhongguo Shehuikexueyuan Kaogu Yanjiusuo 中國社會科學院考古研究所等編 et al., eds., *Liye gucheng. Qin jian yu Qin wenhua yanjiu* 里耶古城.秦簡與秦文化研究. Beijing: Kexue chubanshe, 210–217.

Tianchang Shi Wenwu Guanlisuo 天長市文物管理所 and Tianchang Shi Bowuguan 天長市博物館. 2006. "Anhui Tianchang Xi Han mu fajue jianbao" 安徽天長西漢墓發掘簡報. *Wenwu* 文物 11: 4–21.

Tianshui Fangmatan Qin jian 天水放馬灘秦簡. 2009. Published by Gansu Sheng Wenwu Kaogu Yanjiusuo 甘肅省文物考古研究所. Beijing: Zhonghua shuju.

Tong Weimin 仝衛敏. 2013. *Chutu wenxian yu "Shang jun shu" zonghe yanjiu* 出土文獻與《商君書》綜合研究. Vols. 16–17 of Gudian wenxian yanjiu jikan 古典文獻研究輯刊, edited by Pan Meiyue 潘美月 and Du Jiexiang 杜潔祥. Taibei: Hua Mulan chubanshe.

Tongzhi 通志. By Zheng Qiao 鄭樵 (1104–1162). Electronic *Siku quanshu* 四庫全書 (e-Siku) edition .

Vankeerberghen, Griet. 2007. "Rulership and Kinship: The *Shangshu dazhuan*'s Discourse on Lords." *Oriens Extremus* 46: 84–100.

Venture, Olivier. 2008. "L'écriture de Qin." In Alain Thote and Lothar von Falkenhausen, eds., *Les Soldats de l'éternité: L'armée de Xi'an*. Paris: Pinacothèque de Paris, 209–215.

Wagner, Donald B. 1993. *Iron and Steel in Ancient China*. Leiden: Brill.

——. 2008. *Ferrous Metallurgy*. In Joseph Needham, ed., *Science and Civilisation in China*, vol. 5, pt. 11. Cambridge: Cambridge University Press.

Waldron, Arthur. 1990. *The Great Wall of China: From History to Myth*. Cambridge: Cambridge University Press.

Wallace-Hadrill, Andrew. 1982. "*Civilis Princeps*. Between Citizen and King." *Journal of Roman Studies* 72: 32–48.

Wan Changhua 萬昌華 and Zhao Xingbin 趙興彬. 2008. *Qin Han yilai jiceng xingzheng yanjiu* 秦漢以來基層行政研究. Ji'nan: Qilu shushe.

Wang Aiqing 王愛清. 2007. "'Sishu' xintan" "私屬"新探. *Shixue yuekan* 史學月刊 2: 28–32.

Wang Guihai 汪桂海. 1999. *Han dai guanwen shu zhidu* 漢代官文書制度. Guilin: Guangxi jiaoyu chubanshe.

Wang Guowei 王國維 (1877–1927). 2004. *Jiandu jianshukao jiaozhu* 簡牘檢署考校注, annotated by Hu Pingsheng 胡平生 and Ma Yuehua 馬月華. Shanghai: Shanghai guji chubanshe.

Wang Huanlin 王煥林. 2007. *Liye Qin jian jiaogu* 里耶秦簡校詁. Beijing: Zhongguo wenxian chubanshe.

Wang Hui 王輝. 1990. *Qin tongqi mingwen biannian jishi* 秦銅器銘文編年集釋. Xi'an: San Qin chubanshe.

———. 2000. *Qin chutu wenxian biannian* 秦出土文獻編年. Taibei: Xin wenfeng.

———. 2002. "*Qin chutu wenxian biannian xubu 1*"《秦出土文獻編年》續補(一). *Qin wenhua luncong* 秦文化論叢第 9: 512–549.

Wang Hui 王輝 and Cheng Xuehua 程學華. 1999. *Qin wenzi jizheng* 秦文字集證. Taibei: Yinwen.

Wang Hui 王輝 and Wang Wei 王偉. 2006. "*Qin chutu wenxian biannian xubu 2*"《秦出土文獻編年》續補(二). *Qin wenhua luncong* 秦文化論叢第 13: 203–266.

———. 2008. "*Qin chutu wenxian biannian xubu 4*"《秦出土文獻編年》續補(四), *Qin wenhua luncong* 秦文化論叢 15: 226–266.

Wang Hui 王輝 and Yang Zongbing 楊宗兵. 2007. "*Qin chutu wenxian biannian xubu 3*"《秦出土文獻編年》續補(三). *Qin wenhua luncong* 秦文化論叢第 14: 256–278.

Wang Jianhua 王建華. 2007. "Huanghe zhongxiayou diqu shiqian renkou nianling goucheng yanjiu" 黃河中下游地區史前人口年齡構成研究. *Kaogu* 考古 4: 63–73.

Wang Mingqin 王明欽. 2004. "Wangjiatai Qin mu zhujian gaishu" 王家台秦墓竹簡概述. in Sarah Allan (Ai Lan 艾蘭) and Xing Wen 邢文, eds., *Xinchu jianbo yanjiu* 新出簡帛研究. Beijing: Wenwu chubanshe, 26–49.

Wang Shaodong 王紹東. 2007. "Lun tongyi hou Qin lizhi baihuai de yuanyin ji yu Qin chao suwang zhi guanxi" 論統一後秦吏治敗壞的原因及與秦朝速亡之關係. *Xianyang Shifan Xueyuan xuebao* 咸陽示範學院學報 22.3: 15–22.

Wang Weihai 王威海. 2006. *Zhongguo huji zhidu—lishi yu zhengzhi de fenxi* 中國戶籍制度—歷史與政治的分析. Shanghai: Shanghai wenhua chubanshe.

Wang Xiaoguang 王曉光. 2012. "Tianchang Jizhuang mudu heiji yanjiu ji shuxie shijian xintan" 天長紀莊木牘黑跡研究及書寫時間新探. *Jianbo yanjiu 2010* 簡帛研究 2010: 89–98.

Wang Xiaoxuan 汪小烜. 2004. "Zoumalou Wu jian huji chulun" 走馬樓吳簡戶籍初論. *Wu jian yanjiu* 吳簡研究 1: 143–159.

Wang Xueli 王學理. 1994. *Qin yong zhuanti yanjiu* 秦俑專題研究. Xi'an: San Qin chubanshe.

———. 2009. "Jianping *Qin du Xianyang kaogu baogao*" 簡評《秦都咸陽考古報告》. *Qin Han yanjiu* 秦漢研究 3: 258–266.

———, ed. 1994. *Qin wuzhi wenhua shi* 秦物質文化史. Xi'an: San Qin chubanshe.

Wang Xueli 王學理 and Liang Yun 梁雲. 2001. *Qin wenhua* 秦文化. Beijing: Wenhua chubanshe.

Wang Yanhui 王彥輝. 2003. "Cong Zhangjiashan Han jian kan Xi-Han shiqi si nubi de shehui diwei" 從張家山漢簡看西漢時期私奴婢的社會地位. *Dongbei shida xuebao* 東北師大學報 2: 13–20. Rpt. in *Qin Han shi luncong* 秦漢史論叢 9: 232–146. Xi'an: San Qin chubanshe. 2004.

Wang Yundu 王雲度 and Zhang Liwen 張立文. 1997. *Qin diguo shi* 秦帝國史. Xi'an: Shaanxi renmin chubanshe.

Wang Zhongshu. 1982. *Han Civilization*. New Haven and London: Yale University Press.

Wang Zijin 王子今. 1987. "Qin ren quzhizang fangxiang quwo shuo" 秦人屈肢葬仿象窀卧說. *Kaogu* 考古 12: 1105–1106, 1114.

———. 2003. *Shuihudi Qin jian Ri shu jiazhong shuzheng* 睡虎地秦簡《日書》甲種疏證. Wuhan: Hubei jiaoyu chubanshe.

———. 2005. "Lun Qin Han Yongdi zhushi zhong de Yandi zhici" 論秦漢雍地諸時中的炎帝之祠. *Wenbo* 文博 6: 20–25.

———. 2008. "Qin Han 'xiaonüzi' chengwei zaiyi" 秦漢"小女子"稱謂再議. *Wenwu* 文物 5: 70–74.

Watson, Burton, trans. 1961. *Records of the Grand Historian of China: The Shih chi of Ssu-ma Ch'ien*. 2 vols. New York: Columbia University Press.

———. 1993. *Records of the Grand Historian. Vol. 3: Qin Dynasty*. Hong Kong: Chinese University of Hong Kong Press.

Webster, David. 2002. *The Fall of the Ancient Maya: Solving the Mystery of the Maya Collapse*. New York: Thames and Hudson.

Wei Huaiheng 魏懷珩. 1982. "Gansu Pingliang Miaozhuang de liang zuo Zhanguo mu" 甘肅平涼廟莊的兩座戰國墓. *Kaogu yu wenwu* 考古與文物 5: 21–33.

Wei Qingyuan 韋慶遠. 1982. *Qing dai nubi zhidu* 清代奴婢制度. Beijing: Zhongguo renmin daxue chubanshe.

Wen Xia 文霞. 2007. "Cong Qin Han nubi jianzui kuitan qi falü diwei" 從秦漢奴婢奸罪窺探其法律地位, *Shoudu shifan daxue xuebao* 首都師範大學學報 2 (175): 16–21.

———. 2009. "Jiandu ziliao suojian Qin Han nubi de susong quan" 簡牘資料所見奴婢的訴訟權. *Zhongguo shi yanjiu* 中國史研究 3 : 173–176.

Wilbur, Clarence Martin. 1943. *Slavery in China during the Former Han Dynasty, 206 B.C.–A.D. 25*. Anthropological Series, vol. 34. Chicago: Chicago Field Museum of Natural History.

Witschel, Christian. 2008. "The *Res Gestae Divi Augusti* and the Roman Empire." In Fritz-Heiner Mutschler and Achim Mittag, eds., *Conceiving Empire: China and Rome Compared*. Oxford: Oxford University Press, 241–266.

Wittfogel, Karl A. 1957. *Oriental Despotism: A Comparative Study of Total Power*. New Haven: Yale University Press.

Wu Hung (Wu Hong) 巫鴻. 2006. "Mingqi de lilun he shijian" "明器"的理論和實踐. *Wenwu* 文物 6: 72–81.

Wu Xiaoqiang 吳小強, ed. 2000. *Qin jian Ri shu jishi* 秦簡日書集釋. Changsha: Yuelu.

Wu Yi 吳毅. 1999. "Qin chao suwang yuanyin xinlun" 秦朝速亡原因新論. *Baoji Wenli xueyuan xuebao* 寶鷄文理學院學報 19.3: 50–55.

Wu Zhenfeng 吳鎮峰 and Shang Zhiru 尚志儒. 1980. "Shaanxi Fengxiang Baqitun Qin guo muzang fajue jianbao" 陝西鳳翔八旗屯秦國墓葬發掘簡報. *Wenwu ziliao congkan* 文物資料叢刊 3: 67–85.

———. 1981. "Shaanxi Fengxiang Gaozhuang Qin mudi fajue jianbao" 陝西鳳翔高庄秦墓地發掘簡報. *Kaogu yu wenwu* 考古與文物 1: 12–38.

Xianyang Shi Wenwu Kaogu Yanjiusuo 咸陽市文物考古研究所. 1998. *Ta'erpo Qin mu* 塔兒坡秦墓. Xi'an: San Qin chubanshe.

———. 2005. *Renjiazui Qin mu* 任家咀秦墓. Beijing: Kexue chubanshe.

Xie Duanju 謝端琚. 1987. "Shilun woguo zaoqi tudongmu" 試論我國早期土洞墓. *Kaogu* 考古 12: 1097–1114.

Xijing zaji 西京雜記. 1985. Compiled by Ge Hong 葛洪 (283–343). Beijing: Zhonghua shuju.

Xincai Geling Chumu 新蔡葛陵楚墓. 2003. Published by Henan Sheng wenwu kaogu Yanjiusuo 河南省文物考古研究所. Zhengzhou: Daxiang chubanshe.

Xing Yitian. See Hsing I-t'ien.

Xu Pingfang 徐萍芳. 1999. "Kaoguxue shang suo jian Qin diguo de xingcheng yu tongyi" 考古學上所見秦帝國的形成與统一. *Taida lishi xuebao* 太大歷史學報 23: 301–306.

———. "The Archaeology of the Great Wall of the Qin and Han Dynasties." *Journal of East Asian Archaeology.* 3 (1–2): 259–281.

Xu Weimin 徐衛民. 2005. "Fajia sixiang yu Qin wangchao miewang guanxi xinlun" 法家思想與秦王朝滅亡關係新論. *Xibei daxue xuebao* 西北大學學報 35.4: 130–133.

Xu Zhaochang 許兆昌. 2006. *Xian-Qin shiguan de zhidu yu wenhua* 先秦史官的制度與文化. Harbin: Heilongjiang renmin chubanshe.

Xu Zhi, Fan Zhang, Bosong Xu, Jingze Tan, Shilin Li, Chunxiang Li, Hui Zhou, Hong Zhu, Jun Zhang, Qingbo Duan, and Li Jin. 2008. "Mitochondrial DNA Evidence for a Diversified Origin of Workers Building Mausoleum for First Emperor of China." *PLoS ONE.* 3.10: 1–7.

Xu Zhongshu 徐仲舒. 1936. "Jinwen guci shili" 金文嘏辭釋例. Rpt. in *Xu Zhongshu lishi lunwen xuanji* 徐仲舒歷史論文選輯. Beijing: Zhonghua shuju. 1988, 502–564.

Xu Zhuoyun (Hsü Cho-yün) 許倬雲. 1980. "You xinchu jiandu suojian Qin-Han shehui" 由新出簡牘所見秦漢社會. *Zhongyang yanjiuyuan lishi yuyan yanjiusuo jikan* 中央研究院歷史語言研究所季刊 51.2: 226–229.

———. 1998. "Gudai guojia xingcheng de bijiao" 古代國家形成的比較. *Beifang wenwu* 北方文物 3: 1–7.

Xunzi jijie 荀子集解. 1992. Compiled by Wang Xianqian 王先謙. Beijing: Zhonghua shuju.

Yakobson, Alexander. 2003. "*Maiestas*, the Imperial Ideology and the Imperial Family: The Evidence of the *senatus consultum de Cn. Pisone patre.*" In *Eutopia*, Nuova Serie III, 1 -2, Roma: 75–108.

Yamada Katsuyoshi 山田勝芳. 1993. *Shinkan zaisei shūnyū no kenkyū* 秦漢財政收入の研究. Tokyo: Kyūko shoin.

Yan Buke 閻步克. 2001. *Yueshi yu shiguan: chuantong zhengzhi wenhua yu zhengzhi zhidu lunji* 樂師與史官: 傳統政治文化與政治制度論集. Beijing: Sanlian shudian.

Yan Changgui 晏昌貴. 2005. "Qinjiazui bushi jidao jian shiwen jijiao" 秦家嘴

卜筮祭禱簡釋文輯校. *Hubei daxue xuebao (zhexue shehuikexue ban)* 湖北大學學報 (哲學社會科學版) 1: 10–13.

Yan Xinzhi 晏新志, Liu Yusheng 劉宇生, and Yan Huajun 閏華軍. 2009. "Han Jingdi Yangling yanjiu huigu yu zhanwang" 漢景帝陽陵研究的回顧與展望. *Wenbo* 文博 1: 25–33.

Yang Hua 楊華. 2011. "Qin Han diguo de shenquan tongyi: chutu jianbo yu 'Fengshan shu,' 'Jiaosi zhi' de duibi kaocha" 秦漢帝國的神權統一——出土簡帛與《封禪書》、《郊祀志》的對比考察. *Lishi yanjiu* 歷史研究 5: 4–26.

Yang Yiping 楊以平 and Qiao Guorong 喬國榮. 2008. "Tianchang Xi Han mudu shulue" 天長西漢木牘述略. *Jianbo yanjiu* 簡帛研究 2006. Guilin: Guangxi shifan daxue chubanshe, 195–202.

Yang Zhenhong 楊振紅. 2010. "Songbo Xi Han mu buji du kaoshi" 松柏西漢墓簿籍牘考釋. *Nandu xuetan* 南都學壇 5: 1–8.

Yang Zhenhong 楊振紅. 2011. "Cong chutu 'suan,' 'shi' jian kan Liang Han Sanguo Wu shiqi de fuyi jiegou–'suanfu' fei danyi shuimu bian" 從出土"算"、"事"簡看兩漢三國吳時期的賦役結構—"算賦"非單一稅目辨. *Zhonghua wenshi luncong* 中華文史論叢 1: 35–58.

Yang Zuolong 楊作龍. 1985. "Han dai nubi huji wenti shangque" 漢代奴婢戶籍問題商榷, *Zhongguo shi yanjiu* 中國史研究 2: 27–30.

Yantie lun jiaozhu 鹽鐵論校注 (ca. 50 BCE). 1996. Compiled and annotated by Wang Liqi 王利器. Beijing: Zhonghua shuju.

Yates, Robin D. S. 1985/7. "Some Notes on Ch'in Law." *Early China* 11–12: 243–275.

———. 1987. "Social Status in the Ch'in: Evidence from the Yün-meng Legal Documents. Part One: Commoners." *Harvard Journal of Asiatic Studies* 47.1: 197–236.

———. 1995. "State Control of Bureaucrats under the Qin: Techniques and Procedures." *Early China* 20: 331–365.

———. 1997. "Purity and Pollution in Early China." In *Chung-kuo k'ao-ku-hsüeh yü li-shih-hsüeh cheng-ho yen-chiu (Integrated Studies of Chinese Archaeology and History)*, symposium series of the Institute of History and Philology, Academia Sinica, no. 4, ed. Tsang Chenghwa. Taipei: Institute of History and Philology, 479- 536.

———. 1999. "Early China." In Kurt Raaflaub and Nathan Rosenstein, eds., *War and Society in the Ancient and Medieval Worlds: Asia, the Mediterranean, Europe, and Mesoamerica*. Washington, DC: Center for Hellenic Studies, Trustees for Harvard University, and Harvard University Press, 9–46.

———. 2002. "Slavery in Early China: A Socio-cultural Perspective." *Journal of East Asian Archaeology* 3.1–2: 283–331.

———. 2006. "The Song Empire: The World's First Superpower?" In Philip Tetlock, Richard Ned Lebow, and Noel Geoffrey Parker, eds., *Unmaking the West: "What-If?" Scenarios That Rewrite World History*. Ann Arbor: University of Michigan Press, 205–240.

———. 2007. "The Rise of Qin and the Military Conquest of the Warring

States." In Jane Portal, ed., *The First Emperor*. Cambridge, MA: Harvard University Press / London: Trustees of the British Museum, 30–57.

———. 2008. "Le Premier Empereur, la loi et la vie quotidienne en Chine ancienne." In Alain Thote and Lothar von Falkenhausen, eds., *Les soldats de l'éternité: L'armée de Xi'an*. Paris: Éditions de la Pinacothèque de Paris, 183–189.

———. 2009a. "Chinese Law, History of: Eastern Zhou, Ch'in State and Empire." In Stanley N. Katz, ed., *The Oxford International Encyclopedia of Legal History*, vol. 1. Oxford: Oxford University Press, 406–412.

———. 2009b. "Chinese Law, History of: Han Empire (206 BC–AD 220)." In Stanley N. Katz, ed., *The Oxford International Encyclopedia of Legal History*, vol. 1. Oxford: Oxford University Press, 412–418.

———. 2009c. "Law and the Military in Early China." In Nicola Di Cosmo, ed., *Military Culture in Imperial China*. Cambridge, MA: Harvard University Press, 23–44; 341–343.

———. 2009d. "Mutilation in Chinese Law." In Stanley N. Katz, ed., *The Oxford International Encyclopedia of Legal History*, vol. 4. Oxford: Oxford University Press, 196–197.

———. 2011. "Soldiers, Scribes and Women: Literacy among the Lower Orders in Early China." In Li Feng and David Branner, eds., *Writing and Literacy in Early China*. Seattle: University of Washington Press, 352–381.

———. 2012. "Bureaucratic Organization of the Qin County of Qianling 遷陵 in the Light of the Newly Published *Liye Qin jian (yi)* and *Liye Qin jiandu jiaoshi (diyi juan)*." Paper presented at the Fourth International Conference on Sinology, Institute for History and Philology, Academia Sinica, June 20–22.

———. 2012/13. "The Qin Slips and Boards from Well No. 1, Liye, Hunan: A Brief Introduction to the Qin Qianling County Archives." *Early China* 35–36: 291–330.

Ye Shan 葉山 (Robin D. S. Yates). 2008. "Zu, shi yu nüxing: Zhanguo Qin Han shiqi xiaceng shehui de duxie nengli" 卒、史與女性: 戰國秦漢時期下層社會的讀寫能力. *Jianbo* 簡帛 3: 359–384.

Yin Shengping 尹盛平 and Zhang Tian'en 張天恩. 1986. "Shaanxi Long Xian Bianjiazhuang yihao Chunqiu Qin mu" 陝西隴縣邊家庄一號春秋秦墓. *Kaogu yu wenwu* 考古與文物 6: 15–22.

Yin Zaishuo 尹在碩. 2003. "Shuihudi Qin jian he Zhangjiashan Han jian fanying de Qin-Han shiqi houzi zhi he jiaxi jicheng" 睡虎地秦簡和張家山漢簡反映的秦漢時期後子制和家系繼承. *Zhongguo lishi wenwu* 中國歷史文物 1: 31–43.

Yinwan Han mu jiandu 尹灣漢墓簡牘. 1997. Published by Lianyungang shi bowuguan 連雲港市博物館 and Shekeyuan Jianbo Yanjiu Zhongxin 社科院簡帛研究中心. Beijing: Zhonghua shuju.

Yoffee, Norman. 2005. *Myths of the Archaic State*. Cambridge: Cambridge University Press.

Yongcheng Kaogu Gongzuodui 雍城考古工作隊. 1980. "Fengxiang Gaozhuang Zhanguo Qin mu fajue jianbao" 鳳翔高庄戰國秦墓發掘簡報. *Wenwu* 文物 9: 10–14.

Yoshinami Takashi 好井隆司. 1992. *Shōkun sho kenkyū* 商君書研究. Hiroshima: Keisuisha.

Yoshimoto Michimasa 吉本道雅. 1995. "Shin shi kenkyū josetsu" 秦史研究序說. *Shirin* 史林 78.3: 34–67.

———. 2000. "Shō Kun henhō kenkyū josetsu" 商君變法研究序說. *Shirin* 史林 83–84: 1–29.

You Yifei 游逸飛. 2011. "Liye Qin jian 8–455 hao mufang xuanshi" 里耶秦簡 8–455 號木方選釋. *Jianbo* 簡帛 6: 87–104.

Yu Haoliang 于豪亮. 1985. "Qin lü congkao" 秦律叢考. In idem, *Yu Haoliang xueshu wencun* 于豪亮學術文存. Beijing: Zhonghua shuju, 131–145.

Yu Weichao 俞偉超. 1985. *Xian Qin liang Han kaoguxue lunji* 先秦兩漢考古學論集. Beijing: Wenwu chubanshe.

———. 2002. *Gushi de kaoguxue tansuo* 古史的考古學探索. Beijing: Wenwu chubanshe.

Yu Zhenbo 于振波. 2005. "Han dai de duguan yu liguan" 漢代的都官與離官. *Jianbo yanjiu 2002–2003* 簡帛研究 2002–2003: 221–227.

———. 2007. *Zoumalou Wujian xutan* 走馬樓吳簡續探. Taibei: Wenjin chubanshe.

———. 2010. "Qin lü zhong de jiadun bijia ji xiangguan wenti" 秦律中的甲盾比價及相關問題. *Shixue jikan* 史學集刊 5: 36–38.

Yuan Anzhi 負安志. 1984. "Shaanxi Changwu Shangmengcun Qin guo muzang fajue jianbao" 陝西省長武上孟村秦國墓葬發掘簡報. *Kaogu yu wenwu* 考古與文物 3: 8–17.

Yuan Lin 袁林. 2000. *Liang Zhou tudi zhidu xinlun* 兩周土地制度新論. Changchun: Dongbei shifan daxue chubanshe.

Yuan Yansheng 袁延勝. 2008. "Tianchang Jizhuang mudu suan bu yu Han dai suanfu wenti" 天長紀莊木牘算簿與漢代算賦問題. *Zhongguoshi yanjiu* 中國史研究 2: 105–118.

———. 2009. "Jingzhou Songbo mudu ji xiangguan wenti" 荊州松柏木牘及相關問題. *Jianghan kaogu* 江漢考古 3: 114–119.

Yuan Zhongyi 袁仲一. 1983. "Cong Qinshihuang ling de kaogu ziliao kan Qin wangchao de yaoyi" 從秦始皇陵的考古資料看秦王朝的徭役. *Zhongguo nongming zhanzheng shi yanjiu* 中國農民戰爭史研究 3: 42–55.

———. 2008. "Qin taowen zongshu" 秦陶文綜述. *Qin wenhua luncong* 秦文化論叢 15: 1–36.

Yue Qingping 岳慶平. 1985. "Han dai 'fu'e' shitan" 漢代"賦額"試探. *Zhongguoshi yanjiu* 中國史研究 4: 29–43.

Yuelu shuyuan cang Qin jian (yi) 岳麓書院藏秦簡(壹). 2011. Edited by Zhu Hanmin 朱漢民 and Chen Songchang 陳松長. Shanghai: Cishu chubanshe.

Yuelu shuyuan cang Qin jian (er) 岳麓書院藏秦簡(貳). 2012. Edited by Zhu Hanmin 朱漢民 and Chen Songchang 陳松長. Shanghai: Cishu chubanshe.

Yunmeng Shuihudi Qin mu 雲夢睡虎地秦墓. 1981. Published by Yunmeng

Shuihudi Qin mu bianxiezu 雲夢睡虎地秦墓編寫組. Beijing: Wenwu chubanshe.

Zang Zhifei 藏知非. 2002. "Zhou Qin fengsu de rentong yu chongtu: Qin Shihuang 'kuangchi yi su' tanlun" 周秦風俗的認同與衝突—秦始皇"匡飭異俗"探論. *Qin ling Qin yong yanjiu dongtai* 秦陵秦俑研究動態 4: 8-18.

———. 2005. "Zhangjiashan Han jian *Zouyan shu* suojian Qin Han zhunu guanxi shixi" 張家山漢簡奏讞書所見秦漢主奴關係試析. *Qin wenhua luncong* 秦文化論叢 12: 559-573. Also published in *Shixue xinlun: Zhuhe Zhu Shaohou xiansheng bashi huadan* 史學新論: 祝賀朱紹侯先生八十華誕, ed. Henan daxue lishi wenhua xueyuan 河南大學歷史文化學院, 465-476. Kaifeng: Henan daxue chubanshe.

Zaoqi Qin Wenhua Lianhe Kaogudui 早期秦文化聯合考古隊. 2005. "2004 nian Gansu Li Xian Luantingshan yizhi fajue de zhongyao shouhuo" 2004年甘肅禮縣鸞亭山遺址發掘的主要收獲. *Zhongguo lishi wenwu* 中國歷史文物 5: 4-14.

Zaoqi Qin Wenhua Kaogu Lianhe Ketizu 早期秦文化考古聯合課題組, Zhao Huacheng 趙化成, and Wang Hui 王輝. 2007. "Gansu Li Xian Dabuzishan zaoqi Qin wenhua yizhi" 甘肅禮縣大堡子山早期秦文化遺址. *Kaogu* 考古 7: 38-46.

Zaoqi Qin Wenhua Lianhe Kaogudui 早期秦文化聯合考古隊 and Cao Dazhi 曹大志. 2008a. "Gansu Li Xian san zuo Zhou dai chengzhi diaocha baogao" 甘肅禮縣三座周代城址調查報告, *Gudai wenming* 古代文明 7.

Zaoqi Qin Wenhua Lianhe Kaogudui 早期秦文化聯合考古隊. 2008b. "2006 nian Gansu Li Xian Dabuzishan 21 hao jianzhu jizhi fajue jianbao" 2006年甘肅禮縣大堡子山21號建築基址發掘簡報. *Wenwu* 文物 11: 4-13.

———. 2008c. "2006 nian Gansu Li Xian Dabuzishan jisi yiji fajue jianbao" 2006年甘肅禮縣大堡子山祭祀遺跡發掘簡報. *Wenwu* 文物 11: 14-29.

———. 2008d. "2006 nian Gansu Li Xian Dabuzishan Dong Zhou muzang fajue jianbao" 2006年甘肅禮縣大堡子山東周墓葬發掘簡報. *Wenwu* 文物 11: 30-49.

Zeng Jia 曾加. 2007. "*Ernian lüling* youguan nubi de falü sixiang chutan" 《二年律令》有關奴婢的法律思想初探. *Xibei daxue xuebao (zhexue shehuikexueban)* 西北大學學報(哲學社會科學版) 1 (37.1): 43-47.

———. 2008. *Zhangjiashan Han jian falü sixiang yanjiu* 張家山漢簡法律思想研究. Beijing: Shangwu yinshuguan.

Zhang Binglin 章炳麟 (1869-1936). 1977. *Zhang Taiyan zhenglun xuanji* 章太炎政論選集. Edited by Tang Zhijun 湯志鈞. Beijing: Zhonghua shuju.

Zhang Chunlong 張春龍. 2009. "Liye Qin jian zhong huji he renkou guanli jilu" 里耶秦簡中戶籍和人口管理記錄. In Zhongguo Shehuikexueyuan Kaogu Yanjiusuo 中國社會科學院考古研究所 et al., eds., *Liye gucheng: Qin jian yu Qin wenhua yanjiu* 里耶古城·秦簡與秦文化研究. Beijing: Kexue chubanshe, 188-195.

———. 2010. "Liye Qin jian zhong Qianling Xian xueguan he xiangguan jilu" 里耶秦簡中遷陵縣學官和相關記錄. *Chutu wenxian* 出土文獻 1: 232-234.

Zhang Chunlong 張春龍 and Long Jingsha 龍京沙. 2009. "Xiangxi Liye Qin jian 8–455 hao" 湘西里耶秦簡8–455號. *Jianbo* 簡帛 4: 11–15.

Zhang Fentian 張分田. 2005. *Qin Shihuang zhuan* 秦始皇傳. 2nd ed. Beijing: Renmin chubanshe.

Zhang Gong 張功. 2006. *Qin Han taowang fanzui yanjiu* 秦漢逃亡犯罪研究. Wuhan: Hubei renmin chubanshe.

Zhang Hua 張驊. 2003. *Da Qin yitong: Qin Zheng Guo qu* 大秦一統:秦鄭國渠. Xi'an: San Qin chubanshe.

Zhang Jinguang 張金光. 1994. "Qin huji zhidu kao" 秦戶籍制度考. *Hanxue yanjiu* 漢學研究 12.1: 75–99.

———. 2013. *Zhanguo Qin shehui jingji xingtai xintan* 戰國秦社會經濟形態新探. Beijing: Shangwu yinshuguan.

Zhang Junmin 張俊民. 2003. "Qin dai de fuzhai fangshi—du Xiangxi Liye Qin dai jiandu xuanshi" 秦代的付債方式—讀湘西里耶秦代簡牘選釋. *Shaanxi lishi bowuguan guankan* 陝西歷史博物館館刊 10: 288–292.

Zhang Linxiang 張林祥. 2008. *'Shang jun shu' de chengshu yu sixiang yanjiu* 《商君書》的成書與思想研究. Beijing: Renmin chubanshe.

Zhang Quanmin 張全民. 2004. *Zhouli suojian fazhi yanjiu* 《周禮》 所見法制研究. Beijing: Falü chubanshe.

Zhang Rongqiang 張榮強. 2004. "Shuo Sun Wu huji jian zhong de 'shi'" 說孫吳戶籍簡中的'事.' *Wujian yanjiu* 吳簡研究 1: 203–221. Wuhan: Chongwen shuju.

Zhang Rongqiang 張榮強. 2010. *Han-Tang jizhang zhidu yanjiu* 漢唐籍帳制度研究. Beijing: Shangwu.

Zhang Shilong 張世龍. 1988. "Lun Qinshihuang 'fenshu' wei 'kengru'" 論秦始皇"焚書"未"坑儒". *Zhongguo renmin daxue xuebao* 中國人民大學學報 3: 114–120.

Zhang Tian'en 張天恩. 1990. "Bianjiazhuang Chunqiu mudi yu Qianyi di wang" 邊家庄春秋墓地與汧邑地望. *Wenbo* 文博 5: 227–231.

Zhang Weixing 張衛星. 2002. "Qin yu Xi Han jia de chubu bijiao" 秦與西漢甲的初步比較. In Wu Yongqi 吳永琪, Yang Xumin 楊緒敏, and Qiu Yongsheng 邱永生, eds., *Qin Han wenhua bijiao yanjiu—Qin Han bingmayong ji Liang Han wenhua lunwenji* 秦漢文化比較研究—秦漢兵馬俑暨兩漢文化論文集. Xi'an: San Qin chubanshe, 250–270.

———. 2004. "Qin jian zijia kao" 秦簡貲甲考. *Qin wenhua luncong* 秦文化論叢 11: 290–304.

Zhang Weixing 張衛星 and Ma Yu 馬宇. 2003. *Qin jiazhou yanjiu* 秦甲胄研究. Xi'an: Shaanxi renmin chubanshe.

Zhang Xiaofeng 張小鋒. 2004. "Shi Zhangjiashan Han jian zhong de 'Yubi'" 釋張家山漢簡中的'御婢.' *Chutu wenxian yanjiu* 出土文獻研究 6: 125–129.

Zhang Yujin 張玉金. 2011. *Chutu Zhanguo wenxian xuci yanjiu* 出土戰國文獻虛詞研究. Beijing: Renmin chubanshe.

Zhang Zixia 張子俠. 1991. "'Fenshu kengru' bianxi" "焚書坑儒" 辨析. *Huaibei meishiyuan xuebao* 淮北煤師院學報 2: 41–48, 18.

Zhangjiashan Han mu zhujian (er si qi hao mu) 張家山漢墓竹簡(二四七號墓).

2001. Published by Zhangjiashan Han mu zhujian zhengli xiaozu 張家山漢墓竹簡整理小組. Beijing: Wenwu chubanshe.

Zhangjiashan Han mu zhujian (shiwen xiuding ben) 張家山漢墓竹簡(釋文修訂本). 2006. Published by Zhangjiashan ersiqi hao Han mu zhujian zhengli xiaozu 張家山二四七號漢墓竹簡整理小組. Beijing: Wenwu chubanshe.

Zhanguo ce zhushi 戰國策注釋. 1991. Annotated by He Jianzhang 何建章. Beijing: Zhonghua shuju.

Zhao Huacheng 趙化成. 1987. "Xunzhao Qin wenhua yuanyuan de xin xiansuo" 尋找秦文化淵源的新線索. *Wenbo* 文博 1: 1–7, 17.

——. 1989. "Gansu dongbu Qin yu Jiang Rong wenhua de kaoguxue tansuo" 甘肅東部秦與姜戎文化的考古學探索. In Yu Weichao 俞偉超, ed., *Kaogu leixingxue de lilun yu shijian* 考古類型學的理論與實踐. Beijing: Wenwu chubanshe, 145–176.

——. 2011. "Beida cang Xi Han zhushu *Zhao Zheng shu* jianshuo" 北大藏西漢竹書《趙正書》簡說. *Wenwu* 文物 6: 64–66.

Zhao Huacheng 趙化成 and Gao Chongwen 高崇文. 2002. *Qin Han kaogu* 秦漢考古. Beijing: Wenwu chubanshe.

Zhao Huacheng 趙化成, Wang Hui 王輝, and Wei Zheng 韋正. 2008. "Li Xian Dabuzishan Qin zi 'yueqi keng' xiangguan wenti tantao" 禮縣大堡子山秦子"樂器坑"相關問題探討. *Wenwu* 文物 11: 54–66.

Zhao Ping'an 趙平安. 2009. "Xinchu "Shi lü" yu "Shi Zhou pian" de xingzhi" 新出《史律》與《史籀篇》的性質. In Zhao Ping'an, *Xinchu jianbo yu gu wenzi gu wenxian yanjiu* 新出簡帛與古文字古文獻研究. Beijing: Shangwu yinshuguan, 87–297.

Zhao Shugui 趙書貴. 1985. "Shilun liang Han nubi wenti yu nubi zhengce" 試論兩漢奴婢問題與奴婢政策. *Shixue yuekan* 史學月刊 4: 25–30.

Zheng Liangshu 鄭良樹. 1989. *Shang Yang ji qi xuepai* 商鞅及其學派. Shanghai: Guji chubanshe.

Zheng lun jiaozhu 政論校注 [2012], by Cui Shi 崔寔 (ca. 103–170 CE), annotated by Sun Qizhi 孫啟治. Beijing: Zhonghua shuju.

Zheng Zhimin 鄭志敏. 1997. *Xi shuo Tang ji* 細說唐妓. Taibei: Wenjin.

Zhongguo Kexueyuan Kaogu Yanjiusuo 中國科學院考古研究所. 1962. *Fengxi fajue baogao* 灃西發掘報告. Beijing: Wenwu chubanshe.

Zhongguo Kexueyuan Kaogu Yanjiusuo Baoji Fajuedui 中國科學院考古研究所寶雞發掘隊. 1963. "Shaanxi Baoji Fulinbao Dongzhou mu fajue ji" 陝西寶雞福臨堡東周墓發掘記. *Kaogu* 考古 10: 536–543.

Zhongguo qingtongqi quanji 中國青銅器全集. 1998. Vol. 7 (*Dong Zhou* 東周 1). Beijing: Wenwu chubanshe.

Zhongguo Shehuikexueyuan Kaogu Yanjiusuo 中國社會科學院考古研究所. 2004. "Xi'an shi E'panggong yizhi de kaogu xin faxian" 西安市阿房宮遺址的考古新發現. *Kaogu* 考古 4: 3–6.

Zhongguo Shehuikexueyuan Kaogu Yanjiusuo 中國社會科學院考古研究所 et al., eds. 2009. *Liye gucheng: Qin jian yu Qin wenhua yanjiu* 里耶古城·秦簡與秦文化研究. Beijing: Kexue chubanshe.

Zhongguo Shehuikexueyuan Kaogu Yanjiusuo Wugong Fajuedui 中國社會

科學院考古研究所武功發掘隊. 1996. "Shaanxi Wugong Xian Zhaojialai Dong Zhou shiqi de Qin mu" 陝西武功縣趙家來東周時期的秦墓. *Kaogu* 考古 12: 44–48.

———. 1985. "Qin Han Yueyang yizhi de kantan he shijue" 秦漢櫟陽遺址的勘探和試掘. *Kaogu xuebao* 考古學報 3: 353–380.

Zhou Fang 周芳. 2013. *Kengru pingyi* 坑儒平議. Guilin: Guangxi Shifan Daxue chubanshe.

Zhouli zhushu 周禮注疏. 1991. Annotated by Zheng Xuan 鄭玄 and Jia Gong-yan 賈公彥. In *Shisanjing zhushu* 十三經注疏, compiled by Ruan Yuan 阮元. Beijing: Zhonghua shuju, 1: 631–940.

Zhu Fenghan 朱鳳瀚. 2012. "Beida cang Qin jian *Cong zheng zhi jing* shuyao" 北大藏秦簡《從政之經》述要. *Wenwu* 文物 6: 74–80.

Zhu Honglin 朱紅林. 2005. *Zhangjiashan Han jian* Ernian lüling *jishi* 張家山漢簡二年律令集釋. Beijing: Shehuikexue wenxian chubanshe.

Zhu Shaohou 朱紹侯. 2008. *Jungong juezhi kaolun* 軍功爵制考論. Beijing: Shangwu yinshuguan.

Zufferey, Nicholas. 2003. *To the Origins of Confucianism. The Ru in pre-Qin times and during the Early Han Dynasty.* Bern: Peter Lang.

Zürcher, Erik. 1982. "Prince Moonlight: Messianism and Eschatology in Early Medieval Chinese Buddhism." *T'oung Pao* 68.1–3: 1–75.

Contributors

HANS VAN ESS, Professor, Ludwig-Maximilians-Universität München

LOTHAR VON FALKENHAUSEN, Professor of Chinese archaeology and art history, UCLA

HSING I-TIEN, Professor, Institute of History and Philology, Academia Sinica, Taipei

YURI PINES, Michael W. Lipson Professor of East Asian Studies, the Hebrew University of Jerusalem

POO MU-CHOU, Professor of History, Chinese University of Hong Kong

TENG MINGYU, Professor, Research Center for Chinese Frontier Archaeology, Jilin University

GIDEON SHELACH, Louis Frieberg Professor of East Asian Studies, the Hebrew University of Jerusalem

ALEXANDER YAKOBSON, Professor of History, the Hebrew University of Jerusalem

ROBIN D. S. YATES, James McGill Professor, departments of East Asian Studies and History and Classical Studies, McGill University

ZHAO HUACHENG, Professor, School of Archaeology and Museology, Peking University

Index

Page numbers in *italic* type refer to illustrations, tables and maps.

www.ingramcontent.com/pod-product-compliance
Lightning Source LLC
Chambersburg PA
CBHW030634270326
41929CB00007B/79